American Lions

American Lions

The 332nd Infantry Regiment in Italy in World War I

Robert J. Dalessandro & Rebecca S. Dalessandro

Schiffer Military History
Atglen, PA

Acknowledgements

This project could never have been possible without the resources of the U.S. Army Center of Military History in Washington, D.C. and the Army Heritage and Education Center at Carlisle Barracks, Pennsylvania. The matchless collections of the National Army Museum, the Military History Institute and the Army Heritage Museum provided the authors endless opportunities to understand the complexities of the American Expeditionary Forces and the American Army in Italy. The staff of the Center of Military History was always ready to help with this project – our particular thanks go out to Dr. Jeff Clarke, Mike Knapp, Dr. Charlie Cureton, Alan Bogan, John Paschal, Alan Archambault, Julia Simon, Carrie Sullivan, James Tobias and Jane Smith Stewart. The Army Heritage and Education Center staff was ever helpful especially, Melissa Wiford and Molly Bompane who assisted with this project from its inception. Brooke Anderson kindly provided materials from his collection including the roster of the 332nd reprinted in this volume for the first time. Lisa Long and Jon Haas at the Information and Reference Department, Ohio Historical Society were always willing to dig deeper and find any obscure document we requested on short notice. Our thanks, also, to the professionals at the Military History Institute; particularly Dr. Richard "Dick" Sommers, the late Dr. Art Bergeron, Rich Baker, and Louise Arnold-Friend. At the Army Heritage Museum, Roger Durham, Jay Graybeal, Mike Mirra and Chris Semancik were of immeasurable help to the project and always willing to go the extra mile to assist. Thanks to Osvaldo Amari and Cimee Trincee for allowing us to publish the photograph of their Italian Army ancestor and his brother Bruno Costa, a soldier in the 332nd. Numerous individuals and collectors provided advice and made their personal collections available to us for our research into the AEF in Italy. Ron Northrup, Gus Radle, Gil Sanow, Jim Frasca, Steve Wagner, Major (Ret) Terry R. Morris, Major (Ret) Charles R. Snyder, Jr., Herb & Beverly Goodman, Roger Cirillo, Jack McKinney, Michael Albanese Roberto Patrignani and Furio Lazzarini have been particularly helpful; grateful thanks to Majors Ginger Shaw and Shane Reilly and to the tenacious researching skills of Brandi Buchman and Ryan Witte. Special thanks to Ralph Doerres, Jr., the son of the First Sergeant of L Company, whose willingness to share information about the regiment proved to be of invaluable help to the project. Jenny Davenport, Director of Client Services at Rendigs, Fry, Kiely, and Dennis, LLP made the original copy of August A. Rendigs important account of the regiment available to us. Thanks to our Editor, Bob Biondi for making this all so easy. Finally, to the late Peter Schiffer, a man of vision whose love for art and antiques and history has enriched our world.

Dedication

To those who inspire future generations of Americans and to the men and women of the Armed Services who have put their lives on the line for over 230 years so that the American people might enjoy their freedom.

"Those who long enjoyed such privileges as we enjoy forget in time that men have died to win them."
— Franklin D. Roosevelt.

Book design by Robert Biondi.

Library of Congress Catalog Number: 2010931236.

Printed in China.
ISBN: 978-0-7643-3518-1

We are always looking for people to write books on new and related subjects. If you have an idea for a book, please contact us at the address below.

Published by Schiffer Publishing Ltd.
4880 Lower Valley Road
Atglen, PA 19310
Phone: (610) 593-1777
FAX: (610) 593-2002
E-mail: Info@schifferbooks.com.
Visit our web site at: www.schifferbooks.com
Please write for a free catalog.
This book may be purchased from the publisher.
Please include $5.00 postage.
Try your bookstore first.

In Europe, Schiffer books are distributed by:
Bushwood Books
6 Marksbury Ave.
Kew Gardens, Surrey TW9 4JF
England
Phone: 44 (0)20 8392-8585
FAX: 44 (0)20 8392-9876
E-mail: info@bushwoodbooks.co.uk
www.bushwoodbooks.co.uk

Contents

Introduction

This is the story of one American regiment and their service in World War I. It is the chronicle of a very unusual regiment and of the men who served as its members.

So many histories focus on grand strategy and watershed events that reshape the world in which we live; this account does not. It is the story of World War One and the 332nd United States Infantry Regiment, which is recounted using the voices of those who served in that regiment.

It was not our intention to write this book, but the men of the regiment led us to document their story, or perhaps it is more correct to say that several men of the regiment hoped that their story would be told.

This volume began one day, while browsing through the largely un-mined collection of Veteran's Surveys housed at the Military History Institute at Carlisle, Pennsylvania. Allow us to give you a little background before we continue. Early in 1967, the Military History Institute began sending surveys out to veterans. These surveys were no more than several mimeographed sheets asking esoteric questions about the veterans' service. The idea in 1967 was to capture the remembrances of all the living Spanish-American War soldiers. Working with the Veterans Administration, the Military History Institute obtained a list of Spanish-American War Veterans, mailed out their surveys and waited to see how many were returned.

As the weeks passed, something amazing and unexpected happened. Not only did the veterans return the surveys, they generously shared more than what was asked of them. The completed questionnaires arrived in the standard envelopes provided by the Institute, but a great number were packed in scores of boxes! The boxes contained wartime photographs, personal letters sent to loved ones at home, uniforms, weapons, captured flags, and a range of personal mementos that had been connected with their service and were important enough to keep for a period of almost seventy years. No one at the Military History Institute expected this response. Through this survey, they had given the soldiers a voice.

What the staff at the Military History Institute had failed to realize was what these surveys meant to the veterans of a forgot-

The community house at Camp Sherman was a major attraction to the soldiers and was a an important feature of the camp. Courtesy Military History Institute.

ten war; men who were now in the sunset years of life. To them, someone finally cared about their experiences. Someone in the Army, someone in the government, appreciated their service to the Nation. Someone was finally listening to their stories.

As the years passed, the Military History Institute continued to collect. The veterans of the Spanish-American War, who followed their brothers in the Civil War to the last bivouac; no longer answered, but the surveys continued, focused on the next generation and the next and the next. The collection grew.

Today, this voluminous collection resides in acid free, grey boxes, on grey steel shelves, in a secure, temperature and humidity controlled bay. The surveys are filed by time period and by unit. The environment is quiet, sterile, and cold.

Yet in the silence, if you pause to listen, you can hear these men and women speak to you. The story of the 332nd Infantry Regiment is told from their perspective and experience and in their many voices. With only the minimum interruption, which the authors allowed for the sake of a coherent narrative, we begin their story.

Every narrative introduces memorable characters and this one is no different. The veteran's surveys and subsequent research provided the authors with witnesses from across the regiment. This was essential as the headquarters and three battalions of the regiment often had different missions. We drew from across these units to provide a comprehensive look at life in the regiment. In addition to the many published sources, we drew heavily on the unpublished writings of the following men whose recollections were archived in public and in private collections nationwide.

Our introductions begin with Colonel William Wallace. Wallace, a brusque, demanding, regular army officer, cut his teeth fighting insurgents in the Philippines. As second commander of the regiment, Wallace led his men from Camp Sherman to Europe and back.

We will hear from Captain Austin P. Story of Chillicothe, Ohio, Commander of Company I, who ultimately led the second battalion and also from one of his unhappy privates, Henry "Hen" Blank of Dayton, Ohio.

Cincinnatian and Lieutenant August A. Rendigs, Jr., a young Harvard attorney turned soldier, provides us gripping narrative accounts of the Italian adventure, while future writer and poet Lieutenant Harold Speakman softens the view of war.

Ferris Wellman Myrice, a private in Company L from Deshler, Ohio, adds his insightful observations; as F Company private George A. Roberts, a mason who hailed from Columbus, Ohio, provides memorable narratives of his time with the 332nd

The voices of these men are joined by many others, including officers, non-commissioned officers, soldiers, Red Cross workers, and civilians, in their telling of the regiment's story.

The Episcopal Church was located at the center of the camp. Courtesy Military History Institute.

When the 332nd Infantry Regiment was activated at Camp Sherman, Ohio, the regiment was no different than scores of other such regiments being formed around the United States. Like their sister regiments, they trained hard, were forged into a cohesive unit, and became a building block organization, as one of the four regiments ultimately comprising one of the many of the United States infantry divisions joining the American Expeditionary Forces (A.E.F.) in France.

Such was the case with the 332nd. During those early days in the life of the regiment, they worked together, played together, endured hardships, underwent tough training, and formed ties that would last a lifetime. Then, at the appointed moment, they shipped for France and certain assignment to the Western Front. Upon arrival overseas, they marshaled very near the Headquarters of the Commander of the A.E.F, General John J. Pershing. Here they prepared to undergo their final training before going into the front line and here everything changed.

General John J. Pershing vehemently opposed dissipating the strength of the A.E.F by sending troops to reinforce other theaters of war. He was constantly pressured to do so by the allied, and occasionally his own, governments. In two specific instances, Pershing was ordered to take action. As a result, he sent several regiments to supply and assist the White Russian Army engaged in a desperate struggle with Communist forces in Russia, and he sent one regiment to Italy to bolster the flagging morale of the Italian people. The 27th, 31st and 339th Infantry Regiments were to go to Russia.

The 332nd Infantry Regiment was to go to Italy.

1

The Regiment is Formed: Camp Sherman to France

The birthplace of the 332nd Infantry Regiment was Camp Sherman; one of the many large cantonments built to house and train the rapidly expanding army deemed necessary to meet the National Emergency of 1917. The birth date of 332nd Infantry Regiment was fixed by War Department Order as August 27, 1917. The historian of Company D described the moment when he joined the fledgling regiment:

> "It was the afternoon of Friday, September 7, 1917. A truck filled with embryo soldiers ploughed its way across a muddy cornfield at Camp Sherman and came to a stop before a low black building, the future regimental headquarters of the soon-to-be famous Three Hundred Thirty Second Infantry of the United States Army. No flying flags or sounding bugles marked the laying of the cornerstone – only silence broken somewhat by noise from busy tractors and hurrying carpenters as they erected a city of barracks and huts in a sea of mud."[1]

And so, from early September 1917 until May 24, 1918, the regiment would call Camp Sherman its' home. Sergeant Major Joseph L. Lettau, wrote, the regiment received, "All the necessary "Shots in the back", drills, hikes, rifle practice, bayonet work, signaling, tent pitching and kitchen police …"[2] The days at Camp Sherman were anything but restful for the members of the regiment.

Camp Sherman was located adjacent to the south-central Ohio historic community of Chillicothe. The town was the first capital of Ohio in 1803; home to Camp Bull, the western headquarters of the American Army during the War of 1812 and Camp Logan, a Civil War mobilization camp for the 73rd Regiment, Ohio Volunteer Infantry. By 1917, Chillicothe was the center of a productive agricultural region and a quietly industrious town of about 16,000.[3]

As the U.S. entry into the war looked imminent, the War Department started their search for locations to build camps of instruction for the Army. Immediately, the Chillicothe Chamber of Commerce saw an opportunity for both patriotism and profit and moved to locate one of the camps near the town.[4] The community was so eager for the Army cantonment that to sweeten the deal, the town elders offered to add a \$5.00 per acre subsidy to the standard \$15.00 government compensation payment to landowners.[5] Among several prominent Chillicothe citizens involved in the project, Richard Enderlin, who earned the Medal of Honor in the Civil War, conducted many of the negotiations with the government.[6]

The planned location for the camp offered much. Situated adjacent to the Scioto River, the site provided wide expanses of land, an excellent water supply, railroad accessibility and a range of foothills near Mount Logan that would serve as a rifle range. Frank Ward noted that, "it was on June 8th that wires from Washington flashed the word that Chillicothe had landed the camp … citizens who had worked hard to secure the camp were jubilant.[7]

On June 28, 1917, engineers and contractors began the work of building the cantonment. Ward described the transition of the site, as empty fields were replaced by two thousand buildings and twenty miles of streets. "The barracks are two-story structures, built of wooden frames, covered with matched boards. The roofs are constructed of prepared material. All of the structures are electric lighted. Six hundred of them house infantry, 219 are used by the light artillery, forty-six for the engineers, thirty-one for supplies, twenty-four for sanitary trains, sixty-four for ammunition, sixteen for field signal corps, twenty for aero squadrons, six for division headquarters, seventeen for train headquarters, seventy-six for heavy artillery, nine for telegraph squads, and four for the Red Cross headquarters."[8]

The camp had about 12,000 horses and mules with the necessary hay sheds, feeding barns, a grain elevator and a blacksmith shop. It was a self-sufficient facility with its own railroad and dairy farm including a milk processing center. There was an ice plant, a huge bakery, an immense laundry facility, a large hospital, three theaters, eleven Y.M.C.A. buildings, and various other religious fraternal organization buildings. The camp library was established by Chillicothean Burton Stevenson, journalist, author and librarian, who went on to Paris as the European director of the Library War Service. The camp buildings were cavernous structures of green wood; their rooms fragrant with the sweet, fresh aroma of pine.

On July 16, 1917, the War Department officially designated the site as Camp William Tecumseh Sherman. It was named after a famous Ohio native, Civil War Union General William Tecumseh Sherman. He was most notable during his command of the Army of Tennessee for his March to the Sea. The march, which changed the course of the Civil War, lasted from November 15 to December 21, 1864; his destructive path through Georgia and the Carolinas broke the back of the Confederacy.[9] Arguably, he was one of Ohio's most famous soldiers.

Chillicothe's quick transformation is described in the *Illustrated History of Camp Sherman*:

> "...The sudden arrival of many thousands of strange men could have its reaction upon the social life of a community. An abruptly expanded market offered many temptations to the average merchant or landlord, and these temptations were not absent in Chillicothe. But it can be truthfully said that the attitude of the residents of Chillicothe has been an entirely helpful and friendly one.
>
> During the building of the camp over 15,000 workmen and transients looked to Chillicothe for housing accommodations ... here and there instances of flagrant profiteering were discovered; but in general a spirit of patriotic hospitality prevailed, which lasted throughout the period of the war."[10]

Soon after, the camp's population began to swell to a size twice that of the city of Chillicothe, the city elders began to wonder if they had not been somewhat too eager. As with any military camp, undesirable elements often accompanied large concentrations of troops. An area newspaper published the following notice summing up the feelings of the residents of Chillicothe:

> "Disreputable People, Tin-Horn Gamblers, Games of Chance Proprietors, Itinerate Vendors, Cheap Johns, Fakirs, "Fire Sale" Dealers, Fly-by-Night Concerns, Loose Women – all such will waste money paying railway fare to the City expecting to reap a harvest from the troops in the U.S. Cantonment. They will be given short shrift and "Strong Arm" methods will be used to keep them out of Chillicothe."[11]

The Chamber of Commerce was fervent to make the point. A follow-on article titled "Drastic Action promised to Keep Undesirables from the New Camp." The article stated:

> The Chamber of Commerce took quick action today to let it be known that undesirables are not wanted in this city, and that drastic action will be taken against camp followers. With the selection of Chillicothe as one of the places for an army training camp it was decided the usual followers will try and find a haven here. Mayor and all city and county officials have pledged their united effort to keep the town clean. If present laws are not stringent enough, more drastic ones will be enacted.[12]

The efforts paid off; although Camp Sherman certainly had a seedier side. The City Fathers had managed to curtail much of the vice associated with Army stations. The citizens of Chillicothe spread their arms wide to provide their new guests with a pleasant welcome:

> "Hospitality was spontaneous and personal, as well as through organized effort. Hundreds of families opened their homes for the entertainment of soldiers, particularly at Christmas time. Funds were raised for two downtown Army Clubs, one in a three story building at Paint and Water Streets and the other for colored soldiers at 18 West Market Street. Six hundred splendid girls and women banded themselves together to form the Girls Patriotic League and drove away the loneliness of many a homesick soldier. The spirit of hospitality culminated on November 30, 1918, when "Chillicothe Day" was held. The whole city opened its doors, the theaters distributed 13,000 free tickets, and the churches fed from 7,000 to 8,000 men.
>
> Churches were particularly helpful. Most of them held special socials and entertainments for soldiers from time to time, and were delighted to aid the men at the camp. The fraternal organizations had frequently open nights when all were welcome, and provided jitney dances several times a week."
>
> "... it is doubtful if any other national army or national guard training camp held so high a place in the hearts of the people of the state in which it was located. Camp Sherman was peculiarly Ohio's, and every man, woman, and child in Ohio, came to look upon it as their own."[13]

The 332nd Infantry Regiment was one of the four infantry regiments that formed the 83rd Division. The War Department established the 83rd Division on August 5, 1917 at Camp Sherman, Ohio. Colonel Wallace, the second commander of the regiment, described the regiment as being composed of "Mainly Ohioans with a sprinkling of Pennsylvanians."[14] The 83rd Division had the same composition and selected "Ohio Division" as its' nickname.[15]

The cadre for National Army Divisions were drawn from the standing National Guard Divisions. These National Guard Divisions were formed prior to the war for service on the Mexican Border. They provided a pool of experienced officers and men to staff the newly formed organizations. The initial lottery for the conscription of American men, aged 21 to 30, levied as part of the Selective Service Act, quickly supplied men for the new National Army. Additionally, many men with previous military service, volunteered to report for service prior to their draft call. They were the early fillers of the National Army Divisions including the 83rd.

Later the Division adopted a shoulder sleeve insignia in 1918 which mirrored this Ohio tradition consisting of a black triangle with vortex down, the gold letters, "OHIO" forming a monogram within a gold circle.

The new division was commanded by the sixty-two year old Major General Edwin Forbes Glenn. A native of North Carolina, Glenn was educated at the U.S. Military Academy at West Point, New York graduating with the Class of 1877. He was described in the *Camp Sherman Souvenir* as "a big man, both physically and mentally."[16] Long past his prime, Glenn had spent much of his Army career away from troop assignments.

As a captain, he commanded an expedition of exploration to Cook's Inlet and other points in Alaska, then served as the Judge Advocate, an Army lawyer, at headquarters in Manila, Philippine Islands while many of his classmates attained laurels fighting the insurrection. After promotion to major and a brief command, he returned to the United States and spent the next five years in staff and training assignments. Returning to the Philippines in 1908, he commanded a small post in Malabang.

In March 1911, Glenn's fortunes reversed. Promoted to colonel, he took command of the 23rd Infantry Regiment stationed at Fort Bliss, Texas. Selection to the Army War College followed in 1913, and an assignment for a second command, the storied 18th Infantry Regiment, at Deming, New Mexico. During his scant six months of command, Glenn gained some combat experience when he took the regiment into action along the Mexican Border.

In April 1917, he was reassigned as Commandant of the Officer's Training Camp at Fort Benjamin Harrison, Indiana. Here Glenn showed himself as an adept organizer and educator. Promotion in May to Brigadier General was followed just three months later with a second promotion to Major General in recognition of his services.[17]

The division had two infantry brigades assigned, the 165th and the 166th. Each brigade was composed of two infantry regiments and a machine gun battalion. The 165th Infantry Brigade included the 329th and 330th Infantry Regiments and the 323rd Machine Gun Battalion. The 166th Infantry Brigade had the 331st Infantry Regiment, the 332nd Infantry Regiment and the 324th Machine Gun Battalion assigned. Division troops included the 332nd Machine Gun Battalion, the 158th Field Artillery Brigade, the 308th Engineer Regiment and a variety of service and support troops. Those included the 308th Ammunition, Supply, Engineer and Sanitary Trains. The army term "Trains" dated to the nineteenth century was used to denote logistical organizations, located behind the lines, which provided supply and service to the division.

The 166th Infantry Brigade was commanded by Brigadier General Frederick Perkins, an 1883 graduate of West Point. Perkins' career followed that of his superior, with numerous staff assignments and long periods away from troops. In thirty-four years of service, Perkins had never seen combat. He began his career with the 8th Infantry Regiment; however, sickness and recruiting duties kept him away from the regiment during the Spanish-American War. He finally served as a company commander in Cuba after the hostilities ended. For the next six years, he moved with the regiment to various posts including Fort Snelling, Minnesota, Fort Missoula, Montana, and Fort Egbert, Alaska. As a major, he served in the Philippines and at Fort Leavenworth, Kansas. Detailed to the Adjutant General's Office in 1908, Perkins spent the next four years functioning in that capacity in the Philippines, as well as in the States. A promotion to lieutenant colonel followed with duty back to the regiment and service on the Mexican Border. Several months later, he was selected for the War College and returned to Washington, D.C. Promoted to colonel in 1916, Perkins was assigned to San Francisco, California in charge of Military Affairs, Headquarters Western Department. The impending war brought promotion to brigadier general and an assignment as Commander, 166th Infantry Brigade at Camp Sherman.[18]

An infantry regiment in World War I was commanded by a colonel and assigned a headquarters company, three battalions, numbered one through three, a machine gun company with sixteen heavy machine guns, a supply company and a medical and chaplain detachment. Each of the battalions was commanded by majors and consisted of a headquarters and four infantry companies. The companies were led by captains and lettered A through D in the First Battalion, E through H in the Second Battalion; with an attached machine gun company that was added to the 332nd organization, and I, K, L, M and an attached supply company also unique to the 332nd, in the Third Battalion.

The infantry company consisted of a headquarters and four platoons, each platoon had a platoon headquarters and four sections: first section (hand bombers), second section (rifle grenadiers), third section (riflemen), and fourth section (automatic riflemen). The first section had three bomber squads each consisting of one leader, one thrower, one carrier and one scout. The second section had six rifle grenadiers and three carriers. The third section had seventeen riflemen and the fourth section had four automatic rifle teams each consisting of one gunner and two carriers with one corporal in charge of every two guns.

The strength of the regiment was approximately 4000 officers and men. The regiment primarily included men from Eastern Ohio – largely from the cities of Akron, Alliance, Canton, East Liverpool, and Youngstown. There were also men from western Pennsylvania, predominately from the Pittsburgh area.

The 332nd Regimental Commander was Colonel Robert Walter Mearns, a West Point graduate of the Class of 1892. A hard-bitten, Regular Army officer of the frontier style, Mearns knew that much had to be learned before civilians were stamped out into soldiers. Like his superior, Major General Glenn, Mearns was a veteran of the Philippine Insurrection; however, that was where any comparison ended. While Glenn reviewed paperwork in the headquarters in Manila, Mearns cut his teeth with the Philippine scouts fighting insurgents in the steamy jungles where he was cited for valor. Command of a company in the 20th Infantry Regiment followed and then a transfer to Fort Shafter, Hawaii with the company when it returned from the Philippine adventure. Long, hard service in the tropics took a toll and much of the next two years was spent in hospitals or on leave in recovery. He rejoined his company at Fort Douglas, Utah and immediately found himself on duty patrolling the Mexican Border. Promoted to Major, he was assigned as Regimental Adjutant of the 12th Infantry. Mearns received brief fame in 1914 when he was appointed to escort Pancho Villa and General Obregon from El Paso, Texas to Nogales, Arizona and back. May 1917 brought promotion to lieutenant colonel and assignment to Fort Benjamin Harrison, Indiana with duties as a mustering [recruiting] officer. Three months later, he was selected to command the 332nd Infantry Regiment at Camp Sherman with promotion to colonel.[19]

Even under a tough drillmaster like Mearns, the full transition from civilian to soldier was delayed due to a simple supply issue. As noted in the Company D Log, "These drills presented a novel appearance for at the end of the first two weeks, the men had not received their uniforms, consequently, they drilled in civilian clothes minus the coats … By the end of the first week's drill, the appearance of the men had altered greatly. Their bodies were erect; their shoulders, more nearly square, while a better color came into their cheeks; they had already absorbed as much military training as men usually got in thirty days at a Receiving Barracks in peace times."[20]

Frank Ward, editor of *The Camp Sherman Souvenir*, reported that during the first few days of September, General Glenn ordered light initial training as many of the men arriving "were still soft from civilian pursuits."[21] As the recruits settled in and adjusted to military life in barracks, tents and muddy fields, the training schedule became more physically intense.

A typical day began with the bugle sounding Reveille at 6:00 a.m. followed by breakfast thirty minutes later which, according to the History of Company K, "… usually consisted of oatmeal and prunes. Once in awhile we had pancakes and eggs, and always coffee and plenty of bread."[22] Then training began. This included various forms of drill starting at the individual soldier level – school of the soldier in the Army lingo, followed by more drill at the platoon, company and finally regimental level. Between drill, soldiers received classroom lectures from the French, British and American officers assigned to the camp. Various subjects included how to survive trench warfare on the Western Front, French language and the use of grenades and explosives.

Mess Call sounded promptly at noon for a meal "which usually consisted of "… beef and potatoes and one other vegetable. Sometimes we got pork and sometimes the beef was cut into steaks, but more often it was roasted or boiled. About four times a week at noon we received a dessert usually consisting of bread pudding. Often at noon our drink was varied by serving iced tea, milk or lemonade."[23] Dinner was followed by a 1:00 p.m. regimental formation marking the beginning of afternoon training. Normally, afternoon training focused on practical aspects of modern warfare, including bayonet instruction, signaling, machinegun and rifle familiarization, and bombing; the quaint moniker used for grenade throwing. A regimental formation and inspection followed at the end of the training day, usually around 4:30 p.m., and soldiers were then released for organized sports. At retreat, which sounded at 4:50 p.m., honors were rendered to the flag which signaled the end of the official training day.

Supper Mess Call sounded at 5:00 p.m. and "… was nearly always the best and most varied meal, and we enjoyed it for this reason, also because it marked the end of a busy, tiresome day. In the evening there were passes to Chillicothe or games and reading material at the "Y" or boxing bouts in the big squad rooms along with school for N.C.O.s."[24] Soldiers finally called it a day with Taps at 10:30 p.m.[25]

After a period of barely two months spent adjusting to the rigors of solider life at Camp Sherman, the regiment boarded trains. The History of Company K recalled, "On November 22nd, the regiment entrained for Camp Perry [Ohio], near Toledo, for rifle practice. Most of us had a strange foreboding feeling that we were going to miss Camp Sherman, but none of us dreamed what the trip would really mean to us."[26]

Captain Austin P. Story, I Company Commander, described this formative period. "Intensive training followed the organization of the regiment and since the rifle range at the foot of Mt. Logan was not ready until early in 1918, the regiment was sent to Camp Perry, Ohio on Lake Erie for target practice. Terrific winter weather struck while the regiment was at Perry, the temperature dropped to as low as 21 degrees below zero. The men were in tents with stoves in them but nevertheless there was much discomfort to say the least."[27]

Communities near Lake Erie suffered frequently from what locals described as the "lake effect." Winter storms were more severe in the area and snow accumulation was always greater than in the central areas of Ohio. Such was the case on November 23, 1917, when Camp Perry was struck by a blizzard. Many soldiers who participated in training exercises at Camp Perry reported that the experience was extremely miserable and uncomfortable. They huddled in squad tents while the ground surface alternated from snow and ice to mud. During their encampment, the log from Company D noted the illnesses attributed to these conditions: "when a suspected case of smallpox appeared every man in the camp had to be vaccinated. Vaccinations were made while there was a heavy snow on the ground and the temperature hovering around the zero mark. Miniature blizzards made it impossible to go out on the range. The men were inadequately clothed to resist this severe weather. At this time Corporal Arthur C. Nelson contracted the disease which caused his death."[28]

Soldiers in Company K recorded that, "On the second day there our camp was covered with a heavy snow, then came persistent zero weather with freezing winds off the lake, and for whole days and nights we did nothing at all but alternately freeze and roast according to whether our tent stove was red hot or not. We did very little firing, and this little was done under the most adverse conditions."[29]

The weather continued to be problematic as the regiment trained. Finally, "Thanksgiving came. This was the first holiday the regiment had had. Fifty percent of the men were allowed to go on pass to their homes. For those who could not go there was a turkey and stuffin' dinner that still lingers pleasantly in the memory … The training rushed to a whirlwind close in a spell of good weather and on December 11, Camp was struck amid a roaring blizzard which swept in off the lake."[30]

After nearly a month of hellish conditions, the regiment finally left Camp Perry. Captain Story noted, "Under great difficulties the camp was struck, the regiment put on a train and returned to Camp Sherman. One distressing incident of the return was that a steam line broke in a car full of mules and when the car was opened up it was found that all the mules had been killed by the live steam." Story continued, "About this time Colonel Wallace replaced Col. Mearns as regimental commander."[31] Selected for promotion to brigadier general, Mearns left the regiment on short notice to assume command of Camp Beauregard, Louisiana.

Much like his predecessor, Colonel William Wallace was a Regular Army officer of the old style. At fifty-one years of age, he was a capable, rigorous, no-nonsense leader who demanded excellence from both his officers and his men. Tough and experienced, sometimes impatient, he was an intelligent and articulate officer who, also, certainly knew how to swear like a trooper. Commissioned in the 7th Infantry Regiment in 1891, Wallace served as a first lieutenant in the Spanish-American War and was wounded at El Caney in Cuba, where he received a brevet promotion to captain for gallantry in action. After his recovery, he saw service in the Philippines, California and at Fort Leavenworth, Kansas. While assigned with the regiment at Fort Leavenworth, he met Bessie Keller. Marriage followed in 1896 and a year later, twins Henry and Cordelia were born. At the outbreak of the war in 1917, Wallace was attached to the West Virginia National Guard. He served on the committee which selected the site for Camp Sherman. Promoted to colonel in August, 1917, Wallace proved to be a tough commander throughout his service with the 332nd Infantry Regiment until demobilization in 1919. He was known to his troops by names that including "Wild Bill" and "Colonel Billy."

Upon the return of the regiment to Camp Sherman from the frigid exercise at Camp Perry, training continued apace. Wallace proved to be a demanding trainer and continued to build on the increasing levels of competence within the unit, adding regimental drill, mock trench raids and advanced tactical maneuvers to the individual skills that now became second nature to his soldiers.

Training progressed and Colonel Wallace and his officers were generally pleased with the improvement. However, earlier deploying divisions sent to France required trained men to be reassigned from the 332nd. Captain Story noted that, "It was most discouraging to the Officers from Colonel Wallace down to have to train units and then have the men transferred to other camps or divisions for overseas service. It was estimated that we must have trained over 12,000 men before we finally moved out of Camp Sherman."[32]

"About 10 days before leaving Camp Sherman for France, nearly three thousand draftees joined the 332nd to replace similar numbers sent to other organizations. Officers of rank felt that sailing time was near so I asked that new men be sent to the target range to receive the par-excellent instruction of Colonel "Sandy" McNab. Drill instruction could take place almost anywhere but range work required facilities that might not be immediately available in France. General Glenn, the Division Commander, with his usual broadminded practicality agreed. As rifle instruction was being completed the Regiment gathered up and entrained for overseas duty."[33]

Lieutenant Colonel A.J. "Sandy" McNab was known throughout the army as the best rifle marksman in the country. In fact, shortly after the 332nd left Camp Sherman, McNab was sent to France to set up a rifle training program for the entire A.E.F.

The 332nd was armed with the U.S. Enfield Rifle M1917, or M-17, as the soldiers came to call it. This was not the "standard" weapon of the Army in the First World War. That weapon was the M1903 Springfield Rifle – the famous '03 Rifle. However, the Springfield Arsenal was unable to keep up with the meteoric expansion of the Army. They simply could not produce enough '03 Rifles to meet the requirements of the deploying American Expeditionary Forces divisions. The answer to this acute logistical problem came in the form of a contract that Britain had with several U.S. companies for the manufacture of rifles prior to our entry into the World War. Winchester, Remington Arms and a factory contracted by Remington Arms in Eddystone, Pennsylvania were manufacturing British P14 rifles. These weapons were being produced in caliber .303, the British standard caliber. Secretary of War Newton Baker quickly realized that if these factories could manufacture the P14 in caliber .30-06, the standard caliber of American issue ammunition, the rifle problem would be solved. American industry immediately answered his call and devised a simple method to convert the rifles. Thus, the M-17 Enfield rifle joined ranks with the '03 Springfield as an issue weapon of the AEF. Secretary Baker further decided to arm all of the National Army Divisions with M-17's, simplifying logistics rather than issue any one division two different types of rifles. Thus, as a National Army Regiment, this was the primary weapon of the men of the 332nd.

Private George A. Roberts, one of the new inductees from F Company summed up his view of this period: "Hiked over to Mt. Logan to the rifle range for a week to improve in marksmanship, then returned to camp for more instructions in squads east and west and trigger squeeze. After five weeks of hard drilling, of bayonet practice, signaling, physical development and hiking, the next move was to entrain for the first lap of the trip to Europe."[34]

The Historian of Company K added, "The last few weeks were busy ones. Every man was completely refitted in clothes and equipment. Off the range again a new and more intensive drill schedule was started; all passes were annulled, and every man and officer worked literally night and day. The months at Camp Sherman had taught us many mechanical things, but the lesson that got home to most of us was not taught on the drill field or in the lecture room, but in our daily life – that the American civilian, given even a very little training, becomes a soldier, who, either considered as an individual, a company or an army, cannot be beaten when his cause is just."[35]

During this preparation period, soldiers and their families sensed that the departure date for Europe was imminent. Ferris Myrice, a private in L Company, wrote that on May 12th, Mother's Day, there were "visitors galore-Received my first pass-7-17 uptown with mother."[36] Some mothers were not as fortunate during their visit to the camp. As noted in the

Company D. Log, "Mother's Day brought both joy and grief. On that day the camp was filled with mothers and relatives of soldiers who had journeyd (sic) from near and far to see their loved ones about to depart for overseas service. The intensive training schedule, a consequence of the intended immediate departure for overseas, along with the probable military crisis on the European battlefront, necessitated training without a break. Many mothers returned to their homes, their hearts saddened that they were unable to see their sons at all, or were, at least, not able to spend but a very little time in final companionship. "Carry On' was the order of the day. It became more and more apparent as the days passed that soon the regiment would be starting for "Over There."[37]

So, after nearly eight months of extensive training, the 332nd Infantry Regiment began its' anticipated journey to answer the call to arms that would take them to the "Big Show" in France. Members of Company D reported that:

> "At 8:45 a.m. on May 25, the company entrained, and started for the seaboard via the B&O Railroad. Upon reaching Parkersburg, West Virginia, an enthusiastic greeting welcomed the trains, while the American Red Cross served palatable and appetizing food and drinks. This heartfelt greeting of welcome and farewell, at once, was the beginning of a long series of its kind which were to add a spirit of patriotic fervor and fan into a breeze the fires of patriotism which often are dormant in the heart of a disciplined soldier.
>
> When again at Grafton, W. Va., the same hearty expressions of regard were demonstrated as at Parkersburg; when every village and hamlet along the route proved its loyalty by various patriotic manifestations; and finally, when [in] Philadelphia, that proud old city of true Americans, displayed its real feeling by shrieking whistles, clanging bells, and exultant hurrahs – well, every man felt a strange and new awakening as though his very soul, accustomed to looking down into the black caverns of cold earth, had suddenly been turned face upward to the sunlight and there beheld a new and hereto unseen divinity, the unconquerable spirit of one hundred millions of people. It is by no means an easy task to journey four thousand miles from home to fight a foreign foe on foreign soil; but to fight, to die if necessary for such people, such homes, and a land that believes in one, that is back of one till the last glowing ember fades into darkness, ah! That is not hard; that is easy for a man. The route was through the mineral rich hills of West Virginia, to the Apalachin (sic) foothills of Cumberland, Maryland; over the mountains to the Potomac, and to Washington, D.C., to Philadelphia, via Baltimore; thence to New York City, and finally to Camp Merritt, where Company D arrived at 9:00 p.m. Sunday May 26th."[38]

Lieutenant August A. Rendigs, Jr., who was second in command of H Company, described the departure:

> "... Tourist Pullmans for the men and Standard Pullmans for the officers, and the cars were soon filled with our boys in Khaki. Then they leaned out of the windows, and a few, whose folks were still there, were permitted to mingle with them on the cinder path along the siding. A few of the boys whose sweethearts were there, paid no attention whatever to the conventions, but boldly put their arms around the girls' waists and strolled up and down in plain view of everyone... Promptly at 12 noon, the train's wheels began to move ... Then a mighty cheer went up – it seemed as if everyone desired to give vent to a pent-up emotion ..."

He continued, "As twilight settled down ... a chorus of boyish voices could be heard ... throughout the long train, singing ... – "My Old Kentucky Home", "Back Home Again in Indiana", and the song of our regiment, "Ohio". And to us in the last coach it sounded fine and beautiful ..."[39]

Captain Austin Story remembered the journey as a "... comfortable trip in Pullmans."[40] Private Henry S. Blank agreed saying in a most satisfied manner which was quite unusual for him, "rode...on sleeping cars by way of West Virginia ... the best service we have enjoyed anywhere."[41] But perhaps their travels are best illustrated in a History of Company E poem: "Towns on the road sure treated us fine; What they gave made our faces shine. A merry old ride all along the way, Our first big jump in the U.S.A. Lem-on-ade, and fine grape juice, A cig-a-rette, or a piece of fruit, Post-al cards – a favor or two, Things went fine, and we never got stewed. 'Twas hel-lo girls, and hel-lo boys, A merry hurrah, to everybody's joy; From the time we left to the time we 'rived, We can safely say "'twas one fine ride."[42]

Beginning on Friday, May 24, 1918, several trains carried the units of the 332nd Infantry along various routes: some through Buffalo, Utica and Syracuse, New York; others on a more southerly path. The greetings and receptions given along the way were much the same, though. Lieutenant Rendigs recounted his experience, "People ran to their windows to call to us, and little children to their gates to wave their little flags and shout to our boys ... we stopped at a suburb of Philadelphia, where we were met by the Red Cross, who served sandwiches, doughnuts, fruit and coffee to the boys and gave them flowers."[43]

Unknown to most of the regiment's members was that their final stateside destination was to be Camp Merritt, New Jersey. Camp Merritt was named in honor of Major General Wesley Merritt, a distinguished veteran of the Civil War and commander of the first Philippine Expedition.[44] Camp Merritt was one of the principal staging areas for troops prior to embarkation. The cantonment served the Port of Hoboken, one of the major seaports used for troop movements. Here soldiers underwent the preparations necessary prior to sailing overseas. Officers conducted final inspections, troops were issued any missing or replacement equipment, and men were manifested on outbound troop transport ships waiting to join convoys to England and France. Lastly, troops boarded trains or ferries destined for the Hoboken docks and the passage across the Atlantic. Normally, soldiers could expect a short stay at these embarkation camps before departure.

Camp Merritt was located across the Hudson River from New York City. Rather than enjoying a sightseeing tour of the area, Sergeant Major Lettau reported that "After a weary twelve days here of endless clothing checks, physical examinations and dripping letters to loved ones, we proceeded to Hoboken, crossed the river to the majestic "*Aquitania*," second largest ship afloat, and went to our-er-staterooms."[45]

Members of Company K recalled their time at Camp Merritt somewhat differently, "It was about noon when we arrived in Closter, a small town in New Jersey, and we hiked to our barracks in Camp Merritt, only a short distance from the station. Here we spent ten days. Each day taking hikes for about three hours and really enjoying it as the country was so different from what we had been accustomed to, and the cool breezes from the Atlantic Ocean were a stimulant to our pep, which was already quite high. The remainder of the time we spent placing our identification tags, extra shoelaces, etc., in an orderly manner on our bunks so the C.O.'s [Commanding Officers] could determine when we were properly fitted for overseas service. When equipped we were given more freedom and also allowed passes to New York City. We do not know what the individuals did when they were out on those twenty-four hour passes, but we did take for granted that they had a good time. This did not last long, for at noon on June 5 orders came in that no more passes were to be issued and we were to be confined to the area of our barracks."[46]

Leave in the city was described by Lieutenant Rendigs. "Arrived in New York, the party separated into little groups and followed their various bents. The average man had at least one big meal and "took in" some good theatre … slept that night between clean sheets, had a wholesome breakfast according to their means, a short morning shopping expedition, and it was time to return to camp."[47]

In his typical disgruntled tone, Private Blank of I Company wrote of yet another experience. His journal entry noted, "Arrived at Camp Merritt May 24 at 8:30pm Merritt being a rest camp until we arrived there. We broke the record. We drilled and it was better than Sherman." Later he added, "Dutch Engle King visited me June 2 at Merritt. We were promised passes but found it was all Bull like everything else in the Army."[48]

Ferris Wellman Myrice, a private in L Company recorded his trip from Camp Merritt. He noted that, "Thursday – up early breakfast – Policed up hike with full pack about 2 miles to Dumont station – Erie R.R. New York – across Hudson on a Ferry boat to Cunard dock and then on board the *Aquitania* – Bottom deck – "G" – Hell – hot etc. farthest from the propeller – *Carpathia* first to the *Titanic's* aid – lying alongside, walked deck for two hours watching crap and poker games – $100 a throw."[49]

One officer's experience on the *H.M.S. Aquitania* was significantly different as described by Lieutenant Rendigs, "… a large, comfortable room, containing two handsome, mahogany, single beds, with dressers and chairs to match, and was to be occupied by our captain together with another from the Third Batallion (sic) … our own quarters… a small state room along the outside of the ship, containing four permanent bunks, two on either side, with a wash stand and coat rack between them, Everything was scrupulously clean and neat, the steward service proved to be very good … We also noted the Colonel's and General's quarters in passing, – each had a small suite."[50]

Myrice was correct, the *Carpathia* was indeed berthed next to the *Aquitania* in New York that day. A few weeks later, on July 17, 1918, while traveling as part of a convoy, the *Carpathia* was torpedoed off the east coast of Ireland by the German submarine U-55. She quickly listed to port and sank bow first, passing into history. The ship which had rescued the *Titanic* shared her fate if not her circumstances; all but five hands would be saved by the vigilant crew of the HMS *Snowdrop*.

The *Aquitania* was the longest serving Cunard liner of the time. The Cunard Line initially planned to operate the ship on the North Atlantic route to New York convoying alongside the *Lusitania* and *Mauretania*. Exercising great caution in the light of the recent Titanic disaster, the company ensured that lifeboat accommodations were provided for all those on board. The *Aquitania's* original passenger accommodations were far superior to anything seen on liners before her launching; quickly establishing her one of the best-known of Cunard luxury liners.

Much fanfare was planned for the *Aquitania* when she left Liverpool on her maiden voyage in May 1914, bound for New York. The event was overshadowed by a tragedy on the day before the launch. A German submarine attack caused the tragic loss of the liner *Empress of Ireland*, and the one thousand souls on board. The *Aquitania* made two more commercial passenger voyages to New York before the outbreak of the World War. Immediately upon the opening of hostilities, she was requisitioned by the British Government to serve as an armed merchant cruiser and was commissioned into the Royal Navy in August. After colliding with the ship Canadian in a fog weeks after her first deployment, the Royal Navy concluded that the *Aquitania* was too large for service as a cruiser. By 1915, she was serving as a troopship ferrying British soldiers to the ill-fated Gallipoli campaign. In 1916 and 1917, she served intermittently as a hospital ship: U.S. entry into the war brought the *Aquitania* back into service to transport the American Expeditionary Forces to Europe. Joseph Doyle in *The History of Company K* writes:

> "After receiving our bunk assignments we took advantage of the opportunity to look this transport over, and I am sure no one met with disappointment. With more than eleven thousand men aboard she seemed more like a small city than a steamship. Just now we began to have a sneaky feeling we were going somewhere, and that somewhere was not going to be in the United States. Had it not been for the boat drill and getting lost on our way to the mess hall we should have had a thorough knowledge of the ship by the time we sailed on June 8.
>
> It was 8 o'clock in the morning when a little tug came down the river and hooked onto the transport. As she began to move slowly away we were ordered from all decks, so our only means of seeing New York fade from sight was through a small port hole or a little scratch made in the black

paint that covered every tiny piece of glass that served as an opening for daylight. It was near noon before we were allowed on deck again to watch the destroyers and sub-chasers darting here and there on the water, reminding one more of a faithful dog hunting for his master than boats as a means of protection for us. But what a burden those life belts were to us, ten steps from our bunk without one and we were stopped by the guard, and at night it was nowhere but under our head. True, we knew they might be a means of saving our lives some time, but we did not have the feeling that the subs were going to get anywhere near us, so why wear them? At 4 o'clock our mascots turned back and we were alone at sea.

From the deck the next day nothing was to be seen except now and then a lone ship far in the distance, and things began to seem a bit monotonous. But we had become pretty tired from the intensive drilling, and found no trouble at all in sleeping. Soldiers are not supposed to get tired, and the commander saw to it that we were given the manual of arms, target practice, etc., on the decks, even though the boat at times was at an angle that made it impossible to stand at attention. This continued day after day with moving pictures in the mess hall and small group gatherings to keep our minds occupied during the evenings."[51]

Late in the afternoon, the day the regiment sailed, the soldiers witnessed an unusual phenomenon a solar eclipse. One can only imagine the thoughts that passed through the minds of the men watching as they made their way off to war. But there were other distractions as well. Second Battalion Sergeant Major Joseph Lettau added:

"We were too much filled with curiosity to explore this huge vessel to think much of the coming dangers. We lay next to the pier until the morning of June 8th, when to our disgust we were ordered below until the ship should have cleared the harbor. So, we left America without even the slight consolation of wafting a kiss to Miss Liberty, whose features we were not to see for ten, long, weary months.

Besides the 332nd Infantry, there were aboard Major General Glenn with his staff and about 2000 men of medical units. To our great surprise, and a twinge of misgiving, we had no escort after the first day out and this, with the U-boats spreading terror along our coast. At this time, even Coney Island had been darkened at night. However, the "*Aquitania*" had speed as well as grace and it would have required a fast U-boat to drive a torpedo into her side as she sped on her zig-zag course.

The weather was perfect and we proceeded without adventure until the fourth day out when someone sighted what he thought was the periscope of a submarine. (I think he must have been a Medic!) At any rate, his loudly voiced cry started a small panic which might have reached disastrous dimensions had not word suddenly come that the object sighted was a floating buoy used by the transports for a target in practice firing.

Some of the most intensely interesting minutes aboard were spent watching the little three inch guns which every few minutes turned on their pivots as they followed each suspicious looking object in the water. There were not enough gunners, so several doughboys were detailed to render assistance. Besides these guardians of the public welfare, the regular guard was stationed at various points on the ship, the companies taking their turn at guard duty.

By way of showing the submarines what they thought of them, our excellent band gave several greatly enjoyed concerts on the open deck.

On the morning of June 15th, Ireland was sighted and, before noon, we had passed up the river Mersey and stood on land once more in the city of Liverpool, England."[52]

Private Myrice recorded his view of the voyage in several terse journal entries, "June 8, Called to quarters at 7:45 – ship started at 8:10 – just saw about – of statue of Liberty – on guard 15 out of 24 hours – Mess certainly rotten. Bloomin Hinglish starve us and then sell us food at high prices. In bed with a dizzy feeling – a fine watch is kept – a destroyer lead the way – a plane also watches over us. June 10 All's well – I watch the sea about half my time. spend the rest – reading. Water – wild water – blue-black one instance pure white the next Saw a school of flying fish – the fish were 4 or 5 inches long. June 11 With a cork preserver for a desk – all on top as yet – they say its our last night to sleep without clothes – on this trip. Real danger zone tomorrow. On cleaning up detail with squad today. June 12 A mine sighted. – Orders, sleep with clothes on. danger zone. Danger everywhere – but one never realizes it. A trifle homesick. June 13. This old sea is sure rocking the boat. June 14 Land sighted sure looked good. One of the convoys sighted a sub – not so good. Sea looked green. so near Ireland, I suppose."[53]

Private George Roberts reported a similar story,

"Left port at 8:15 a.m. convoyed by two submarine chasers and an airplane for a day, when they turned back. A sharp lookout was kept for U boats. Boat drills were held daily and life belts were worn all the time on that trip. It was quite an uneventful trip except on two occasions, once when the "Watch" thought they had sighted a Sub., and again when we met a boat that was repairing the Atlantic Cable. This boat was a little slow in returning our salute, or pass, and we had all guns trained on her and probably would have fired on her had she not answered just when she did. June 13 found us one day ahead of our schedule which made it necessary for our boat to travel in a circle for an entire day while waiting for the English convoys which did arrive sometime during the night. We lived in a place called "Glory Hole" down on F deck, which is somewhere near the bottom of the boat, had bunk inspections daily, spent the time trying to drill, practice sighting and trigger squeezing; were not allowed on deck after dark. The meals were simply rotten so I lived mostly on candy and crackers which I purchased at the canteen. June 14 Had a glimpse of the coast of Ireland about sunset."[54]

Private Henry Blank was unimpressed as he noted, "Left New York City June 6, from 47th St. Docks, Arrived Halifax June 9 after a some-what rough ride. Fed the fish [got seasick] twice on the way. Left Halifax June 9 in the afternoon, with 14 other boats besides escorts."[55]

The Company D log added:

> "On the evening of June 14 a setting sun broke through the western clouds and a shaft of golden sunlight exposed to view the southeast coast of Ireland. That night the Irish Sea was crossed and in the morning the *Aquitania* rested on a choppy estuary covered with white winged fishing boats, at the mouth of the Mersey River. Liverpool lay in front. Unable to enter the river mouth at ebb tide, the *Aquitania* anchored outside, and at noon, on the crest of a high tide, bore its burden of khaki up the river and at 2:00 p.m., June 15, the 332nd set foot on European soil."[56]

Docked in Liverpool and safely on shore, the 332nd was welcomed by, "... an English band, composed entirely of boys save for the band leader, arrived on the scene and regaled us with a few of our popular airs, "Over There", "Keep The Home Fires Burning", and a few others ... Then began our march through the city to the depot on the other side. We were enthusiastically greeted by crowds all along the line of march... we reached the railroad station, and here again we were greeted by a large, hospitable, crowd and another brass band of boy musicians." recollected Lieutenant Rendigs.[57] Before the trains left the Liverpool station, some of the men of the 332nd received cards distributed by the British Army with the official Imperial welcome from His Majesty, King George IV.[58]

Pleased with his initial impression of England George Roberts wrote,

> "June 15 Arrived Liverpool, England; this city being up the Mercey (sic) river some distance from the sea. Marched thru the city to the depot where trains were waiting. The English railroad system seems to be a good one, but the engines are much smaller than ours and very powerful. The cars are divided into four parts, each part accommodating eight persons; the cars have side door entrances. This was the Midland Railway. There are no railway crossings in England; the highways are bridged over the tracks.
>
> Our ride thru England was one I shall never forget; it lasted far into a beautiful moonlight night. It did not get dark until late and the sunset back of those ancient farms presented a scene of grandeur and picturesque beauty, rare to behold. Most of the farm houses were built of stone or brick and covered with green ivy. The fields were small, well cultivated and fenced in by ancient stone fences; the whole a thrifty and beautiful country, inviting and interesting. Our journey took us thru Derby and Birmingham and to South Hampton June 16th at 2 a.m. where we walked to the rest camp at the edge of the city, which was a very quiet place with practically no lights as a precaution against air raids."[59]

By contrast, Henry Blank simply noted, "Not sure on the date. Rode across England in some dinky cars ... After several days experience with English meals & sanitary ideas – in a bucket and let it stand for 24 hours before empting it."[60]

Sergeant Major Lettau much taken with England, painted a somewhat different view,

> "Our stay here was confined to a walk from the pier to a railroad station about two miles away. The English cordially welcomed us and sent us off with a boy's band conducted by a genial, elderly man.
>
> The ride from Liverpool, in the peculiar little English coaches, took us across the rich farm lands of Southern England. We passed through so many tunnels that, when I think of England, I think of tunnels broken here and there by little towns containing little brick houses bordered by pretty little gardens most neatly kept.
>
> Arriving at Southampton, we hiked miles to a "Rest Camp." I would not dare mention these two words in the vicinity of a doughboy for, it is true, we do not understand the English language as our English friends do. Imagine yourself and twelve others occupying a tent made for eight and this tent luxuriously furnished with a – wooden floor and a tent pole. Then imagine resting on a bed consisting of the contents of your pack, namely, two blankets, one mess kit, one shelter half, one rope, one tent pole, five pins, one suit of BVD'S, two pairs of socks and a pair of shoe laces. Keep your picture moving and imagine the task of collecting your property in the morning and making a neat roll. And this is what they call a "Rest Camp!"
>
> We began to take war seriously. "If this is a rest camp," we thought, "why –" but figure it out for yourself. Indeed we were glad to leave Southampton on the cattle boats which awaited us."[61]

Lieutenant Rendigs described their preparation for departure: "Just before noon we received word that we were to leave that afternoon for France and that our battalion was to move at four o'clock. This was a surprise to us, as we had expected at least a short sojourn in England, but those were the days when the need of troops was indeed pressing, and we were to commence training in France at once. After a very frugal dinner, which left us with the impression that food was scarce in England, – an impression that we afterwards learned was correct, we strolled about the camp and visited the Y.M.C.A. and the camp Canteen. At the latter place we obtained beer and ale ... Our men soon learned of this place and the absence of any restrictions against drinking, whereupon the Canteen became immensely popular and there was scarcely standing room inside. Upon visiting the "Y", we found it filled with English and American soldiers, some of them swapping yarns, others playing a small Victrola and piano in opposite ends of the room, while still others were busily engaged in writing home. It was good to see how quickly and readily our soldiers fraternized with the English, this fraternization and good feeling occurred whenever we came in contact with them thereafter. It was soon time to move again, so promptly at four o'clock, in a drizzling rain, we began our march to the docks."[62]

The moment had finally come! After long months, the 332nd was entering the last portion of their journey to France. George Roberts reported that, "Leaving the camp at 4 P.M. we marched thru the city to the docks where we boarded the boat "*Viper*" to cross the English Channel. The boat was much overcrowded, dirty and old. We passed the Isle of Wright [sic], saw many ancient castles, and also many boats that had been disabled by U-boats or mines."[63]

In addition to the *Viper*, other transport boats that ferried the regiment across the English Channel to France included the *Archangel* and the *Prince George*, the latter, according to the *History of Company K*, "... would have been a disgrace to the worst freight car in the United States, and there was barely room enough for our packs in the hold, not thinking of sleeping room."[64]

The History of Company E offered a humorous account of their voyage with this poem; "Sleep aboard was but a dream, Piled in a corner, or 'gainst a beam; On top of packs, and about the floor, When all settled, of space there was no more. Some men slept on the deck they said, One man slept on another fellow's head, Some fellow's hot and other men cold; a devil of a boat a hundred years old.[65]

The 332nd United States Infantry Regiment landed at Le Havre, France early in the morning of June 17, 1918. Their adventures in Europe had only just begun.

Major General Edwin F. Glenn, Commander of the 83rd Division, U.S. National Army, posed mounted for this Camp Sherman portrait. Courtesy Military History Institute.

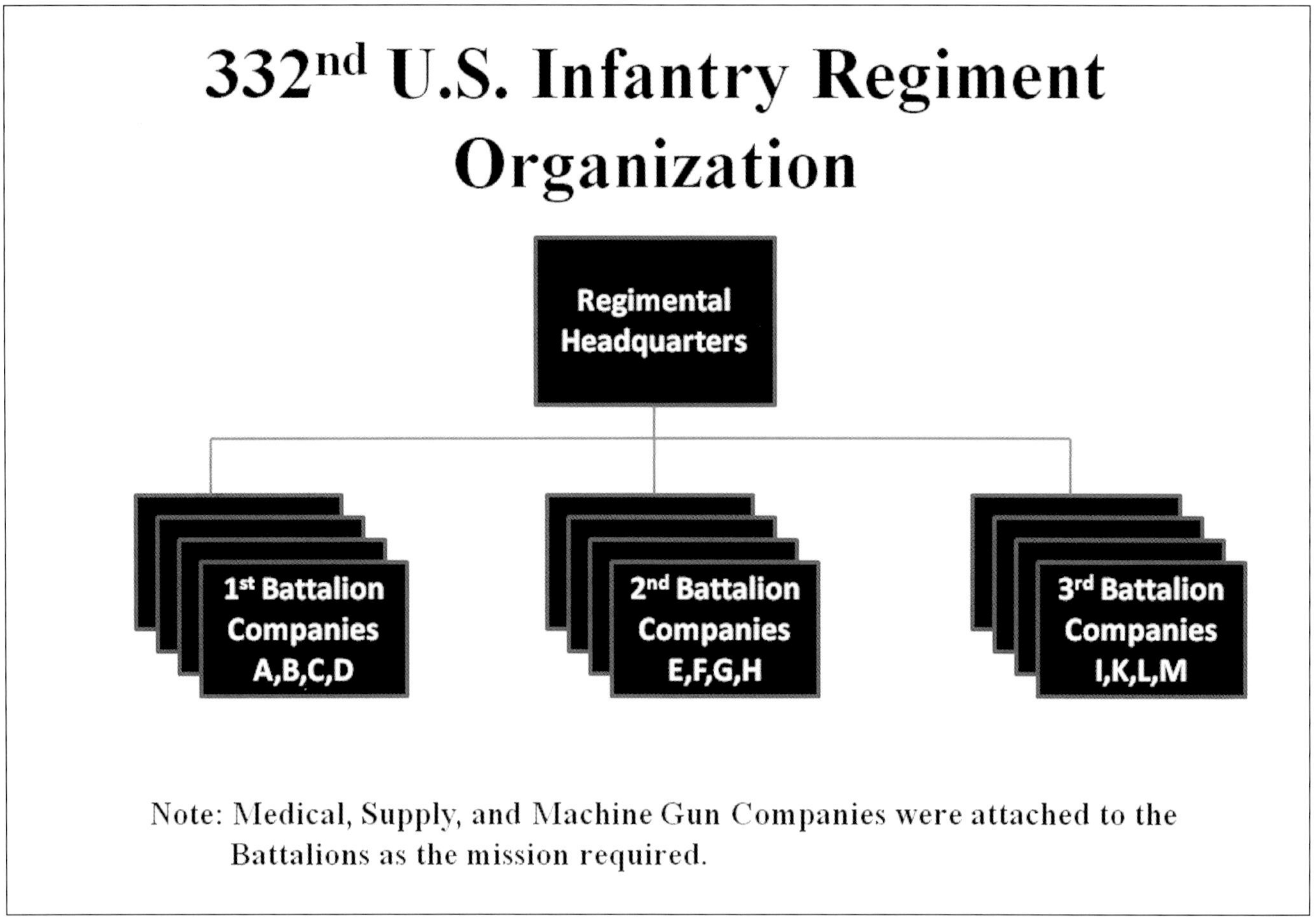

The 332nd Regiment's Organization.

The Railroad Station at Camp Sherman. From here the regiment departed for Camp Merritt and France. Courtesy Military History Institute.

A view of Camp Sherman showing the vast area of the cantonment. Courtesy Military History Institute.

This image shows camp buildings under construction. A building went up at Camp Sherman every twenty minutes during the early days of camp construction. Courtesy Military History Institute

Another view of the camp. Note the recruits in formation in front of the barracks buildings. Courtesy Military History Institute.

New inductees arrive at the camp and assemble in front of their barracks. Courtesy Military History Institute.

Opposite
Top: A group of the Army's newest soldiers pose in front of a Camp Sherman barracks. Having yet to be issued their uniforms, they wear Army-issue raincoats over civilian clothes and have their new mess kits and cups ready for a fine Army meal. Courtesy Military History Institute.

Bottom: Wearing freshly issued uniforms and loaded down with equipment, new soldiers move into their barracks. Courtesy Military History Institute.

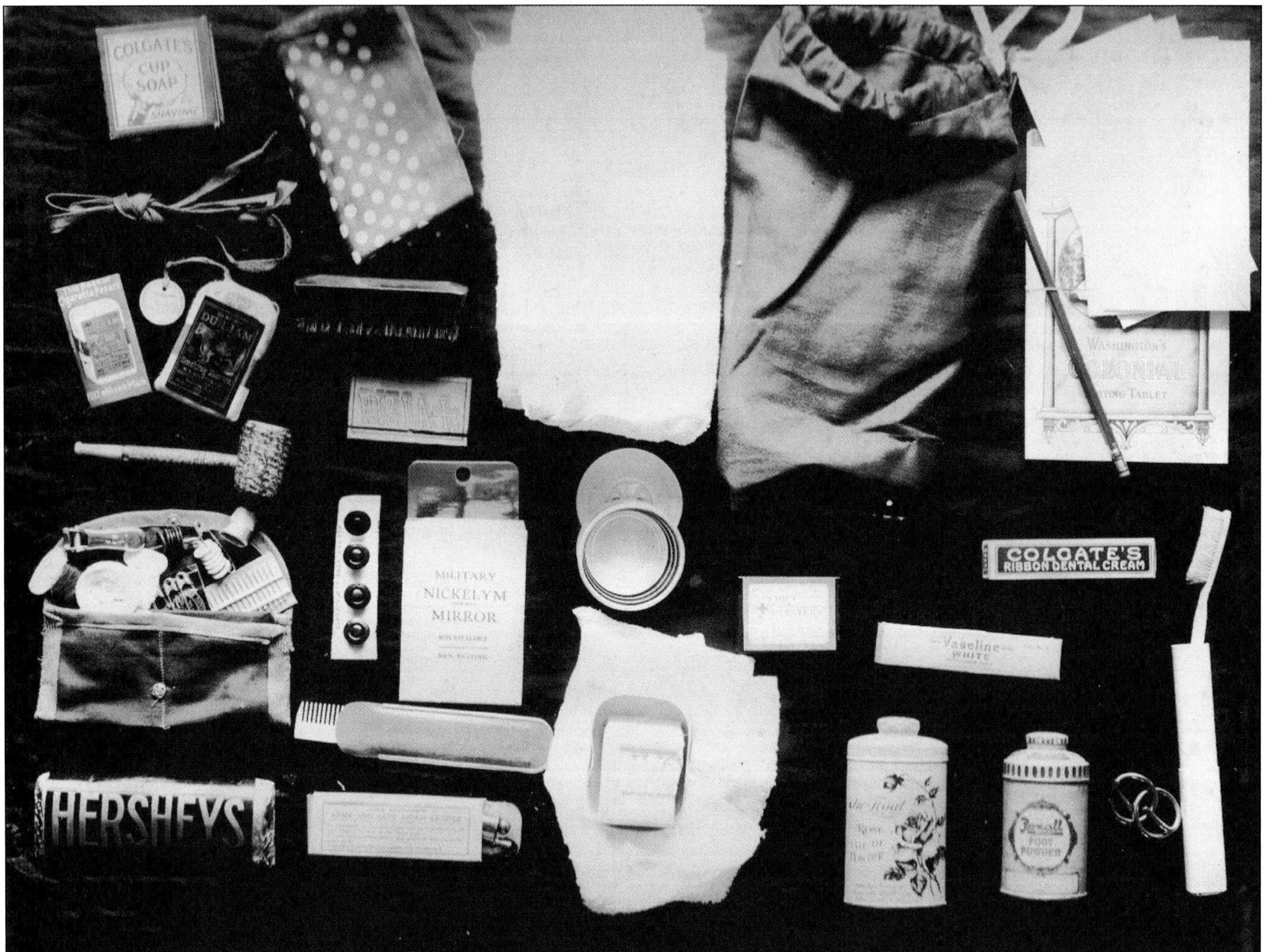
COLGATE'S
CUP
SOAP
SHAVING
WASHINGTON'S
MILITARY
NICKELYM
MIRROR
COLGATE'S
RIBBON DENTAL CREAM
Vaseline
WHITE
HERSHEYS
FOOT
POWDER

Opposite
Top: Physical fitness became one of the first orders of business. Here a company takes unit fitness training. Courtesy Military History Institute.

Bottom: Komfort Kits were issued to each soldier and contained a variety of items to make life in camp bearable. Courtesy Military History Institute.

Right: Several specialist trainers were assigned to the camp including (left) Johnny Kilbane, featherweight champion of the world who was the boxing instructor and (right) British Captain De Brissoe Owen, the bayonet fighting instruction officer. Courtesy Military History Institute.

Major Woodcock of the British Army supervised machine gun training. Courtesy Military History Institute.

French officers were also assigned to the camp. Here Lieutenant Michel poses for the camera. Courtesy Military History Institute.

Sergeant John H. McClanahan was the best shot in camp. McClanahan was a Regular Army soldier who fought at Montdidier-Noyon; Aisne-Marne; St. Mihiel and Meuse-Argonne and went on to accept a commission as a Second Lieutenant in the 103rd Engineers, 28th Division. Courtesy Military History Institute.

Camp Perry was struck by a blizzard on November 23, 1917. This image, taken from a panoramic photograph, shows the soldiers of the 332nd Infantry digging out the next morning. Courtesy Private Collection.

Another section of the same panoramic photograph. Note the primitive mess hall at center and line of soldiers waiting for chow. Courtesy Private Collection.

Colonel Robert W. Mearns, the first Commander of the 332nd Infantry Regiment. Mearns had been promoted to Brigadier General by the time this portrait was taken at Camp Beauregard, Louisiana in February 1919. Courtesy Military History Institute.

Machine gun training at Camp Sherman. Note that the soldiers are wearing the blue denim fatigues with the driver's cap. Courtesy Military History Institute.

Soldiers firing at the completed rifle range at the foot of Mount Logan. Courtesy Military History Institute.

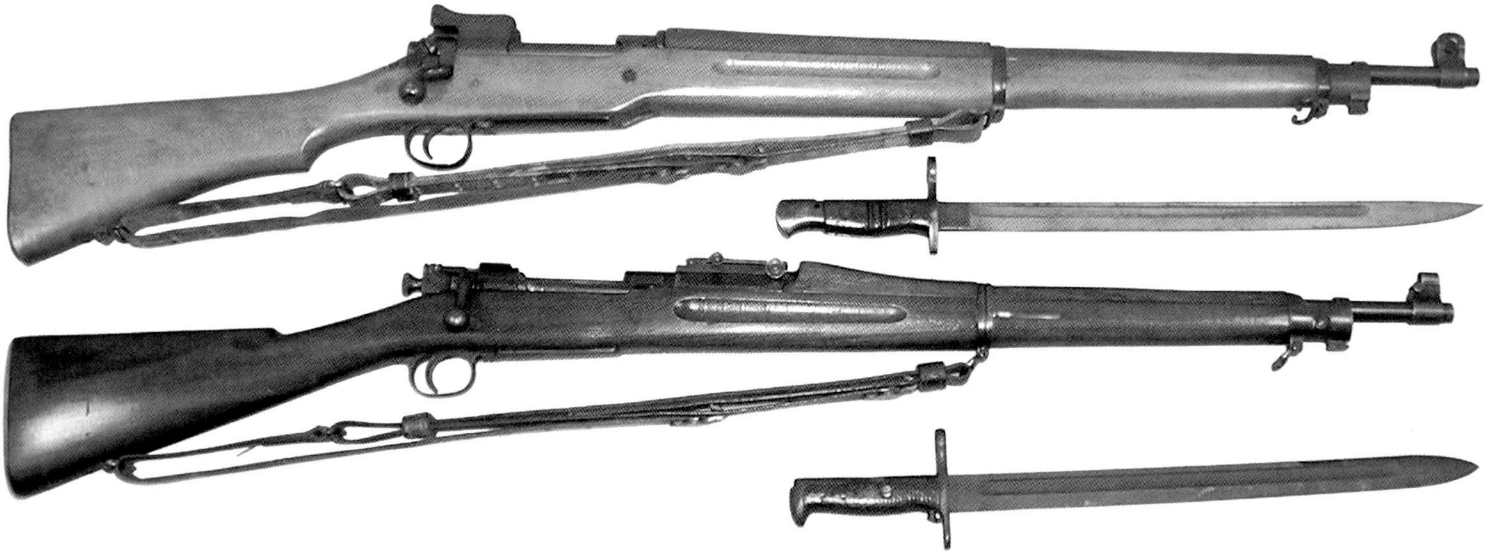

Above: The comparison between the M1903 Springfield (bottom) and the M1917 Rifle which the 332nd was issued (top). The Springfield was the "standard" U.S. Army weapon, the M1917 was adopted as an emergency measure for National Army units. Courtesy Army Heritage Museum.

Right: This close-up of the two bolt action assemblies (M1917 at top, M1903 at bottom) further illustrates the differences between the two rifles. Though the M1917 was reliable, its awkward action made it unpopular with soldiers. Courtesy Army Heritage Museum.

Rifle firing at Camp Sherman. Note the trench positions built to simulate firing on the Western Front. Courtesy Military History Institute.

Many dignitaries visited Camp Sherman; here Pennsylvania Governor Brumbaugh reviews the troops. Courtesy Military History Institute.

Former President Taft and Former Governor Judson Harmon are entertained by Brigadier General and Mrs. Frederick Perkins. Courtesy Military History Institute.

One of the members of the French Military Mission instructs a class on bombing. Courtesy Military History Institute.

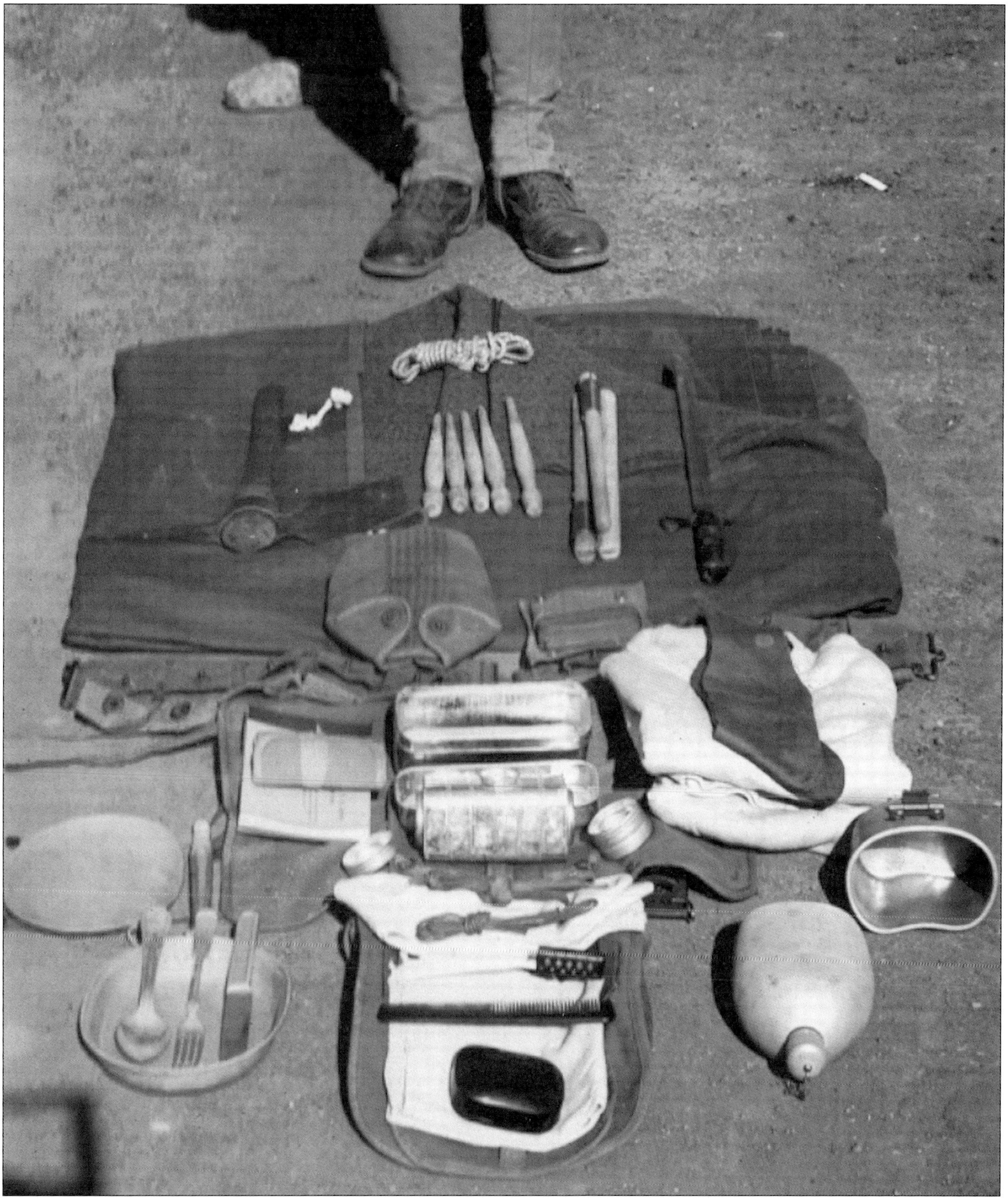

Opposite
Top: Soldiers undergo bayonet training at Camp Sherman. Note the British officer, probably Captain De Brissoe Owen, in the foreground conducting the training. Once again, the soldiers are wearing the blue denim fatigues. Courtesy Military History Institute.

Bottom: Two newly minted soldiers stand equipment inspection. Courtesy Military History Institute.

Above: A closer view of the equipment laid out for inspection. Courtesy Military History Institute.

Soldiers give bombing a try! Courtesy Military History Institute.

Final machine gun training at Mount Logan before departing for Europe. Courtesy Military History Institute.

Bridge over the Scioto River built by B Company, 308th Engineer Regiment. Courtesy Military History Institute.

Another view of the bridge. Courtesy Military History Institute

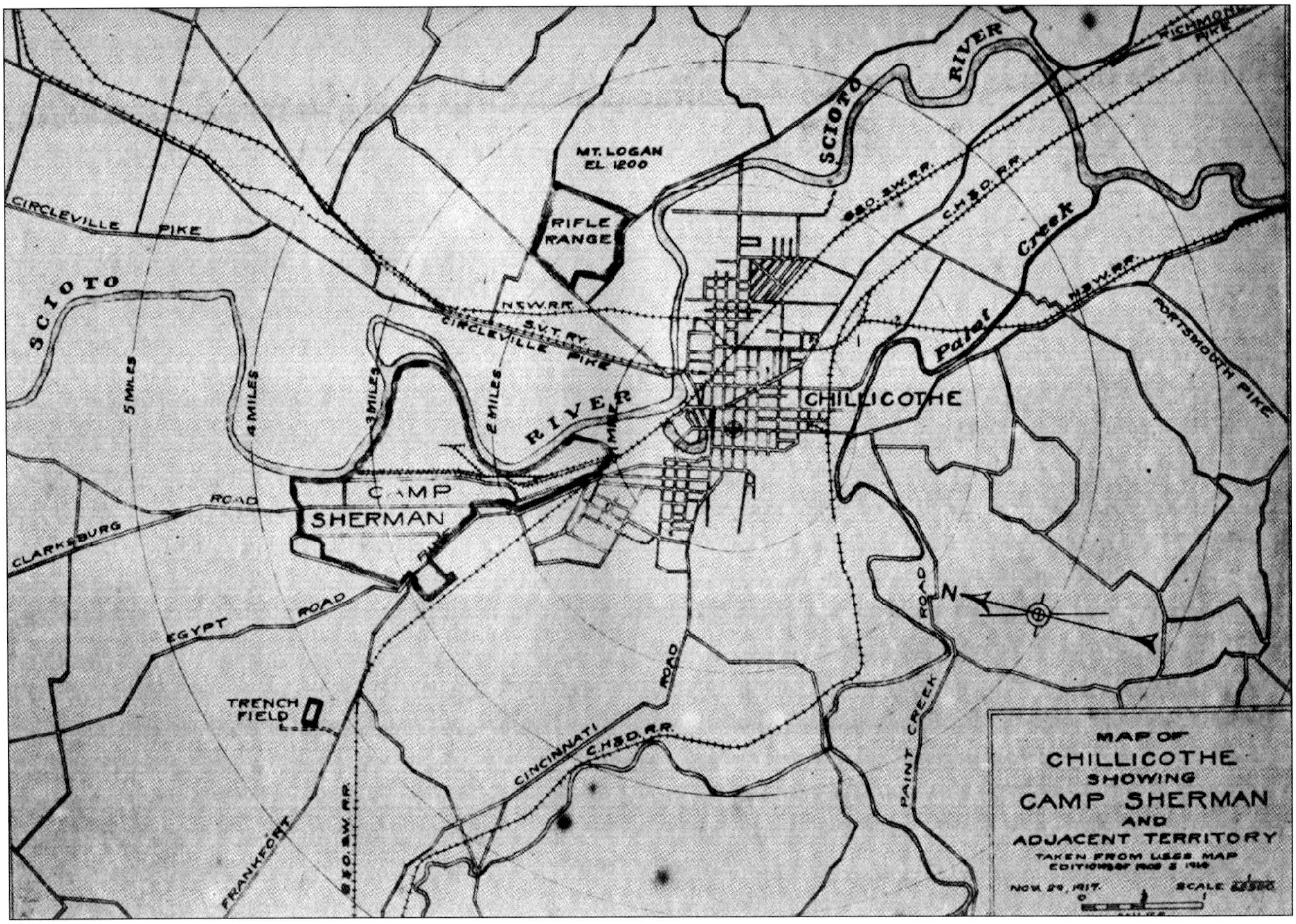

Map of Camp Sherman, Ohio. Courtesy Military History Institute.

Gas Mask training at Camp Sherman under the supervision of a British NCO. Courtesy Military History Institute.

Brigadier General Frederick Perkins, 166th Infantry Brigade Commander. Courtesy Military History Institute.

Colonel William Wallace was the second commander of the 332nd Infantry Regiment. He would command the regiment for the remainder of the war. Courtesy Military History Institute.

The HMS Aquitania was the largest ship in the Cunard Service and transported the regiment to France. Courtesy Military History Institute.

When troops leave Camp Merritt, New Jersey for embarkation overseas they break camp at an early hour, march to Alpine Landing, where they board a boat and are taken to the embarkation pier, Hoboken. Soldiers waiting at Alpine Landing for the boat. Courtesy National Archives.

End of hike from Camp Merritt to Alpine Landing. Courtesy National Archives.

Opposite
Top: Troops from Camp Merritt boarding boats at Alpine Landing. Courtesy National Archives.
Bottom: Leaving the ferryboat "Catskill" at Hoboken. Courtesy National Archives.

WOMEN
15601

Another view of soldiers leaving the ferryboat "Catskill" at Hoboken. Courtesy National Archives.

An unidentified member of the 332nd sits for a studio portrait most likely rendered at Camp Sherman, Ohio. Note the "332" clearly visible on his collar insignia. Courtesy Private Collection.

2

"France at last, and news too incredible to believe!"

"FRANCE AT LAST!" was the way Sergeant Major Lettau characterized his initial feeling when he set foot on the Continent. He continued:

> "Early on the morning of June 17th, 1918, our little cattle boat, having safely traversed the submarine-infested channel, steamed into the ancient harbor of Havre [Le Havre]. In the gray morning not much of the town could be seen and, anyway, we were too busy to admire the scenery."[1]

Company K, had left one platoon at the docks to help unload the baggage. They, "... quite enjoyed the mixture of workman (sic) there, which was made up of Chinese, Sengalese, Indians, German prisoners of war, British Soldiers and what not."[2]

The scene in Le Havre was described in *Company D, The Company Log*: "The shops were poor and barren; they were not American shops. French flags, with some of all allied nations, hung from the window ledges of old, black, stone buildings. A cheer greeted a French "Barbara Fritchie"[3] as she unfurled a large American flag before the ranks of Co. "D." American flags were conspicuous throughout the city."[4]

Certainly France did not agree with Private Henry Blank any more than England; he tersely noted, "Arrived at Harve ... after a night on a channel cattle boat. Marched to rest camp there ... Sold water for wine at one dollar a bottle. Meals still getting worse. Saw a Zeppelin in flight."[5]

Private George Roberts, Company F., impressed at first, soon began to see the toll that three years of war had wrought on the French people: "Arrived at Le Havre, France; the Harbor was a very busy place, reminding us of the way they do things back in the good old U.S.A. The streets of the city were narrow and very dirty, and we saw many hard looking sailors and fishermen there. Passing thru the city we beheld many sad sights such as old men, women, and children in rags, many of them looking as if they had been getting only half enough to eat.[6]

Private Ferris Myrice was also struck by the plight of the inhabitants; to him the French were "... very much "down at the heels" ..."[7]

Sergeant Major Lettau continued his observation of the regiment's first glimpse of life in France:

> "Companies were formed and trucks loaded and we started for the camp, our eyes wide with curiosity, for we were in France, that land of which we had heard so much for the last two years. I retain an impression of a dusty, aged, wasted city of old brick and stone buildings. The shopkeepers signs were interesting and – mysterious. As we moved away from the business district we passed many piles of ammunition and cannon guarded by Algerian soldiers. It was edifying to see these colored soldiers snap to attention.
>
> Everywhere, however, our passage was marked for the absence of anything like a greeting from the natives. We wondered. In America, on the train, racing to the coast, whistles shrieked, bells rang and people cheered. In England, bands played and people loudly applauded. Yet, here in France, to whose immediate aid we were rushing, no word of welcome came to us. It was grim. Did France think that America was too slow? Was France too sorrowful at her losses? Did she think that these dressed up shopmen, farmers and clerks were poor substitutes for her own brave who had died in the vain attempt to stem the German tide? Whatever her thoughts, we saw nothing to confirm the prevalent idea that the French are an excitable people.
>
> Continuing through the winding streets, up and down hills, we came to a sandy, wire-enclosed field containing a few wooden buildings and many tents. It was a dreary looking place and the painted signs giving directions to be followed in case of an air raid failed to put any humor in the situation.
>
> Outside the barbed wire fence, which held us prisoners, a sentinel paced up and down. On the street, there were

at all times several boys waiting and begging for food or cigarettes. At meal time the number increased and with them came women and girls begging for food. A walk around showed us that the camp was scarcely more than a makeshift and we hoped we would not remain long."[8]

Lieutenant Rendigs described meeting a widow and her young son during their march through the city. recalled that:

"... the little fellow ... upon our leaving, thrust a small bunch of roses into my hands as he smilingly bade us, "Au revoir, Messieurs". We cordially shook hands with mother and son, and thanked them for their courtesy, – the mother smiled sweetly and replied that she was only too glad to do what little she could for "the brave Americans who had come so far to help my country." And as we resumed our march, ... our first impressions of France took a more favorable turn."[9]

Private George Roberts, Company F, was not as fortunate as his sergeant major. Apparently, his company did not have the benefit of motor transport to get to the camp; "We marched up a long hill to a camp at the edge of the city, passing thru some attractive residence districts on the way. That camp was made up of camouflaged tents and anti-air raid trenches, an English canteen and a YMCA hut. We were not allowed to leave camp because the Rainbow Division had caused so much disturbance when passing thru there a year previous to our arrival."[10] [The 42nd Division or "Rainbow Division" was composed of National Guardsman from across the country. It included the 165th Infantry Regiment, also known as the "Fighting 69th" – a name the regiment retained from its original designation, the 69th Infantry Regiment, New York Army National Guard. The regiment was a predominantly Irish-American regiment from New York City and one can only guess what sort of mischief these soldiers managed to create at the rest camp on one of their first nights in France!]

Fortunately the regiment did not stay long in this rest camp, Sergeant Major Lettau remembered that:

"About noon of the 18th, we moved from this camp. Luckily, for us, we were first at the train and upon discovering that eight men and all their equipment, irrespective of rank, excepting commissioned officers, were to be jammed into one compartment made for eight to sit in, and that we were to spend the night there, we began to consider the matter seriously. Before long, one of the boys unfolded a plan and, a moment later, three busier Sergeants Major than we three could not have been found. We turned "baggage smashers" and in a few minutes, a whole second class compartment was empty, and later, some of the officers discovered that there were as many as three of them to a compartment.

Our ride across France took us close to Paris but as we passed at night we did not see it. France is beautiful. There was the same orderliness that we noted in England except that there was more evidence of recent neglect. The hedges along the tracks, which in other days had been so well kept, now showed lack of attention. Cattle were few and far between and no young men were seen, except those in uniform.

On the afternoon of the 19th we arrived at a town named Foulain. However, we remained in the cars until darkness. We saw no reason for wasting these daylight hours but later learned that troop movements were allowed only under cover of darkness.[11]

Company D's Log described their trip differently than that of the headquarters staff of the Second Battalion, "Darkness and rain were falling fast as Co. "D's" column entered the freight yards of Le Havre, and formed up against a long line of box cars. On each car was a sign in French: 8 Chevaux (8 horses) and 40 Hommes (40 men). ["40 and 8's" and "Sidedoor Pullmans", were the derisive name doughboys gave the workhorse boxcars of the French Railway system, they were ubiquitous on the Western Front. They were the principal means of moving troops from marshalling areas] Not forty but thirty-five men were placed in each car, which, with the full equipment each man carried, made conditions very crowded. Lights were forbidden, and in the pitch of darkness there was great confusion. Rations consisting of corned beef, canned tomatoes, beans, and hard tack, sufficient for three days' travel, were loaded into each car.[12]

F Company was not privy to the relative luxury of their sergeant major. George Roberts remembered that "we got 36 men inside believe me it was some jam."[13] Henry Blacnk from I Company agreed, "Rode form here [Le Harve] in box cars about 35 men in a car. Some men had to stand at night as there was not enough room to sleep at once."[14]

These "much beloved" French boxcars had other surprises in store. As the men piled into the cars, it began to rain, adding to the discomfort of the crowded space; "The roof leaked and water poured through on this jumbled and distorted mass of humanity. The box car had three flat wheels that never bumped in unison; there was no extra charge for the up and down motion."[15]

There were some enjoyable moments on the ride, as well. Private George Roberts was fortunate enough to catch a glimpse of some of the famous landmarks. He wrote that, "Passing thru the outskirts of Paris we saw the Eifel (sic) Tower, Capitol Dome, and the very beautiful surrounding country, interesting indeed to all of us."[16] Private Ferris Myrice also recorded that they were, "Off for the front in a box-car. Fine scenery – the people all seem to be beggars. "biscuit" is about all one could hear about the track – Women washing about the Seine River."[17]

Members of the Third Battalion remarked about the pathetic begging as the journey by train gave them "... a good chance to look over the "mademoiselles" and to share our issue of hard bread with the dirty, ragged little children who stood by the way shouting "Bisque – Americana bisque." The more we saw, the more the horrors of war were brought before us, and we would all much rather have landed in the front lines where we could have gotten a crack at the Germans than in that little town of Foulain, some 250 miles south and east of Paris."[18]

Up to this point, Sergeant Major Lettau had ardently avoided the foot marches most of the other members of the regiment had been obliged to endure during their short European foray. At Foulain, his luck ran out:

"The companies, except one, were formed and marched away into the dark, silent, rainy night. As usual, we attended to the loading of our boxes and when this was accomplished, we climbed aboard the truck. Just about this time, however, the officer who had been left behind to supervise the loading of supplies, saw us on top of the truck. With angry voice he wanted to know what we were doing there and before anyone mustered up courage to present an alibi, he ordered us off, leaving only a half dozen aboard to unload the baggage. Sorrowfully we climbed down, but we left our packs on the truck and we felt that we had "slipped one over" at any rate.[19]

The journey aboard the rain soaked and cramped trains lasted through the night and now in the early morning hours, the regiment formed for the march to their more permanent billeting locations:

"After a half hour of confusion and haste everybody was outside in formation, arms stacked and equipment on their backs, the men waited, one hour, two hours, "Fall in," came the order, and before dawn had come a long column crossed the Marne and moved snake-like out over the winding roads of the upper Marne region, leaving Foulain and the railroad in the valley.

Marching with full equipment for hours, up and down hill, is about as pleasant as having one's teeth pulled, but it is not nearly so pleasant as that, if the head of the column, not sure of his route, changes his mind and retraces his steps after an hour's aimless wandering. Such a system of exercise does not improve one's disposition, either. The country was rugged, the roads winding, and dispositions in utter ruin."[20]

Private George Roberts also commented about the officers getting them lost: "Arrived at Foulain; took a fifteen mile hike with heavy packs and without breakfast, getting lost enroute and finally ending up at Lanques Haute, Marne County, where we were billeted in barns and sheds, and of all the places we had seen this one took the record for dirt. The streets had not been cleaned for many years and the main pastime of the people seemed to be driving horses, cows, sheep, and goats thru the main street."[21]

Sergeant Major Lettau recalled that:

"The rain had ceased and the night was now truly beautiful. The stars above shone brightly and as we marched up the valley alongside a silvery canal, flanked on both sides by cool, whispering trees, we found it difficult to believe that a desperate battle raged a few miles away.

We walked at a good pace for fifty minutes and then rested ten minutes, according to the army marching rules. Of course, we smoked a cigarette, the doughboy's best friend, and enjoyed for the time, the coolness and quiet. It was difficult to get up and continue the march, and long before the next rest period came, our feet were dragging. How those lads with heavy packs stood it, is difficult to understand. Remember that for about forty hours we had been riding in a space that scarcely permitted stretching. When the order came for the second rest period, the stars as interesting phenomena had lost their charm. Even a cigarette was unattractive. We wanted to lie down and sleep, sleep, sleep. When the order to fall in came again, we stumbled to our feet and actually "fell in." The next hour was torture. Never did we want rest so much. Now and then we sighted a town ahead and our spirits rose, but always, it seemed, our town was further on. "Why are there so many hills in France?" "Will we never get to that – town?" "Is the Captain on the right road?" These thoughts filled our minds and I believe some of the boys walked in their sleep. This condition was not exceptional, it was the general feeling.[22]

E Company's poet, Cyril Littlefield wrote, "For getting lost we had to pay, Major walked us half the way, Without any rest, at a rapid pace, Up hill and down 'till we thought it was a race; Men dropped out and men laid down, Worst hike then we were ever on. Two days and nights without any rest, A hike like that was a hell of a test."[23]

The *History of Company K* recounted, "… But we kept on hiking, thinking every time we rested that our next stop would be our destination. But after seven hours of this without water passed we halted in a small village and proceeded to get into sleeping quarters. Those hay lofts and chicken sheds we pulled for billets that night afforded the best beds we ever had, and our appreciation was so great that we did not stop to remove our wet clothes, caused by the drizzling rain we had hiked through, to dry them out."[24]

Not every unit of the 332nd Infantry got lost, or hiked for the seemingly endless hours. At the evening arrival of Company H in Foulain:

"… Huge motor trucks were waiting, but these were quickly filled by the four companies of the Third Battalion, and it became apparent that we should have to remain in this place for the night. Leaving a platoon in charge of Lieut. Quensen, to unload and guard the baggage, the captain marched the remainder of the company up the winding road until we reached the main highway. Here we halted, and the captain and I went up the road to the left for about a half a mile until we came to a small tavern, which, with its lights, shining through the windows, looked most inviting to us, standing outside in the cheerless, drizzling rain, and with darkness already upon us. We entered the tavern, where we found a large bar-room with long, wooden tables and benches, occupying every foot of space, with dingy, smoky lanterns swinging overhead. The benches were comfortably crowded with French poilus indulging in their national beverage, and in the intervals between gulps giving vent to their feelings in an outburst of song. A neat looking bar-maid and an old woman, presumably her mother, were busily engaged in moving from table to table and replenishing the quickly drained glasses and tumblers of the poilus. No notice was taken of our entry, I managed to get the bar maid away from her duties long enough to tell her by means of a sort of "pigeon French" that we wanted accommodations for men and officers for the night. At first she did not think it possible to accommodate so many, but finally we agreed to put up a platoon in the large bar-room, another one in a large summer-house outside, and to quarter the third one in a barn across the road. She also furnished a large room for two of the officers upstairs, and the other two officers slept on chairs in a private dining room adjoining the large bar-room. Our arrangements completed, we quickly placed our men, who having eaten their supper on the train, were soon fast asleep on the benches, tables and chairs, and some curled up in their overcoats on the floor. Arising reluctantly early the next morning, we found the rain still coming down, but our trucks were waiting for us outside on the road. We quickly filled them with our men, and were off on the journey toward a little village called Ageville, where we were told we were to be billeted while in training."[25]

This time Private Ferris Myrice, having caught a ride on a truck from Foulain was feeling quite lucky. "... After miles of riding in a truck thru magnificent country and finally dropped off at 10 P.M. at Essy Les Eaux. They say its a typical French town – a regular mud hole houses and barns combined. The street and barnyards are "one" and a very dirty and smelly "one". Billeting in an upper room – fine, rain came thru the roof and on my clothes.[26] Another private in Company L, Raymond L. Shade, wrote, "June 22nd. Without detraining moved on south about four miles to Foulain and here detrained and were moved by U.S. Army trucks to Essey Les Eaux a distance of about ten miles. Here we were billeted in different quarters some in houses some in barns, others out in tents anywhere there might be any available space ..."

Meanwhile, a much relieved Sergeant Major Lettau reported,

"Everything ends, and at last we had climbed our last hill and had arrived in the muddy street of a quaint little, stone-housed town. Lights began to twinkle here and there and people came out to see their first American soldiers. It was 2 A.M. I understood that we were going into billets, but it seemed impossible to find room for one thousand men in these few houses. At length, several detachments moved away. Some of these men climbed ladders and disappeared into attics and hay lofts; others passed from view into cellars and barns. "So these are billets?"

After our Detachment had stood in the road many minutes, we began to realize that unless we ourselves found a place to sleep, we would very likely be there in the road until daybreak. Therefore, we marched up the street and found a newly constructed wooden building, entered it, picked up the softest looking piece of wood and "went to bed."

We who stopped in Mandres were fortunate as the Second and Third Battalions were stationed four or five miles beyond Mandres.

In the morning, after a breakfast of canned willy, canned tomatoes and crackers, we located Regimental Headquarters." [The canned beef issued as field rations to AEF soldiers resembled modern corned beef. Soldiers quickly tired of its tasteless monotony and derisively dubbed it Canned Willy, Canned Bill, Bully-Beef and Monkey Meat.]

Later, we learned that there were rooms for some of us. We had pictured a hay loft at best but when we found that we had drawn rooms containing real beds, we were pleased beyond description. Two of us were billeted in the home of an old lady who smiled and talked incessantly, but since our French was in its infancy and had not reached the talking stage, we could only grin at her and say "Wee, wee" whenever it appeared time. However, we got along famously.

When the lady finally bowed herself out, we examined the room. The bed drew our attention immediately. It was not six feet long (I am, and I know the bed was not) and it stood about four feet from the floor. The odd thing about it was a sort of feather-bed on top of the covers. We could never learn to use it as a cover but always lovingly put it upon the floor whenever we did not fear the lady's coming. One of the covers was made entirely of heavy, exquisite lace, pretty to look at, but not half as warm as our "three thin blankets."

There were two pictures on the wall, both of young soldiers, and we knew why the old lady was so kind to us. A dresser and a stand with bowl and pitcher completed the room. Simple it was, but a mansion compared to what we expected.

The companies were put to work immediately. Those men who had offended were given the task of rendering a town sanitary that had been unsanitary since the first man and his cow had come to live there. The others embarked upon a six weeks training schedule, the author of which, evidently, had never heard of relaxation. From early morning, when the bugle blew "Assembly," khaki clad youths came down ladders, out of cellars, out of barns and out of houses, and throughout the day, pausing only at noon, American cries and activities resounded through the ordinarily quiet village until nightfall. Our service at the front, it appeared, would begin at the expiration of these six weeks."[27]

83rd Division Headquarters was located at Montigny Le Roi; 332nd Infantry Regiment HQ was in Mandres with Headquarters Company and the entire First Battalion; at Lanques was Supply Company, Machine Gun Company, Second Battalion Headquarters and Companies E and F; Companies G and H were at Ageville; Donnemarie was home to the Third Battalion Headquarters along with I and K Companies; Essey les Eaux is where Companie L and M were billeted. The remainder of the Division, which had sailed with the 332nd were housed in several other villages to the east and south of nearby AEF Headquarters at Chaumont. The First Battalion were in Mandres. It was a town which D Company soldiers aptly described as, "... a quaint rural village, of simple country folk where cows live in close proximity to the family, and the pigs are on speaking terms with the children."[28] Those Doughboys were astonished that, "In these ordinary French peasant homes the door opened from the kitchen into the cow stable, and from the parlor into the manure pile." Second Battalion Companies E and Company F, Private George Roberts' company, were billeted in Lanques. He described the place in some detail:

> "The population of Lanques is probably about two hundred. Two famous roads lead into this town, the one built by Caesar, the other built by Napoleon. In the center of the town is a large watering place where stock is watered, the people drink, and the women wash their clothes. The houses and barns are all huddled together and it is quite a problem to tell just where the houses leave off and the barns begin. We were very downhearted to find such dirty places to live in but we got busy and soon had everything cleaned up in regular Yankee style. The people were very poor as the men folks had been away for about four years fighting for their homes and country. The women and children always seemed eager to assist us in any way possible. The women washed our clothes at very reasonable prices, and they all helped us in our efforts to learn their language. Two little girls had a regular school for us every evening, and on Sundays, teaching us French."[29]

Companies I and K of the Third Battalion were located in Donnemarie where Company K members described the town:

> "It was noon the following day when most of us arose to find that we were in an antiquated village where something happened in 1738 as indicated by the date on an old rough stone monument located at the center of the village. Certainly "Donnemarie" was that old at least, for to look at the weathern-worn, crumbled, old stone buildings, dwellings, barns, chicken sheds and all combined, we should not have been surprised to see the date on the village monument to read 1738 B.C. Even the people were very ancient in their ways, as they walked about on wooden shoes."[30]

Private Ferris Myrice of Company K described the setting of Essey les Eaux where he was billeted: "Evening and all is well – about ½ mile from the village – seated on a stone – such a beautiful country, but oh! what a dirty town. The people sure do need help – why can't they keep their homes, streets and selves looking as beautiful as their hills, fields and cattle? The people did not expect us last night – thot [sic] the Germans had broken thru – but all O.K. this A.M. all smiles and willing to help all they can, which is very little – they themselves have nothing but work. Only one good looking girl in town – "school marm" and she talks a little English – very much monopolized by officers – no chance for privates. Just a trifle homesick for U.S.A., home and friends. May this war – end and end quickly, here's a prayer at least – Bon Soir." The next day, he wrote, "Up and drill until noon after dinner we cleaned the town or I should say started to – I am afraid the cows had a hard time finding their homes – for we sure did make a hole in the years of dirt and manure lying around on the street. The place doesn't look half bad now Trouble with that squad of mine – I wish it was in Heaven. Tomorrow is Sunday but – I suppose it will be shovel manure all day. Firing could be heard today – must be some guns."[31]

The regiment quickly settled down to a daily training routine. Company I's history simply stated, "We worked hard at Donnemarie, at first, because we expected to go into the lines in a short time, and later, when we learned our regiment had been selected to go to Italy, because we wanted America's representatives to be the best soldier on the Italian front."[32]

Sergeant Major Lettau noted that, "... practically the same events took place at each little town. At stated times, the different companies leaving their stations, met on the line of march and when a prearranged point was reached, skirmishes and trench maneuvers were executed. The noon meal was served in the field from the rolling kitchens. Drinking water was frowned on while marching and at the conclusion of a march there were generally many thick tongues, parched throats and black lips. ... During June a party of commissioned and non-commissioned officers were sent to the Infantry school at Chatillon-sur-Seine, there to further their education in matters military."[33]

Private George Roberts detailed the period of preparation for the front: "The next few weeks were spent at real training, using the columns of half platoons digging imaginary trenches and doing double time while wearing gas masks, until we were all sick of it, and in our spare time, which of course was not much, we helped the people with their work. One evening I helped two old women unload some hay and when this was done they took me inside and gave me a nice big drink of good wine; after that I was always ready and glad to help any of them."[34]

First Battalion's D Company also reported an arduous routine:

> "Drilling began in dead earnest on the following day, June 22, the work being done on the Macadam pike just west of the village. The schedule which started very early consisted of "School of the Soldier," "Close Order," "Open Order," "Manual of Arms," "Aiming and Sighting," "Range Finding" and "Bayonet Drill." ... The first day's drill was a stiff schedule and each day thereafter, as long as the 332d remained in Madres, a heavy day's work from early till late was carried out ...
>
> On July 2, the regiment ceased work on the road west of Madres, and began to drill on the stone covered top of the hill overlooking the village. The ascent always made an arduous task, and afterwards, without resting, a strenuous gruelling [day] began in musketry and all phases of open order battle practice, the work lasting from early morning till 5:30 p.m. Semaphore and wigwag practice followed

for an evening period from 7:30 to 8:00. Long wearisome days brought constant work with little or no recreation. Departure from Mandres was forbidden...

Drill on the hilltop now started in dead earnest; trench digging, bombing, gas training, the French system of attack, were added to the already heavy schedule, the training being done under the intensely hot sun. The regiment rapidly prepared to lay claim to being the best trained organization in the A.E.F. During this intensive drill no canteens were worn by Co. "D" men, except on the all day hikes when one canteen full of water was allowed each man for the whole day ...[35]

Free time for the 332nd was depicted by Sergeant Major Lettau as:

> Generally, in the evening, the boys wrote letters and read the Paris edition of the "Chicago Tribune" and the "New York Herald." Also, the thirst was quenched. The water was under the ban of the Medical Officer unless it was purified by the addition of hypo-chloride of lime. This water was placed in a lister bag hung upon a tripod and was liked less than the various "vins" and brandies offered in the vin shops, especially since most of these little shops were presided over by mademoiselles. During the day no drinks could be sold to Americans, but after the companies were dismissed, until taps, the shopkeepers reaped a harvest of francs ... Our excellent band made the evenings happy for French and Americans with splendid concerts on the "Square."[36]

Lieutenant Harold Speakman, described some of his duties and experiences in France:

> "The battalion commander has appointed me town major, familiarly known as the "T.M." Every town where American troops are billeted has a T.M. He must, it seems combine the best qualities of a policeman, an ambassador and a nursemaid. He must also be a hotel clerk, as just repayment to the townspeople for the daily use of their houses and barns rests with him. Fortunately for all concerned, the T.M. is allowed two assistants, and, thanks to that, the citizens of the Little Village have a much better chance of receiving their correct payments at the end of the month than if the T.M. himself made the calculations.
>
> There has been a review for the mayor. It was a gala occasion. The band of the regiment came up from its own village and played a smashing American march as the battalion passed in review. The mayor, wearing the tricolored band of office about his shoulders, stood in the shadow of the old church and saluted with all the pride of France as the platoons passed by in the sunlight. After the review the troops were formed in the court between the church and the fountain, and the mayor, surrounded by our soldiers and his own people, addressed the battalion in a simple and affectionate manner.
>
> The company devotes much of its spare time to writing letters. There may be as many as fifty or sixty a day in each of the four platoons, all of which must be censored before being sent to battalion headquarters ... Sometimes it is not easy to cross out a word or phrase carrying so much of interest, ... It is not an ungracious task, for, in the first place, one is glad that the letters are being written, and in the second place, a single line in a man's letter may bring a better understanding of than days of study...
>
> Yesterday, I visited Chaumont, the headquarters city of the American forces in France. There were some roof-tiles of glass to be bought and a few other articles which had been broken by our soldiers ... The horse was Jeanette, owned by the knife-maker at the top of the hill. ... Jeanette is a large, comfortable-looking animal, somewhat moth-eaten, and about the color of an old army blanket. She has astonishing poise – and no temperament at all. ... The most annoying whip in the world wouldn't make Jeanette trot up hill. ... An ancient "wagonette" was procured from a farmer at the other end of town, and finally, with the aid of bits of wire and string and rope, this strange vehicle and Jeanette were somehow assembled. ... At last, being able to move without any parts dropping off, we started merrily on our journey. The day was fine. Messengers from the front flashed by on motorcycles at sixty miles an hour. Great O.D. limousines filled with immaculate staff officers speeded past, and up above, great tri-colored bird-of-war hummed along in patrol formation. ... Just as Jeanette and I had come to an agreement about halting in fron of the Y.M.C.A., a gray touring car rolled up from the opposite direction and stopped next to us. I climbed out of the rigging back of Jeanette and reached terra firma at the same moment that an American officer of high rank descended from the touring car. He looked at Jeanette and the sea-going craft behind her, and at me. Then he smiled – broadly – returned my salute and passed on, still smiling. Now, while I certainly wanted to be loyal to Jeanette, etc., I found myself turning somewhat red about the ears. However, General Pershing's smile had been kindly. ... In the headquarters city there is activity everywhere. Belgian, French, English, and American officers, French Colonials, Canadians, East Indians, and Algerians pass in an ever-interesting and colorful procession. ... The streets are swarming with traffic of every description. ..."[37]

On June 30th, General Pershing visited the regiment. On the face of it, his sudden appearance was not unusual; Pershing was known to inspect units of the A.E.F. with little or no notice. His policy was to show the flag by being seen, which resulted in frequent visits and inspections. The A.E.F. Headquarters was only about six miles from where the 332nd was billeted. Pershing's reputation for being a stickler for discipline and requiring a high standard for the uniform appearance of the men was well known by the soldiers of the 332nd. Sergeant Major Lettau commented that, "On June 29th we were told that General Pershing was coming to review us. That meant a night of polishing guns, cleaning quarters, grounds and clothes. When he came, the next day, Premier Clemenceau accompanied him. General Pershing smiled and spoke to the boys as he passed along the line. He looked like a man capable of doing big things."[38]

However, unknown to the members of the 332nd, however, was that Pershing's visit culminated months of negotiations, entangled with Army politics, which would cement an important Pershing decision.

Colonel Wallace described the event, "We had been here (the French villages) for a short time when who should come along like a rocket but General Pershing and His Excellency Monsieur Clemenceau, the Prime Minister. Six companies were paraded immediately – inspected carefully by a big staff of inspectors – and then sailed away."[39]

Clearly, Pershing was impressed with what he saw in the regiment for he summoned Major General Glenn and Colonel Wallace to his headquarters:

> "[The] next day General Glenn and I were ordered to report to General Headquarters. Whether I was to be cashiered or promoted neither he nor I knew. When there the Chief of Staff, General McAndrews said "Colonel your regiment has been selected to go to Italy. Prepare it. General Glenn, your Division becomes a depot." Shells burst over my head since then, but none created half the inner commotion as did those two sentences. Glenn's beautiful division practically disbanded and I, securing a prize coveted by every officer and man in France. 'Fortuna della Guerra'."[40]

Wallace was not privy to the politics that drove Pershing's decision. With the stroke of a pen, Major General Glenn and the "Ohio" Division were finished. Glenn would never have a combat command; his career was effectively ended. Additionally, Pershing had relegated the 83rd Division to the status of a Depot Division. In the language used by the staff at War Department Headquarters, the division had been skeletonized. Its purpose would be to fill combat divisions with new soldiers arriving in France as replacements. Instead of earning battlefield laurels as a cohesive unit, Ohio's 83rd Division (redesignated as the 2nd Depot Division) was no more than a stopping place on the way to the front.

There were several factors that influenced Pershing's decision. The principle reason was the culmination of many years of bickering between two powerful Army factions – one led by Pershing's senior general, Leonard Wood and the other led by Pershing himself.

Major General Leonard Wood, born one year before the Civil War, was somewhat of an anomaly in the Army. In lieu of a West Point education, he attended Harvard Medical School and received a medical degree after an internship at Boston City Hospital. He joined the Army with a temporary appointment as a contract surgeon in 1884, which he parleyed into a permanent appointment as an assistant surgeon in the regular army. In 1886 he was assigned in Arizona as a participant in the final operations against the Apaches. Later, for his distinguished conduct during the Geronimo campaign, he was a recipient of the Medal of Honor.

By 1895, Wood had successfully served in a wide range of medical assignments in the west, which resulted in a position at Army Headquarters in Washington, D.C. With this new posting came a promotion to captain with duties as assistant attending surgeon for all senior government officials, including the President of the United States. Leonard Wood's star rose with this new post and he used it to cultivate powerful Washington connections that he would rely on for the rest of his life.

When the Spanish-American war broke out, Wood secured a colonelcy in the 1st Volunteer Cavalry Regiment; Teddy Roosevelt's famous Rough Riders. His service with the regiment in the fight at Guasimas and San Juan Hill brought him rapid promotions; first to brigadier and then to major general. When the hostilities ended, he was appointed the military governor of the city of Santiago where he served until 1902.

His regular army appointment to brigadier general was secured in February 1901 with promotion to major general following in December. That promotion included a transfer to the Philippines, where he served as governor of the Moro Province and then commanded the Philippines Division.

Recalled to the States in 1908, Wood served as Commander of the Department of the East; then as special ambassador to Argentina for that country's centennial celebration. Upon return from that assignment, he was appointed as Chief of Staff of the Army on April 22, 1910 serving in the highest army position for four years.

By the eve of the World War, Leonard Wood was an outspoken proponent of military preparedness which often placed him in conflict with the Wilson Administration. When the U.S. entered the war, he worked to establish and improve the Officer Training Camp at Plattsburg, New York. Wood visited Europe in 1917-1918 to observe Allied Operations.[41]

Years of bitterness between Wood and Pershing and their respective allies erupted when Pershing was appointed the Commander of the American Expeditionary Forces and ended with General Wood's visit to Europe. From the time of Wood's arrival in England, until he finally met with Pershing at A.E.F. headquarters at Chaumont, he used his highly placed connections to speak to anyone or any group of people who would listen to him. Wood's message was that American soldiers were not prepared for war because President Wilson's policy of American neutrality and the deficient leadership at the War Department had led to military unpreparedness: the A.E.F and its commander, General John Pershing, could not deliver victory. Wood suggested that only one man, a man of great military experience, could possibly reverse the outcome to one of success. That man was "America's Ablest Soldier": none other than Major General Leonard Wood himself.[42] Wood darted through the European social circles conveying his misplaced message.

Although some of his beliefs may have had merit, many regular army officers, including John J. Pershing, viewed Wood as no more than a curmudgeonly fellow, far past his prime, who used political connections and bombast to forward both his own career and his personal interests. He was a man to be watched but not trusted.

By the time he arrived at A.E.F. Headquarters, Pershing had had enough. In that decisive meeting, the then four-star Pershing simply commanded, "You will say nothing!" Secretary of War Baker suggested, in order to placate Wood's powerful allies in Washington, a command for Wood in Italy as a compromise. Pershing replied by cable, "Regardless of his physical unfitness if sent to France or Italy it would introduce a disturbing factor in an already difficult situation as he would certainly endeavor to undermine the structure that only loyal co-operation could build or maintain…Having his own political ambitions always in mind, he would, without question, endeavor to lay a foundation for his own political future. No matter what he promised, he would never be subordinate to discipline under his former junior. His entire Army career has fully demonstrated that loyalty is not a trait in his character. Both his reputation and character inspire only mistrust, even among those who know him best. He is unscrupulous, and I should have no confidence in him in the conduct of operations nor under any other circumstances. He would carry out orders only if suited to his purpose. He is superficial in military knowledge and training and inclined solely to the spectacular."[43] This June 1918 cable ended Wood's bid for an A.E.F. combat command in Italy; he quietly faded from the national scene.

Pershing's allies considered Major General Glenn to be a "Leonard Wood Man." Austin Story verified this assessment when he recounted a visit with General Glenn at Camp Sherman in 1920:

> "… he told me of a most interesting happening. Sometime in the Spring of 1918, General Glenn had occasion to visit the chief of Staff in Washington. He told me that as he was leaving the Chief's office, the Inspector General of the Army entered. The Inspector General said, "Just a minute, Glenn, I want you to hear what I am to report to the Chief of Staff. Your division (the 83rd) is the best National Army Division in the country." Then in a sad voice, General Glenn said to me "And then, by God, they made it a Replacement Division when we reached France".
>
> The reason for this is hard to fathom, but I believe there were two political factions in the Army and unfortunately General Glenn was one of the "outs". Later I was convinced that Glenn was a supporter of General Wood, and the Pershing faction was bitterly opposed to him"[44]

Age and fitness for combat command became another key factor that worked against Edwin Glenn's continued command of a combat division. In 1918, Glenn, a very portly sixty-two year old graduate of the West Point class of 1877, did not project the appearance of a "fighting" general. Both Secretary of War Baker and General Pershing were continually focused on the fitness of the A.E.F. division commanders; many lacked the youth and vigor which both believed were necessary for the trials of command on the Western Front. In fact, Pershing had reluctantly passed over one of his closest friends for command, Major General J. Franklin Bell; a result of Bell's health and Pershing's policy on older generals.

Given that Pershing was not disposed to give his friends dispensation from the age rule, there was no hope for Glenn; he was easily characterized in the "too-old and too-unfit-to-command" category. Lacking any meaningful connection to Pershing, an exception to the standard rule was out of the question. It is likely that Pershing had made note of Glenn's situation long before the June inspection of the 332nd in France. While the 83rd Division was still training at Camp Sherman, Glenn had visited A.E.F. headquarters as part of a delegation of division commanders. One of Pershing's many purposes for their trip to France was to assess the fitness of each of them for combat command. Pershing probably made a mental note on the status of each of the commanders during this visit, so before Glenn ever returned, the decision to convert the 83rd Division into a depot division may have been made.

The final factor addressed in the meeting that day was the need for a single, well-trained regiment to serve in Italy. Colonel Wallace's article in Ohio Doughboys in Italy best summarizes the background:

> "The debacle of Capporetto, which drove the Italian Army across Vittorio Venetia to the western banks of the Piave River, was one of the disasters of the World War to the Allied cause. Although France and England felt its indirect results, Italy was to bear the full brunt in the loss of territory, men and munitions. But uneasiness in the Allied Councils was at once manifest over the lowered morale of the Italian Army and civilians. German propaganda, before the drive of the Central Powers into Italy, had helped bring about the defeat at Capporetto and nearly lost to Hun vandalism the treasured city of Venice. The Germans planned their propaganda in masterly fashion and much better than usual. It was well timed, for at the moment many Italians were ready to believe anything was preferable to a continuance of mouldy (sic) war bread and macaroni "slum."
>
> Socialism and anti-war feeling (before Italy joined the Allied forces) were strongly intrenched (sic) from toe to strap of the Italian boot. Continued warfare, with its irksome penalties produced in the minds of the discontented, a feeling of war-weariness like that which overthrew the Russian giant. German propaganda guns were turned toward this vulnerable morale salient in the Italian nation. Then followed Capporetto, and beguilers and beguiled were in the state of self-satisfaction which gave them the seeming right to shout: "I told you so." So lowered was Italian morale that everyone who understood the situation was worried lest still darker times might follow.
>
> The Italian Minister of War had a happy thought. At a meeting of the Supreme War Council, in Paris, February 6, 1918, he asked Pershing to send a battalion of Americans to Italy. A battalion was all he requested – not for the strength a battalion might exert in a military way, but for bolstering up the weak-kneed in the Italian Army and civilian population. The Italian Minister strongly urged that such American units be sent directly to an Italian port as tangible proof of the co-operation of the American nation. He was certain that the effect would be electrical upon all classes in Italy,

especially the large number of Italian Americans who had returned to their native soil.

Pershing evidently thought well of the proposal, and cabled asking for instructions. Four months later, he received from Washington the following cablegram: "Reference to shipment of one regiment of American Infantry to Italy, the Secretary of War directs that you ship one regiment from your command for that purpose" ... Italy had asked for one battalion and received three – a regiment."[45]

The reorganization of the 83rd Division from a combat division to a depot division offered Pershing exactly what he needed to fulfill his promise to the Italians: a well-trained, well-led regiment. Three of the 83rd Division's four regiments were to be dissolved and the soldiers used as "fillers" for other divisions. The 332nd Infantry Regiment would remain active and form the nucleus of the A.E.F. in Italy – they would become Pershing's, regiment on the Italian Front. Word did not take long to get out, "The next day a rumor went forth that we were scheduled to go to Italy as a propaganda regiment to encourage the Italians. As this rumor gained credence, the study of French lost ground and many copies of "French for Soldiers" went to the bottom of the barracks bags."[46]

Lieutenant August Rendigs described the reaction of his battalion to the rumors, "no one paid any attention to them at first, but finally they became widespread and seemed to have an element of truth in them ... The men were all very enthusiastic. It meant a break in the routine, a change in scenery, and an opportunity for travel in another country."[47]

Lieutenant Speakman added, "... the regiment is going to Italy. Whether it is founded in good faith on an order reposing among some General's private papers, or whether it was darkly conceived in the brain of a Kitchen Police, no one can tell. Whichever it is, it has the whole regiment by the ears!"[48]

With the 332nd Infantry as the only surviving regiment of the 83rd Division, the first order of business was to fill the regiment with the best soldiers available before their departure for Italy. Captain Story of I Company remembered how this was accomplished:

"Then followed a month of disorganizing, organizing and equipping, and since the regiment was to represent the "cream of the crop," one day each of us company commanders was told that we should weed out any in our outfit that we would like to get rid of and march them over to the village where the 331st Infantry was billeted and there each captain had his company lined up. Then each of us was to pick out good-looking men from the corresponding company. I thought that Company I of the 331st looked rather small but we did our best and marched our selections back to our company. It was then found that each 331st captain had hid his best men out in the nearby woods. So the next day we marched our former selectees back and then out of the augmented Company I of the 331st, I picked another and better looking group. So I believe we did have the best bunch of soldiers in the A.E.F."[49]

July 4th, brought a respite from hard work, the regiment was, "awakened before reveille by our band which, in two separate sections, marched around the town endeavoring to see which section could make more noise. During the day athletic games were staged and prizes were given to the winners."[50]

The following week, the regiment received another more welcome surprise visitor. Elsie Janis, the *"Sweetheart of the A.E.F,"* and one of the period's greatest entertainers, performed for the regiment. The visit was all the more special in that Elsie hailed from Columbus, Ohio and loved to open her shows for Ohio troops Ohio State University yell "Wah hoo, Wah hoo, Rip, Zip, Bazoo, I yell like Hell, O.S.U."[51]

The soldiers remembered that night well, "... our boys came from all the nearby towns to see her."[52] "... [she] came to our neighborhood and provided an evening's entertainment we shall never forget. In a natural amphitheatre, a rude wooden stage with improvised lights, was built. The hillside was dotted with the "flowers" of the American army, the 331st in overseas caps, the 332nd in campaign hats. Both regimental bands were near the stage and they kept everyone in good spirits. A truck drove up and a piano was unloaded and placed upon the stage. Shortly after, Miss Janis and her mother arrived in a limousine, and from the moment the door of the car opened until she left the stage, everyone had a wonderful time. Miss Janis sang several songs, new to us, and her parodies and accompanying antics were greatly enjoyed."[53] It was a night the regiment would never forget.

Morale boosting mail from the states arrived a few days later on July 10, "We had our first mail delivery since arriving overseas and believe me it surely was good to get letters from the folks back home. One will appreciate a letter so much more when he is far away from home, especially when in a strange land where he neither understands or speaks the language spoken there. In the mail today was a big, fat letter for Rupert from one of his old friends in Columbus, Ohio, and it was a real treat, for there was a closely typewritten three page letter itself, and folded in it were the clippings of news items from Columbus papers, also some wit and humor clippings that helped to produce a few smiles"[54]:

"On July 14th, France's Independence Day, another holiday was declared. We were free to go anywhere possible in the twenty-four hours. In order to bring the holiday spirit to the whole regiment, the band was sent around to the various towns. In each town a short concert was played and at the Second Battalion headquarters it co-operated in a pleasant program of speeches and songs attended by the French people as well as the soldiers."[55]

Disappointed at his transfer from H to F Company, Lieutenant Rendigs remarked:

"... accompanied the Major and his adjutant back to Ageville, to attend a celebration there in honor of the day, – it was a French holiday. ... The celebration at Ageville started at seven in the evening, and took place in a large field in the lower [e]nd of the village, which had been used as a drill field by Companies G & H. Of course the entire village turned out for the occasion, and after a review of G & H Companies by the Major and the Mayor of the village the entire assemblage, French and Americans, gathered around a small platform which had been erected for the occasion, and, seating ourselves on the grass, we carried on with the rest of the program. There were appropriate addresses by the Mayor of the Village and M. Le Cure, and appropriate responses by our Major and the Chaplain of the Battalion, who spoke in French. At the conclusion of the addresses there was music by our Regimental Band, which had been imported for the occasion, and then there were songs by our soldiers which were warmly applauded by our French friends, although they understood nothing of what had been sung. Then the French gave times three lusty "Viv l'Amerique" for the Americans, and the Americans, not to be outdone, gave the same number for the French."[56]

Many of the soldiers of the 332nd reveled in the decision. Private Myrice boasted, "... About 50 of us serenaded the town paraded the streets etc. "We are going to Italy – we're going to Italy – why? We are tired of wading in the cow – "[57]

Lieutenant Rendigs happily concurred, "One morning we were finally notified to pack up at once and send off all but the absolutely necessary baggage in preparation for our journey to Italy. The men were all very enthusiastic, ..."[58]

Private Roberts noted, "... on July 25th we were all set for sunny Italy. On this date we left Lanques and marched back to Foulain, fifteen miles, where we again climbed into side door pullmans and said "Goodbye" to beautiful France."[59]

General John J. Pershing, Commander of the American Expeditionary Forces in Europe; his stormy relationship with Major General Leonard Wood led to a regiment being "readily available" for service in Italy. Courtesy Library of Congress.

Pershing with American and French officers at AEF Headquarters, Chaumont, France. Courtesy National Archives.

Above: American Expeditionary Forces Headquarters at Chaumont. Courtesy Library of Congress.

Left: Pershing's nemesis, Major General Leonard Wood. His bombast as an outspoken critic of Pershing and the A.E.F. saw him sidelined to duties in the states. Courtesy National Archives.

Below: The 332nd dubbed themselves "Boxcar Tourists." This cartoon addressed their travels in France and Italy; it pays tribute to the soldier's love of the ubiquitous French "40 & 8's".

Stationing of the Regiment in France

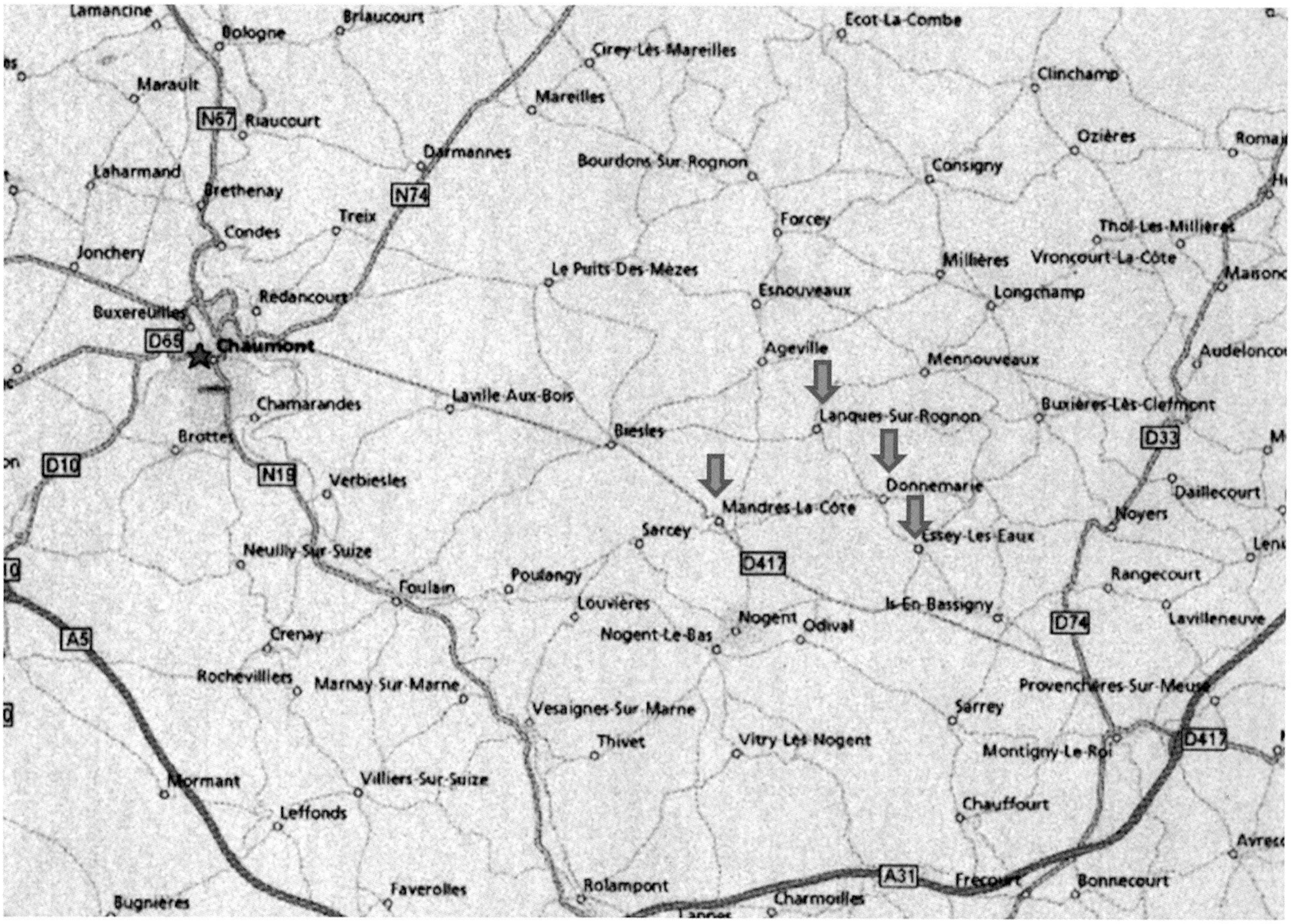

The regiment was stationed in several towns as none of them were large enough to hold the entire unit. First Battalion was in Mandres, Second and Third Battalions and Supply and Machine Gun Companies were scattered in Essey-les-Eaux, Donne Marie and Lanques.

Elsie Janis, the "Sweetheart of the A.E.F.," was one of the most popular entertainers of the day. During the war, she toured France, performing for the A.E.F. Later in life, she remembered that tour as the most important contribution she made. Courtesy Library of Congress.

Elsie Janis performing for the troops. Although these soldiers are probably not from the 332nd Infantry, the show they attended would have had the same presentation. Courtesy National Archives.

Two views of Elsie Janis performing. Courtesy National Archives.

General Pershing's first official visit to 83rd Division Headquarters at Montigney le Roi, France, June 23, 1918. Left to right: Major General Edwin F. Glenn and General John. J. Pershing. Courtesy National Archives.

A G Company soldier becomes acquainted with two mademoiselles in Ageville, France. Courtesy Military History Institute.

Sergeant Major Joseph L. Lettau was the regiment's chronicler; Lettau published "In Italy with the 332nd Infantry" in 1921. "In Italy" is the single best period volume on the regiment. Courtesy Military History Institute.

An unidentified 332nd soldier cozies up to French locals in Ageville, France. Courtesy Military History Institute

First Lieutenant August A. Rendigs, Jr in a commanding studio portrait. Courtesy Rendigs, Fry, Kiely & Dennis, LLP.

Above: A G Company soldier cleans up manure in Ageville, France. Courtesy Military History Institute

Top right: This copy of Soldiers French Course belonged to Private Cannoll Stillwell, a G company soldier. Courtesy Private Collection.

Right: Carried to France in expectation of a long stay there, Private Stillwell took time to fill out the "Soldiers Identification Card" in the flyleaf. Courtesy Private Collection.

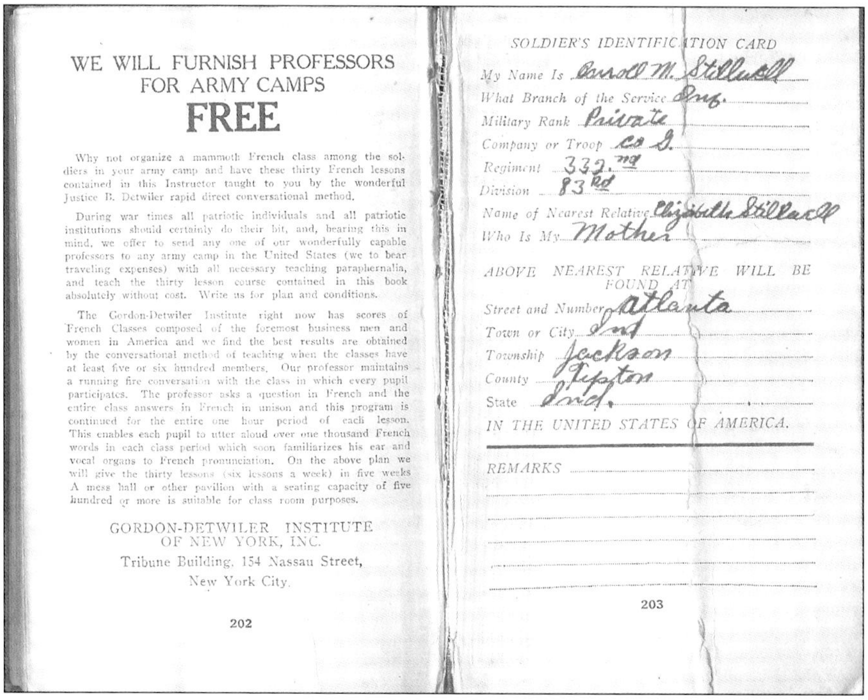

WE WILL FURNISH PROFESSORS FOR ARMY CAMPS

FREE

Why not organize a mammoth French class among the soldiers in your army camp and have these thirty French lessons contained in this Instructor taught to you by the wonderful Justice B. Detwiler rapid direct conversational method.

During war times all patriotic individuals and all patriotic institutions should certainly do their bit, and, bearing this in mind, we offer to send any one of our wonderfully capable professors to any army camp in the United States (we to bear traveling expenses) with all necessary teaching paraphernalia, and teach the thirty lesson course contained in this book absolutely without cost. Write us for plan and conditions.

The Gordon-Detwiler Institute right now has scores of French Classes composed of the foremost business men and women in America and we find the best results are obtained by the conversational method of teaching when the classes have at least five or six hundred members. Our professor maintains a running fire conversation with the class in which every pupil participates. The professor asks a question in French and the entire class answers in French in unison and this program is continued for the entire one hour period of each lesson. This enables each pupil to utter aloud over one thousand French words in each class period which soon familiarizes his ear and vocal organs to French pronunciation. On the above plan we will give the thirty lessons (six lessons a week) in five weeks A mess hall or other pavilion with a seating capacity of five hundred or more is suitable for class room purposes.

GORDON-DETWILER INSTITUTE
OF NEW YORK, INC.
Tribune Building, 154 Nassau Street,
New York City.

202

SOLDIER'S IDENTIFICATION CARD

My Name Is Carroll M. Stillwell
What Branch of the Service Inf.
Military Rank Private
Company or Troop Co G.
Regiment 332nd
Division 83rd
Name of Nearest Relative Elizabeth Stillwell
Who Is My Mother

ABOVE NEAREST RELATIVE WILL BE FOUND AT
Street and Number Atlanta
Town or City Ind
Township Jackson
County Tipton
State Ind.
IN THE UNITED STATES OF AMERICA.

REMARKS

203

3

Italy: the Regiment Trains

On July 25, 1918, the 332nd Infantry Regiment, with attached medical and supply units, began the journey to Italy. The departure dates varied as the Second Battalion was the first to board the trains. The remaining battalions followed in separate cars within a period of a few days. Private Walter Hart of Company D noted that although the soldiers traveled in different elements, "our impressions were the same as everybody in the 332nd got, since all entered over the same route."[1]

The official mission of the regiment was twofold: "to build up Italian morale and to depress that of the enemy by creating the impression that a large force of Americans had reached that front and was preparing to enter the battle line and to take an active part in the fighting."[2]

Rumors and speculation were displaced by a briefing on the mission. Corporal C.O. Littlefield wrote, "The purpose was explained in that we were bound to morally uphold the traditions of the U.S., and were to set a good example, for but one regiment was going. It was at this time that the saying " Wallace's Circus" became popular, due to the fact that our future gave promise of continued parading and exhibiting of American physique and ability, with apparently no front line experience,- what use, it was asked would 4,000 men be to Italy as a unit? So we boarded the train with the well established orders to say nothing about where we were bound"[3]

Company K wrote: "On July 26 we marched to Foulain, where we boarded what they might call a train, made up of third class coaches, box cars and flat cars, and as we only had to put 40 men on a car it almost left room for everyone to stand up. But we didn't mind that very much, for we were traveling. A soldier is happy when he is going someplace, it doesn't matter where."[4]

"The train of box cars with its human freight began to move and the 332nd commenced another lap of its nomadic career."[5] The 332nd was on the way to Italy. Most of the boys rode in the same "high style" as the trip between Le Have and Foulain; however, Sergeant Major Lettau, ever ready to improve on comfort, figured out that there was a better way:

"There was about thirty motor trucks and two touring cars fastened on flat cars, and these trucks filled with canvas tents looked more inviting to us than the notorious box cars marked "40 HOMMES, 8 CHEVAUX".

This journey, which was to occupy three days and two nights, was remarkable for its changing scenes and climates. Leaving Foulain about 3:00 P.M. July 25th, we proceeded in a southeastern direction, reaching Gray about twilight. Drawing forth our canned willy, crackers, tomatoes, etc., we had "dinner." Upon completing this luxurious repast we pulled a canvas tarpaulin over us and put our "bedroom" in shape.

[Soldiers of every period enjoyed using derisive names for their rations. WWI was no exception. Lieutenant Harold Speakman recalled, "... even good food has special names of its own. Food in general is "chow." Stew is "slum" or "Slum-gullion." Coffee is "Java." Salmon – and there is a lot of it is "gold-fish" or"sea-turkey." Corned beef is "corned willy," and canned meat of almost any variety is "bully-beef," "canned African," or "monkey meat." In barracks when the mess is ready, the cook simply makes the announcement, "Come and get it!" and there is never any doubt about what he means."][6]

Sergeant Major Lettau continued, The evening air was growing colder as we approached the mountains, but we slept comfortably even though we had allowed ourselves the luxury of removing shoes and puttees.

While we had taken care of ourselves in this manner, the boys in the box cars were anything but comfortable. The French box car is not the large one we see on American railroads and it was only by taking turns at lying down that anyone got any sleep."[7]

During the trip to Italy, soldiers of the regiment became true "boxcar tourists"; their written memories bearing a greater resemblance to travel journals rather than war diaries. "Our Company reached and passed the Reyssouse River at Bourg the morning of July 27th. The early hours were chill and damp. From Bourg the route led to Amberieu, where after a half-hour stop, the train backed up to enter the Alpine Pass – the same as was used by ancient conquerors. The extremity of the Alpine Pass looks down upon the plains of northern Italy – and the memory of that afternoon shall forever remain a cherished recollection in the war annals of every man lucky enough to be there."[8]

George Roberts, too, marveled at the prospect unfolding before him:

> "When passing thru the Alps we beheld the most beautiful and gorgeous scenery of our trip … Arrived at Torino, Italy, where we stopped long enough to parade; the people almost went wild over us all along the route. We were met at Milano by the Red Cross who issued us hot coffee, sandwiches, cigarettes, and chocolate, all of which we thoroughly enjoyed. All along the way the people treated us with candy, cigarettes, and eats of different kinds. Sleep and rest were almost impossible on account of the crowded conditions, nevertheless we enjoyed the trip immensely, realizing the unusual opportunity we were having. The natural picture was too wonderful to take in at a glance, and I can still see those snow capped peaks, the mountain streams, the waterfalls, and the gorgeous colors of the sun's rays illuminating almost secluded peaks of solid rock, causing them to sparkle like precious jewels. This is a part of our trip never to be forgotten. No more picturesque or magnificent scenery could be imagined than we beheld there where the sun, mountains, waterfalls, and lakes all combined to form one panorama of nature's greatest spectacle."[9]

Aix-les-Bains was another remarkable waypoint along the route:

> "… that most renowned watering place of Europe, nestling amid Alpine crags on the edge of the beautiful Lake Bourget, was reached at 5:00 p.m. A gorgeous sunlight flooded the mountains and pierced the crystal depths of the lake. Another hour of tingling wonderment and the troop train came to a standstill in cosmopolitan Chambery. Clouds rolled over the mountain sides and soon rain was falling fast.
>
> Within the station area a queer crowd was passing to and fro. Peasant mountaineers, bearing (apparently) all their earthly possessions, jammed the passageways and excitedly jostled their neighbors for the right of fullest personal liberties. Soldiers from all Allied countries stirred through the crowd, some returning from leave, others newly arrived. Chambery is near the heart of France's most attractive scenery. Here was the American Red Cross as though to give the men one last farewell on French soil. Only a short delay, one last glance at the great cross surmounting the highest mountain overlooking the city, and the troops waved its adieu to Chambery. A drizzling rain fell.
>
> The next stop half an hour later was made at Montmelian, nestling in the shadow of Mt. Savoie, Mt. Glazier, and Mt. Montmelian. By this time the rain had ceased. Heavily leaved trees dripped with water so recently fallen; the atmosphere was charged with the odor of fir and summer flowers.
>
> Here half an hour's delay to wash and clean up permitted some of the men to climb a little hill to a spot where a more commanding view of the mighty snow-covered crags could be had. The scene was an inspiring one. A great trinity of walls rose to the very heavens. "Look," said an English Red Cross nurse, "and if the sun comes out you'll see Mont Blanc." Then as though to gratify the sensibilities of every man, a ray of golden sunset pierced the dark gray mass of clouds wrapping the crest; the clouds dispersed and slowly fell away from the mountain crest, unfolding a crystal shaft sparkling in the golden shaft of light …
>
> The engine shrieked. These pioneering American soldiers scrambled to find their places on the train. Darkness fell fast down in the valley. The train moved in to the night and into the region of never ending snow. A region of eternal ice is cold; it is needless to say this night, the last on the soil of France, was not a comfortable one."[10]

The doughboys were fascinated with the both with the beauty of this area and the engineering of the railroad and commented on the many tunnels along the route, "Saturday – riding thru the Alps – They sure are wonderful but I believe U.S. has some just as fine. – The sides are all cultivated very far up grapes – wheat and corn are raised thru here. We see snow on the mountain top – just before leaving France – sure are a number of tunnels around this country arrived in Italy about 3:15 P.M. This country sure is a revelation to me – Seems much more progressive to me than some other countries Being the first troops here every one seems to be out watching us parade in Turin."[11]

An enthralled Lieutenant August Rendigs noted: "… we reached the summit of that great natural boundary between France and Italy and started its descent. It was a beautiful moonlight night and the towering grandeur of the majestic Alps with their snow-capped peaks glittering in the brilliant silvery light, together with the foaming mountain streams that dashed wildly down the sides of the rocks over innumerable waterfalls, made a picture that we shall never forget."[12]

Another reality struck the members of the regiment. There was a remarkable difference between the lackluster reception the 332nd had received in France and the festive rejoicing that they encountered in their welcome to Italy. Captain Story captured the mood, "We were cheered, pelted with flowers and fed until there was no doubt in our minds that the Italians were glad to see us."[13] Even as Sergeant Major Lettau poked a little fun at his hosts' curious manners, it was clear that he was touched by their outpouring of gratitude – the Americans had finally arrived. "The Italians have a way of waving the hand in greeting that furnished much amusement. The arm is held up, palm of the hand inward and the hand is rapidly opened and closed. Shouts of "Viva l'Americani!" accompanied each move of the fingers. The boys were quick to reply and answering shouts of, "Viva l' Italia," came from them. Later in the night we entered Turin and here again were delightfully received. We ourselves could not realize what our presence meant to these people."[14]

Harold Speakman recalled his journey through Italy:

> "Here the mountains meet the plains, here rainbow lakes reflect the purple hills, here the land is a land of vineyards and sunlight and prospering cities. The platoons sit in their "side-door Pullmans" (boxcars), with their feet dangling above the flying rails and their hat-brims and hands loaded with flowers and Italian flags which have been showered on them. They are high- spirited and wonderfully care-free in the way only a child or soldier can be, with all the enthusiasm of explorers entering a new enchanting country.[15]

As the trains passed through the towns of Torino, Vercelli, Novara, Milano, Bergamo, Brescia and Verona, the soldiers, described the enthusiastic townspeople lined along the route to welcome them with heartfelt rejoicing in a festive spirit of celebration.

Lieutenant Rendigs described their arrival in Turino:

> As we slid along side the station platform we were greeted by prolonged cheering from the large crowd gathered there to greet us, and a delegation of high military and civic officials came hurrying up to welcome us while an Italian band blared forth the "Star Spangled Banner". Hundreds of women and young Italian girls went along the side of our train distributing small Italian flags and flowers among our men. We were requested by the officials who greeted us to parade through the town, so after a short interval devoted by the men to cleaning up and putting their equipment in order, we detrained and formed in [a] column of squads in front of the station.
>
> "Preceded by a couple of Italian bands and escorted by the officials we began our march, which took us through the principal business section of the city … although the hour was yet early, we were greeted by enormous crowds that lined the streets and cheered frantically for our men and for our nation. Many little groups gathered on the small balconies … and threw huge masses of flowers in our paths and down upon us. Young women and children darted out of the crowds to place a small bouquet with an Italian flag in some doughboy's hand or eagerly grasp a hand as our boys marched by. We were genuinely surprised and touched by the warmth and sincerity of our welcome and returned to our train more than satisfied with the wonderful welcome and demonstration that we had received."[16]

As the trains resumed their passage through the towns, jubilant celebrations continued along the route. Even prior to their arrival at their final destinations, the soldiers' feelings of mutual kinship with the Italian people grew. This was demonstrated by Company D as they were welcomed in Milan:

> "In the city's outskirts, over vacant lots, down street and avenue, thousands rushed to the train, waving, shouting, cheering. Children clambered over railroad cuts and up embankments, only to see the last car go by. Ahead and high above the tracks a monster viaduct was filled with expectant, anxious, overjoyed people.
>
> "As the shrieking engine entered the train shed, a long line of Italian troops stood at "Present Arms," while an Italian military ban played the "Star Spangled Banner." A mighty cheer went up from the masses in the shed – a cheer immediately taken up by the crowd without.
>
> Beautifully gowned women and girls rushed forward bearing garlands of fresh flowers as if a great conqueror had come. Companies "C" and "D" soon formed their ranks; the gates swung open and the parade began amid the exultant cheers of a grateful race.
>
> Flowers, generous and costly tributes to the American Army and People, were hurled upon the marching troops. They came from bystanders, from porches and windows above, – they seemed to rain from the very heavens; they fell upon and around the men till the route became one harmonious blend of odor and color. Elegantly dressed women and men, crowding every available inch of space, every window, every door, vied with one another in cheering loudest. The din increased as the march proceeded.
>
> Young men and young women walked beside the ranks, grasping the hands of the men as though the latter might be creatures of divine origin. Women alternately wept and cried for joy, while above the noisy turmoil rose the happy ejaculations of the crowd, drunken with emotions of enthusiasm and good will, "Viva l'America! Viva l'America!"
>
> Men embraced and kissed one another, then fell to cheering madly. Voices of women, tears streaming down their faces, were choked by sobs.
>
> Tighter and tighter grew the pressure of the dense crowd on the flanks; then, suddenly, as the column swung into the "Piazza del Duomo' and passed "Il Duomo," the flanks could stand the pressure no longer. The crowd, now uncontrollable, almost bore the men from their feet in a mad frenzy to honor these first combatant American troops in Italy. The exultant cries continued, "Viva l'America! Viva l'America!"
>
> The irresistible pressure shattered the ranks. The stiff wall of reserve of the Anglo-Saxon could no longer resist the mighty flood of human emotion the surged against it and in that sublime moment, seizing the inspiration of the hour, the men in khaki spoke for America, and cried back, "Viva l'Italia! Viva l'Italia!
>
> … Dazed by this reception, the companies made their way back to the station where the magnificent piazza without was packed by tens of thousands of the city's happy and enthusiastic populace … The troops boarded the train. The sun was setting on the blue horizon. The strains of the "Star Spangled Banner" flooded the station and fell upon the concourse assembled without. Every man stood at salute. The train began to move and a mighty cheer went up from the crowd. …"[17]

Sergeant Major Lettau wrote, "our next and final stop was Villa Franca. Here, amid great enthusiasm, we detrained. The American Red Cross surprised us with hot coffee and doughnuts and never was a lunch more appreciated. While we ate, American aviators [These aviators included a man who would become the most iconic of New York Mayors, Captain Florello LaGuardia, then leading the American Air Service detachment in Italy] flew above us, doing amazing stunts."[18]

At Villafranca, Colonel Wallace, his staff and the portion of the regiment that accompanied him, were welcomed by Brigadier General Charles G. Treat, Chief of the American Mission to Italy and General Pecori Giraldi, Commander of the Italian 1st Army. General Treat was Commander of Base Section 8 and had responsibilities that included oversight of all the Services of Supply (S.O.S.) logistical troops that operated from a series of bases scattered around northern Italy. His subordinate units included an Army Air Corps training base, Base Hospital 102 in Vicenza, the port at Genoa, motor transport and repair facilities, and a supply depot. With the arrival of the 332nd in his area, General Treat became Wallace's immediate superior. A West Point graduate of the Class of 1882, Treat was widely respected for his sound diplomatic abilities, cheerful disposition and cordial manners.[19]

He would prove to be the perfect counterbalance to Wallace's more bellicose nature; Treat was content with the arrangement of Wallace commanding the regiment without his interference, performing his role as higher commander largely in a ceremonial manner.

Brigadier General Treat replaced Major General Eben Swift, a West Point graduate of the Class of 1876 shortly before the regiment arrived. Swift was "continued on active duty" beyond retirement to manage the delicate affairs in Italy. During the course of his long career, which included service during the Indian Campaigns, fighting in the Spanish-American War, duty in the Philippines and as an observer in Manchuria of the Russo-Japanese War, Swift had proven to be one of the great intellects of the Army. He was in the forefront of reform for the military education and staff systems, ultimately serving as the Director of the new Army War College in Washington, D.C. Too old to lead troops in the field, the War Department wisely called on his unique talents to handle the complex problems the Italian Theater presented. At sixty-four, he was more schoolmaster than soldier, but Swift's leadership was a powerful presence in shaping policy in Rome and he arranged for the regiment's arrival.[20]

In addition to the War Department, Major General Swift and successor, Brigadier General Treat, reported directly to the U.S. Ambassador to Italy, Thomas Nelson Page. A member of a prominent Virginia family, Page, a prominent attorney, was well known as an author of short stories and novels which depicted the romance of the antebellum South. He had close ties to fellow Virginian President Woodrow Wilson. As fellow academics, Page and Swift, worked well together; forming an unusually effective State Department/War Department team; given the influence that the two men held in their respective departments, Wallace could be reasonably assured that his command would be free of meddlesome direction from a higher chain of command.

At Villafranca, after a series of welcoming speeches, an Italian Army band played, the crowds cheered and the boys of the 332nd were again showered with flowers and adulation, the units of the regiment then marched off to their billets. The regiment's size dictated that it must be scattered in a few villages and small towns in the vicinity. Regimental Headquarters and First Battalion were billeted in Sommacampagna, Second Battalion and the Field Hospital Number 331 in Custoza, Third Battalion and the Supply Company were in Villafranca di Verona, and the Machine Gun Company was in Fredda at Villa Contini. These places are all located just a few miles southwest of Verona.

Routine duties continued for the doughboys as unprecedented experiences presented themselves in the foreign surroundings. Private Myrice recalled his first days in Villafranca: "On guard, more like war every day to us – our posts (3 of us and a nco) over the ammunition dump – easy – far away from town. We could see airships and [searchlights] – guarding the front during the night. The planes have light on them. We thot they were stars at first, but we could hear the engines. From the room where we are billeted – we can see a big cathedral very near. In the distance are snow capped mountains."[21] *The History of Company K* offered this comment on a soldier's life in Villafranca: "We billeted in a large three-story brick building which was located on the nicest street in town. In these billets we inherited our mosquito nets, which were each night suspended from sky hooks or otherwise in such a manner as to keep the mosquitos and their allies at a comfortable interval from our bodies. The nets proved fairly efficient with mosquitos, but were a desperate failure with fleas and other small animals. Italian fleas are of the small black variety, unusually active, but fortunately desert you as you leave the country."[22]

It was at Villafranca that the regiment was, "... first introduced to Mr. Haare (sic), photographer for *Leslie's Weekly*, and our motion picture career was begun. Mr. [Hare], together with Lieutenant Hill, regimental photographer, earned for us the title of the "Movie" regiment."[23] James H. "Jimmy" Hare was one of the most highly regarded photojournalists of the time. Starting with the Spanish-American War, he had earned a fine reputation recording events of the Russo-Japanese War, the Mexican Revolution and the First Balkan War. On assignment in Italy covering the various aspects of the Italian Front for *Leslie's Weekly*, he often took pictures of the 332nd Infantry.

From the existing accounts, the accommodations for the troops in Villafranca were generally more modest, but no worse, than any of those in Sommacampagna and Custoza. The town was the site of the regional general Italian headquarters. It, also, offered some things that appealed to the the boys of the 3rd Battalion. "The American Red Cross ran a rest house for the soldiers at Villa Franca. There were six rooms attractively furnished, and an old garden, and here our soldiers received refreshments and made themselves at home after their long, hot, and dusty tramps. As a group of these soldiers came in one day singing with much gusto "Hail! Hail! the gang's all here, What the – " etc., an old native who stood admiringly by was heard to remark: "Here come the dear boys singing their national anthem."[24] Private Myrice, Co L, patronized the YMCA. "I sure am getting "many returns" for the ten dollars donation to the "Y" last winter – drank several glasses of lemonade today sure tasted fine."[25] About his first Sunday in Villafranca he wrote: "Many of the boys went to Verona – I prefer to rest – went to church and Y.M. I like to hear [Chaplain Kelly] talk. In the evening I walked around a little – seeing sights. one can see women and girls coming or in town (about 5000 inhabitants) without shoes – think of an American woman doing that – no hose no shoes. one can see very dreams in silk hose and lingerie and French heels and all that a girl uses to dress up. ..."[26]

After the warm welcome by the American Red Cross, the Italian military and the citizens of Villafranca, Lieutenant Rendigs wrote, about his section's billeting:

> "Arriving at the outskirts of the town, we found a long line of Italian motor trucks awaiting us, into which our men quickly scrambled, glad that they were not required to march farther with their heavy equipment. It was raining steadily by this time, but the covered trucks afforded a comfortable shelter from the downpour. A half-hour's ride brought us to the little village of Custoza, nestled cozily among the foothills of a small range of the Alps. Here, after some little delay, we billeted our men in various small houses, and ourselves turned in for the night in a large villa which, standing on the summit of a small hill, commanded the little village which lay directly in front of it. ... The following day, Sunday the 28th, ... [t]wo other officers of our company and I were assigned to permanent quarters with a certain Count Bianchini in a beautiful little Italian villa ...
>
> The villa was but two stories in height but spread over a considerable amount of ground. It was of stucco construction and around the top of the walls on the outside were various paintings and charactures in true Italian style. It stood on a high hill just opposite the large villa where we had spent our first night in Custoza and its approach was through two tall iron gates, flanked on either side by tall concrete pillars with urns mounted on them, giving the gates a rather imposing appearance. In the rear was a beautiful terrace or series of terraces, which gradually dropped down into the valley below. The view from this terrace was most magnificent, commanding as it did miles upon miles of Italian lowlands with their myriad rows of fruit trees and grape arbors, while in the far-off distance could be seen the Alps, towering skywards, the picture being flanked on one side by the beautiful Lac de Garda and on the other by the tall spires of the cathedrals of the city of Verona, some twenty kilometers away. It was very pleasant, during the summer evenings that followed, to sit on this terrace in the cool twilight and contemplate this picture while conversing with our host and his wife, the Countess, who were both most amiable and delightful people. They had three sons with the Italian armies, two of them had been in the service from the beginning of Italy's part in the war, and none of them had been wounded. The Count spoke of them with great pride, and in the stillness of the calm summer evenings, when the faint booming of the great guns could be heard from the Piave front, many miles away, he would never fail to call our attention to them and remark that at least two of his sons were "off there". This would sometimes call tears to the eyes of the countess, but he would quickly assure her that he knew that the boys would be spared and that the war would be over in October and they would then have theirs sons with them again. ... Near Villa Bianchini was a massive stone tomb with its tall shaft visible for miles around, ..."[27]

The billets varied, but compared to those in France, most of the soldiers found themselves in fairly pleasant quarters. Private Roberts' billets were near Lieutenant Rendigs' housing. [At Custoza] "we were billeted in a fine, large mansion on top of a big hill within two hundred feet of the monument which was erected in memory of the battle of Custoza, fought in 1866 against Austria for the freedom of Italy. The base of this monument is filled with skulls and bones of hundreds of men who paid the supreme price in that battle (about two thousand skulls in all). From this hill one can see Lake de Garda, the Alps, and many beautiful fields, vineyards, castles, etc. all so grand and picturesque."[28]

Sergeant Major Lettau found his accommodations in Sommacampagna to be far beyond any expectation. "Our driver took us through the walled streets of the town and set us down before the doors of "The Villa of 1001 Roses." Not knowing where our quarters were to be, we made our bunks on the floor. Right there we became acquainted with the Italian mosquito and of all the mosquitoes we have met, he is the most voracious and insistent. "Cusses" and slaps were heard throughout the night."

Like the other soldiers in the regiment, Lettau set about exploring his new home and the town. He continued:

> [The Villa] "was the property of an Italian Countess [Contessa Livio], widow of an Italian general. The building, of white stone, had a balcony in front from which the Countess often looked down at the curious "Americanos." At the south end there was a large room, very likely a conservatory, the walls of which were covered with what were at one time beautiful paintings. This was the office of the Sergeants Major. At the other end of the building, the Colonel and Adjutant had their desks.
>
> In front of the building the road divided forming a round plot of grass on which were shrubbery, flowers and palm trees. To the left was a thicket of bamboo trees; to the right were majestic palms. Immediately before our entrance was a grape arbor, which, in the hot weather, was very enticing.
>
> The rear, however, was most attractive. Passing across the court, shut in on three sides by the villa, the garage and the servants quarters, one came to a grove of cool, hanging trees. Winding paths bordered by the hedgerows led through this grove to the edge of a steep hill. Here a small balcony of stone had been built and one could see directly below, the white road twining its serpentine course among green trees, past little red roofed village houses presided over by the eternal campanile of the village church. While we sweltered in the sun amid these tropical surroundings,

the mountain tops, visible across the valley, were snow-capped.

Sommacompagna is quite small. When one walked through the streets there was a feeling as of being walled in. The church, the municipio, the vino shops and the houses were made of stone, and walls of masonry extended around the boundaries of each person's property. Five minutes walk took one into the country and the country meant the open fields, for in Italy the farmers live in the towns and go out to work their farms.

Possibly we had come to Italy to cement national relations; to put out any lingering fire of love the Northern Italians had for the Germans; to show Italy that America was at her side.

Nevertheless, as in France, when "Assembly" sounded in the early morning, doughboys, gun in hand, poured from barns, cellars and houses for the daily work. On the hottest days, drills were ordered and borne, but when evening came, the tension was relaxed and until 10:30 the boys had good times.

In this section of Italy there are many irrigation ditches fed by mountain streams, so that the farms are very productive. These streams and ditches were very popular as swimming places after a hot day's drill and along the banks could be seen many future husbands drilling themselves in the art of laundering.

Then, there were the new vinos (wines) and cognacs of Italy to be tried and many pleasant evenings were spent in dingy little shops we would not think of entering at home.

Others, musically inclined, struck up an acquaintance with the owner of a piano and thus amused themselves with the good old American tunes. The Italians generally liked American rag-time. We were made welcome everywhere and in turn thought highly of our hosts.

Some of us were fortunate enough to secure rooms with beds and we felt as if we were going to like the war in Italy. Owing to mosquitoes we found use for the mosquito nets issued by the Quartermaster, for we persisted in sleeping with the windows open despite our "landlady" who insisted on closing them ..."[29]

Quartered himself at the "Villa of One Thousand and One Roses," Colonel Wallace displeased with the regiment's happily situated arrangements. The tough, seasoned field soldier blustered, "I think that Captain Scanland, my adjutant, was embarrassed. His office was sort of a throne room and his clerks and orderlies were stuck around in tapestried shrines along with eminent armored gentlemen. As for myself, I was in sort of an art gallery, with portraits, pianos and mirrors. Then there was a "Salon", Banquet Hall and another dining room with a fountain in a glass case. Upstairs was a really regal suite, but not a bath tub in the place."[30]

Others in Sommacampagna shared their Colonel's dissatisfaction and frustration with the lodging arrangements but from quite a different perspective as they were living in far less splendor. Company D's Log stated that "Billets were found in out-of-the way dismal garrets and gloomy sheds infested with fleas, rats and mice."[31]

American soldiers are known for their ability to adjust, and as the days passed they settled into a somewhat lighter training routine. "We drilled only eight hours a day during our stay there (more east and west and trigger squeeze).[32] In this environment, the soldiers had ample time to enjoy Italy's enticements. "The second Sunday in Villa Franca was a day of events, fifty percent of the company being allowed passes to Verona. Trucks provided by the supply company made the trip in a few hours and upon our arrival there we had a lunch served by the Italian Red Cross, and proceeded without delay to see the town. Some spent the day in viewing art and architecture of former ages, especially the old Roman amphitheater, while others became better acquainted with modern art – "Bella Signorini" of the more lively type."[33] Concerning these "Signorini," Lettau added, "Incidentally, we learned that the Signorinas of Italy are very lovely and that they are not amateurs in dressing attractively. Those of the better class are always chaperoned in the evening. There were many such in company of father, or father and mother, and their deportment and beauty caused hearts to beat, while thoughts of Her in far off America rushed to mind."[34]

Verona was a prime attraction for some of the men, Lieutenant Rendigs wrote:

" Upon reaching the center of the city we found a large crowd of people promenading gaily up and down the principal streets, with many splendidly dressed Italian officers mingling in their midst. It was eight o'clock, and still daylight, and the long broad piazza, which is found in all Italian cities of respectable size, was crowded with little groups of civilians and soldiery, sipping their coffee or liqueurs while carrying on a vivacious conversation. Across the street was a huge arena, built of stone and typical of the Roman arenas that were the scenes of so many Christian massacres in ancient times. ... The arena was circular in shape and inside was a large stage on a level with the entrance. The seats, which were fashioned of huge, wide slabs of stone, ran completely around the arena and were built tier upon tier. ... back to the piazza, and after indulging in the national beverage of the Italians, strolled through the narrow, winding, dimly-lit streets ... During our stroll around the city we attracted a great deal of attention from the people who had, apparently, never before seen Americans, and when we repaired to our rendezvous to board our trucks a great crowd gathered and cheered repeatedly for America and its people. ...

The following Sunday a party of us spent the entire day in Verona and found many places of interest, including a market place with an old-fashioned whipping post that had evidently known frequent use, the old home of the Capulets of Shakespearean fame [Juliet's house and balcony], and a beautiful memorial statue to that ever-famous Italian poet, Dante. We learned to know the location of several good hotels and eating places, and in our subsequent visits to Verona, which occurred occasionally, we became their regular patrons."[35]

Ruminating on the incredible luck of the regiment's posting Lettau wrote, "Thus in work and play the days passed. We loved Italy at this time. It had been impressed upon us that we had been chosen from the entire A.E.F. to represent American soldiery and that upon our actions Americans would be judged. The boys strove hard to maintain this standard."[36]

It was during these glorious summer days, that the regiment had two royal visitors; the King of Italy and England's Edward, Prince of Wales.

Preparation for the first big event started immediately. "It was July 31 that the regiment marched to the aerodrome [at the village of Ganfardine], half way between Villafranca and Sommacampagna, to rehearse for its review by King Victor Emmanuel III. The following morning at 4:45 first call sounded, and at 7:00 a.m. the 332nd marched upon the reviewing field. A large stand, decorated with bunting and flags of all the allied nations, held the many noted persons who attended the review and who represented the nations fighting the Hun."[37] The historian of Company I recorded that, "As the King and his party entered the field, we were called to attention, presented arms and the band played while the King passed slowly down the line inspecting us. He returned to the stand and we passed in review before him. Never have we made a better appearance. In spite of the heat, every man marched erectly with a snappy step in perfect time with the music, and the spectacle as a whole was one which called forth the highest compliments from all who witnessed it, including, in addition to his Majesty and his staff, the U.S. Ambassador to Italy, Thomas Nelson Page, Princes of the Roman Catholic Church, high officers of the British and French armies."[38]:

> "The reviewing stand held the royal party and was beautifully draped with crimson and the flags of the Allied countries. The regiment turned out arrayed in its best, and after some preliminary ceremonies, during which the King, General [Diaz], and a party of notables walked down the entire line, marched in review in a column of platoons headed by Col. Wallace, his staff and the regimental band. An immense throng packed the side lines, and the field was a riot of color in its elaborate decoration. Everything went off smoothly and the men certainly marched well and made a splendid appearance, which was attested by the volume of frantic cheering with which we were greeted as we marched down the long field. The Colonel was highly complimented on the appearance of the regiment, and the Italian papers on the following day gave a glowing account of our performance."[39]

Compared to the excitement and plaudits the regiment won during the Italian King's visit, the Prince of Wale's visit on August 10th was almost anti-climatic. He stopped briefly to lunch with Colonel Wallace at the villa and left. The lightly documented record of this visit was noted by a few Signal Corps photographs and a letter penned the next day to Mrs. Freda Dudley Ward, Edward's first true love and mistress. The Prince remarked, "Yesterday, I motored 2hrs each way to lunch with the Colonel commanding the U.S. Infantry Regiment that arrived in Italy about a fortnight ago at his regimental headquarters near Verona; they are a chery (sic) crowd of d---d good fellows & keener than I ever imagined!! How long will it last is another question but when I asked them what arrangements they had, their reply was the last verse of a very good one step tune "We won't go back till it's over over there!!!" Made me feel very small & I don't at all like the idea of waiting till the war is over before returning to England!!"[40]

Shortly after they had arrived in Italy, dysentery broke out among the regiment. Private 1st Class Wilbert D. Macer of Company C, a twenty-four-year-old florist from Indiana, died of the infection on August 11, 1918. His was the first death in Italy for the A.E.F. Private Myrice recorded the solemn scene at the funeral: "Lined in battalion front with salute as the [hearse] and his company passed. We then marched to the cemetery and stood at parade rest during the firing of the 3 volleys and playing of taps. sure was a grand way to "go across" if it had only been in U.S.A. And then one can hardly realize how his people at home thot (sic)."[41]

Colonel Wallace had stewed long enough about the regiment's high life style. "About the middle of August, our Colonel began to think that fetes and reviews better fitted a conquering army than a regiment so lately civilians. He felt that town life, with the regiment in four different villages, was not good for discipline, and to the utter astonishment and objection of the Italians, civilian and military, we moved, on the 14th of August to a field near Vallegio."[42]

Certainly Wallace had reason to be displeased. As their commander, he was responsible for preparing the regiment for combat; to toughen them for the realities and horrors of war. The present contented lifestyle his soldiers were living in the villages did nothing to further his goals. He explained, "On arrival in Italy the Regiment was billeted in six towns and in some of them occupying widely separated quarters. As a saving of impedimenta billeting may be an advantage to seasoned troops but it is disastrous to rookies. It required four days to make a casual inspection which developed the fact that half the time of half the men was devoted to military housekeeping. It might lead to worse results. I requested permission to go into camp, placing my views before Colonel Rizzoni, Italian liaison officer for the Allied troops in Italy, and our own particular guardian angel. The request was granted, an ideal field at Valleggio near Verona selected, and a commodious camp of new white tents pitched according to pattern. This was the first unpopular move the men were called upon to make."[43]

Some of the men who were not billeted in homes and villas greeted the move with joy stating that, "Thirteen lost its unsavory reputation when, on August 13, 1918, the entire 332nd Regiment arose early and marched to a point 1 km. east of Valeggio on the Mincio River. On August 14, camp was completely and carefully pitched. The change from the stuffy and ofttimes crowded conditions prevalent in the villages to an open air camp was welcome; and from now on till their departure from Valeggio this camp and its surroundings brought much pleasure to the men of the 332nd. The spot was picturesque."[44]

Captain Story recounted, "We were supplied with tents – squad size for the troops – and after our march from Villa

Franca, we proceeded to erect our tents. Never having had the experience of setting up such a camp, it was quite a laborious job and the results left much to be desired as to the regularity and proper alignment of the companies. When Colonel Wallace saw the results, he expressed his displeasure in no uncertain terms and all tents had to be taken down except for "A" company, and then re-erected to be in line with that company. The writer will never forget how tired and discouraged we were when the order was given, but we realized later how important it was to make a good appearance for we would be looked over by the Italian and Allied officers with critical eyes, being the only U.S. troops on the Italian front."[45]

Ferris Myrice was one of those unhappy soldiers. "Hardly any sleep – those bloomin' bites [mosquito bites]. We left at 8 A.M. marched about 7 miles and are now encamped in squad tents, the whole regiment is here – The Col[onel] Just came along said we should move our tents."[46] The next day his frustration continued: "Moving tents – took all day to move about 10 feet – and it doesn't look right yet."[47] And yet another 3rd Battalion soldier, Private Weller Phillips, crabbed, "In camp. Moved our tent about five times today finally got it in the right place. Feel in the bum tonight."[48] Henry Blank noted with his usual dour tone, "Moved to tented city near Villa Franka (sic). Got all set and then had to move again. Aug 14 Moved tents again."[49]

At least, in the *History of Company K*, someone saw some humor in their labors. "In pitching tents we acquired great skill, since among the officers there was so much difference of opinion as to what constitutes a straight line. After striking and pitching tents fourteen times, they were allowed to stand at ease for the duration of our stay."[50] Once the camp was in order Lieutenant Rendigs observed that "It was a novel thing for the Italians, too, to see so large a unit as a regiment under canvas, and the citizens and soldiery came from miles around to see our neatly laid out camp with its wide company streets and canvas homes."[51]

E Company's poet muse, Cyril O. Littlefield, could not resist the final word on the move, "Sixteen days and we pulled up stakes, From billets a hike to take; Six miles away in a big open field, Pitched squad tents and good it did feel. Tents must be in a very straight line, Worked at it hard for a good long time; All up crooked, a mess the claim. That's what they said, 'twas a shame, 'twas a shame. Early next morn we did it all over, tents pulled down, and bunched a little closer, Sighted with eyes, and lined with rope, Chased us around like slippery soap."[52]

With the regiment together again in the bivouac soldiers would dub "Camp Wallace", the Colonel focused on the final training necessary before taking his regiment into combat. The Italian Front offered some unique challenges. Mountainous terrain characterized the area and the regiment would need specialized training in the techniques used in mountain warfare. "A heavy drill schedule began at once. Shade could be found nowhere; the sun's burning rays could not be avoided. The nights spent in the open tents under a boundless sky, glistening with bright stars, amply compensated for the scorching noonday heat."[53] Initially, the regiment "… operated in the region towards the hills to the north of the camp, learning to advance over obstacles such as corn fields, grape vines, plowed ground and deep ditches full of thorn bushes."[54] Wallace noted that when he asked his ally "Colonel Rizzoni if a small force with battle experience could not be sent to demonstrate the methods [of trench warfare] to the entire Regiment … he sent me a large battalion of Arditi for the purpose."[55]

Arditi, literally meaning "The Daring," in Italian, were the perfect selection; created in 1917, Italy's Arditi were similar to Germany's *Stosstruppen* (storm troopers). The Italian *Reparti d'assalto*, or Assault Units, were well versed in small unit tactics, and were designed to conduct trench raids deep into enemy territory. Experts in hand to hand combat, Arditti were ruthless in combat, showing no mercy to their opponents. The 23rd Assault Battalion of Arditi was led by Major Lorenzo Allegretti; his troops immediately awed the Americans. Captain Story said, "These Ardite (sic) were so tough that it was rumored that many of them had come from Italian penitentiaries. In addition to their rifles and grenades, they all had a dagger strapped to their belts and in the handle was a needle like instrument for the purpose, so it was said, to gouge out the eyes of the captured enemy. This battalion had its own band and I can see them yet, early in the morning running to the training field at double time, the band playing all the while."[56]

Not long after the arrival of the Arditi the 332nd was "… assigned to a more spacious training area, – a valley over the hills beyond Valeggio. Here we practiced the Italian system of open warfare, advancing several yards at a time as a platoon or squad column, then forming a skirmish line and opening fire with rifles, automatic rifles, flame throwers, etc."[57] Wallace was a taskmaster, and he ensured that the regiment threw all of its energy into training. "Daily we fared forth to our training ground, a piece of land along the Minco River (which had been selected because its area, about 220 acres, contained nearly every kind of terrain upon which we would ever be called upon to fight, and practiced some phase of battle). When we had become proficient in all the details of combat, we pieced them together and went through several lively scraps, with rifles, auto rifles, machine guns, bombs, trench mortars and light artillery, all being used and nothing simulated except enemy."[58]

Not all moments at Camp Wallace were spent in military instruction; during their off hours, the boys enjoyed the services offered by the YMCA and the Red Cross:

> "At Valeggio the Y.M.C.A was on the job with their army huts, sufficiently large enough for their canteen, reading and writing room, entertainment and motion picture hall. It was their aim to have social gatherings of some kind each night. It was at the Y.M.C.A hut where many enjoyed religious services by Chaplin O'Herron, O'Donnel and Kelly. Miss Bissel, Miss Morris, Miss Fosdick and Miss Richards, of the Y.M.C.A deserve worthy mention for their untiring efforts to make life more pleasant for the boys of the regiment. A class in Italian was conducted with Miss Bissel as instructor.
>
> A the east side of the camp was the American Red Cross Hut. Although built on a much smaller scale than the Y.M.C.A., yet gave to everyone the impression of welcome.

Many a pleasant evening was spent in the little writing room, reading, writing or enjoying lemonade after a day's workout in the scorching sun. All thanks are due to Miss MacIntosh and "Daddy" of the Red Cross for their faithful work in the interest of the boys of the 332nd Infantry."[59]

All manner of activities and assistance were provided. "The days at [Valeggio] with the regiment afforded the "Y" its best opportunity to carry out a well ordered program daily, as a large hut had been erected on the Italian plains, and a sufficient number of workers, including two American women, were on hand to render a well-rounded service. Athletics, movies, minstrels, vaudeville, lectures, religious services, banking, money order department, library, and last, but first to the heart of the doughboy, a well stocked canteen, were among the features of this, the largest "Y" hut built conducted in Italy."[60]

Always on the lookout for something better than army food and some way to pass the time after a long day's drill the doughboys would "... go to the little town of Vallegio. It had nothing to offer except the usual little wine shops and grocery stores where we showed a decided fondness for the Swiss chocolate and almonds. Occasionally, someone would go out into the country and bring back enough eggs, tomatoes, potatoes, etc., so that a few of the boys could enjoy a "real" meal in a Signora's kitchen."[61]

Swimming in the River Mincio was a relief for the soldiers of the 332nd, The Company [D] Log noted that, "The regiment continued intensive training through the late summer; each man, already overtrained, began hoping that the impending day would soon arrive when the big drive in Italy would begin. At the close of the day's heavy, and by this time, monotonous drill, the men spent their evenings on the streets and in the small shops of Valeggio, or bathed in the clear, swift waters of the Mincio."[62]

Sergeant Major Lettau recalled the swimming and an exasperating turn of events, "Near the camp was an irrigation ditch about five to seven feet wide and about four feet deep. About a mile away was the Mincio River, a real mountain stream. We bathed in both places, but one day, the Powers that were, decreed that the enlisted men should swim in the ditch, for "Officers Only" were allowed in the River. It is superfluous to reproduce the comment, but let the reader think of nearly 4000 men in a ditch, in which clothes also were washed, while for less than two hundred officers, there was a large river."[63]

Colonel Wallace was acutely aware of his important diplomatic and Italian morale building mission. Thus, he staged a party and show at the camp. "... it was proposed by the officers and men that a minstrel and boxing show be given in which we might all return our numerous social obligations. During the stay at [Valeggio], I had reduced social functions to the minimum. Nevertheless, some invitations had to be accepted. The officers had been entertained at messes when they visited the trenches and by commanders on their way to them. The British non-commissioned officers entertained ours at their mess on Lake Garda and all were indebted to the [Arditi], who had entertainments for them. It was expedient to have the matter over and done with at once rather than spread over a considerable period of time, and besides it meant a really creditable affair. I approved of it."[64]

The gala affair was on Saturday night, August 24, 1918; Lieutenant Rendigs remembered:

> "It was decided to give a minstrel show and garden party about this time in honor of the Italians and other Allied troops in the vicinity. The affair was worked up from "home talent" and was given on two successive nights, the first one for our own and the Allied officers and the second for the Americans and Allied soldiery. A stage was erected and a large area was fenced in with beautifully ornamented trellis, inside of which are placed a number of small tables and several hundred chairs. Dozens of Japanese lanterns strung overhead provided the illumination, and the regimental band, covertly hidden by a bower of palms, furnished the music. All of our own officers attended the first night to act as hosts to our brother officers of the Allied armies, about three hundred of whom attended as our guests. The affair took on the nature of a garden party, with a cabaret, and the never-ending variety of liqueurs and drinks of all kinds was necessarily present. The minstrel show "got across" in fine shape, and the other "stunts" were liberally applauded. In fact the whole affair was a great success, quite different from the Italian parties, and therefore agreeable to them."[65]

Private Phillips wrote, "The officers are having a show tonight for the officers of the Allied armies here. There are Italian, French, British and Scotch officers here. And the privates are not allowed to even look on at a distance. It gets rottener every day."[66] Sergeant Major Lettau, noted, "The performance was a regulation American minstrel show and was a great credit to the boys who took part in it. Besides the minstrel show proper, there were sketches by two clever cartoonists, several vocal solos, a violin solo and dances. This may sound ordinary by considering the time, the circumstances and the place, it will be seen how extraordinary it was."[67]

The day after the officers' party Private Phillips went to Sunday services, "In camp. Sunday and a day of rest ... Was over to hear Chaplain O'Donnell this evening. He is a very good speaker."[68] Lieutenant Speakman described Father Charles Leo O'Donnell, their Catholic chaplain as "... somewhat under average height and somewhat under thirty, erect though rather slight, with a serious kindly face behind large, metal-rimmed glasses. It is a face of humility and strength and gentleness."[69]

During his studies at Notre Dame, O'Donnell was considered an, "... excellent debater, with splendid powers of rebuttal."[70] After studying at Harvard for a short time, he attended Catholic University where he received his doctorate in English. He returned to Notre Dame and there was ordained a priest in 1910. Father O'Donnell was one of first to sign up when, priests at the University were asked to volunteer as chaplains. In the summer of 1918, Father O'Donnell was assigned to the 332nd Infantry Regiment. It was only a matter of time before the devout debater O'Donnell crossed swords with Wallace, "Father Charles O'Donnell was sent to Italy to accompany the American forces there. His experiences were not very gratifying. His commanding officer had no idea of religion and less appreciation for morals. On one occasion, after this officer had quite brazenly advised his men to satisfy all the lusts they desired, Father O'Donnell, with two other chaplains, went to protest. This commanding officer had cultivated the habit of leaning back in his chair, closing his eyes, and emitting a stream of sulphurous curses and coruscating blasphemies, during which the protestor was supposed to disappear. This day, he fell into his routine, but when he opened his eyes, Father O'Donnell was still there. Anyone who recalls Father O'Donnell's facile tongue well remembers that Father O'Donnell did not have to curse to be effective. It is quite safe to say that that commanding officer had never been taken apart quite so neatly."[71]

That Sunday, many of the regiment's officers traveled to Venice. Lieutenant Rendigs recounted the trip:

> "We arrived there about eleven o'clock in the morning and were cordially greeted at the station by the American Consul and General & Mrs. Treat. The Consul took the entire party in charge and piloted us on board a large power boat for a hasty tour of the Grand Canal and the other beautiful waterways which make Venice different from any other city in the world. After paying our respects to the Italian Admiral in command of that district, who presented each of us with bronze medals commemorative of our visit, we journeyed to a small island near by and there took a dip into the salty but wonderfully warm Adriatic. Wherever we went we were escorted by our band, which had made the journey with us, and were received by large crowds of Venetians who gave us a hearty welcome – the first American [Army] Officers to visit their beautiful town.
>
> ... After lunch we were the guests of honor at a reception in the Municipal Council Chamber, tendered us by the City Fathers, where addresses were made in behalf of both Italy and America and much excellent champagne was drunk. An interesting feature of this reception was the appearance, as an invited guest, of an aged Italian in a bright red uniform, and wearing many medals. He was treated with great deference and on being presented to him we learned that he was a veteran who had fought with the Italian patriot, Garibaldi, for the Italian independence. He was very proud of his uniform, and in it presented a most picturesque and striking character. Having drunk to the health of every American and Italian hero, both dead and alive, we left the party, broke up into various small groups and roamed the city at will, visiting all of the famous places of interest.
>
> At five o'clock we stood in front of the famous Lions of St. Mark and listened for a few minutes to our regimental band rendering a concert to several thousand musically inclined and thoroughly appreciative Italians. After an hour in one of the numerous gondolas with which Venice abounds, we had our evening dinner in one of the bright little restaurants that line the Grand Canal, and then after a short stroll through the darkened streets retired to our hotel..."[72]

In addition to the nearby training area at Borghetto, the regiment underwent instruction around the village of Custoza, just a few kilometers to the northeast of Camp Wallace. "The Custoza region was pitted by trenches and dugouts, and covered with barbed wire entanglements in preparation for any military exigency that might arise from a successful attack by enemy forces from the Trento area."[73] Lieutenant Rendigs related his experience of the trenches at Custoza:

> "The various battalions and companies alternated in acquiring the training, and the nature an variety of it held our interest very closely. The first time that our turn came to go to these "play trenches", as we called them, we marched out as a battalion at three in the afternoon, but had not gone very far when a terrific hail and thunderstorm came up. We were obliged to halt because of the intensity of it, and, since there was no shelter available, stood in huddled groups on the open road. It lasted for about an hour and by that time we were all soaking wet and thoroughly convinced that we were experiencing real war-time hardship...took over our section in orderly fashion, at eight o'clock. The system employed was for two platoons of each company to occupy the front line, with the other two platoons in reserve. After holding for a period of four hours, the platoons in the line would be relieved by the platoons in reserve in order to give every one an opportunity for training. The first night was, of course, miserable, and what sleeping was done was in our wet clothes; but the next morning the sun came up warm and early, and dried us out, which was great relief. During our tour in these trenches, which lasted forty-eight hours, everything was done to bring the reality of trench warfare home to us. The automatic rifles and trench mortars were put in place and manned at all times, a line of outguards was established and a system of countersigns and paroles was arranged, patrols and working parties were sent out, rockets and very-lights were profusely used, telephonic communication was established between all points and battalion headquarters, gas alarms were used and even aeroplanes circled overhead during the day in order to determine the visibility of our positions and how well the men kept under cover. The men enjoyed the novelty of the. work, it made our training seem real to us, and, though tired out, they were somewhat regretful when our first tour of duty came to an end and we were relieved by the First Battalion. However, we made two other trips to these trenches during the following two weeks, both times for forty-eight hours."[74]

On September 11th, while in the Custoza trenches, a humorous incident occurred which ended quickly, but became an enduring part of 332nd lore. Roberts explained, "After we reached our destination we had to sleep out in an open field, and during our stay in these trenches we ate grapes which we picked from a vineyard nearby. The joke of it was, we thought we were stealing the grapes but had to pay for them about four months later."[75] Private Ferris Myrice added that, "We make a raid – on a grape arbor – it was sure "stripped."[76] Private Shade added, "In the trenches nothing doing, only standing guard. over the top twice and come back with hat full of grapes."[77] Roberts noted the result of the grape stealing incident; the men ended up paying restitution for the grapes (privates 3 Lire each; officers 5 Lire each). It was from this incident that one of the nicknames of the regiment arose: "The Grape Eaters."

Regular athletic competitions were held at Valeggio to keep up the morale of the soldiers and to "show the flag" as part of Wallace's larger diplomatic mission. Baseball was very popular and some of the men had experience in the Big Leagues. On Saturday afternoon, September 7, 1918, the championship was held at "Camp Wallace"; First Battalion would play 2nd Battalion. As the regimental band provided music, doughboys packed around the field and perched in the surrounding mulberry trees. Generale Pecori Giraldi, some of his staff and other officers represented the Italians along with a few young Italian women. The second battalion emerged victorious and was crowned the regimental champions.

There were other competitions as well. "While at Valleggio, it was felt that the men were in need of recreation and plans for a track team were formed. ... A Regimental track team was now formed. It toured Italy, competing in meets at Verona, [Florence], Bolonga and Rome. ... Little or no attention had been given to track work until we reached Villa Franca, Italy, and not then until we received an invitation from the French soldiers to compete in three events of a field meet they were holding in Verona, Italy. We accepted even though we had only one week to train ... As a result of this there developed a demand for a Regimental track team, which was obtained through a process of elimination, first the Company, then the Battalion, then the Regiment." One company's athletes dominated the 3rd Battalion track meet: "Company "I" was practically the whole works in the Regimental meet too, having five winners out of a total of nine single men events, and furnished most or the members of the relay teams. ... We were beginning to feel sorry by this time and didn't enter the high jump and pole vault, wanted some other Company to have a look in"[78]

The Drill Schedule for the day during this period included:

Monday A.M.
7:00 to 7:30: Physical exercise, running, jumping obstacles so as to develop agility and endurance of soldiers.
7:30 to 8:00: Instruction in use of Gas Mask.
8:00 to 8:15: Rest.
8:15 to 9:00 : Company combat drill; including debouching from departure trenches. Attacks against points of resistance.
9:00 to 10:00 : Bolt manipulation with magazine floor plate, magazine spring and follower removed.
10:00 to 10:15: Rest.
10:15 to 10:45: Platoon close order drill and Manual of Arms.

P.M.
2:50 to 3:30: Position and aiming exercises.
3:30 to 5:30: Developing company strong points.

Tuesday Schedule the same as for Monday except;

8:15 to 9:00 A.M.: Period devoted to giving platoons an opportunity to go over carefully their particular phase of the company combat drill of the previous day, using Gas Masks,
7:30 to 8:00 A. M.: Bayonet instruction.

Wednesday Same as Monday, except the period 8:15 to 9:00 during which time instructions will be given company specialists.

Thursday Same as Wednesday, except 7:30 to 8:00 bayonet instruction.

Friday Practice march under assumed tactical situation.

Saturday Trenches.[79]

Captain Story described a training exercise:

> "On the occasion of our last visit, a [battalion] of [Arditi], accompanied by a detachment from our own battalion, under my command, put on a night attack against the position held by the American troops. It was interesting, instructive, and one that I shall remember, because it resulted in the first reward for bravery given to an American soldier by the Italian government. The Italian major was in command of our attacking force, and he decided to make a frontal demonstration with heavy rifle fire against the American position, while the main attack was to be made against their left flank, with view to encircling it. I divided my detachment into two parts and sent half of it under two officers with the Italians, who were to make the frontal demonstration, while another officer and I took the remaining part and accompanied the major with his [Arditi], who were to make the flanking movement it was arranged that both forces were to be in position and the frontal attack made at quarter before two in the morning, while at the same time our flanking force was to begin its encircling movement, reserving our fire, however, until we were actually discovered by the American. Blank cartridges were used to make the attack more realistic, and promptly at the appointed hour our force on the left center opened a heavy fire, attempting to distract the attention of the "enemy" while we encircled their flank. At this point occurred the incident which showed the pluck of one of our sergeants.
>
> As our troops on the center opened fire, they began a slow advance through the inky darkness against the "enemy's center". A small stream, about ten yards wide but very deep, [paralleled] the American position, and only two fords were available for crossing it at the point where the frontal attack was developing. As the men crawled slowly forward, one of the Italians, in his excitement, and not seeing the stream, crawled directly into it and went under. Immediately a great [commotion] arose and his comrades sent up a number of very-lights [flares fired

from pistols that are used for battlefield illumination], all the while dancing wildly up and down on the bank of the stream and chattering volubly instead of trying to render some real aid to their unfortunate companion. Sergeant Richardson, of Company H, seeing the commotion, and realizing that the Italian was drowning, quickly dashed off his helmet, but with his gas mask, still in place, tied on his chest and his belt full of ammunition, jumped into the stream and swam to the rescue of the Italian soldier, who had apparently given up and gone down for the second time. As he came up, Sergeant Richardson grabbed him, but the Italian, with the proverbial habit of the drowning man, clasped the Sergeant around the neck in such manner as to pull them both under together. The sergeant, however, broke the Italian's hold and managed to swim to the bank with him, where willing hands pulled them out of danger. The Italian was given first aid and then sent to the hospital, where he eventually recovered, while the Sergeant was none the worse for the mishap. An Italian colonel who was present as an observer immediately pressed forward and, warmly congratulating the sergeant, took his name and organization and assured him that his promptness and courage had undoubtedly saved the life of the Arditii. About a month later the sergeant was publicly decorated on a field near Verona with the Medal Militaire, which is the second highest decoration obtainable by a soldier in the Italian army. He was the first American so honored, and rightly deserved the decoration, acting courageously and promptly as he did, without stopping even to remove his heavy and cumbersome equipment.

In the meantime our attack on the right flank was developing and after being discovered by the "enemy", we opened a heavy fire, cut through their wire entanglements, and jumped into the trenches where many mimic, humorous, hand-to-hand [encounters] took place The Italian major promptly declared the attack a success and the positions won, while the American major promptly decided that the attack had failed and that we were all prisoners. After some good-natured bantering back and forth we called it a night's work and the Italians retired to their billets near by, while we went back to our respective organizations, where we arrived just as the day was dawning. It had been a hard night and we were all glad enough to eat breakfast of hot mush, bread and coffee, and then to snatch a few hours' sleep on the hard, but welcome, ground. The next night we returned to our camp, and upon arriving there found that "Dad" Butler, of the Red Cross, and his Assistants, had prepared a great amount of hot coffee and some tempting biscuits which they immediately proceeded to serve to our boys. This refreshment would have been welcome at any time, but coming as it did, after two strenuous days and nights, with a twelve mile return march for a climax, the men felt as if it were something that had been sent from heaven. "Dad" was one of the characters of the Camp, and, by his kindness and indefatigable labor in behalf of the men, endeared himself greatly to all with whom he came in contact."[80]

Our last trip to the "play trenches" had been the best of all and we now felt fit and eager to take over a real sector on the Italian front and to put into practice those lessons which we had long been studying and for which we had been diligently trained. Rumors now became current that we were about to see the "real thing", the field officers were sent here and there along the Italian front for short stays, – it was safe to pick out a suitable sector, – and the entire camp was all agog with curiosity and eagerness to go into action. …Sunday, we were officially notified that our battalion had been chosen to take over a quiet sector on the Piave front. The news spread through the camp like wildfire and our men were everywhere jubilant, while the men of the other two [battalions] were correspondingly downcast. It was announced, however, that it was probable that in the near future the other two battalions would also be sent into the line at different points, the plan being to impress the Austrians with the idea that there was a large number of American troops in Italy, which it was hoped would have a depressing effect on the morale of the enemy and would be good propaganda for the Allies. …As soon as our major received his orders he assembled our officers and gave us the plan which called for our moving early the following Tuesday morning to the city of Treviso, which was the largest town nearest to that part of the Piave front for which we were bound. …"[81]

Sergeant Major Lettau noted:

"These good times, however, were not to last, for on the 11th of September we said goodbye to our Second Battalion which had been selected to hold a sector of the Italian line on the Piave River. With moist eyes we watched them march away. How many of them, our comrades of a year, would return? But they, led by the band, stepped away lightly with shining faces. I know that even mortal battle was more welcome to them than that that (sic) soul-deadening drill in the hot sun. Hourly we awaited news from them, but beyond a few meagre (sic) reports that they were successfully occupying the trenches, we heard little.

From what I have been able to learn, however, they went into their sector and held it. With characteristic American love of action, their quiet sector was hardly bearable. For Americans to stand silently in the trenches and watch enemy shells and aeroplanes pass overhead without replying was unheard of. However, "to take a shot," as many wished would have called down upon them the merciless rebuke of the Italian General under whose orders they were. No unauthorized shooting was allowed. So, our gallant Second chafed and obeyed orders as good soldiers do."[82]

It took a couple of days for the entire Second Battalion to get out of Camp Wallace and convoy to the Front. The scene was recalled by Lieutenant Rendigs:

"On Tuesday morning,…we arose bright and early, made up our packs, fell in and prepared to march out to

Villafranca on the first leg of our journey to the front. The entire regiment turned out to see us march away, and [finally], headed by our regimental band playing "Hail, Hail, The gang's All Here", and "There'll Be A Hot Time In the Old Town Tonight", we started off. The Colonel and his entire staff took up an advantageous position to witness our departure, and there was a world of pride in his look as he wished each platoon "good luck" as it came by and admonished our men to "give 'em hell, boys!" The boys were all jubilant with never a thought for the morrow, although here and there there was a more serious countenance, reflecting the thought that possibly some of that group would not return. After marching about a mile down the main highway the band opened up into two lanes and permitted us to pass through while they rendered our old favorite "OHIO".

About eight in the evening, just as dusk was deepening into night, we saw numerous tiny red flashes, high up in the air all along our left, but at apparently a great distance. No sound could be heard but we knew these flashes to be the bursting of the shrapnel shell, probably fired by the anti-aircraft guns. These flashes could be seen for about an hour and this fact, together with the appearance of long hospital trains carrying wounded on their way back from the front, made us quick to believe the reports that we had heard of a sudden re-opening of activity along the entire Italian front. Many thought that we were arriving just in time and fully expected to be sent into the front line that very night; but I cherished no such Illusions on that subject. We reached Treviso shortly before midnight and quickly detrained. Here we were met by Major Everson, who had preceded our coming, and were quickly formed up as a battalion and marched out. After marching about an hour and a half through business streets and wide avenues lined with beautiful trees we came, finally, to a huge, long, brick building which had formerly been used as a cavalry barracks by the Italians Here we [billeted] in the best way that we could for the night, sleeping on the cement floor, wrapped in our coats, since our baggage had not yet arrived."[83]

Upon the departure of the Second Battalion, the atmosphere at Camp Wallace was a mix of sadness and expectation. "The ground where their tents had stood was leveled, along with the streets and clever gravel designs before the tents. From this it was plainly evident that the second battalion would not return to the Valeggio camp, and with this indication there was revived in the men the hope for early action and a change from the depressing influence of constant training. The men were stale and overtrained by severe, intensive drills for long hours every day in the hot sun."[84]

Lieutenant Rendigs noted:

"... what I saw there convinced me that at last we were in the danger zone and nearing the front line. There was scarcely a single business block that did not have at least two buildings in complete ruins. There were huge towering piles of debris to be seen on every side, with many bent and twisted iron girders protruding from underneath, showing the powerful effect of the raiders' bombs ... Machine guns and anti-aircraft weapons were mounted at every point of vantage, and the roofs of all of the taller buildings are continually used as observation posts. I was informed that the Austrian raiders came frequently, almost always at night, and that usually there were [some] casualties ... Upon returning to our barracks I caught my first glimpse of one of the sausage-shaped observation balloons tugging lazily at its anchor to the northeast of us. It was thought to be an Italian, but farther to the left could be seen several oval-shaped ones in a curved line, which indicated the Austrian positions. That night before retiring we were instructed in the alarm to be given in case of an air raid directed at us, and were assigned different sections of a field nearby, where we were ordered to take our commands and cause them to lie down at scattered intervals. This was done in order to fool any possible night-rider, who would undoubtedly bomb the barracks if he could get low enough to see them. ..."

Next morning we drilled for a little while and then put on a battalion review in preparation for an expected visit from the [Duc] d'Aosta, Commander of the 10th Italian Army Corps, of which we were a part. He came the following day and, after a formal review of the battalion, he made a short friendly address to our officers. He was a very amiable old gentleman, a cousin of the King of Italy, and held the rank of Lieutenant General ..."[85]

With the Second Battalion in their final training on the line, Colonel Wallace kept up the relentless pace for the balance of the regiment through the month of September. According to Private Hart, "All methods of warfare known to the modern world were presented to the 332d in a practical way of the bombing range; artillery, flares, gas, shrapnel bombs, gas bombs, smoke bombs, automatic rifles, trench mortars, machine guns, rifle grenades, and liquid fire – all were used in maneuvers. By the close of summer the 332d was doubtless one of the most highly trained regiments in the U.S. Army."[86] Then tragedy struck. Myrice reported:

"Friday the 13th and it sure was unlucky for the 3rd Battalion – we went out to the field where the maneuvers are held and watched the Italians prepare and then we began our part of the days work. Several trench mortars were going to send over a barrage, they were slow in getting started. Major McKinney asked the reason and the Lt. [lieutenant] in charge replied that he was waiting on an orderly, just then he appeared and the Lt. told the major he would start in two minutes. Then things started – By pure accident or carelessness a shell went straight up and down – exploded among the men mostly officers – one – a gunner was killed – inst.[instantly] six others are reported as dying later and several more are not expected to live – including Major McKinney and Lt. Bails. Lt. Carter of M. Co – has died – the first Lt. I really knew – and that anything of I met him at the range in Sherman in my early days "over there". – A fine chap lost for U.S. I often wondered what I would do when I saw dead and wounded lying all around – I surprised myself, I felt no inclination to faint etc. – I even helped to bind a wound for Nayer. Our officers and men did fine in such a time. L. Co was lucky only a few slight scratches – where much of the shrapnel hit – the NCO's were standing a few minutes before. – We receive word that the Sammies [British slang for Uncle Sam's Soldiers] are going after Metz [France] – heres hoping they get it and soon – I've seen all of war…war is sure hell."[87]

The reported number of casualties differed in various reports. Most agree that there were six soldiers killed: Lieutenant Marion Leslie Carter, Company M, Anthony J. Bently and Clayton Samuel Gochnauer, Headquarters Company; Private John R. Jones and Corporal Frank "Monk" Simon of Co I. Fifty others were injured.

Captain Story observed the accident which, "… resulted in the death of one officer and five men and the wounding of fifty others. The wounded were rushed by ambulance to the 331st Field Hospital located in Sommacompagna. Lieutenant Colonel Boyer had one foot amputated, Major Charles McKinney of our (3rd) battalion had a piece of shell go through his carotid arteries, but Lt. John Sargent sat by his side during the ambulance ride, pinching the artery with his fingers and after surgery, Major McKinney made a complete recovery but was out of action for the duration of the war."[88] "On September 14th there was a great military funeral when the dead were lovingly laid to rest in the Italian cemetery at Villa Franca."[89] Weller Phillips, a private in Captain Story's company, wrote about the funeral in his diary, "… The King sent a special representative and also the Pope. Generals – there were many. It certainly was a beautiful ceremony and the Italians sure did good."[90]

Lieutenant Rendigs continued the description of his journey"

> That day, the Second Battalion "Marched on to Varigo (sic) near to the front and there got our last training before going into the trenches. As the buildings are all damaged by the artillery fire it was very dangerous to chance living in them, therefore we pitched our pup tents and slept on the ground, which is nothing new for us now. We almost broke our necks the next few days watching aeroplane battles. While here we learned to make barbed wire entanglements and then crawl thru them without losing all our clothes. We also learned to throw bombs and dig real trenches. The Ardities, to which we are now attached, put on some war stunts for us which we repeated after them and showed them up somewhat."[91]
>
> "… a beautiful September morning, warm and sunshiny, and as we marched along the well-camouflaged roads leading to Varago everyone was in the best of spirits. We marched in single file on either side of the road and a staggered platoon formation was used with the platoons about fifty yards apart. The advantages of this formation were, of course, apparent, – it made our visibility to aerial observers practically nil, in case of a bursting shell it reduced the chances for casualties, and, lastly but very important, it left open a wide space in the center of the road for the constantly flowing stream of camions passing back and forth. As we neared Varago we passed a myriad of wire obstacles and obstructions ready to hold back the enemy in case of an offensive, and we saw many large holes in the ground and many a wall in ruins, which we recognized as the work of the enemy artillery. We reached Varago about ten o'clock, and to our great joy found that the Y.M.C.A. was on the job as usual and had already established a canteen in an old house and was ready for business. The four companies in the battalion were quickly [billeted] in four different parts of the little village, with battalion headquarters about the center, the idea being, of course, to reduce casualties in case of a direct hit. One of the platoons occupied an old church with a huge gaping hole, the height of a man, in its side, – mute testimony to the efficiency of the Austrian artillery, – while in the small room occupied by the sergeants of my own platoon was a beautifully carved hole boarded up in the ceiling, directly over their heads. These "punctures" caused a great deal of amusement to the men, who immediately began betting that "they couldn't do it again." All of the men were comfortably [billeted], however, with the exception of one platoon, which was obliged to sleep in pup tents for lack of [billeting] space. The tents were hidden under a row of trees and well camouflaged, so their only danger was from a stray shot."[92]
>
> "We had been in Varago about ten minutes when, all of a sudden, we heard a loud explosion followed by a terrific crash, and on looking toward the direction of the noise, saw a cloud of dust and splinters rising heavenwards about two hundred yards on our right. We realized that for the first time we were being fired upon and in actual danger; and it gave us the thrill, I suppose, that might be termed "comes once in a lifetime". The first explosion was quickly followed by a succession of others, all of the shells striking about the same place, and we thought at first that the Austrians had learned of our coming and were giving us a warm welcome. A minute later we were greatly surprised by a terrific reverberation which caused the ground to shake under us and the windows to rattle noisily as we grasped the fact that the well-concealed Italian battery near by was replying to the Austrian fire. In a few minutes a merry artillery duel was in progress, and then, to make things more interesting, a couple of Italian aeroplanes came up from somewhere behind us and started for the Austrian lines. We also noticed for the first time that we were now in front of a line of Italian observation balloons which soared high in the air directly in our rear.
>
> The two aeroplanes, on reaching the Austrian lines, were immediately greeted by salvos of shrapnel from the Austrian anti-aircrafts' and little white puffs of smoke, – "cream puffs" the boys later termed them, – denoting the shrapnel burst, could be seen bursting all around the Italian planes. The mission of the Italians was plainly one of observation in order to locate the enemy guns so they were not to be driven off thus easily. suddenly a pair of Austrian aeroplanes could be seen mounting skywards

and we knew that at last we were to see an aeroplane duel, Higher and higher came the Austrians, but the Italian planes kept up their work of circling round and round, trying to locate the Austrian artillery and paying apparently no attention to their oncoming adversaries. Finally the Italian anti-aircraft guns on our side of the river opened up, but their fire fell far short of the Austrian planes, who were directly above the Austrian lines and heading straight for the Italians, who by this time had joined forces, evidently preparing to meet the Austrians. The opposing planes were now quite close and suddenly the pat-pat-pat of the machine guns, followed by tiny puffs of white smoke, told us that they were using their own weapons. Then began a series of dipping and circling and other difficult [maneuvering] on the part of both sides, each of them apparently jockeying for a position where they could score a direct hit with their machine guns on their adversaries. The firing of the Austrian anti-aircraft guns was now merely desultory, since they dared not fire with the planes grouped as they were, because of the danger of hitting their own pilots. Finally the Italians seemed to gain the advantage, for suddenly one of the Austrian planes took a downward course, circling slowly like a bird with a broken wing, and, closely pursued by an Italian plane, passed out of sight below the tree tops. The Italian immediately rose again under the hot fire of the Austrian antis and joined his comrade who was still circling, dipping and shooting at the remaining Austrian plane. As soon as the other Italian regained his altitude safely and it was apparent to the Austrian that he would have to fight two, he turned tail and fled, much to the delight of our onlookers, who howled their approval as if the combatants might hear them. By this time the artillery duel had ceased and the Italians, apparently satisfied with their work, turned back toward our own lines pursued by the Austrian shrapnel-bursts until they were out-distanced. As they passed over our heads, high up, with their motors humming, they reminded me of two big roosters, who, having vanquished their opponents were now returning to crow about it. Of course this aeroplane duel, combined with the artillery firing, convinced us that we had found an interesting spot and formed the sole topic of conversation for the rest of that morning.

I was told by some of the men that there was a battery of Italian 75's down the road toward the front, and another about three hundred yards to our left, and I determined to pay them a visit. Accompanied by an interpreter I visited the battery which had done the firing and found it slightly back of the main road five hundred yards from our billets. There were four guns,-75's – and all of them well concealed beneath arbors of young trees. Each one was set down about a foot below the surface of the ground, which afforded a natural shock-absorber for the recoil in the rear. There were hundreds of shells, high-explosive, gas and shrapnel, concealed in dugouts nearby and there were dugouts and protective shelters for the artillerymen if it should become too hot for them. The officer in charge of the battery was a young Italian lieutenant, and he courteously explained to me the workings of the gun, and regretted his inability to fire one then, but said that if I would come later he would be glad to permit me to do the firing, which is easily done by pulling on the end of a long rope attached to a lever, which discharges the piece. I subsequently made several trips to this battery for that purpose, but never succeeded in getting there at the right time, since it could only fire upon receipt of telephoned orders from Division Headquarters.

That evening, immediately after supper, a great swarm of Italian aeroplanes went over the Austrian lines and were immediately greeted by the Austrian "archies". Scenting the probability that the Italians had gone over with the view to directing artillery fire, I immediately made my way to the other Italian battery which had been firing frequently during the afternoon and which, from the noise, I knew to be directly to our left and front. Before I reached the position it was belching forth its missiles in quick succession, in response to the direction of the Italian planes. I found this battery to be 105's, and at a splendid location, with an observation post situated in the top of a high tree which stood directly above it. During a momentary cessation of firing I obtained permission from the battery commander to mount to this observation platform, which I did by means of a series of wooden ladders placed there for that purpose. Upon reaching the platform with another officer we found ourselves about a hundred and twenty-five feet above ground and could easily see the Piave River in front and to our right with the Austrian lines in the underbrush on the other side. Just then the battery immediately below us began firing again and the shock of the explosions, which were deafening, caused our tree to sway from side to side. The firing proceeded about five minutes, during which time we could see the shells falling in a small village back of the Austrian lines and throwing up great clouds of dirt and debris, when suddenly half a dozen Austrian aeroplanes, in battle formation, could be seen coming toward the Italian planes, which at that moment were hovering over our lines [signaling] the effect of the shots to the Italian artillery. Before the enemy planes gained contact with the Italian planes, however, the Italian anti-aircrafts opened up from positions all around us and plastered the air in the vicinity of the Austrian planes with shrapnel "cream-puffs". Between the unbroken reports of the Italian "archies" all around us and the terrific crashing of the big guns directly beneath us, we found conversation impossible on that little observation platform which was swaying precariously from side to side, and, to make things more interesting, the bits of shrapnel were dropping all around us from our own anti-aircraft guns, because by this time the Austrian planes were directly overhead and the black Maltese crosses could be plainly seen on the bottom side of the lower planes. We decided to go below and take shelter in the Battery Commander's concrete bombproof, which we hastily did and found him glad to see us come under cover. The Austrian planes turned and [paralleled] the Italian lines for a short distance, but the firing of the Italian guns became too hot for them and they finally circled back over their own lines. The Italian planes, which had been hovering around in a state of indecision, turned and went back over our heads, the artillery ceased firing, and the incident was closed."[93]

The Second Battalion visited the sector of the Piave trenches, of which they were to assume control, in order to acquaint them with the lines of defense. Rendigs continued:

"[Visits to the front] … was carried out by companies, one company going up every morning early, spending the morning in becoming acquainted with the sector, and returning about noon. Bright and early one September morning our Company started out in a staggered platoon formation, every man of course wearing his helmet and with his gas mask in the "alert' position. We proceeded through the village of Maserada en route, which was nothing more than a mass of ruins, and a little farther on were met by a quartet of Italian officers who acted as our guides, one for each platoon. The platoons then went ahead at ten-minute intervals in order not to become "bunched" or to attract the attention of the enemy, and when it came time for my platoon to move forward we did so in single file on either side of the road. We had gone only two hundred yards when a large shrapnel shell burst overhead about twenty-five yards in rear of the end of the platoon. It sounded like a thunderclap and was the first indication that the Austrians were about to shell the road. I looked around, intending to order my men to take cover, but no need for that – they were scurrying into large drainage ditches along either side of the road like rabbits into their holes. The next "card" we received from the enemy was also an "overshoot" but was a high-explosive and buried itself deeply in the ground in rear of the tail of the platoon, showering dirt and stones on several of our men. I deemed it advisable to move from there, and so we crawled [cautiously] forward for about ten minutes, keeping well under cover in the drainage ditches. The Austrians continued to [lambaste] the same place, so we finally emerged from cover and took the road, which was swifter going and from which we eventually branched off onto a footpath which brought us directly to the third line of defense.

At this point the platoon was halted, while the sergeants, our Italian guide and I went forward to a vantage point to gain a birdseye-view of the entire sector. We saw a large flat strip of low country with the Piave River about a half mile to our front, the stream being about five hundred yards wide at that point, apparently shallow, and with several small islands and sandbars dividing it in the center. The first line of defense was a high, wide dike which had been constructed in pre-war days of earth and concrete, and which had been converted into an excellent defensive breastworks with numerous small dugouts, rifle and machine gun pits evenly distributed all along the line. We were informed by our guide that this dike, together with a second one called the "Royal Dike", which formed the third line of defense for that sector, had been there for many years and had been very useful in checking the rise of the river which occurred perennially in the springtime, caused by the large quantities of snow and ice melting in the mountains and flowing down into the Piave. The "Royal Dike", in the shelter of which we were then standing, was exactly similar in construction to the first line of defense and formed the "Linea Reserva" for the sector. Its dugouts were built directly in rear and sheltered by the dike, were of several rows of sand bags and timbers, [strongly] constructed and large enough to accommodate about eight men, but not, it must be confessed, with a great deal of comfort. In rear of this third line, at a distance of about two hundred yards, was a high mound of earth resembling a small hill and extending about four hundred yards in length. This served to shelter a half company and constituted a sort of [strong] point and second reserve line, but could also be used as Brigade Headquarters in the event of action: From the "Royal Dike" or third line the three large communicating trenches of the sector zig-zagged their way forward, connecting this third line with the "Linea Reincalzo" or "Line of Supports" constituting the Second Line of Defense, and continued on with many sharp- angles until they reached the first line. This "Linea Reincal[z]o" was the only line of defense which was entirely in the form of a trench dug into the ground, – the other two lines of defense being the two dikes which rose above ground.

Of course all of the communicating trenches and a number of "saps" leading out to outposts and numerous strong points were in the form of dug-in trenches, and all of them were so arranged that they could be used to advantage as a defensive position with barbed wire obstacles which could easily be dragged down into the trenches, thus effectively blocking any further penetration, [paralleling] their entire course. Directly in rear of the second line and about in the center of the sector was Battalion Headquarters, with small rooms for the major and his adjutant, a dining room, kitchen, and an office, all well protected with many layers of sand bags, timbers and dirt, with small saplings planted overhead at irregular intervals to effectively camouflage it from aerial observation. Here, too, the first-aid and medical dressing station was located with sleeping accommodations for the doctors and their corps of attendants. Between the lines of defense was a veritable myriad of barbed wire entanglements which, stretching in every direction and criss-crossing at every conceivable angle, appeared absolutely impossible of penetration. The sector which we were to take over was bounded on the left by Communicating Trench G5, and on the right by the [Salettuol] Road which was the chief artery of transportation to the rear and considered the most important single highway on the entire Piave front. We were charged with the defense of this road in conjunction with the battalion on our right, and the orders given us before going into the trenches were to hold it to the last man against any possible attack of the enemy. The reason for its strategic importance was because it led directly into Treviso and opened up the way to Venice, which city the Austrians were very desirous of taking. Regimental Headquarters was just to one side of this road, inside our future sector, and was a very large and well-constructed position.

Having gained a general idea of the sector, we brought up the platoon and proceeded to a thorough inspection of the three different lines of defense with their communicating trenches. Upon reaching the first line we found a series of outposts on an island in the center of the stream, in front of the left flank of the sector. This island was connected with the main land by a small foot bridge which could be hastily withdrawn or destroyed should the enemy ever-gain possession of the island. Only our Italian guide and I were permitted to visit this island [because] in so doing we were obliged to expose ourselves to the view of the enemy and it was not deemed wise to take over an entire platoon, and thus run the risk of drawing the enemy's fire. We found the island well protected with barbed wire entanglements and with several bomb proofs to afford shelter against enemy fire. After rejoining the platoon we inspected the front line carefully, made note of the rifle pits, the emplacements for the one-pounders and machine guns, the numerous dugouts, which were not very well constructed, and-the gas sentinel stations with their accompanying appliances, for the giving of gas alarms. These latter I was particularly interested in. I found two sentinel posts in the front line, one toward either flank, both were well revetted with sod and fitted with the Italian alarm devices. These were very crude and consisted of two small empty shell cases suspended from a small frame which, in case of alarm, were to be repeatedly struck with a bayonet or some other steel object, giving out a clanging noise which was far from loud enough. In addition to these were two special rockets for each post which, when they worked, were excellent, sending up a distinct yellowish flare and the head, in coming down, giving out a loud whistling noise like an old-fashioned whistling cannon-cracker, only much louder. The difficulty with them was that they seldom worked. These were the only alarms that the Italians used, and it seemed to us that they were trusting too much to luck. In addition to these gas alarms each line of defense was fitted up with numerous large brush-piles to which were fastened four pitch and tar bags which in case of a gas attack were to be lighted-and thus aid to disperse the gas quickly. This was an old precaution but a very good one.

After finishing up with the front line we moved back to the second line and, on going through the communicating trenches, found them well kept, wide and, fitted up in many places to be used as a firing trench if the occasion should arise for such a use. The second line we found to be a trench proper with a number of firing bays and several strong points. Although an-Italian company was [billeted] in the second-line, no attempt was made to man the firing bays or strong points so long as the Austrians were not attacking or showing any signs of doing so, and the only observation post in the entire second line was immediately in front of Italian headquarters and well elevated in order to give its occupants a good view of the enemy's line. Occasionally, too, a lookout would be established in a tall tree that was left standing for some unknown reason near battalion headquarters. The third line of defense, the "Royal Dike", proved of exactly similar type and arrangement as the first line, but no lookout whatever was kept in this line since it was only intended to house the troops in reserve. Two gas sentinel posts were, however, maintained in this line because of the known tendency to use this weapon, particularly against reserves.

By the time we had concluded our inspection it was noon, and we hurried back to Varago and dinner, well satisfied that we were to occupy a fairly good sector, although the dugouts, as-we had found them were neither overly clean nor comfortable, to say the least. Our inspection of the trenches had been made without incident, although twice we had taken shelter as the enemy had sent over some of his 105's, but fortunately both times they had exploded too far away from us to do any damage. A few days later I took the entire gas personnel of the battalion to the trenches for another visit, and this time we made detailed sketches of the position of the gas alarms; sentinel posts and wood defenses with an idea of improving their location and condition. On this occasion I met both the brigade and regimental gas officers and exchanged ideas with them. On September 23rd, which happened to be the first anniversary of military service for many of the older service men of the battalion, Company F was ordered to take over the front line trench that night and hold it several hours, to gain experience in how to take over the reliefs etc. I was to accompany them and take over the gas sentry posts with our own gas personnel.

We left Varago for the trenches about seven in the evening and had only just started when a terrific thunder storm broke over us, lasting for an hour, and drenching every one to the skin. After the storm had spent its fury it settled down to an all night rain with intermittent downpours to enliven the evening's entertainment. No more miserable a night could be imagined for the taking over of a line of trenches, but we plugged ahead, trying our best to keep up our spirits. Upon arriving at the trenches it was quite dark, but we managed to flounder through the mud and water to where our guides awaited us. The different platoons of the company were then conducted to different parts of the line to relieve the Italian platoons, and I accompanied the captain and major to battalion headquarters to meet the battalion gas officer. Upon our arrival there, after plunging through mud and water up to our knees in the trenches, we were warmly welcomed by the Italian major who immediately set before us some excellent coffee and cognac, which warmed the cockles of our hearts. I then proceeded with the Italian gas officer to make a complete tour of the gas sentry posts, replacing the Italian gas sentinels with our own men. Having completed this duty we returned to battalion headquarters, which was warm and comfortable despite the miserable weather outside, and waited for word to come in that the complete relief of the Italians by our forces had been made. This word arrived at eleven o'clock, and once again I made a tour of the trenches, this time accompanying the two battalion commanders for the purpose of inspection. The inspection of the sector being completed, I quickly withdrew my gas sentinels, who were again replaced by the Italians, and we started for Varago by the shortest possible route, which was also the most dangerous.

However, we were all feeling so miserably low that we didn't count danger, and arrived at our billets about two A.M. on the morning of the 24th after a most miserable expedition. The company came in about an hour later, but, although all the men were thoroughly sopping wet none of them any the worse off the next day except in the matter of shoes, which refused to go on the men's feet until they had been worked over for an hour or more. Each man had only one pair of shoes with him, and so the program the next morning was held up for a short time while the men sat around wrestling with their obstinate "Number Elevens". Each company in the battalion had its turn in taking over the sector for one night, and then it was announced that in all probability the next evening, Saturday September 29th, the battalion would take over the sector as a whole from the Italians and would hold it for an indefinite period."[94]

From the time that the 332nd Infantry Regiment relocated to Valeggio until the middle of September, the Machine Gun Company was reorganized and increased in strength through the reassignment of men from the other companies, thus doubling their firepower capability. Near the end of August the Machine Gun Company went to advanced training at the Italian machine gun school in the Berico Hills south of Vicenza. At Villa Montruglio the men learned and perfected techniques on their own and Italian guns. Before their training was concluded a platoon was assigned to the Second Battalion for duty at the Piave. The rest of the company, upon completion of their instruction, rejoined the regiment at Valeggio on September 16th.

In honor of Italian Unification Day the men of the 332nd Infantry Regiment had the day off. Sergeant Major remarked, "... 'B' Company and the Band went to Rome to participate in the annual September 20th celebration. With them were several of our best athletes [for the international military track meet]. When the Americans arrived in Rome, the Italians wondered why they had come. However, seeing they were there, they offered an Italian barracks to them. Besides this incident, the most noteworthy event was the disappointment of being in Rome with no money, for many of the boys were robbed in this barracks of the few lires they had."[95]:

"... to Pesehiera, situated on Lake Garda, beautiful, crystal, blue Lake Garda. Like many Italian towns, Pesehiera boasts a splendid old wall, relic of the days of battle. The town itself held us just during the time required to eat lunch, for there was a boat making a trip around Lake Garda sometime after lunch and we could not miss that trip. The lake extends up into Austria, that country controlling the northern end while Italy controls the southern. It is fed by streams from the melted snow of the mountains, the bases of which meet the water. The shores are very rocky and when the boat docked at the little landings, the dancing waves could be seen lapping over the doorsteps of the stone houses built on the very edge of the land. The villages are beautiful and quaint beyond comparison. The picturesque dress of the people; the ornamented though poor stone houses; the little donkeys; the blue, crystal-clear water all about, with the mountain peaks above hidden by clouds, made an [unforgettable] picture. Many of these simple villagers had never seen an American soldier and when we approached a town, at least half of the population turned out to stare at us and wave a greeting in their peculiar, backhanded way. On hillsides facing the lake, many pretty homes have been built, always of stone, while vines and shrubbery are so well trained and trimmed that these dwellings look like fairy palaces."[96]

Private Myrice enjoyed his day off, "Friday – Italian holiday – part of the Battalion go to Lake Garda I soon saw all the city I wished and went swimming in the lake. – Then by good fortune was given a long ride in a "rig" with a couple of [sergeants]. We took pictures and ate grapes. Watermelon later."[97]

Private Raymond Shade, described the final phases of the training at Valeggio as, "...out for field [maneuvers] under barrage 3 inch guns and trench mortars. trench mortar bursted over my head but luck was with me. shakey tho (sic)."[98] A few days later, under similar circumstances, another fatal accident befell the regiment; Private Phillips recorded the incident, "Monday, September 23, 1918 In camp. Was out on battle maneuvers today. Another man killed today. By rifle or automatic rifle fire. He was from K Company. We are having more casualties here than we would on the front."[99] The soldier killed in that training accident was Wojciech Bialy.[100]

Private Walter Hart remembered the day when "Camp Wallace" was finally abandoned by the last elements of the regiment, "The command came on Wednesday, October 2, to destroy the gravel designs around the tents, to level the ground, and to fill in the streets of the camp. That night pup tents covered the former camp site now transformed by picks and shovels to a rough area of torn and irregular earth. The 332d had at last received the long-awaited order to go to the front."[101]

With the Second Battalion going forward Sergeant Major Lettau stated:

"It was generally thought that the First or Third Battalion would go up to relieve them in a few weeks. The Colonel's idea in occupying these trenches was to reserve a place for the Americans when the day of battle came. However, before this plan could be carried out, the tents at Vallegio were struck and the regiment was moved to Treviso by train and the Second Battalion was ordered from the trenches so as to join the regiment at Treviso.

Regimental Headquarters remained till the last. Everyone except about twenty of us had gone.

We were to follow in trucks with the records, boxes, etc. It was sad and lonesome to look at the former site of a living, bustling camp, now deserted and dead. Only a few fires, burning rubbish, remained to mark the place. With the coming of daylight, we loaded the trucks and set out for Treviso.

The trip occupied the entire day but it was pleasant in every respect. On passing through a village one could always get hot coffee, chocolate and fresh bread which helped our canned meals considerably.

It was evening when we reached our troops billeted in an Italian barracks on the outskirts of Treviso. Having no definite orders to proceed we remained for the night. In the morning we received orders to go to a villa outside of Treviso, which we did. The name was Villa Angelica.[102]

"On October 4th we broke camp and moved to the Piave front."[103] With months of intensive training and hard work behind them at Camp Sherman, in France and Italy, the 332nd was finally moving into the line. The ultimate test for the regiment, the test of combat, now loomed before them. Colonel Wallace's boys were about to advance into history.

Brigadier General Charles G. Treat with American Red Cross nurses in Villafranca, Italy. July 27, 1918. Courtesy National Archives.

Officers that arrived in the first troop train, marching thru the streets of Villafranca. Left to right: General Pecori Giraldi, Colonel Wallace, commanding the 332nd Infantry. Brigadier General Charles G. Treat, Officers of the Allied Armies in Italy and Officials of Villafranca, Italy, July 27, 1918. Courtesy National Archives.

Above: A portrait of Major General Eben Swift as a lieutenant colonel; Swift was the senior American officer in Italy. Courtesy Military History Institute.

Right: This map illustrates the American activities that Brigadier General Treat controlled in Northern Italy. Courtesy Military History Institute.

Opposite
Top: The new arrivals, accompanied by an Italian band, march through the streets of Villafranca. Courtesy National Archives.

Bottom: Colonel Wallace (left) and Brigadier Treat (right) led the parade through Villafranca. Courtesy National Archives.

Above: One of the Caproni aero planes flying over Villafranca, welcoming the first Americans, Villafranca, Italy. July 27, 1918. Courtesy National Archives.

Right: Piloting one of the Caproni aero planes was Captain Fiorello LaGuardia, future New York City mayor, flying for the American Air Service. Courtesy Library of Congress.

Below: Line of Italian trucks carrying the first American troops to arrive in Italy to their billets. Villafranca, Italy. July 26, 1918. Courtesy National Archives.

Above: View of Italian band playing while first American troops to arrive in Italy leave for their billets in trucks. Villafrance, Italy. Courtesy National Archives.

Right: Officers of the First Battalion, 332nd Infantry receiving coffee, doughnuts and cigarettes from the American Red Cross, Villafranca, Italy, July 28, 1918. Courtesy National Archives.

WELCOME TO OUR SOLDIERS IN ITALY

SPECIAL U. S. ARMY NUMBER OF

THE RED CROSS BULLETIN

OF THE AMERICAN RED CROSS IN ITALY

(CROCE ROSSA AMERICANA IN ITALIA)

ROME ITALY

VOL. I — AUGUST 15, 1918 — *Special*

First American Line Troops arrive in Italy

SOLDIERS MAKE FINE SHOWING WHEN REVIEWED BY KING OF ITALY

Somewhere in the Italian war zone: July 1918. — At last the American fighting troops are on Italian soil. The question that has been asked repeatedly of every American in Italy for the past seven months: « When will your soldiers come? » has now been answered They are here.

They have been welcomed with fraternal cordiality by thousands of Italians and they have had the honor to pass in review before the King of Italy, attended by the Prime Minister, the General commanding the armies of Italy, and many other Italian military notables as well as the American Ambassador, the General Commanding the American Military Mission to Italy, the Acting Commissioner of the American Red Cross, and other distinguished representatives of their own country, America, and her Allies.

The historic importance of the occasion of the arrival of American fighting troops to take their places at the Italian front was recognized by every one privileged to take any part in the welcome of the soldiers from the United States. General Diaz made the announcement of the event in an order of the day to his armies and the news was carried to all who could read and to those who could not read, so that today there is probably not a person in all Italy who does not know that soldiers from the United States are on Italian soil.

Everywhere the American officers and men have been, through all the towns and cities they have passed and stayed long enough for the inhabitants to get a glimpse of them, they have been received with demonstrative enthusiasm. When at the end of the journey the men in numerous detachments detrained, every man wore in his sombrero or pinned to his blouse an Italian flag, or carried in his hands flowers, the gifts of the delighted people who had already come to regard them as old friends.

Of course, every one will be asking ow many men have arrived and equally, of course, the answer cannot be given. But there are enough to make a fine showing — big, stalwart, husky young men, most of them from the middle West and they were all glad to be in Italy. « Oh, boy! We never had such a reception as this, not even back home », is the way more than one expressed it.

Best of all, of course, was the welcome given by the Italian people, the Italian Red Cross and other Italian organizations which did all that it was possible to do. But hardly second in its appeal to the sentiments of the men was the touch of home they found at every stopping place. The

THE REVIEWING STAND

FIGHTING MEN IN KHAKI RECEIVE SPLENDID WELCOME EVERYWHERE

American Red Cross in Italy had its agents, officers, men and women, to greet t e American soldiers and offer them those small comforts that in war time mean so much — coffee and lemonade, and doughnuts and cigarettes and good hot soup. There wasn't a chance for the men to get homesick or hungry. They all had their rations in plenty, but they took pleasure in filing past the Red Cross stands with their cups and hands extended, and their cups and hands were well filled before they got past the American women in Red Cross uniforms.

There were Bersaglieri troops always on hand as a guard of honor and a Bersaglieri band to play them in as the trains arrived and Italian officers of high rank who watched the Americans with manifest approval as they went about the big business of detraining with the snap and energy officers love to see in their men. There was no idling, no lethargy anywhere, but the American and Italian soldiers found moments in which to get together and learn to know each other in that quick way soldiers have. The Americans could not speak Italian and the Italians could not speak English, but they understood each other.

Home Service

The Home Service and Communication Bureau of the American Red Cross has been designated by the War Department in General Orders No 17, as a body authorized "to relieve .... the anxieties of soldiers who are worried about their families, and to promote the comfort and well being of those families". In accordance with this order the Department of Civil Affairs of the American Red Cross in Italy has organized such a bureau to follow up the requests of soldiers and seek all possible information for them concerning their families. Its field representatives also follow up in the hospitals the cases of all sick or wounded members of the American Expeditionary Force, including soldiers, sailors, aviators in training, American Red Cross personnel, etc., etc., and, with the approval of the Commanding Officer communicate all details to the relatives at home.

A. R. C. Hospitals in Italy

There are four American Red Cross hospitals in Italy: one at Milan, under the supervision of Miss de Long, in connection with the Nurses' Center that has been established there; one at Genoa, under Miss de Graw; one at Rome where Miss Sparrow is supervisor, and one at Florence. With the exception of the last named, all the hospitals are functioning. They are entirely at the service of the U. S. Army and Navy, the American Embassy, the Y. M. C. A., the A. R. C., and in short, of any Americans in Italy who may be engaged in foreign war service. With the exception of the Genoa hospital, which has been more particularly militarized, patients will be received without any formality if direct application is made by the organization under which they are serving, to the person in charge of the patient or hospital, or to the local American Red Cross office.

Left: The American Red Cross printed a special bulletin to celebrate the arrival the 332nd Infantry Regiment in Italy. The headline trumpets, "First American Line Troops arrive in Italy."Courtesy Rendigs, Fry, Kiely & Dennis, LLP.

Officers and men of the 3rd Battalion, 332nd Infantry receiving coffee, doughnuts and cigarettes at the American Red Cross. Villafranca, Italy, July 28, 1918. Courtesy National Archives.

Train arriving with the 1st Battalion, 332nd Infantry Regiment. The first American troops in Italy. Villafranca, Italy, July 28, 1918. Courtesy National Archives.

3rd Battalion, 332nd Infantry marching along a street in Villafranca. The historical castle of Villafranca of Verona is seen in the background. Villafranca, Italy, July 28, 1918. Courtesy National Archives.

Officers of the 3rd Battalion. Major McKinney commanding in the center with glasses. Villafranca, Italy, July 28, 1918. Courtesy National Archives.

Above: Prince of Wales and Colonel William Wallace walking through the gardens of the Villa. Headquarters of 332nd Infantry at the Villa of 1001 Roses in the village of Sommacompagna, Italy, August 11, 1918. Courtesy National Archives.

Right: General Charles Treat, of the American Mission in Italy talking to an English Colonel at an Aviation Field between Villafranca and Sommacampanga, Italy, August 1, 1918. Courtesy National Archives.

Below: Officers of the 2nd Battalion, 332nd Infantry Regiment, left to right: Captain Demprey Meldrum; First Lieutenants Sales, Chamberlain, Hyre, Miller, Craig, Queensen, Moldenhouser, Clinger, Rubin, Connely; Second Lieutenant McLain, First Lieutenant Rendegs; Second Lieutenants Sparkling, Dunbar, Speakman, McMasters, Coffman, Brown, Higgins and Chalders. Borghetto, Italy, August 15, 1918. Courtesy National Archives.

Prince of Wales, Colonel William Wallace, Commanding Officer, American Expeditionary Forces in Italy and Countess Lavinia Bocca Trezza, owner of the Villa of 1001 Roses in the village of Sommacompagna, Italy, August 11, 1918. Courtesy National Archives.

Funeral of Private First Class Wilbert Macer, Company C, 332nd Infantry Regiment who died of pleurisy. He was the first Soldier of the A.E.F. to die in Italy. In the old cemetery of Villafranca. Colonel William Wallace and Captain F.M. Scanland stand by the coffin. Cemetery of Villafranca, Italy, August 12, 1918. Courtesy National Archives.

Lowering Macer's coffin. Courtesy National Archives.

Grave of Wilbert Macer in the extreme northwest corner of the Villafranca Cemetery. August 17, 1918. Note that Macer's ID tag is nailed to the cross as a temporary marker. Courtesy National Archives.

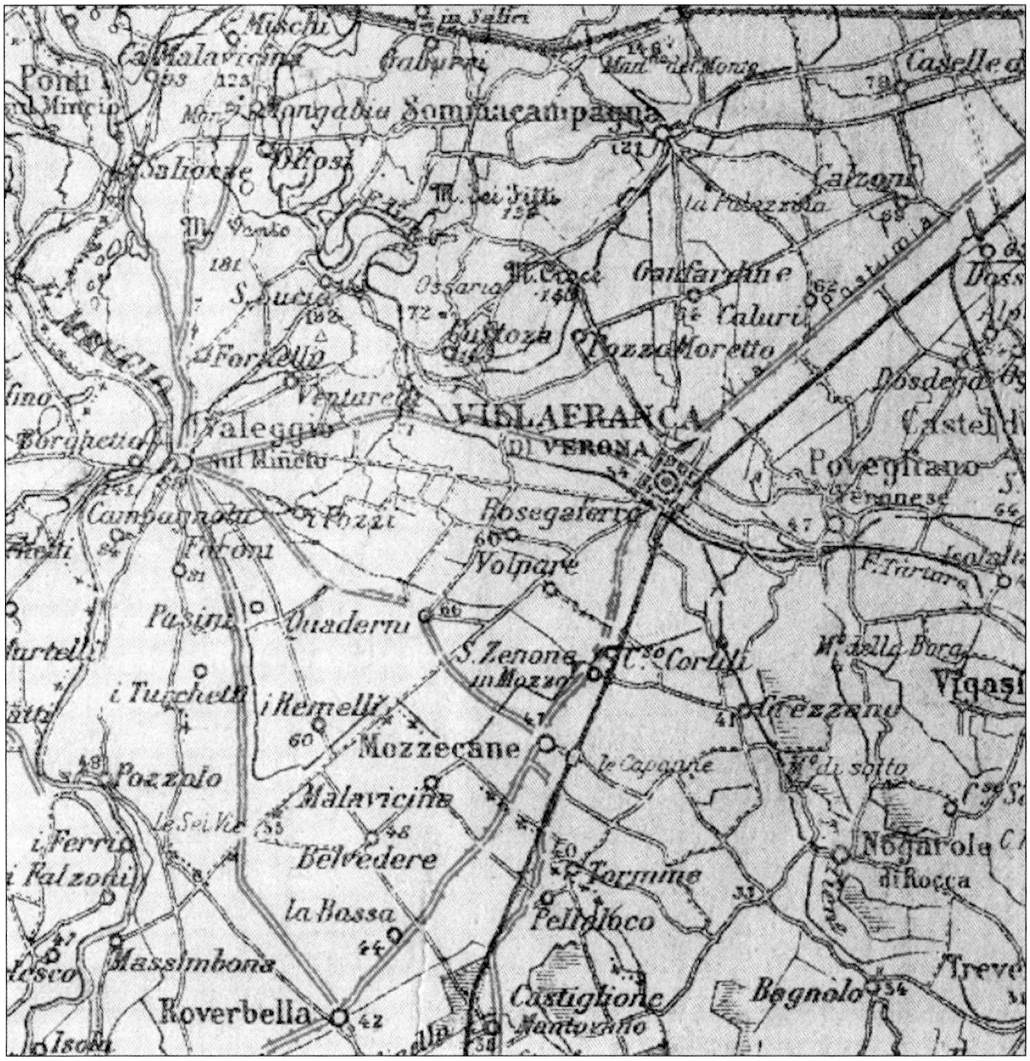

Right: A U.S. Army issue cloth map, carried by Captain Story, shows the area the regiment was initially assigned. Courtesy Military History Institute.

Below: This map belonged to an American Ambulance Service driver. Villafranca is visible at center left, southwest of Verona. Courtesy Military History Institute.

Right: Second Battalion of the 332nd Infantry Regiment on a hike. Major W.G. Everson commanding (1st officer on horseback). Borghetta, Italy, August 18, 1918. Note the Italian soldier standing guard on the bridge to the left. Courtesy National Archives.

Below: Company F, 332nd Infantry following their colors. Borghetto, Italy, August 15, 1918. Italian children follow the soldiers to the right as a civilian watches. Courtesy National Archives.

Above: The King of Italy visits the 332nd Infantry Regiment. King Victor Emmanual was photographed with Ambassador Thomas Nelson Page at a review held at an aviation field between Villafranca and Summacampagna (sic), Italy, August 1, 1918. Courtesy National Archives.

Below: King Emmanuel of Italy, Ambassador Thomas Nelson Page, Brigadier General Charles G. Treat, Colonel Wallace, and officers of allied mission in Italy inspecting troops of the 332nd Infantry. At aviation field between Villafranca and Summacompagna (sic), Italy, August 1, 1918. Courtesy National Archives.

Above: King Emmanuel of Italy, Ambassador Thomas Nelson Page, Brigadier General Charles G. Treat, Colonel Wallace, and officers of allied mission in Italy on the reviewing stand. Aviation field between Villafranca and Summacompagna (sic), Italy, August 1, 1918. Courtesy National Archives.

Below: Group of Italian officers visit the 332nd camp near Veleggio, Italy. August 24, 1918. Courtesy National Archives.

Above: The 332nd Band marches through a crowd in St. Marks Square, Venice, Italy, August 25, 1918. Courtesy National Archives.
Below: The band of the 332nd Infantry Regiment playing in Venice, Italy. August 25th 1918. Courtesy National Archives.

Funeral procession of William E. Evans, Company H, 332nd Infantry Regiment who died August 26, 1918. Buried in the cemetery at Villafranca, Italy, August 26, 1918. Courtesy National Archives.

Evans's coffin is lowered into the grave. Villafranca, August 26, 1918. Courtesy National Archives.

In mid-August, Colonel Wallace decided to move the regiment out of the four different villages where they had been quartered. He moved the regiment to a field outside of Veleggio. In this view, men of the 332nd prepare their new camp. August 13, 1918. Courtesy National Archives.

Rows of tents stand in lines in the new 332nd field camp. Soldiers quickly named the encampment "Camp Wallace." Courtesy National Archives.

Yankee troops, attending a machine gun school in Italy, running through a smoke cloud on the maneuver grounds. Courtesy National Archives.

Group of American and Italian officers. Right to left: Lieutenant Arme Ferrero, Captain Ammi Pagnani and Lieutenant H.L. Neil Italian Machine Gun School near Barbarano (sic), Italy. September 6, 1918. Courtesy National Archives.

Americans studying Italian Armored car. Italian machine gun-school near Barbarano (sic), Italy. September 6, 1918.

Sammies and Arditi watching a game. Camp near Veleggio, Italy. September 7, 1918. Henry Blank made an entry in his journal stating that, "Second Battalion won ballgame 3 to 1." Courtesy National Archives.

Italian and American officers watching the game. Camp near Velleggio, Italy. September 7, 1918. Courtesy National Archives.

Group of Italian and American Officers. Left to right: Captain Rietti, Lieutenant General Ferrari, Lieutenant Treves, Colonel Tacoli, General Pecori Giraldi, Lieutenant Colonel Boyers, Lieutenant Colonel Accorgi, and Captain Maino Righ Camp near Veleggio, Italy. September 7, 1918. Courtesy National Archives.

Group of Italian and American Officers. Left to right: Captain Vaugh, Captain Scanland, General Ferrari, General Percori Giraldi, Colonel Tacoli, Colonel Gregory, Captain Vieth, Major McGraw and Lieutenant Treves. Camp near Veleggio, Italy. September 7, 1918. Courtesy National Archives.

View of 332nd Infantry field camp, one mile east of Valeggio, Italy. Courtesy National Archives.

Colonel William Wallace, Commanding 332nd Regiment and his staff. Camp near Valleggio, Italy. September 7, 1918. Courtesy National Archives.

Company E, 2nd Battalion visited the trenches on the Piave River, near Verago, for observation. They were the first American combatant troops on the Italian line. September 16, 1918. Courtesy National Archives.

Company E at the front. Courtesy National Archives.

Another view of Company E along the Italian Front. Courtesy National Archives.

Opposite
Top: Company E at the front. Note that the men are armed with P-17 Enfield Rifles. Years later, Captain Story noted this in his veteran's survey. Courtesy National Archives.

Bottom: Company E, in a communication trench, returning from an observation post on the bank of the Piave. Front line on the Piave, near Varago, Italy, September 16, 1918. Courtesy National Archives.

Opposite
Top: Left to right: Lieutenant Brown, Lieutenant Moldrum, Captain Johns, Major William Everson, Mrs. Shank, Major General DeAngelis (Italian Army), Mr. Shank (American Council at Palermo, Sicily), Lieutenant Brant. Front Row: Lieutenant DeVaughn, Lieutenant Hill, Captain Varvaro, Mrs. Camera (Nurse), and Captian Mindchalchi. Headquarters Second Battalion. Varago, Italy. September 16, 1918. Courtesy National Archives.

Bottom: Members of the 332nd throwing bombs. Headquarters 2nd Battalion, near Varago, Italy. September 16, 1918. Courtesy National Archives.

Right: Right to left: Major William Everson, Major General DeAngelis, American Council Samuel H. Shank, Headquarters Second Battalion, near Varago, Italy. September 16, 1918. Courtesy National Archives.

Below: Through the window of a ruined house, a Yankee sentry scans the nearby Austrian lines on the Piave. Courtesy National Archives.

While things are quiet in the heat of the day, these Yankee infantryman in a trench beside the Piave are taking a little rest. Courtesy National Archives.

Preparing to start a little commotion among the Austrians. Yankee Infantryman, in a front line trench on the Piave, screwing down the detonators of some hand grenades which they are about to hurl into the nearby Austrian lines. Courtesy National Archives.

The original Signal Corps captions reads: "Where Italy turned the tide of war. The River Piave which marks the spot where our allies turned the tide of war and held the onrushing horde of Teutons. It is again the scene of terrific fighting with the Italians against aggressors." Courtesy National Archives.

King of Italy and Major William Everson. Headquarters Second Battalion, near Varago, Italy. September 18, 1918. Courtesy National Archives.

Members of the Second Battalion in front line trenches. Piave Sector, Varago, Italy. September 28, 1918. Courtesy National Archives.

Another view of the Second Battalion along the Piave Front. September 28, 1918. Courtesy National Archives.

Group of American and Italian officers, in front line. Left to right: Captain Dickerson, Lieutenant Zappi, Captain Pedrom, Lieutenant Baldare and Lieutenant Chamberlain. Front line on Piave Sector, near Varango, Italy. September 28, 1918. Note that most of the American officers are in shirt sleeves, having discarded the tunic. Courtesy National Archives.

Members of the Second Battalion in front line trenches on Piave sector. Note the improvised carriers used to move "Dixies" filled with rations to the front. September 28, 1918. Courtesy National Archives.

American soldiers in Italian mosquito masks and gloves. Front line on the Piave. September 28, 1918. Courtesy National Archives.

Scene of outpost on the Piave River. Front line on the Piave near Varango, Italy. September 28, 1918. Courtesy National Archives.

American soldier in outpost, Piave Front. Note the P-17 Enfield rifle. Courtesy National Archives.

25386
U.S.
OFFICIAL

Group of machine-gun officers in machine gun outpost. Right to left: Lieutenant Berry, Lieutenant Rubino, and Lieutenant Miller, commanding the machine gun detachment from the Second Battalion. Front line on the Piave. September 28, 1918. Lieutenant Miller wears infantry branch insignia with the numbers "332" clearly visible above the crossed rifles. Courtesy National Archives.

Opposite
Top: No Man's Land from front line. machine gun outpost, used for infilading No Man's Land in the Piave Front. Italy. Courtesy National Archives.
Bottom: Second Battalion men receiving food in outpost on the Piave Front. September 28, 1918. Courtesy National Archives.

Left: This "typical" 332nd soldier on the Italian Front contrasts starkly with his Western Front brethren. He stands in a shoulder high trench in shirt sleeves with helmet chin strap placed on the visor of his helmet. His Mills belt, incorporating the M1911 pistol magazine pouch, was regularly used by mounted troops. We can assume he carries a M1911 automatic pistol in addition to the P-17 rifle. He has a British Small Box Respirator. On the Western Front, such casual exposure to the enemy would have seriously risked his survival. Courtesy National Archives.

Below: Major William Everson (eighth from left), Brigadier General Charles Treat (sixth from left), and Mr. Ray S. Baker (fourth from left) at Second Battalion Headquarters on the Piave Front. September 30, 1918. Courtesy National Archives.

Opposite
Major Carboneselini and Major William Everson referring to map. Second Battalion Headquarters on the Piave Front. September 30, 1918. Courtesy National Archives.

View of Headquarters 332nd Infantry at Villa Angelica, near Treviso, Italy. October 12, 1918. Courtesy National Archives.

View across the Piave River. Courtesy National Archives.

During their stay near Verona, many of the soldiers visited the monument of skulls at Custoza. Courtesy private collection.

Standing in front of the YMCA in Custoza. Courtesy Military History Institute.

G Company soldiers visit with the natives in Custoza. Courtesy Military History Institute.

Visting with some of Custoza'a local beauties. Courtesy Military History Institute.

A soldier snaps a photo of several soldiers in the First Century AD Roman Arena in downtown Verona, Italy. This was a popular attraction for soldiers of the regiment visiting the city. Courtesy Military History Institute.

The Marketplace, Verona, Italy. Courtesy Military History Institute.

Mess time at "Camp Wallace." Courtesy Military History Institute.

Company G Officers relaxing in front of their tent at "Camp Wallace." Left to right: Captain Dempsey, Lieutenant Coffman, Lieutenant Conelly. Courtesy Military History Institute.

Two soldiers sit on a wall in front of the ruins of an old Roman Bridge. Courtesy Military History Institute.

The Second Battalion Track Team. Courtesy Military History Institute.

The original caption reads "All In." Courtesy Military History Institute.

Italian Bersaglieri Infantry and the 332nd U.S. Infantry in Italy, by H. Charles McBarron. Executed as part of a larger series created to show uniforms of the U.S. Army throughout history, McBarron illustrated combat action on the Italian Front. Members of the 332nd appear wearing the wool tunic; an uncommon practice for the regiment while in combat. Courtesy Army Art Collection.

Right: Inside the ossuary at Cutosa; these skulls, were a great curiosity to the soldiers of the regiment. Lieutenant Harold Speakman remembered in his tome From a Soldiers Heart; "I have visited the monument on the hill to the north. It is erected to the memory of those Italians who fell there in an unfortunate battle with their old foe, the Austrian, in 1848; and what is more, the very gentlemen are there themselves, for in the monument's vault are two thousand odd skulls – some of them very odd indeed with the bullets and pieces of shell that destroyed them hanging out of holes in their craniums by bits of string." Courtesy Private Collection.

Often acerbic B Company artist and private Fred G. Reinert captures the arrival of the regiment in Italy in his favorite medium, the cartoon, from his pamphlet, "With the 332 Reg in Italy". Courtesy Private Collection.

Fred G. Reinert's pen and ink self portrait. Reinert documented the adventures of the regiment's First Battalion with his unique drawings; from his pamphlet, "With the 332 Reg in Italy". Courtesy Private Collection.

On the trip from France to Italy, the regiment's soldiers were fascinated with the long tunnels they encountered in the Alps; from "With the 332 Reg in Italy". Courtesy Private Collection.

The arrival in Italy was filled with excitement; the regiment's soldiers met Italian girls, tasted Italian wine and were attacked by the ferocious local flies and mosquitoes; from "With the 332 Reg in Italy". Courtesy Private Collection.

As the 332nd soldiers drilled long hours under the Italian sun, they gained greater respect for their campaign hats; from "With the 332 Reg in Italy". Courtesy Private Collection.

Italian women were of great interest to the boys; from "With the 332 Reg in Italy". Courtesy Private Collection.

Foraging for grapes proved to be problematic for the regiment; following the Armistice, every member's of the regiment's pay was garnered to recoup a local farmer's losses resulting from a grape expedition during training in Italy; from "With the 332 Reg in Italy". Courtesy Private Collection.

Figs, a popular food dating back to Roman times, were everywhere in Italy and the doughboys quickly grew to love them; conversely, bathing in the freezing mountain water steams never fully caught on; from "With the 332 Reg in Italy". Courtesy Private Collection.

Many local Italian girls took in laundry but according to Private Reinert, the prettier ones seemed to attract more customers; from "With the 332 Reg in Italy". Courtesy Private Collection.

On August 1, 1918, the regiment was reviewed by the Italian King, Victor Emmanuel III, this event and the unusual Italian Arditi, who trained along with the 332nd, did not escape Reinert's pen; from With the 332 Reg in Italy. Courtesy Private Collection.

Stereotypes based on immigrant Italian-Americans, did not play out in Italy; from "With the 332 Reg in Italy". Courtesy Private Collection.

4

"Put in the Americans!"

"The hike from Valeggio to Villafranca on the afternoon of October 3, was made in ideal weather conditions. At the station there was but a very short delay in entraining, after which the route led eastward toward Verona and the Piave River. Speculation as to the destination was rife. Vicenza was reached and passed; the course proceeded eastward in the darkness broken by flashes of intermittent light on the northern horizon. A dull reverberating roar spread over the plains around; the flashes and the sound spoke plainly of the gigantic struggle for mastery of the Alpine peaks. At 2:30 a.m., October 4, the order, "All out" came. The air was chill; the darkness, intense; the silence, oppressive, except for the sound of heavy artillery wreaking its deadly wrath on the giant walls of Grappa.

The buildings took strange and fantastic shapes in the morning dark, while the silent uninhabited streets spoke more of death than life. The first battalion marched to large cavalry barracks, a bale of straw was distributed to each squad and in a little time each man lay on the floor in the spot where a few minutes before he had stood in the ranks.

Their senses steeped in sleep; the men did not awake till they were ordered to police the unsanitary camp area at 8:00 a. m. "Where are we?" was on the lips of everyone. "Treviso" came back the answer. No one asked "Where is Treviso?" A glance about made such a query needless.

An Italian guard stood at the gate in the high wall around the barracks. A large drill field lay outside, west of the gate. Across the drill field, 300 yards away, the main highway was filled with troops and supply trains; artillery caissons rolled swiftly forward, drawn by clattering, banging tractors; automobiles bearing Allied officers of various ranks, but all with serious mien, dashed by. Bersaglieri [riflemen on bicycles] pedaled their way cleverly through the congested areas; small mules borne down with machine guns, ammunition, and supplies, were being fed in the shadow of the trees that lined both sides of the road. Aeroplanes darted low across the terrain, or, circling magnificently, rose steadily upward, seeking the best camouflage the sky and clouds offered. Others came from the shadow of one cloud to disappear in the heavy vapor of another. Austrian airmen manoeuvred warily to outwit their clever Italian enemies. A battery of anti-aircraft guns, concealed almost in the shadow of the barracks, opened fire. There now could be no question about the location of Treviso – this was the Italian front.

The Alps rose in full view to the north. The front lines could easily be discerned by the position of mammoth observation balloons placed at great heights and visible for miles in the direction of both mountains and sea."[1]

Since his arrival in Italy, Colonel Wallace became increasingly aware of the importance of his "Propaganda Regiment" mission. Considering this as one of his primary duties, he planned to deceive the Austrians as to the true size of the American force in Italy. Wallace hoped that he might be able to convince the enemy that instead of the Americans providing one regiment, there was at least a division in Italy. Perhaps, he could persuade the Austrians to believe that this lone division was the vanguard of many more to follow. Wallace's spectacular success as a master of military deception would have few equals in modern warfare. It was certainly commensurate with the deception operation prior to the Normandy Landings in World War II which caused the Germans to prepare for a fictional landing at Calais. Wallace's guile earned the regiment its other nickname, "Wallace's Circus."

The plan was hatched shortly after the Regiment's arrival in Italy and Wallace implemented some unusual tools to affect the ruse. He saw that members of the regiment were encouraged to organize athletic teams, minstrel shows, vaudeville shows and boxing bouts. These shows would be sent out to tour "as many different places at approximately the same time as could be arranged"[2] The 332nd Regimental Band would also tour as widely and frequently as possible, playing American jazz and ragtime to mesmerized Italian audiences. An old fashioned man, Wallace didn't understand the jazz phenomenon, terming the genre, "wild man music," but he was willing to monopolize on its immense popularity.[3] Noting that jazz and ragtime had not yet reached Italy when the regiment arrived, its popularity spread like wildfire in France thanks to American Regimental bands that introduced the music there. More and more requests for performances streamed in with Wallace loathe to disapprove any which crossed his desk. Before long, it seemed that Americans were performing all over northern Italy. Only a very large American troop presence could have this reach.

Once the 332nd left camp, Wallace redoubled his efforts. When the regiment moved forward he deployed a new tactic:

> "At Treviso, in air view of the enemy, the Regiment was frequently dispersed over considerable areas to conduct small maneuvers. To swell the multitude every man turned out, even the cooks to their disgust. Uniforms were changed in as many ways as possible. The marching incident to all this was absolutely necessary to harden the command for what it must shortly be called to endure. That the maneuvers attracted the attention of the enemy was shown by their dropping some nine hundred bombs in the vicinity of Treviso one night. Had there been as many Americans in the neighborhood as we wanted them to believe some of us would have been hurt. As it was not a scratch, and the woods were as full of our troops the next day as ever. The men took their first baptism of fire with calmness arguing well their battle efficiency, all the noise and fireworks in the world was not going to scare them."[4]
>
> "To give our training a final touch, and as we learned later, to deceive Austrian Intelligence, every day for the last 10 days, each company would start out from Treviso for a hike of 10 to 15 Kms and back by a different road. Each day we would change our uniform slightly – one day campaign hats, another helmets, another overseas caps, etc. For ten days the roads of this part of northern Italy were covered by marching Americans and Austrian Air Intelligence reported over 100,000 Americans on the Italian front, when there was only one regiment of 4,000."[5]

The uniform changes were aided by the addition of some new items, including the British trench jerkin, which is a sleeveless leather vest lined in blanket wool. Company K recorded that:

> "At this period of our existence we became real "overseas" men by reason of the Supply Sergeant finding for each and every one of us one of those chic French creations – the American Overseas Cap, which is very serviceable, but of no value as a cap. At the same time we became attached to Tommie's jerkin."[6]

The deception operation had succeeded beyond anyone's wildest dreams. After the Armistice, Wallace noted, "When I told the Austrians there was only one regiment of Americans on the Italian Front, they would not believe me. They "knew" there were at least 300,000 of them."[7] The Allies had convinced the Austrians that Pershing had sent multiple divisions, amounting to least one or two Corps, to the Italian Theater. Wallace's efforts had produced a phantom army of American reinforcements which had wrecked Austrian morale and led to an early capitulation of enemy force.

Wallace's Circus, with its associated maneuvers, may have impressed the Austrians, but they didn't sit well with the soldiers. Ever content, Private Blank wrote, "Another hike, longest yet. We are getting a good screwing." The next day he noted with disdain, "Another long hike after a bad night, [there was an Air Raid on the 332nd that night] the canteen rubbed the skin off my ass. This being the fifth day hiking."[8] Wallace's activities quickly attracted the attention of the Austrian Air Service who dispatched a force of bombers to mitigate some of the growing American presence. Lettau described the experience:

> "On the night of October 22nd, I retired early. My sleep was unbroken until about 11:00 P. M. when I was awakened by an awful concussion which seemed just a block away. It appeared to my startled senses that a part of the earth had in some way torn loose from the main body and was hurtling through the sky. I do not remember of sitting up in bed, but I suppose I did. The first object to meet my startled gaze was my roommate running toward the window. Exclaiming, "What's that!" I bounded from the bed and, gaining the window, peered anxiously at the heavens for, in a flash, I realized it was an air raid. Despite the din and roar of the guns far and near, we could hear the hum of the motors but could see no planes. A machine gun across the street in a building with its rapid "tat-tat-tat," sounded ridiculously like a woodpecker drumming on a tree and in spite of the danger caused much amusement. A block or so away, a big gun boomed every few minutes while for miles around guns of all sizes spoke.
>
> The sky was dotted with the beams of powerful searchlights, which tried to locate the invaders. While the moon was bright, there were many small black clouds swiftly moving across the sky. It was an ideal night for a raid. We listened to the guns and watched the flares and then wondered at the silence in the building. Upon investigation we found all of the boys in the yard below looking up at the sky. We joined them. The great lights still searched the heavens, the beams reminding one of a boy's mirror shining on the ceiling of a room. Far up, black little puffs of smoke from the shells of the anti-aircraft guns floated around and, sometimes, we mistook them for aeroplanes. Again, far above, a small flame would burst forth and drop and all would be dark again.
>
> It was not long however before we saw the folly of standing in the open, for shrapnel from our guns rained upon the ground near us, sounding like horseshoes as they struck the pavement. As soon as the "rain" was over, the boys ran out to collect souvenirs, these consisting of rusty, jagged pieces of iron, some eight inches long.
>
> Without seeing the aeroplanes, we retired to the straw ticks, somewhat disappointed. Nevertheless, before we could get to sleep, the big gun up the road spoke again

and the chorus of smaller ones followed. Again we rushed from the room to follow the lights, the flares and the smoke clouds. This time our curiosity was rewarded with the sight of a plane. In the searchlight's ray, the whole body of the plane looked as if it had been dipped in phosphorus. It gleamed. I have no idea how fast that little body moved across the sky. Shells were bursting all around it and we expected every moment to see it fall, a mass of flames. But it proved too fast for the gunners, as it at length scurried behind a cloud out of the grasp of the searchlight. I shall never forget that plane, hurrying like a living thing to its haven behind the cloud. This thrilling scene enacted, we once more returned to resume our sleep.

However, we were again aroused when the raiders returned. This time the attack was short.

To our surprise, we learned in the morning, that no great damage was done and we heard with joy that not an American in any of the three outlying barracks was hurt. These boys were not allowed out of the barracks and, as one lad put it, "I lay flat on the floor so tight against the wall that I thought I'd push the wall out.

We thought, at that time, that the planes were out to bomb roads and supplies but we were told later that they came over to "get" the English and Americans. In fact, an Austrian aviator who had been in the raid was indiscreet enough to boast about it in Fiume to some of the Third Battalion men when they were in Fiume. When he came to he thought he had collided with the moon."[9]

As the regiment's men continued their relentless marches, Wallace saw that special training on combat river crossings was added to the regiment's activities. He was preparing the men of the 332nd to force a rapid crossing of the Piave River. In the few days prior to going into the line, two notable events occurred; the presentation of a stand of colors by the New York Sons of Italy and a visit on Columbus Day by American Federation Labor President, Samuel Gompers:

"Monday, October 7, brought a new experience. That day orders came to make packs. This order being executed, the men of the 332nd practiced crossing the swift current of the Sile River in small boats handled by the men themselves. This training, according to report, was in preparation of an assault over the Piave into the face of the enemy on the east bank. In a short time, after several days' practice, the crossing was made safely and quickly. The evening of the same day, a Stand of Colors, the gift of the Italian Colony in New York, was formally presented to the 332nd men assembled in formation on the drill field to receive them."[10]

"October 12, Columbus Day, was made notable by a visit of Samuel Gompers, President of the American Federation of Labor. He stirred the hearts of the men by an eloquent plea for the emancipation of millions in the bondage of political slavery, for the enthronement of political righteousness, and he paid fine tribute to the men who fell so gallantly on the bloody Western Front. Mr. Gompers concluded his concise and inspiring address by a magnificent appeal to the men of the 332nd to act courageously in the task they were about to undertake. His assurance that the folks back home were sharing the trials and pains of the age along with their soldiers aroused in the men a more intense enthusiasm to "do something": In the period from June 8 to October 7, the men had not seen or heard the voice of an American citizen: Mr. Gompers, speaking for the American People, bearing his message direct from home, gratified an intense longing."[11]

Movement to the Treviso front was accompanied by orders assigning the regiment to General De Angelis' Italian 31st Division with a mission to force a crossing of the Piave River when the offensive began.

This action was to be a part of a larger Italian Vittorio-Veneto offensive. The Italian staff had formulated this planned attack at the end of September, adding the final touches into early October. It called for an attack along two axes. The main attack would fall along the Piave River conducted by Eighth, Tenth (of which the 332nd Infantry Regiment was a part) and Twelfth Armies, reinforced by British and French divisions. Their objective was to capture the city of Vittorio-Veneto which sat astride Austrian lines of communication between their forces operating in the mountains to the north and those forces on the Adriatic plain to the south of the city. If the operation was a success, it would drive a wedge between the two Austrian armies turning the flank of both forces, separating one from the other and causing havoc on both forces' logistics. The secondary attack fell to the Italian Fourth Army; they were to penetrate the Austrian front at Monte Grappa to the west, in order to stabilize the Italian left flank.[12]

October 24th was selected as the opening day. Captain Story reported that:

"... the big push" started. Artillery, hub to hub, from Venice to the mountains opened up a terrific bombardment of Austrian lines. Our regiment was part of the 10th British Army under Lord Cavan. On the night of October 28th we were called out and moved to the banks of the Piave River. A Scotch Highland regiment forded the crossing of the river with rather heavy losses. We moved up to the river. Pontoon bridges were being blown up as fast as they could be put in, so we were held up for two days more. However on the last day of October, we made a crossing at the island of Papadopoli [Grave de Popodapoli], the enemy was now in full retreat and all of the battle that we saw was ground stained yellow by the explosives and many dead men, horses and mules. We passed through the ruin of Cimdolma at 9 p.m. and bivouacked at Vazzola. The following day we moved across the Monticcano through Cadogne and Cajarine. Here we reached the front line and slept until midnight."[13]

A member of Company D recounted, "As they marched in the direction of the Grave de Popodapoli, a large island in the Piave, every man of the 332nd felt a thrill at the sight before him. An artillery barrage was being laid over the Piave such as never before had been experienced on the Italian Front. Brilliant flashes of light silhouetting the mountains, illuminated the summit of Mt. Grappa, 5500 feet above and twenty-five miles distant. Toward the mouth of the Piave, thirty miles away, mighty flashes of radiant incandescent fire from the Allied naval guns in the Adriatic made a spectacle so appalling that one stood transfixed with awe. The regular and mighty roar of cannon was on every hand. A wall of flange rose on three sides."[14]

Although the fighting occurring all around the regiment was thrilling, at this point, the Italian 31st Division was still in reserve, so Colonel Wallace, chafing to get his boys into action, found his regiment relegated largely to an observer's role in the action. After the Highlanders opened a crossing of the Piave, the 332nd joined the Allied footrace in pursuit of the fleeing Austrians. Where was the glory in all of this? The men began to wonder openly if the 332nd would ever win laurels before hostilities ceased.

Ferris Myrice observed, "Its somewhat different being in reserve – than doing "squads right." We have advanced to within 2 1/2 miles of the Piave R. and are awaiting orders. When we arrived here yesterday we were near the artillery. Observation balloons were within a few yards of us. After lying along the road (a very conjested (sic) one) for about 12 hours – orders were given to fall in – and out – and pitch tents. We peacefully sleep during the night. Artillery has stopped firing. Many hundred of "Jerries" pass us. – writing home by candle light – lying under my shelter half – here's hoping the bed will be soft to night (sic)." The next day he continued, "Up at 5:30 – start to cross the Piave – takes us 8 hours to reach it. We start crossing at 3:50 – and arrive on the other side at 5:20. We see our first real signs of war – drowned horses wounded and dead Tommies and Jerries. some had lain for 3 days – ammunition of all kinds everywhere. shell holes and signs of mustard gas. The Tommies and Hell Ladies [Scottish Highlanders wearing kilts, thus ladies] must have given them "Hell" – A large town just on this side of the river was "ruined". After hiking for several hours we pulled into a field and pupped tented all night -corn stalks for a bed. P.S. People are coming back to their home, homes that are nothing but stone piles. Note (afterwards) we were several miles beyond Aust[rian] Rearguards at different times."[15]

Everything had changed while Myrice penned these lines. The 332nd was selected to be the vanguard of the corps. Wallace and his battalion were going into action; they would lead the final push against Austria.

Captain Story remembered:

> "We were on the move again at 2 a.m [October 25th]. Our regiment was now in advance guard for the entire Italian Army on the front and the 3rd Battalion was to be the point. The morning of Nov 2nd, our battalion was to lead the regiment and we were to meet the other battalions at a certain crossroad at a certain time. Imagine our surprise when arriving at the crossroad, we found the rest of the regiment waiting for us. We were over 15 minutes late for the rendezvous, Since they had been marching in column of squads, believing our battalion was ahead and nothing between them and the enemy, it can be imagined what a vulnerable position they were in. Colonel Wallace had had other occasions to lose his temper [Wallace, the icon of the rough and tumble, Regular Army soldier, was known throughout the regiment for his short fuse temper and flair with profanity], but nothing equal to this situation. He immediately put our major [Major Vaughn] under arrest, sending him to the rear of the regiment. He then appointed me battalion commander and ordered us to double time to a position far enough ahead to act as a proper point."[16]
>
> "The "Sectore Americano" has suddenly become the livest (sic) spot on the Italian front and the little town of Salettuol is the crossing place for the British, Italians and Americans. We push on from; October 28th, and march through the old sector and cross the Piave at the very spot where Lieutenant "Dug" Meldrum [As Regimental Intelligence Officer, Lieutenant Meldrum conducted a reconnaissance of the Austrian line prior to the regiment moving forward] waded the river in gathering information just a few days before. The Austrian lines are shattered and we are over the river and on our way in the last crushing "drive" of the war so far as our end of the game is concerned.
>
> Colonel William Wallace is ordered to take his Regiment as the Advance Guard of Lord Caven's Corps, made up of two British Divisions, 31st Italian Division, and the 332nd Infantry. November 1-3 are days of marching and fighting and we never hesitate until we find ourselves the first Infantry soldiers at the Taglimentia River, late in the afternoon of November 3rd. We halt with the Second Battalion on the right, including the blown-up bridge, Third Battalion on the left, and the First Battalion in reserve. It is a wild night.
>
> Colonel Wallace was at the end of the bridge and Major Scanland was ordered to take his Battalion across at 5.40 A. M. The Austrians were telling Captain Austin Story, who commanded the Third Battalion, that an Armistice was to go into effect, but Story replied, "We're going to blow you up – get your heads down."[17]

The Company D Log recorded that:

> "At midnight a momentous event took place, when "Dad" Butler, representing the American Red Cross, arrived in the darkness bearing a box of crackers and a packet of Sweet Caporal cigarettes for each man. The men received these presents with expressions of deep gratitude, for they were hungry; they knew the difficulties and obstacles "Dad" had overcome in getting up front the rear; they kept and always will keep him in admiration and esteem merited only by one who hazards himself that he may serve others."[18]
>
> "During the night the boys crawled over the pieces of the bridge and took up a position on the Austrian side of the Taglimentia. Promptly at the time set the artillery opened up and the Second Battalion, with Companies E, F,

G and H in reserve, deploy, and the Machine Gun detachments in position rise from the Austrian side of the river and absolutely surprise the enemy. Colonels Wallace and Everson were at the bridge and the enemy tore up trenches in that position. They ranged their pieces too far, thinking the Americans were on the far side of the river. Hence, most of the bullets went over the heads of our troops. In less than twenty minutes the Second Battalion smash through, and the Austrians break and run for their lives."[19]

Major Scanland's official report to Colonel Wallace stated:

> At 4 p.m. of the 3rd of November 1918, orders were given by Signor General De Angelis, commander of the 31st Division, to cross to the western side of the river Tagliamento, and to occupy an advance position at the bridge. We arrived at the bridge at 5 in the afternoon, and learned that there was approximately one battalion of the enemy occupying a defensive position east of the Tagliamento. I held my battalion in readiness to cross that river at that point. Orders were given to reconnoiter the enemy position with the result that information was brought to the effect that the position was held by a force of 500 men.
>
> At 3:15 in the morning of the November 4th, we received orders to force our passage across the river with the entire battalion, deploy on a front of about 1600 meters, and join on the left bank of the river. This formation was ready at 5:15 A.M. The advance commenced at 5:20. The enemy opened up at first an intermittent rifle fire, followed minutes later by machine gun fire. We continued our advance with the aid of our machine guns and attacked the enemy position at 5:45. It became necessary to use hand bombs to dislocate the enemy from machine gun emplacements. The entire line advanced 500 yards to the eastern bank of the Tagliamento, and the battalion was then reorganized and continued towards Codroipo. One company was designated as the advance guard and one company with two platoons on each side of the road, forming a strong patrol aided by automatic rifles, and exploited the terrain for a distance of 2000 yards on each side of the road. When the column advanced for about a mile and a half, it encountered heavy shrapnel fire from the enemy, and it was necessary to seek cover on the sides of the road in order to continue the advance. During the march to Codroipo, we were disturbed by enemy machine gun fire, which was answered by our machine guns, 5 of which were with the advance guard. We reached Codroipo at 9 A.M. captured the city, seized about 2,500,000 dollars worth of munitions, arms and vehicles. During the march we also captured a 77 m/m gun.
>
> At 3 P.M. two companies of the battalion advanced, deployed on a front of 1400 meters, with the left wing on Villa Orba and the right on Treviso Udine Railroad, the other two companies returning to Codroipo as guard for the captured material.
>
> The morale of the troops excellent; discipline perfect; liaison consistently maintained.
>
> Losses: 1 corporal dead [Corporal Charles A. Kell of G Company], 1 sergeant and six men wounded. Enemy losses: 25 dead and 22 prisoners.
>
> The sanitary corps rendered excellent service, the losses having occurred during the first part of the battle.[20]

During the action, Lieutenant August Rendigs had been detached from F Company and placed in charge of chemical defense for the battalion. This posting provided a unique view of the action, which he carefully recorded"

> "The plan of attack was laid out as follows: We were to rest on our arms until three-thirty the following morning, at which time we were to cross the island in the center of the stream by means of a temporary bridge that was being constructed by the Italian engineers. No resistance was anticipated at this point, the island in question having been seized by the platoon of Americans who had, earlier afternoon, been turned back from the far side of the river by the Austrians. Upon arriving at the island, Companies E, F, and G were to take up a skirmish line with five pace intervals between them, guiding on the bridge as the center, with Company H in reserve. We were then to lie in wait until the order to attack was to be given, and in advancing were not to fire unless fired on by the Austrians. This order was given to give the enemy an opportunity to surrender should they so desire. In the meantime an Italian battery of artillery was to be brought up and we were also to be strengthened by a platoon of our own machine guns. The number of Austrians opposing us was uncertain but it was thought to be about two battalions. Having been given the plan of attack, we returned to our men and gave them our information instructing them to get as much rest as possible between that time and three-thirty in the morning …
>
> We officers spent the waiting hours in alternatively dozing and conversing about the coming event, and speculated freely as to how large the forces of the enemy were and how strong a resistance they would put up.
>
> Finally three o'clock came, and shortly thereafter word was quietly passed around to adjust equipment and gas masks and move out across the improvised bridge to the island. The companies moved out in regular order, E company leading, and a silent stream of dark figures was soon passing in single file across the treacherous planks that wobbled and swayed from side to side, threatening to precipitate us into the turbulent waters rushing beneath. The half of the bridge that had not been dynamited was on the enemy's side of the river and was still burning brightly, illuminating the land round about it, but fortunately for us the fire was between us and the enemy, and accordingly we were not silhouetted by it. Upon reaching the island, the companies moved to the positions in the attacking line which had been previously assigned them by the major, with F Company on the left flank, E Company on the right flank and G Company in the center. H Company, in reserve, was formed in platoon columns about two hundred yards in the rear of the attacking line and in about the center of it …

The movement from our bank of the river to the island had consumed about an hour and a half, and it was just five o'clock when runners from all the companies reported that everything was set and that along our entire line the men were lying prone awaiting the order to attack. The time for the attack had been set at five-twenty, and at this moment also the Italians on our right were to move forward. The Austrians were still sending up a stream of flairs along their front, the rain had stopped, and everything was quiet except the roar of the river behind and in front of us as it hurried its way to the sea.

Sharply at five-twenty, the major blew his whistle, and from my station on the right of the pier I could see the long line of figures in khaki rise off the ground and walk slowly forward, preserving their alignment as they had been instructed. They moved perhaps thirty yards before the Austrians discovered them. Suddenly several single shots rang out from the enemy's lines and we could hear the whizz of the bullets as they sped past us, – the Austrians were plainly "overshooting". The first few shots were quickly followed by small volleys and bursts that broke out all along the Austrian lines. Our troops continued their advance slowly for perhaps an additional twenty yards, and then, at the word of command, flung themselves prone on the ground. The Austrians began using machine guns and from either flank of their line these terribly efficient weapons began to sputter. They were still shooting over our heads, but presently they must have discovered their error, for they began using "tracer" bullets, which, in leaving a thin trace of flame behind them, enabled the Austrians to see where their fire was going. Accordingly they adjusted their range and soon the leaden bullets began to dig up dirt and gravel near us.

Several of them struck telephone and telegraph wires which had fallen to the ground and gave off a sharp metallic sound, and riccochetted (sic) into the ground nearby. Still we thought their range was too high to damage our troops, who were advancing, but in this we were mistaken, for at this point our first casualty was brought in by the stretcher-bearers. It proved to be Sergeant Pahlau, platoon sergeant of the second platoon of F Company. He had been shot in the groin and was bleeding profusely, though not suffering greatly, he said …

By this time the combined rifle and machine gun fire from the Austrian lines was exceedingly intense, and the Americans were obliged to halt again. They waded through the river, which was waist deep in places, and were lying on the opposite bank close to the water line. The Austrians were still over two hundred yards away, behind an embankment, but at this point our troops opened up a lively fire. This did not seem very effective, for the Austrians continued their fire more intensely than before.

Runners from Company G came in breathlessly and panted out the information that their company could not advance farther because of the terrific machine gun fire on their flank. The major sent back word ordering that bombing squads [squads equipped with grenades] be sent out at once to encircle the machine guns and destroy them, and directing the company to continue the advance. The medics at this point sent out an appeal for more stretcher-bearers and twenty-five men from H Company were brought up on the double-time to assist in bringing in our wounded, who, the medics reported, were lying around in great numbers. It was apparent that the Austrians were getting the better of the argument and that further advance without artillery or machine-gun support would be costly. The major accordingly directed the machine-guns be brought up from the reserve and that they get into action at once. He decided also to ask the Italian general, who was observing the action from the river bank in our rear, for artillery support, and the Italian liaison officers were engaged in writing the request when, all at once, the battery of its own initiative opened a fire with a tremendous salvo of 75's [75mm Field Artillery guns] … The combined effect of our artillery and machine-gun fire was disastrous for the Austrians; the firing from that time on became less intense and ineffective.

At this stage the major ordered me to go forward to Captain Dempsey, commanding G Company, and indicate to him the direction and manner in which to continue the advance, furnishing me with a map for that purpose and giving me the necessary instructions. I took with me a corporal and an orderly, to both of them I repeated my instructions and outlined the proposed advance on the map which I held, so that in the event of my being disabled they might "carry on". We started forward but had gone only a few yards when we saw the line in front of us charge toward the Austrians and go over their dike, yelling and howling at the top of their voices. Instantly the firing ceased, and from that time on we went forward undisturbed by any of the enemy's bullets. We passed several of our wounded men, but as they were being taken care of by our stretcher-bearers we did not stop, waded through the river, which was waist high at that point, and finally ran up the bank and crossed the dike, where we came upon Capt. Dempsey and our troops lying prone in skirmish line, awaiting the order with which we brought.

Light was just breaking, and on consulting my watch I discovered that it was six o'clock, the engagement having lasted just forty five minutes. Capt. Dempsey received his orders and prepared to carry them out, informing me in the meantime that his company had lost one man killed and several wounded in the action. The one man who had been killed had been struck by a machine gun bullet in the center of his forehead while he had been advancing, which had split his skull in two, killing him instantly. He had been a corporal [Corporal Charles A. Kell], well thought of by his men and officers, and proved to be the only fatality of the engagement."[21]

George Roberts had a soldier's view of the action. He described the crossing in his journal:

"At 3:30 A.M [November 4]. we started for an island in the middle of the river and crossed over on the burned timbers of the old bridge. This was a dangerous job but all were successful in getting over safely. After reaching the island we formed a skirmish line, Company E and a part of Company G were on the right of the bridge, the balance of Company G and all of Company F on the left of the bridge, while Company H was held in reserve. There was also supposed to be a battalion of Italians on our right and left flanks, and another battalion in the rear as reinforcements. At 5:20 we started forward, the Italians were supposed to furnish us an artillery and machine gun barrage but they failed us. At first the Austrians began to greet us with rifle shots, and then with machine gun fire.

This fire came from all directions except from behind us. Tracer bullets went flying over our heads making red or blue streaks as they went whizzing by. Flares went up making everything as light as day, but we advanced just the same. We would advance about twenty-five yards then drop to the ground again. Machine gun and rifle bullets were whizzing by us by the thousands but our men showed wonderful coolness and courage and the finest kind of discipline. Once I faltered for just a minute and wondered what we were into, and if I would pull thru OK, then I thought of home and the dear ones so far away. At that very time my Lieutenant gave the command "Charge," and then I forgot everything except that command. As we neared the bank I could see by the light of the burning bridge that at each advance a few of our boys failed to go forward. We then gave the Austrians some machine gun fire and made the final rush. When we received this order I heard a machine gun man say, "Cease firing, there go the dough boys," and we certainly did go some, yelling like Indians, and to our surprise and disappointment those Austrians had taken a sudden departure except a few who did not get the chance.

Our casualties at this time were one dead and about twenty wounded, and among the wounded was my sergeant, Dutch Pahlan. It will always remain a mystery with me why more of our men did not pay the supreme sacrifice in that drive. After advancing several hundred yards we waited for lesion (sic) [liaison] with our flanks but our Italian allies were nowhere to be seen. They came triumphantly forward with their banners unfurled about an hour later. The Austrians afterward boasted that they were not afraid of the whole Italian army, and would have marched on to Rome had it not been for the Americans and the English. Alone as we were after going over the top the Austrians could have outflanked us and wiped out the entire battalion. Our Major said afterwards, "My heart went down to the depths when I learned the facts, for it was only pure, downright, damn jackass, American luck that pulled us thru. "Our breakfast that morning was a small piece of dry bread. We continued the advance, capturing Codroipo and three other towns. At Codroipo the Austrians fired on us with machine guns and a few one pounders but soon got cold feet and beat it out of the place. Here we captured more than $2,500,000 worth of supplies such as heavy and light artillery ammunition, rifles, knives, wagons, etc., then continued the advance, capturing Gorisippa and San Lorenzo, then returned to Codroipo where we went into camp. The people were overjoyed to see us and looked on the American soldiers as the saviours of the world. They had suffered horribly under the German yoke and their town and buildings were left in a badly damaged condition. Many of the women and young girls had been indecently handled, and practically all the food stuffs, livestock and personal property had been confiscated. That night we went to bed (out in a field), tired, footsore, and hungry, for we had had little to eat except some corn we had obtained from a nearby field. Our kitchens were not allowed to cross the river although traffic was opened shortly after we had crossed. Dad Butler of the Red Cross had chocolate, cakes and cigarettes for us but our Colonel would not allow him to bring them up to us, although (sic) we were very weak from hunger. Why our Colonel did this we could never understand."[22]

Lieutenant Rendigs concurred with Roberts critical assessment of Colonel Wallace's leadership, liberally adding:

> "Our men had had nothing to eat but reserve rations for several days and as the kitchen arrived with a prepared meal, in the company of the other two battalions, they were greeted with prolonged cheering. Our colonel, however, was impatient to be on, and being a man who cared nothing for the welfare of his officers and men, ordered us to advance at once. We were accordingly obliged to move out in the rear of the other two battalions, without having any supper whatever, with our kitchen following along in our wake, unable to serve the food they had prepared. I mention this incident here merely as one of many similar happenings which showed the utter disregard on the part of the colonel for the welfare of his command. This, being the state of affairs, made him the most hated and despised officer in the regiment in the opinion of the officers and men. He was utterly incompetent for the commission with which he was entrusted, and it was only because of the competency of his officers and non-coms that the regiment was able to make a good record and that he himself was able to retain his command, a fact, however, that he was not intelligent enough to recognize."[23]
>
> "The pursuit is organized and followed with such rapidity that the Austrians never attempt to establish a new position. Our boys pushed on through Codroipo, where over two million dollars' worth of supplies are captured, and then on to the line held when the Armistice went into effect at "fifteen hours, November 4, 1918. It was glorious to see the boys smash through and to hear their yells and to feel that the war was about over. A British aeroplane flew over and dropped a pennant to which was fastened – "Well Done." Most of the night was spent by the 332nd in handling the prisoners, of whom there were many thousands. The Austrian Generals were amazed when informed that there had never been but one combat Regiment of American soldiers in Italy. They reported that it was suspected that we had at least six Divisions.

Following the attack, the regiment consolidated in Codroipo. Here, Lieutenant Rendigs continued his narrative:

> "At three o'clock the battalion was assembled and addressed by the major, who thanked it for the courage and valor displayed during the engagement and deplored the loss of the one man who gave his life while in the performance of his duty, and the wounding of the sixteen others. The major informed us further that in capturing Codroipo we had taken one of the greatest Austrian ammunition dumps and one that included $2,500,000 worth of munitions and small arms and that he wanted everyone to have a souvenir of some kind, and so would throw open the doors of the arsenal to that end immediately after the meeting was dismissed. This statement was greeted with prolonged cheering on the part of the men, which again renewed when we were told that in a day or two we should probably start through the rest of Italy and then through Austria and then attack Germany from the Austrian border. The battalion was then dismissed, and the men ran, joyously cheering and scrambling to be the first to get to the arsenal for the souvenirs. On going there we found thousands upon thousands of trench knives, swords, rifles and fire-arms of all sorts, so that it was apparent that there would be more than enough for all the men. Passing through one door and out another, most of the men selected an assortment of knives, swords and rifles that were necessarily abandoned later when we took up the advance. That night, after supper, which consisted of a fresh supply of reserve rations brought up to us, the men sat around in little groups and fought over again the scenes of the night before and the early morning, until weariness and sleep, stealing upon them like a shadow in the night, shrouded the bivouac in quiet silence, save for the audible breathing of the sleepers."[24]

Major General DeAngelis, in G.O. No.6335, expressed his appreciation of the 2nd Battalion in the trenches and said, "I am pleased to express to you my feelings of satisfaction, and I beg you to tribute in my name a solemn approval of Major Wm. G. Everson, Commanding Officer of that Battalion." The British Commanding General decorated Colonel William Wallace with the British D.S.O. [The Distinguished Service Order], and expressed his appreciation of the Regiment. Major Frank Scanland was decorated with a silver medal for his splendid service in leading his Battalion across the Taglimentia. Decorations were awarded to Colonel Wallace, Lieutenant Colonel Everson, Major Scanland, Major Burch and Captain Story. Several war-crosses and medals are distributed among the enlisted, and we all feel that it was a glorious celebration and we are really glad to be alive and able to take part in the festivities:

> The terms of the Armistice gave us the right to use the roads of Austria, and the right of requisition, and, with the Austrian Army on its back, there was nothing between us and Berlin. We were ordered to proceed by forced-marches to a point designated as "the back door of Germany." We pushed on through Rivolto, La Santissima, Pozzuolo, Lavaria, Buttrio, Orsaria, Ipplis and Carmons. Colonels Wallace and Everson went into the mountains as far as Tolmino.
>
> Then, we are halted by the news on the 11th of November that the Armistice had been signed with Germany. The war is over and we thought our travels at an end except for the homeward journey. We yelled and sang and rolled on the ground like a bunch of school kids."[25]

Samuel Gompers, the famous American labor leader, visited the 332nd while they were headquartered at Villa Angelica. He addressed the Regiment from the rear balcony of the villa. Sergeant Major Joseph Lattau noted that Gompers, "paid us a visit. The band played in his honor and his face brightened to hear the familiar rag-time. He gave a short address on the value of teamwork." Courtesy National Archives.

Gompers poses for a photograph in front of the villa with Colonel William Wallace and Brigadier General Charles G. Treat. Note the 332nd Colors in the background. October 12, 1918. Courtesy National Archives.

After departing the 332nd Infantry Headquarters, Gompers visited the Front Line. Accompanied by Brigadier General Treat and Colonel Montelini, Commander of the 256th Italian Infantry Regiment, he inspects an American position. Courtesy National Archives.

Platoon of E Company, Second Battalion marching along the Royal Dyke. Third line of the Royal Dyke Trenches in sector held by the Americans on the Piave River. Near Varango, Maserada, Italy, October 5, 1918. Courtesy National Archives.

Detachment of E Company, Second Battalion repairing wire in front of third-line trenches in sector held by Americans on the Piave River, October 5, 1918. Courtesy National Archives.

Italian soldiers instructing Americans on how to cross river in pontoons. Third Battalion at the Sile River, Porto di Fiera, Italy. October 6, 1918. Courtesy National Archives.

Another view of river crossing training. Note the overloaded craft in the middle background. Courtesy National Archives.

Brigadier General Treat and Colonel Wallace on the review grounds at the Italian Rest Camp near Treviso, Italy. October 7, 1918. Courtesy National Archives.

Allied Officers inspecting the regiment on presentation of the flag. Review Grounds at the Italian Rest Camp near Treviso, Italy. October 7, 1918. Note the regimental colors at right. Courtesy National Archives.

Right: Chaplains Doherty and O'Donnell, Second Battalion, on the Review Grounds at the Italian Rest Camp near Treviso. October 7, 1918. Note crosses that Major Doherty wears on his shoulder epaulettes. Chaplain O'Donnell would become President of University of Notre Dame in later years. Courtesy National Archives.

Below: Chaplain (Major) Doherty presenting a flag from the New York Sons of Young Italy to officers and NCOs of Company I, the Color Company, Review Grounds at the Italian Rest Camp near Treviso, Italy, October 7, 1918. Courtesy National Archives.

Right: The Regiment's Machine Gun Company on a hike between Treviso and Padova. October 25, 1918. Courtesy National Archives.

Below: The Machine Gun Company passes a column of British Cavalry (on right). Treviso, Italy. October 25, 1918. Courtesy National Archives.

Group of Allied Officers at the review and decoration of Czecho-Slovak Regiment, near Albardo, Italy. General Graciani is the man with the gray beard at left. Courtesy National Archives.

Above: The 332nd Regimental Band waits to play before a review. The Bandmaster Calvin Sims stands at center holding his baton. Courtesy National Archives.

Right: General DeAngelis, Commanding Officer of the 31st Italian Division, reviews the regiment on the road between Treviso and Varago, Italy, just before the Americans leave for the front. October 25, 1918. Courtesy National Archives.

Above: The 332nd soldiers felt that they got more of their full share of marching during the Wallace's Circus adventures as expressed in this cartoon.

Right: Private Ira J. Moll, Company F, Second Battalion. Private Moll wounded October 2, 1918, was the first American soldier to be hit by enemy shell fire in Italy. The photo was taken at the 331st Field Hospital near Treviso. October 24, 1918. Courtesy National Archives.

Below: American troops of the 332nd Regiment crossing the Piave River, near Grave di Papadopoli, Italy, on a pontoon bridge. October 31, 1918. Courtesy National Archives.

Left: Captain Austin P. Story Commanded I Company during the advance on the Piave. When his battalion commander was placed under arrest by Colonel Wallace, Story was elevated to Command of the Third Battalion. Story sits at the center of this image taken from a panoramic photograph. Courtesy Military History Institute.

Below: Another view of the Regiment crossing the Piave. Courtesy National Archives.

In another Italian Front anomaly, a mounted Colonel Wallace and his staff watch the regiment move forward near Grave di Papadopoli, Italy. Courtesy National Archives.

Headquarters Company crossing at Grave di Papadopoli on the afternoon of October 31, 1918. Courtesy National Archives.

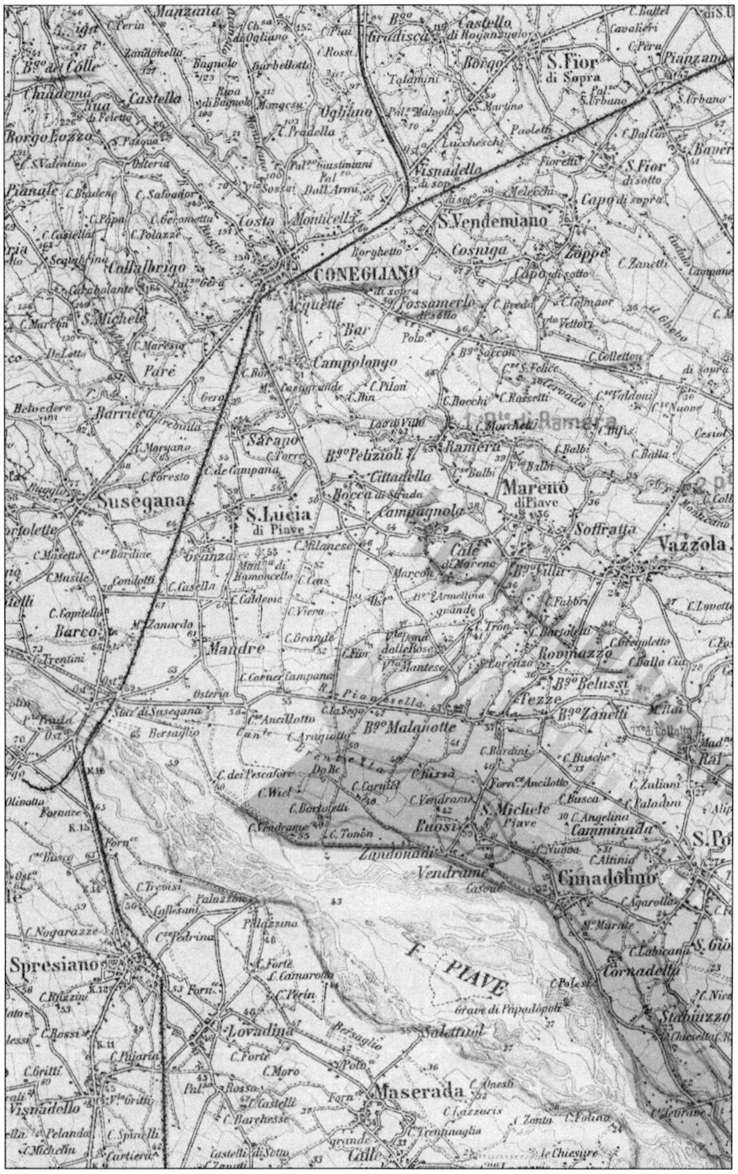

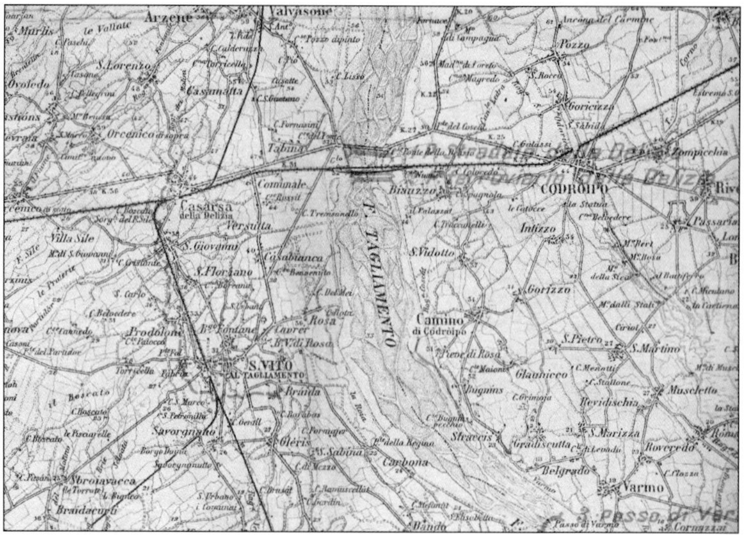

Left: Captain Story's Army issue cloth map shows Grave di Papadopoli, the island in the Paive River. Here the 332nd spent the night before their famous advance across the Taglimento River. The regiment would follow the railroad north and east toward the top right of the map. Courtesy Military History Institute.

Above: Captain Story's Army issue cloth map shows the crossing point of the Tagliamento River. Note the town of Codroipo just east of the crossing. This was the first town that the 332nd liberated. Courtesy Military History Institute.

Below: A 332nd soldier stands guard at a dump of ammunition, ordnance, and engineer's supplies captured by the regiment. Codroipo, Italy. November 5, 1918. Courtesy National Archives.

Major Scanland took command of Second Battalion after Major Everson was promoted; in this view, he studies a map with his adjutant, Lieutenant Hamilton at Codroipo. November 5, 1918. Courtesy National Archives.

Austrian prisoners on the road between Codroipo and Pordenone. November 7, 1918. Courtesy National Archives.

Another view of Austrian prisoners, November 7, 1918. Courtesy National Archives.

Supply Company kitchen, Ipplis, Italy. November 10, 1918. Courtesy National Archives.

Field camp near Ipplis, Italy. Company G in foreground. November 9, 1918. Courtesy National Archives.

Above: Austrian prisoners helping American soldiers saw wood. Field camp near Ipplis, Italy. November 9, 1918. Courtesy National Archives.

Right: Men of the Machine Gun Company assembling a captured Austrian machine gun. Field camp near Ipplis, Italy. November 10, 1918. Courtesy National Archives.

Cooks of the Machine Gun Company making use of a captured Austrian field kitchen. Field Camp near Ipplis, Italy. November 10, 1918. Courtesy National Archives.

Americans throwing bombs, Field Camp near Ipplis, Italy. November 10, 1918. Courtesy National Archives.

Captured Austrian supply train. Village of Ipplis, Italy. November 10, 1918. Courtesy National Archives.

Second Battalion leaving in trucks. Field Camp near Ipplis, Italy. November 12, 1918. Courtesy National Archives.

United States Army ambulances crossing Italian pontoon bridge. Tagliamento River near Pordeone, Italy. November 12, 1918. Courtesy National Archives.

The route of march of the 332nd from Treviso into Austria.

Bridge on the Tagliamento River, near Pordenone, Italy, in flames after being struck by enemy shell fire. November 5, 1918. Courtesy National Archives.

Along the Piave River Line; a quiet time in the front lines. Courtesy Military History Institute.

G Company soldiers on the Piave River Line in a dugout. Courtesy Military History Institute.

Automatic gun emplacement. At right note the Chauchat in .30/06 caliber as evidenced by the straight magazine. Courtesy Military History Institute.

Right: In trenches along the Piave River Line. Courtesy Military History Institute.

Below: The Tagliamento River bridge. At 5:40AM on November 4th, Wallace ordered Second Battalion to cross the destroyed bridge. In less than twenty minutes, Major Scanland's Battalion accomplished the mission at the cost of one dead and six wounded. Courtesy Military History Institute.

The regimental colors of the 332nd Infantry Regiment. Courtesy Ohio Historical Society.

CORP. CHAS. A. KELL.

The first Canton boy from the 332nd infantry to be killed in action in Italy was Corporal Charles A. Kell, 25, according to word received late Thursday night by his sister, Mrs. J. E. Franklin, 706 Eighth street NE, from the war department at Washington.

He died November 4, or just a week before the armistice was signed.

The last word that relatives received from him was a letter dated October 19, in which he said that he had been in the trenches for the past 15 days and had no rest in that length of time. He was then in a rest billet. It is believed by his sister that shortly after the rest he was again sent to the front.

In the 332nd infantry are about 600 boys from Canton and Stark county. He was with Company G which is composed largely of the Canton boys from the north draft board.

Corporal Kell left with the Canton contingent in September, 1917, and sailed overseas in June. The regiment went first to England, then to France and later to Italy. It was not until the last few weeks of the war that the infantry went into action with the Italians against the Austrians on the last drive before the enemy surrendered.

Corporal Kell is survived by two sisters, Mrs. Clyde Wilson and Mrs. Franklin, both of Canton. Before entering the service he was employed at the Cleveland-Canton Spring company's plant.

The obituary of Corporal Charles A Kell of Canton, Ohio. Kell was the only soldier in the regiment killed in combat. Courtesy Private Collection.

Inscription in Corporal Charles A Kell's bible. Courtesy Private Collection.

Returned to his family, Kell may well have carried this bible during the attack on the bridge. Courtesy Private Collection.

Above: Private Reinert, captures the regiment's feelings during the many long marches leading up to the final offensive and the move to the Piave River, corn stalks were often used to camouflage soldiers' tents from air observation; from "With the 332 Reg in Italy". Courtesy Private Collection.

Top right: Private Reinert sketched the Allied soldiers he encountered, including Italian and British Highland troops or "Hell Ladies," while moving forward during the offensive; he also documented their adversaries the Austrians; from "With the 332 Reg in Italy". Courtesy Private Collection.

Right: Commenting on haphazard Italian truck drivers, and the foibles of river crossing training, Reinert juxtaposed the calm of the Italian washerwomen; from "With the 332 Reg in Italy". Courtesy Private Collection.

5

Armistice and Occupation

The cease-fire did not bring an end to exertions for the regiment. On the contrary, the regiment was about to be a chess piece in the game of world politics. The Treaty of London signed in 1915, brought Italy into the war as one of the Allied Powers. The terms of the treaty promised the Italians "spoils of war" that included several areas that were not historically Italian. The Dalmatian Coast, Trentino, Alto-Adige and Trieste were included in this category. Most of the population of these areas was either of German or Slavic ethnicity. Additionally, following their acquisition of Trieste, only one other commercial port remained on the Dalmatian coast – Fiume. With Wilson supporting Yugoslavian self-rule, Fiume might be granted to the new Yugoslavian state and offer serious competition to Italian commerce along the coast. The Italians realized that they could preempt this situation by immediately seizing the port of Fiume before the armistice deadline. In the race to redraw the map before terms could be signed, the 332nd would find themselves entangled in the dispute. Captain Story reported:

> "The regiment rested for a short time on the banks of the Tagliamento, but not for long. Since the terms of the armistice provided that the Italians were to hold all territory that they could reach at a certain time, we started on what was known as our "long march." From 10 A.M. of the 6th to 7 A.M. of the 7th we marched without a real stop. Since we were now a part of a large Italian Army, our march consisted of "stops and starts" and more "stops and starts" but none of the stops long enough to sleep or eat …
>
> The morning of Nov 7th after two hours rest and a light breakfast pressed on to Lovario where we spent the night. On Nov 9th we crossed the Natisone River and went into camp on the plains of Ipplis, where we stayed for three days. On the 12th we again rolled up the packs and set out – this time across the Austrian border – in the town of Cormons where we were billeted in Austrian barracks.[1]

While the regiment rushed to stabilize the front and redraw the map of Europe to the advantage of their Italian allies, Wallace hurried back to Padua to meet with Brigadier General Charles G. Treat, the Head of the American Mission in Italy. At this meeting Wallace received his post-Armistice instructions. These orders would not be favorably received among his men who were now hoping of a swift return home to loved ones.

Sergeant Major Lettau noted, "With the German signature to the armistice, the war ended for us. Some dreamed that for them the famous saying, "Heaven, Hell or Hoboken by Christmas," would come true."[2] However, this dream was not to be. The Army had other plans for the men of the 332nd Infantry Regiment; their work was not complete. Before the regiment was reunited in March 1919, the soldiers of the regiment would be scattered along the northeastern frontier of Italy. First Battalion would garrison Treviso, Second Battalion Cattaro, Dalmatia with a detachment in Montenegro, and Third Battalion would be quartered in Fiume. "Wallace's Circus" had excelled in war, now they would be tested in peace. The regiment's new mission was peacekeeping; an assignment for which none of the men were trained. This was an assignment Wallace must have well understood from his service in the Philippines. The next few months would offer many challenges.

The first of these was morale. The war was over and the question on everyones' mind was – When do we go home? The answer was not so simple. Sergeant Major Lettau addressed this issue:

> "On November 18th the Third Battalion packed up and entrained for Fiume to do international police duty. Gone then were the glimmering hopes of an early departure, for the rumor persisted and seemed to have foundation that the First Battalion and Headquarters were bound for Trieste. However, so I have heard, the Colonel prevailed upon the American Mission, at Padua, that our place was in Treviso where our supplies lay in warehouses.

Accordingly, early Sunday morning, November 24th, with great joy in our hearts, we were ready for the return to Treviso. The companies were to walk … However, the packs were put upon American trucks so that they were unburdened to that extent."[3]

With his days in combat behind him, Sergeant Major Lettau rejoiced when he discovered that, "Headquarters Detachment was fortunate in being allowed to ride upon the trucks which carried the office equipment and some officers' bedding rolls. The trip was one to be remembered."[4]:

When we started, the day was pleasantly brisk but not cold. Leaving at eight o'clock we traveled without adventure until we reached the Livenza River. Here the bridge had been blown up and a pontoon had been built in its place. When we started across an Italian Lieutenant stopped us, saying that the pontoon was not strong enough for our heavy trucks. All argument was of no avail. We were in a strange country and to make a detour of several miles, as he suggested, would cause us endless trouble. Even while we talked an Italian truck crossed the pontoon towing a second truck. We pointed to the two trucks crossing at one time, but we received only his maddening smile and a refusal. Some of the boys in the party were in favor of emulating one of our Sergeants who, during our advance, was bringing food to us. As the story goes, this Sergeant's trucks were approaching a pontoon when an Italian Colonel ran out with arms wildly waving, while he voiced a loud refusal. The Sergeant was a man of few words. He knew that the regiment was in need of food and he thought the pontoon was strong enough. Having faith in his judgment and cause, he displayed his automatic and, motioning the trucks forward, backed the Colonel across the whole pontoon. The pontoon creaked and trembled under the heavy trucks but, fortunately, no mishap occurred.

Our errand was not so urgent, so we turned about feeling very bitter, as this appeared to be just another instance of that antagonism to which we had been subjected by the Italians since the day of the armistice.

After following the river for five or six miles we came to a bridge and crossed. It was now nearly dark and we should have been approaching Treviso. With evening, the weather grew colder and, as a pleasure party, our trip was a failure. We reached the Piave soon after and successfully crossed the creaking pontoon.

However, we had not gone a hundred yards beyond when, as we were climbing a hill, both trucks stopped. Upon investigating we learned that both had run out of gasoline. It was a peculiar coincidence.

On either side of us were damp, clay embankments and all about was darkness. What should we do? We were in a strange country and in a poor part of that, so far as replenishing our gasoline supply went. We thought we could borrow a can from one of the many passing Italian FIATS, but no one seemed to have an extra can. Meanwhile, someone, rooting around among the packs and boxes on our truck found a three gallon can of gasoline, but that would not take us to Treviso, which we were told was twenty miles away.

We again resumed our efforts to beg gasoline from the Italians, but when some time had passed without our efforts being rewarded, the boys in loud voices told the countryside what they thought of the Italian nation in general and these Italian drivers in particular. About this time we noticed a can of gasoline in the rear of a truck which had stopped close by. However, when we edged near to lift the gasoline, the driver suspected and moved the can. Fresh outbursts of American oratory hailed this failure but, out of the din rose a voice speaking the American language with a slight accent and the voice asked: "Who wants gasoline?" Before the speaker could have changed his mind, a half dozen answered: "Here!" As he came nearer we saw he had a five gallon can. We thanked this Italian who had been to America, loaded him down with cigarettes and poured the gasoline into our truck. With eight gallons we felt we could make Treviso. Bidding farewell to the occupants of the other truck, with a promise of speedy relief, we set forth.

Without a map we stumbled onward in the darkness. We had traveled several miles along a dark road when, upon reaching the end, we perceived a river but no bridge or pontoon. It was a delicate task to turn the large truck in the narrow road. Retracing our tracks we set out again, fearful now that our gasoline would become exhausted. To add to the discomfort, the snow fell and the night grew very cold. However, we were on the right road and at 10:00 P. M. we entered the gate at Treviso."[5]

The First Battalion at Treviso

Although Sergeant Major Lettau enjoyed recounting his adventures on the road to Treviso, most of the soldiers of the First Battalion who were bound for the city marched there; this in view of the fact that thousands of Italian trucks sat empty and available. Suddenly, America's most fervent ally was not quite so willing to devote assets to their American brothers in arms. The Italians had their eye on a bigger prize. They were shepherding military resources in case the armistice fell apart. Should the opportunity avail itself, the Italians were poised for another Austrian land grab to the east. In war, alliances are held together by common enemies; in peace these same alliances are torn asunder by divergent interests. The two nation states and their contradictory views of post-war Europe, were quickly driving the alliance apart. The First Battalion official report continues:

"The Battalion was detached from the Regiment and marched from Langoris near Cormons to Treviso, Nov. 24th. The march of approximately 80 miles was done in a period of 5 days, in 4 stages, the men being billeted each night in comfortable quarters. The Battalion was accompanied by Rolling Kitchens and hot meals were served throughout the hike. The Battalion arrived in Treviso on Nov. 28th. The country passed through north of the Piave was infested with influenza and by contact many cases developed in the Battalion. The Battalion was accompanied by ambulances which carried the men who took sick enroute ahead to the Field Hospital at Treviso."[6]

Immediately after the Armistice, the specter of the Spanish Flu pandemic hovered throughout America and Europe. Military records noted that it was especially prevalent in the regiment's area of operations. As the soldiers passed through towns and villages, they heard tragic accounts of inhabitants who had been savaged by the virulent flu. By the end of November, the regiment's soldiers too fell victim; there would be a funeral scheduled nearly each day for soldiers who had succumbed to the flu. Convinced that that hard marching and the poor quality of their meals made them more susceptible to catching the dreaded strain, morale in the regiment plummeted.

Taken alone, the First Battalion's official report bespeaks a military move cleanly executed with few problems. However, the soldiers of D Company tell quite a different story. A description of the misery they suffered was recounted in the Company Log:

> "Over mud soaked roads the battalion trudged to the Tagliamento and found its bed almost dry. It was reached and crossed at 12:15 p.m. Without a stop for mess the march was continued till 3:00 p.m., when Fossalta was reached. The distance covered was 32 kms. (App. 20 miles)
>
> Many of the men of the company had been brought forward in trucks and with rations almost gone, and many men ill, the troops remained here the following day, Tuesday the 26th. All those who were able to go were sent out on wood searching parties. The rest made up self-organized "polenta" parties. The people everywhere were in deep distress. Many wretched widows and mothers were found baking their last and only morsel of corn meal in antique kitchen utensils over open fires.
>
> Many men here fell victims to disease and were sent to hospitals. At Fossalta there was little of interest except the old church tower from whose top could be secured a splendid view of the great stretches of the Venetian lowlands clear to the Adriatic."[7]

The march continued until Thanksgiving Day, November 28th when they finally closed on Treviso, with the supply company ferrying the last of the men into town by truck. They described their miserable experience:

> "The regiment had made harder hikes, with much heavier packs than those made on the march from Cormons to Treviso, but lack of food aggravated the difficulties so that each day's march was a tremendous drain on the physical powers of every man; nevertheless, hard and grueling as was the return , there was not a single man, who, feeling that this was the beginning of the end of his stay in Europe, was not perfectly willing to undertake and carry through the effort."[8]

Sergeant Major Lettau added that:

> "During this time the companies were walking to Treviso. On the first day of this tiresome march they covered twenty-seven kilometers. At seven the next morning the march was continued, without a rest for the noon meal, and at 5:00 P. M., another thirty-five kilometers were passed. Here the tired, footsore lads went into billets until 7:00 A. M. of the 27th when the march was resumed and thirty-eight more kilometers were marched. On November 28th, Thanksgiving Day, they enjoyed (?) a dinner of "slum," [a stew consisting of corned beef, hard tack and corn meal] and reached Dosson, a suburb of Treviso at 4:20 P. M. The distance marched this day was thirty-two kilometers."[9]

The First Battalion report continued, covering the period from November 28, 1918 to February 13, 1919:

> "The Battalion with detachments from Machine Gun Co. and Hqrs. Co. took billets at Dosson near Treviso in a large 3 story factory building which was being used as a military barracks. In an out-building there were hot water shower baths to accommodate 50 men at one time. Field ranges were set up and Rolling Kitchens turned in and portable wooden houses erected to furnish shelter for the kitchens and rations. The winter was exceptionally mild. Close order drill was held for 2 hours daily on drill fields about 1/2 hour's march from the barracks. In bad weather 2 hour hikes were taken. The intention was to maintain discipline and keep the Battalion in good physical condition. The drill was supplemented by an athletic program consisting of volleyball, indoor baseball, football, soccer and group games under a Battalion athletic officer with the idea that every man in the Battalion was engaged in some form of athletics. Equipment was furnished by the Y.M.C.A. A Battalion soccer team contended with all the British teams stationed in Treviso making a creditable showing, affecting good sport and adding to the extremely cordial relations between the British and American soldiers in Italy. The indoor baseball league, included a team from each platoon, six games being played daily. I consider that the athletics were very successful and beneficial.
>
> The Battalion had the benefit of the Y.M.C.A. schools at Doson in the following subjects: History, bookkeeping, geography, mathematics, salesmanship and law. These courses were optional and successful. The Y.M.C.A. took over and operated an opera house at Treviso using all available talent including a Battalion minstrel. Shows were had on an average of 3 times a week.
>
> On February 13th, the Battalion entrained for Genoa to join the Regiment."[10]

While the battalions were scattered about, they reached a milestone in their service. "About the first of December we received a red, white and green service stripe from the Italian government which denoted four months service on the Italian front. This was immediately christened the "Macaroni Bar." A few days later, December 8th, we received the American gold "V" for six months overseas service."[11]

Although life had improved immeasurably for the soldiers of the First Battalion after their arrival in Treviso, most of the soldiers believed that:

> "The more they saw of Europe, the more they wanted to see America, and when at night they returned from Venice to Dosson Barracks (Treviso), it was to think and dream, not of famed glories of a fallen empire, but, now that the war was over, to dream of home and a people whose greatness does not rest alone in the deeds of their ancestors, but in the achievements of today and a hope of a better tomorrow."[12]

Second Battalion in Dalmatia and Montenegro

The Second Battalion was tasked with a challenging peacekeeping mission in Dalmatia; one more akin to military operations American soldiers would experience years later when they were dispatched by President Clinton to this same region. They were to act as mediators, stabilizing the situation in Dalmatia by de-conflicting the needs and desires among the Italian, British and Serbian governments, two revolutionary parties, occupation forces and tribal leaders. Shortly after the arrival of the battalion, the situation dictated that in addition to the demands offered them in the capital city of Cattaro, they were additionally required to send a detachment to Cetinje, Montenegro to stabilize the situation there. Wallace wrote that, "The Battalion [Second] which was ordered to Cattaro, Montenegro, has had the most difficult time. It was 1000 miles from Treviso to Cattaro, by rail to Brindisi and boat across the Adriatic. It had been ordered directly from the advance to Maestre (land port of Venice) to embark."[13]

Lieutenant August Rendigs, recounted the trip to Cattaro:

> "The Second Battalion arrived in the harbor of Cattaro, on Thursday, November 28, 1918, after a delightful and uneventful trip across the calm, blue Adriatic Sea. The voyage from Venice required five days, so the S.S. "Argentina", assigned to the Battalion for this particular voyage, could not possibly be classified as an ocean greyhound … Cattaro is the most important port on the commercially unimportant Dalmatian Coast. During its existence through the centuries, Cattaro has seen a variety of rulers. Romans, Byzantines, Bulgarians, Venetians, Bosnians, Turks, Austrians, Spanish, French, Serbians, Montenegrins, English and a few others have had a try at running the place. They did one thing – gave it a delightfully cosmopolitan character.
>
> Consequently we were greeted by a mixture of nationalities found only in a petty Balkan State or a great American City. Our steamer was warped to the pier amid the blaring of a Serbian band and the wild huzzahs of the throng. Major Scanlon (sic), Battalion Commander, immediately reported to the Italian Land Commander in compliance with orders, but this gentleman was seemingly very surprised, as he claimed to have had no prior knowledge of our arrival, but he suggested that the Major report to the Naval Commander. That official likewise was all "at sea" and would give no orders; he suggested that we remain aboard ship pending the arrival of orders."[14]

Upon arrival in Cattaro, Companies E and G immediately boarded American sub-chasers and were taken down the bay about fifteen miles to the town of Zelenika, an Austrian submarine base. Corporal Leslie Bender of Company E noted in his journal that, "Boarded Sub Chaser 93, in the rain, and landed at Zelenika, Cattara (sic) Bay, Dalmatia. Zelenika was the base of supplies, ammunition, etc. for the Austrians. They had 100,000 prisoners working all the time. Now billeted in the barracks of the guard. Among the prisoners are Russians, Serbs, Slavs, and Montenegrins, Men and Women all half starved. Co. E & G are located here."[15] Company F was ordered to Montenegro. Only Company H and the machine gun, medical and supply detachments remained in Cattaro where Battalion Headquarters was established.

Major Southworth, commanding the F Company expedition to Montenegro, explained the background of the conflict in which he was now embroiled:

> "King Nicholas' long reign in his little country of Montenegro had been quite progressive for a near-eastern monarch. He had allied himself by marriage of his numerous children to the royal houses of Italy, Serbia and Russia, and to the nobility of Germany. He had played Italy, Austria and Russia against one another, to the advantage of himself and his kingdom. After the second Balkan war he had acquired some additional territory on the southeast. And early in this century he granted his people a constitution.
>
> But during the World War the king showed some signs of favoring Austria, and it is said that while he was with his daughter, the Queen of Italy, one of his sons appeared in Cettinje, the capital, during the Austrian occupation, and showed himself a strong partisan of the Austrians. Whether or not the king was at his old game of playing both sides against the middle, it is certain that he became unpopular with his people.
>
> After the Austrians had been driven out, the mass of the Montenegrin people, because of the fact that they are Serbian by race and tongue, were in favor of joining the new Serbian Jugo Slav State. So on November 24, 1918 … at a convention in Podgoritza this union was decided on and a committee of five chosen as interim governors of Montenegro."[16]

Lieutenant August Rendigs continued:

> "Our anxiety to learn the drift of developments was not long deferred; on the following morning orders were issued to Company "F" to prepare at once for a trip into Montenegro; Cettinje, the capital, being our assigned destination.

We formed in line on the Cattaro dock; and marching through the little town, under command of Captain Southworth, we slowly proceeded along a tortuous mountain road. The grade was ever-ascending it seemed. Later in the day we were pleased to meet our old friend Major Allegretti, who is well remembered by everyone on the "Sectora-Americano" front on the Piave. He, with a command of Italian troops, was on the way to Cettinje, and would accompany us.

About an hour after our departure, Major Scanlon (sic) was informed by the senior Italian officer that an Italian force had been prevented from entering Montenegro three days previous; and had been fired upon by the Montenegrins. The Italian Commander imparted the further information that he had given orders to go in at any cost; and would overcome resistance by force if need be. Participation in an adventure of this kind was not in our schedule, so the Italian was informed that our force would take no part in offensive operations against either Montenegrin faction."[17]

In fact, Major Scanland was hearing only part of the story from his Italian allies. Captain Southworth recounted that:

"The day after Company "F" had left on its perilous mission, Major Scanland, chancing to be on board an Italian warship in the harbor, learned by accident that a wireless message had been received the night before from the Italian General that the entrance into Montenegro should not be forced. Much surprised at this because the orders given him had been just the contrary, Major Scanland sought the Italian Lieutenant Colonel at Cattaro (the ranking officer at the place) and asked about the dispatch. The Lieutenant Colonel said he had not received it. Major Scanland had been much worried over the mission on which we were engaged, and forthwith told the Lieutenant Colonel in English (probably not translated) just what kind of a------ he was. Thereupon the good Lieutenant Colonel scratched his head and at last recalled that he had received the dispatch. And yet our column had been allowed to proceed under orders that might easily have produced a collision fraught with grave international consequences!"[18]

Meanwhile Lieutenant Rendigs and his men followed a tortuous course up the mountain toward Cetinje:

"The march up, up Mount Lovchen! Who among those of Company "F" will ever forget it? Not one. It is burned – aye, literally frozen – in their memories. The night was dark and a cold, stinging wind added neither joy nor comfort to the trip up the winding mountain trail. The packs were unusually heavy and necessarily so, although wearisome to a degree seldom realized in marching because of the poor road and ever-ascending grade. Full packs, two extra blankets, additional ammunition and overcoat made a load of over 75 pounds. All this we carried while climbing Mount Lovchen on a cold, windy winter night.

Every hour we were permitted ten-minute halts which gave us a short breathing spell; then on we went ever climbing that mountain, the top of which it seethed would never be reached. Many men were compelled to drop out from sheer exhaustion. By the time the mountain top was reached a count revealed the fact that nearly fifty men out of a total of 190 were behind straggling to catch up with those who were fortunate to have the unusual stamina to carry them along with the main body.

About eleven o'clock we arrived at Krystak, a little mountain village at the very crest of Mount Lovchen. This diminutive mountain village consisted of two houses and an Austrian built barrack. The command to halt and turn in for the night was never more welcome than it was that night after the long, zigzag climb laden with an unusually heavy pack. We were soon fast asleep on the straw-strewn floor.

The morning found us on the march again. This time down hill, until the miniature village of Niegush was reached, and where we were met by a party of Serbians. A parley ensued, as the Serbs and Montenegrins opposed the entrance of Italian troops; seemingly they would welcome us alone, but our company they keenly resented. Anyway, we were permitted to go along a little further.

We then started up another steep grade to the top of a second mountain; a five-hour gruelling march. Our noon-day chow was eaten on the crest of the mountain, and during the afternoon we descended to the village of Dubrovik, one mile from Cettinje. Here we had another parley. This time both civil and military officers informed our commander that Americans were welcome, but not the Italians. Cettinje would open her gates and arms to us, but not to our companions. As a result of this talk it was decided that Captain Southworth with Lieutenant Speakman, as interpreter, would accompany the local dignitaries to Cettinje, and there consult the higher nabobs."[19]

Major Southworth recounted the parley:

"... I went on to the capital with Lt. H.S. Speakman, and ascertained, as I had suspected, that the American detachment was being used as a shield for Italian penetration. Returning to the column I persuaded Major Guadeloupe to retire to the top of the pass and await further instructions. Perhaps he consented the more readily as the rocks and mountains along the Cettinje road were swarming with irregulars all armed. They were particularly incensed against Major Guadeloupe because, but three days before, he had promised to withdraw the Italians. It should be said, however, that the Major was ordered back and so had no choice."[20]

Lieutenant Rendigs' narrative added:

"That night a heavy snow fall made us fearful lest we might be snow-bound. We were informed that during winter the roads leading to Cattaro were often blocked for months – a cheering prospect. That night we billeted in huts. The next day found us all in Krystak, where we were billeted in the fairly comfortable barracks, built by the Austrians during their occupancy. As the snow had turned to a pouring rain, Captain Southworth deemed it advisable to return to Cattaro with all possible speed. The Italians also desired to leave the vicinity of Cettinje, where they were so unwelcome.

We returned through the mountains by a better route than that on the outward trip. On November 31 we arrived at our barracks in Teodo, where we remained during our stay in Dalmatia. Teodo is a short distance from Cattaro, on the water front. Thanksgiving of '18 will be long remembered by every man at Cattaro. Coffee without milk or sugar, moldy bread, macaroni, beef and rice, constituted the menu of that festive day. We longingly thought of the fat turkeys, pumpkin pies, "an' everything else" at home, but our sadness was sweetened by the hope that the shores of Dalmatia would soon be seen fading from our view as we would homeward go.

During the week that followed we engaged in close-order drill, and took up a rather comprehensive guard-duty, which included the little village; and its docks, loaded with vast quantities of munitions, war materials, clothing, shoes and four, landed from a number of Austrian battleships that had been captured and were interned in the harbor. We had been requested by the Allied Commission, composed of officers of the American, French and British navies, to furnish daily a large detail for work in unloading large shells and other material from the Austrian vessels and in dismantling and disarming them. This work was soon commenced and in a short time the Austrian vessels were without the wherewithal aboard to sail or fight."[21]

The soldiers remaining in Cattaro continued with duties similar to those that Lieutenant Rendigs described, "The duties assigned Companies "E" and "G" at Zelenika were quite different from "F" Company's. When they came into Zelenika they found the filthiest spot in Europe and, as usual, the characteristic American order to "Police up," was given. The barracks had been occupied by Russian prisoners several of whom were found in the building – dead. Between the barracks, dead horses also were found and all about was filth and debris. Not content with making the town sanitary, those of a mechanical bent made the necessary repairs to the water and electric lighting plants and soon both conveniences were at their disposal."[22]

In January, the F Company detachment returned to the mountains to distribute sacks of flour to feed the starving Montenegrins and once again, to play the role of mediator between the factions. Major Southworth reported a summary of the expedition, but omitted from the record his own act of heroism which brought accolades from his soldiers:

"On General Venel's orders, Company "F" made the second expedition into Montenegro as part of an inter-allied intervention … I can say that our efforts to check further bloodshed were eventually crowned with success. The only serious threat I made to use force was in order to protect the non-combatants in the valley of Njegusi from a fight with, or pillage by, the successful de facto government troops, and here again I was successful. So in due time with the country now quiet, we marched into Cettinje and were given a hearty reception."[23]

Lieutenant Rendigs reported on the critical situation:

"Early in the morning of the ninth we could make out, through our glasses, large parties of armed Montenegrins moving along the top of the surrounding mountain ridges which enclosed Niegush, and it was thought that these parties were about to attack the town. However, they eventually disappeared from view, and we waited to see what would happen. In the afternoon I procured permission from Capt. Southworth to take Corporal Chandler of my platoon with me for the purpose of exploring the surrounding mountains and the passes leading up to them. The Corporal and I went up to the top of the nearest ridge, and discovered a band of revolutionists, numbering about fifty, holding the pass. They were a most picturesque group, ragged, wild-eyed, half starved, with long unkempt beards and moustaches, and closely resembled a group of banditti. They were friendly to us and expressed a desire to lay down their arms and go back to their homes, but said that they were afraid to do so for fear that they would be run down and put to death by the Government Forces …

On January 10th … our labors began to bear fruit. About two hundred revolutionists came in and surrendered their arms to us, and each one received a safeguard from the Serbian Major, Alexandrovitch. An incident to their surrender occurred, which is worth relating. It had been arranged that they would surrender their arms to us at one o'clock in the afternoon, on a small plain near Niegush. At the appointed time the Revolutionists began to appear from different parts of the mountains, and gathered at one side of the plain. A small detachment of the Government Forces suddenly appeared on the opposite side of the plain. Capt. Southworth, Lieut. Speakman and a squad of Americans were standing in the center of the plain, ready to receive the Revolutionists' arms. The Revolutionists, seeing the Government Forces on the opposite side of the plain, became excited, and one of them fired a rifle.

Immediately both forces flung themselves to the earth in skirmish line, and an interchange of shots ensued, with the Americans in between the opposing lines. Capt. Southworth, with rare presence of mind, held up his hand with a commanding gesture, and after about twenty shots had been fired by the two sides, the firing ceased as suddenly as it began. Officers from both sides immediately ran forward and offered their apologies and regrets to Capt. Southworth and the Americans for this untoward incident. Fortunately there were no casualties, but if there had been, it would have taken something more than apologies or regrets to have squared things.

> As soon as the Revolutionists were disarmed they were sent down under guard to Cattaro, to be put to work unloading the flour off of the U. S. Supply Ship "Western Plains", which had anchored there with white flour on board for the relief of the starving Montenegrins."[24]

The American battalion's fleeting presence would stabilize the situation to some degree However, there was no hope that this short lived expedition would yield more lasting results in a region torn for millennia by war. Captain Southworth addressed the challenge with an interesting vignette:

> "The following incident may illustrate much that has been said and written of this proud and picturesque race. At a critical point at the time of negotiations for the surrender by the insurgents of their "army" to us, a grizzled Montenegrin major appeared on the upper reaches of the Lovcen with a large detachment of the de facto government troops. A fight threatened and a few shots were fired, but at my request he obligingly held back his men until I could arrange to send the insurgents to Cattaro; and thus practically ended the "revolution". This same major later welcomed our troops as we marched into Cettinje; and there we met often and he was most friendly and courteous. About that time this story was told me of this major. During the first of the fighting around Cettinje when the City was blockaded (and about the time of my two trips above referred to, through the opposing forms in an endeavor to find some basis on which to negotiate and of which others have written) there came a lull in the battle. This major seized the opportunity to send out a white flag and request a conference with a certain insurgent leader whom he had recognized. In response to the invitation the insurgent came into the major's lines, and was brought to his headquarters. Here the major offered him tobacco, and while the visitor was rolling a cigarette, the major shot him through the head!"[25]

Sergeant Major Lettau felt for the boys of the Third Battalion. He remembered that:

> "Much has been said about the rations received by the boys in Dalmatia and the balance of the regiment was inclined to brand the Second Battalion a lot of discontents. However, too many men of unquestionable character have said that the rations were far from normal to allow such an impression to remain. In the words of an American Major who investigated these alleged conditions: "This ration (the standard ration fixed for American troops serving in the Italian Army, as we were) has not been issued to the United States troops." His statement follows with a list of articles which were not issued. He said: "The meat is of very inferior grade," and "It is sometimes diseased." "Canned meat is old, some issues being put up in the year 1913." "The issues of macaroni and of rice are frequently wormy."
>
> Several men were marked "Quarters" [Soldiers who were on the sick list and not available for duty were confined to their quarters; hence they were in "Quarters" status] because of the ragged condition of their uniforms and others wore raincoats on sunny days to cover their torn breeches. Some of the officers gave men their own clothes. It has also been said that when the French soldiers came to Cattaro, they would not believe that the ragged soldiers were Americans. Many were marked "Quarters" on account of their shoes and I have heard that one lad had boards tied to the bottom of his shoes to keep his feet off the earth. These conditions, especially regarding clothing, were alleviated before the boys left Dalmatia.
>
> The impressions received by the boys were not flattering to the country. "It was dirty, ill kept and contaminated," they said. "The men were very lazy and the women did all the work that was done. The men dressed up and sat in the wine or coffee rooms telling stories throughout the day. The women were held as slaves and it was a common sight to see them descending the mountains with loads of wood upon their backs large enough for a mule to carry."
>
> "... the boys settled down to the dull wait for the glad day when the order would come that would release them from Dalmatia. At last, early in March, the good word came and on the 5th, the Battalion said goodbye to the beautiful but gloomy Dalmatian coast and after four days on the sea, joined the First and Third Battalions at Genoa."[26]

The Third Battalion at Fiume

The Third Battalion, under Captain Story arrived in Fiume on November 19th:

> "Their duty was to aid in the international policing of this difficult territory. Fiume, since the armistice, was jealously watched by both Italy and the new Jugo-Slav state. The real issue probably was, and is, that the Jugo-Slavs consider this port indispensable to their future while the Italians think they should have Fiume as a reward for their share in the war. This being understood, it will be easier to comprehend what difficulties the Americans labored under in a work in which they had no material interest."[27]
>
> "Fiume is an old city, having been known in Roman times. There is, in fact, a Roman triumphant arch built by Claudius II. The modern city of 39,000 population sits in a sort of amphitheatre between the hills and the shore of the Gulf of Quarnera. A large export business contributes largely to Fiume's prosperity as is evident from the wharves, warehouses and steamships to be seen here. It is said that 7,500 emigrants passed through Fiume in 1902 which makes Fiume the cosmopolitan town it is.
>
> With such activities at its gate, it is not surprising to see the many imposing public buildings such as the Governor's palace, the Austrian Emperor's palace and the many large schools and churches. In the northwest part of the city there are fine public gardens. As intimated above, there are two

parts of the town, New Fiume and Old Fiume. New Fiume is a busy, bustling place with wide, clean streets which reminded the boys of American cities.

Old Fiume, however, which is entered through a huge archway, is different. It contains most of the Italian portion of the population and its dark, odoriferous, covered alleys have a medieval air about them. Gloomy, vaulted passages lead from one crooked street to another still more crooked, and a walk through these strange byways was delightful in the surprises met at every step. One saw first a bazaar, then a market scene or an old monument and again, a fountain or a dilapidated old door with a coat of arms. At every turn, as in Italy, there is a little, dark odorous wine room, but the crowd inside is always loud and happy with dances or dice games. The shops in this quarter are open in front. Here is a corn dealer beside an old clothes store, while next door is an image maker. Nearby is a barber shop with its owner in the doorway sharpening his razor. Across the street is a macaroni shop and an artificial flower store.

The fine cafes of Fiume attracted many Americans, for aside from their wares, exquisite Hungarian music was offered and its appealing strains were as enjoyable here as when translated to the American light opera stage."[28]

All that the port of Fiume offered made it an enticing prize to both the Yugo-Slavs and Italians, Captain Story quickly understood that the battalion would have to tread carefully:

"My third battalion played a part in an important political situation. We were sent to Fiume (now Rijeka) from Cormons. Lt.Col. William G. Everson was to accompany us as the diplomatic leader while I was in command of the troops. Everson went ahead and then came back and reported that Fiume was waiting for us with much enthusiasm, Serbian, Croatian and other Yugo-Slav flags flying from all the buildings. Fiume was of great importance to the Yugo-Slav as his only outlet to the sea, however the Italians coveted it although they had a better port of Trieste on the other side of the Istrian peninsula.

After Lt.Col. Everson had left Fiume and while our second battalion was conveniently still in Venice, the Italians placed a platoon from our Co. G commanded by Lt. George Connelly on one of several Italian destroyers and off they went to Fiume across the Adriatic.

It seems that a day or two after the armistice, a Serbian regiment had marched in to Fiume, the Colonel occupying the palace amid the joy of the Yugo-Slav populace. Now watch the crafty Italians. Several Italian destroyers steamed in to the harbor of Fiume and one of them contained the platoon from our Co. G under Lt. Connelly, who knew nothing of the political situation. The Italian Admiral in a conference with the Serbian colonel told him that Fiume was not to be occupied, and if he (the Serb) would withdraw, the Italians would not come in. So the Serbians withdrew to the surrounding hills around Trsat and Susack , and then the Italians landed first our platoon and followed them with Italian marines and soon a whole Italian division. Here then they used us for the first time, knowing that the Serbs and other Yugo-Slavs trusted the Americans and would not fire on them.

It was after that affair, and knowing nothing of it, that our battalion arrived in Fiume and we were mildly surprised to find it full of Italians, and nothing but Italian flags flying. But to us it did not mean much for none of us was familiar in the slightest degree with the political situation, unless it might have been Lt. Col. Everson. As soon as we arrived we hunted up billets, the troops were lodged in large school buildings and the officers in the luxurious S.S. Ferenc Ferdinand, the private yacht of the Crown Prince, whose assassination started the war.

A very affable civilian of evident Italian sympathies took Everson under his wing for proper welcome and entertainment, and that was the last I saw of him until the next morning. The 'fine Italian hand" again, as will be seen.

About nine o'clock that first night in Fiume, an orderly came to my headquarters with an order from the Italian commanding general requesting the senior American officer to report to the palace immediately. I instituted a search for Everson everyplace, sent men all over the town, sounded "officers' call," but no Everson to be found any place. So I proceeded to the palace, knowing nothing of what was doing. I'll never forget that conference, an American captain, an Italian major general (Anfosi), a couple of Italian brigadiers, to say nothing of Italian colonels and lesser officers, interpreters, etc. I was told to have two companies ready at four thirty the next morning to assist in the occupation of the Yugo-Slav towns of Trsat and Sussack. I didn't like the looks of things although I did not know then, as I found out later, that this territory was outside of the Italian zone and was in the Serbian zone as laid out by terms of the armistice, and that the Serbians had just withdrawn to these points. I was inclined to demur and wanted to know the whys of things, which was not very good military discipline, but I was assured that it was on the orders of the Inter-Allied Supreme Command, and knowing that we were a part of the Italian command, I had no choice but obey.

I chose companies K and M for this duty and in the cold grey dawn they were lined up in company fronts and at this point may I digress to tell of an incident that has given me a chuckle every time I think of it. The commander of Co. M was Captain Jasper McKinney, he had been a regular army non-com before the war, a splendid officer if somewhat unique. His order to his men that morning was "with ball cartridges – load! Your mission this morning is" – (then a long pause and each man hanging on the next words) – "is none of your Goddamned business – Squads right – March!"

These two companies were placed at the head of two columns which marched up those hills to Treat and Sussack, occupying those villages without any trouble only finding a couple of machine guns and a one-pounder. Of course we were followed by a battalion or two of Italians who took over the little towns. The idea, of course, was that the people would not object if they saw Americans for at that time we were pretty much liked and trusted by all those factions.

Our battalion (the 3rd) remained longer in Fiume than in any other locality in Europe, but our duties were light, and our stay a pleasant one. It was interesting to watch the rivalry between the Italian and Yugo-Slav factions, each especially tried to gain sympathy and influence of the British and American officers in the city. One day an American soldier was walking down the street with a Yugo-Slav girl, she was wearing the red, white and blue ribbons signifying her Slav sympathies, when an Italian soldier snatched the ribbon from her dress, this caused a fight between a group of Americans and Italians. The Italian carabiniere M.P.s arrested one American and threw him in the local jail. This caused an uproar which led to the release of the prisoner and an apology from General Grazioli before the entire battalion drawn up in review. From then on the city was policed by M.P.s consisting of three soldiers walking around together – an American doughboy, a British Tommy and an Italian carabiniere.

The two factions went to great lengths to entertain the Americans and British. Once a week the Slavs would put on a big party and the Italians would do likewise. Since our officers seemed to enjoy the Yugo-Slav parties more than the Italian, it finally came to a point where I had to assign the proper number of officers to attend the Italian parties. At each there would be dancing, pretty girls and much food and drink. The Serbians took a group of us in the Dalmatian forests to hunt deer for several days. It was a great party and most interesting.

While we were in Fiume a detail of twenty men made a trip to Vienna as guards for a trainload of flour, and during their stay, in the Austrian capital, went through the palace of the ex-Emperor Franz Joseph."[29]

Ferris Myrice was one of the soldiers on that detail, his journal notes that on January 29:

"Volunteered to convoy flour into Austria. Arrived in Trieste at 11 A.M...finally arriving at Vienna 9 A.M ... The night of Jan 31st the train became uncontrollable going down a grade and things were happening for a short time – just missed a passenger train pulling across ahead of us...We billeted in the gym of a school building, fine place. Most everything was closed the next day (Sunday) but I saw about all one could in a day. Wein [Vienna] sure is a Wonderful city...I saw or visited Natural Museum, Hapsburg Palace (the trip thru the palace was worth the hardships of the ride to Wein) We saw the balcony upon which F.J. [Emperor Franz Joseph] stood while making his speech when war was declared. Went to Mass at St. Stevens...Finally ended the day by going home with an Austrian. When I left, his little daughter called me to the side of her bed – where she was waving the American and British flags."[30]

When the battalion moved to Genoa, Myrice would be promoted to corporal leaving the regiment to join a consular company in France, "It looks as tho (sic) the 332nd would beat me home – but – guess this is the only safe way."[31] He confided to his diary; he would miss his many friends in L Company. As the months slowly passed, life for the soldiers in Fiume was a positive experience:

"It was no surprise, therefore, that the American soldiers, fresh from the small towns of Italy and the rigorous campaign, should fall in love with Fiume, especially since the Jugo-Slavs tried to make life so pleasant for them. The girls were very popular with the soldiers and before the battalion left Fiume, there were several weddings.

The regimental band was sent for and on several nights dances were held which were greatly enjoyed. At first, the girls could not understand the American way of dancing, but it was not long before they were one-stepping and fox-trotting as if they had never danced otherwise. In fact, to hear the story from the lips of a Third Battalion soldier, the young ladies of Fiume threw their hearts at the Americans' feet.

At last ... the Battalion rolled up its packs, said good-bye in several languages to the weeping population of Fiume, boarded its "side-door pullmans," and set out for Genoa. They left heavy hearts behind them for the Jugo-Slavs truly loved them, and, when they had gone, I'm sure the Jugo-Slavs realized that truer champions of purer ideals never wore the uniforms of soldiers."[32]

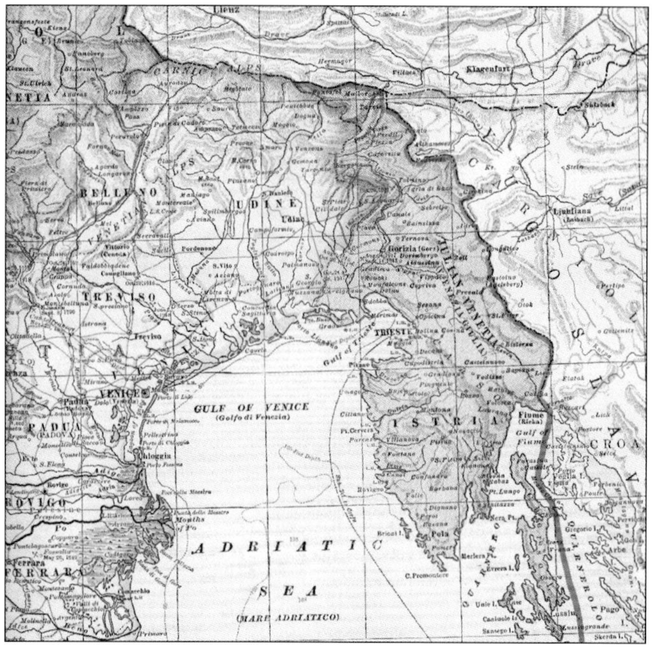

Left: This 1918 map of the Austro-Montenegrin Frontier depicts the area of operations of the Second Battalion. The battalion headquarters remained in Cattaro conducting sporadic operations in Cettigne. Courtesy Military History Institute.

Above: This 1928 map of Northern Italy depicts the area of operations of the First and Third Battalions. First Battalion remained in Treviso while Third Battalion was stationed in Fiume. Courtesy Private Colection.

The Regiment on the road between Ipplis and Brazzano, Italy. November 12, 1918. Courtesy National Archives.

Some of the lucky soldiers traveled by truck on the march between Ipplis and Brazzano. Courtesy National Archives.

The 332nd entering Brazzano, Italy, the first Austrian occupied town entered by U.S. troops. November 12, 1918. Courtesy National Archives.

The next day, the 332nd moved into Cormons, Italy. Courtesy National Archives.

Captured Austrian rolling stock. Cormons railway station, Italy. November 13, 1918. Courtesy National Archives.

Captured Austrian 120cm searchlight. Cormons, Italy. November 12, 1918. Courtesy National Archives.

Italian and American Officers Left to right: Major Birch, General Castagnola, Commander of the 37th Italian Division, Lieutenant Colonel Everson, and Captain Magnus. Cormons, Italy. November 13, 1918. Courtesy National Archives.

Italian and American Officers watching Company A drill. Officers facing directly forward, left to right General Castagnola, Commander of the 37th Italian Division, Lieutenant Colonel Everson, Major Birch and Captain Magnus. Cormons, Italy. November 13, 1918. Courtesy National Archives.

U.S. OFFICIAL

Opposite
Top: American soldiers from the Third Battalion enter Fiume, Austria. November 12, 1918. Courtesy National Archives.

Bottom: The original Signal Corps caption for this photograph reads: With the American troops in Fiume. Fiume and its harbor, as seen from one of the hills, adjacent. American troops who fought beside Italians on the Piave River now find themselves here (on the opposite shore of the Adriatic Sea) in a city which, a little while back, was a base for Boche submarines. The city has a population of about 51,000 and the second best harbor on the Eastern shore of the Adriatic. Courtesy National Archives.

Three U.S. Subchasers in Fiume harbor. November 29, 1918. Courtesy National Archives.

Two companies of the Third Battalion on the southeastern road out of Fiume, Austria. November 22, 1918. Courtesy National Archives.

American Officer talking with Jugo-Slav peasants. Fiume, Austria. November 22, 1918. Courtesy National Archives.

Another encounter between one of the Sammies and the locals. Courtesy National Archives.

Americans posting guard on northeastern hill of Fiume. November 22, 1918. Courtesy National Archives.

Austrian steamship Ferencz Ferdinand, used as headquarters for American Force in Fiume, Italy. November 23, 1918. Courtesy National Archives.

The platoon from Company G, Second Battalion marches down street. Fiume, Austria. November 26, 1918. Courtesy National Archives.

Governor's palace now occupied by Allied forces. Fiume, Austria. November 23, 1918. Courtesy National Archives.

Right: American and Italian guards at the gate of the Governor's palace. Fiume, Austria. November 28, 1918. Courtesy National Archives.

Below: Captured by American patrols, the village of Codroipo; this photograph shows the first American soldiers to enter the village after its capture. November 5, 1918. Courtesy National Archives.

American troops passing over a destroyed bridge on the Noncello River, near Prata di Pordenone, Italy, after it had been repaired by the engineers. November 1, 1918. Courtesy National Archives.

Field kitchen in Fiume, Austria. November 28, 1918. Courtesy National Archives.

Opposite

Top: Soldiers of Third Battalion with American sailors on a U.S. subchaser in Fiume harbor. November 28, 1918. Courtesy National Archives.

Bottom: Henry Blank posed with his fellow squad members of 9th Squad, 2nd Platoon for this photo in Fiume on November 22, 1918. Left to right, standing: John Neal, Nashville, Indiana, Ed Schmidt, Alliance, Ohio, William Market, Put-in-Bay, Ohio, William Quigley, Cleveland, Ohio; sitting: Fred Carter, Columbus, Ohio, Henry Blank, Dayton, Ohio, David Brush, Columbus, Ohio. "Hen" as his numerous friends affectionately called him, was known as the working man's advocate. Courtesy Military History Institute.

Right: American guard silhouetted against bay of Fiume. November 22, 1918. Courtesy National Archives.

Below: After the armistice, part of the regiment was stationed in Treviso, Italy. There, a 332nd soldier snapped this photograph of the John Pitt of Norfolk, Virginia (marked by the small "x"), the YMCA Director. The reverse of this Carte Postale reads, "Mr. Pitt is in charge of the work [of the YMCA] at Treviso and a very fine fellow – at home he is in the shoe business. Treviso Italy Feb 3, 1919." Courtesy Private Collection.

Henry Blank saved this Company "I" Christmas Card. The reference to "Plumber" Blank addresses his fame for complaining to his fellow soldiers about Italian plumbing. Courtesy Military History Institute.

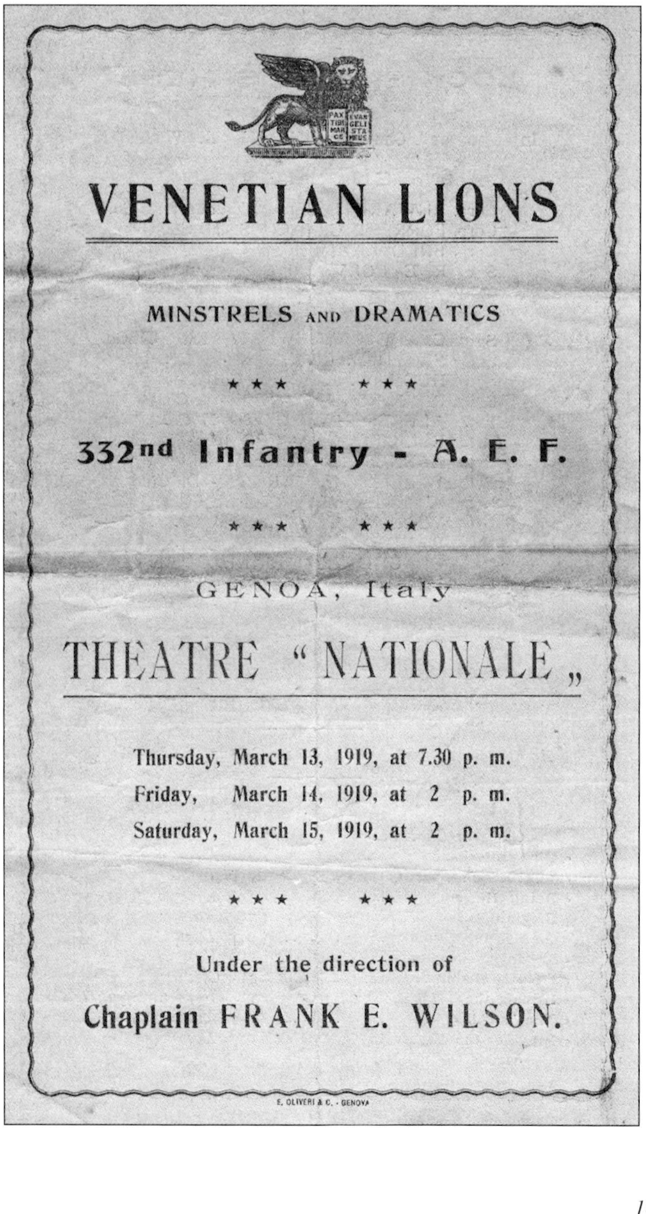

VENETIAN LIONS

MINSTRELS AND DRAMATICS

* * * * * *

332nd Infantry - A. E. F.

* * * * * *

GENOA, Italy

THEATRE "NATIONALE"

Thursday, March 13, 1919, at 7.30 p. m.
Friday, March 14, 1919, at 2 p. m.
Saturday, March 15, 1919, at 2 p. m.

* * * * * *

Under the direction of

Chaplain FRANK E. WILSON.

F. OLIVERI & C. - GENOVA

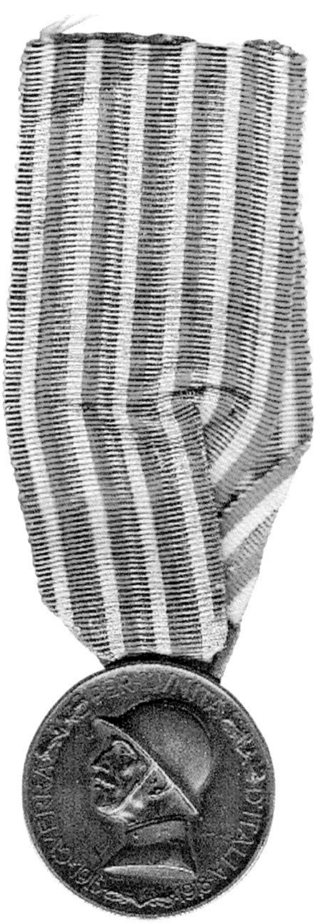

Left: This souvenir program advertises "Minstrels and Dramatics" at a show featuring the 332nd in Genoa. Courtesy Military History Institute.

Above: The regiment was authorized to wear the Italian Commemorative War Medal. Soldiers quickly named the accompanying ribbon for the medal the "Macaroni" Ribbon. Courtesy Private Collection.

A Yankee sentry on Guard at Cormons over recaptured Italian field pieces. November 15, 1918. Courtesy National Archives.

American soldiers and sailor looking at gargoyle in castle courtyard, Fiume. December 1, 1918. Courtesy National Archives.

American machine gun on tower of Terseto Castle. Fiume. December 1, 1918. Courtesy National Archives.

Soldiers pose in front of an Austrian Anti-Aircraft gun in Dalmatia. Courtesy Military History Institute.

A soldier sits on some Austrian Heavy Artillery at Meljine. Courtesy Military History Institute.

The caption on this photo reads; "Shorty Higgins' Artillery." Courtesy Military History Institute.

A Serbian wedding in Dalmatia. Courtesy Military History Institute.

A country church in Dalmatia. Courtesy Military History Institute.

Crew of Hotel Pension. Courtesy Military History Institute.

Taking refreshments. Courtesy Military History Institute.

Natives of Zelenika. Courtesy Military History Institute.

Austrian artillery emplacement in Dalmatia. Courtesy Military History Institute.

A Second Battalion soldier clowns around on an Austrian artillery piece. Courtesy Military History Institute.

On board the Chin Chow. Courtesy Military History Institute.

Left to right: Captains Dempsey and Johns, Lieutenants Hamilton and Bierry. Courtesy Military History Institute.

The Leopolis in Cattaro Bay. Courtesy Military History Institute.

Reigler's Navy captures Castleno, Dalmatia. Courtesy Military History Institute.

Lieutenant Bayles boarding a troop train. Courtesy Military History Institute.

After the armistice, soldier shows were organized to boost morale, as may be imagined, talents, and thus, quality, varied widely; from "With the 332 Reg in Italy". Courtesy Private Collection.

Some of the 332nd soldiers had an opportunity to visit Rome and take in its many sights; from "With the 332 Reg in Italy". Courtesy Private Collection.

Italian towns always drew the soldiers interest; from "With the 332 Reg in Italy". Courtesy Private Collection.

Reinert poked fun at the town of Treviso where First Battalion was stationed during the occupation period; from "With the 332 Reg in Italy". Courtesy Private Collection.

A large one dollar bill with notes following the travels of a soldier of the regiment; making special reference to the disappointing 1918 Christmas dinner menu. This dollar bill most probably belonged to Russell Harbaugh of 1st Platoon of F Company. His name is written on the bill in two places including a notation that he is in 6th Squad, 1st Platoon, Company F of the 332nd Inf or Col Wallace's Circus. Additionally, there are three other names and one set of initials on the bill; each match the names of men assigned to F Company. They include James McKeena, "C.C. Meyers" for Charles C. Meyers and "J. Thomas" for John R. Thomas, finally the initials "L.J.F." appear for Lewis J. Fritz. All of these men were likely assigned to the 6th Squad of 1st Platoon. Meanwhile, the Christmas dinner for the Regimental Headquarters at Treviso was somewhat different. In a December 26, 1918 letter to his brother, Carl P. Hinkle, a cook for the Supply Company, noted that, "We had turkey, stuffed figs, chocolate drops, creamed cauliflower, mashed potatoes, soup and coffee. By the way, we did not serve it in the order named as that is the way it came into my mind." Courtesy Private Collection.

IL MINISTRO DELLA GVERRA

DECRETA

IL 2nd Lt inf

Mclain Chester A.

È AVTORIZZATO A FREGIARSI DELLA

MEDAGLIA ISTITVITA A RICORDO

DELLA GVERRA MCMXV-MCMXVIII

ROMA, ADDÌ 30 Ottobre 1925

IL MINISTRO

Editori Alfieri & Lacroix - Roma-Milano

The Italian War Medal was awarded to members of the regiment. Soldiers quickly dubbed the accompanying ribbon the "Macaroni Ribbon." This award certificate, signed in 1925 by Italian Prime Minister Benito Mussolini, is framed along with the medal and was awarded to Lieutenant Chester A. McClain. Courtesy Private Collection.

6

Together Again and Back to Ohio

On February 10th, orders arrived at the Treviso Headquarters. Sergeant Major Lettau described the scene: "The Adjutant entered our office, looked me straight in the eye and exclaimed: "You're leaving for Genoa tomorrow!"... An advance party was quickly formed and they departed the following day for Genoa to set up accommodations for billeting the troops. Lettau continues, "The stately Hotel Miramare came into view as we turned the corner of the station. High up on the hillside, this massive stone structure stood, a fine looking hotel and a work of art. The desire to see its interior helped us climb the steep hill and when we stood within its marble reception hall and saw its magnificence, we were fearful that a mistake had been made. We could not believe that the doughboys were to have this palace for their billet. The rooms were stripped of beds, carpets and furniture but there were hundreds of mattresses and sheets. Sheets for the 332nd! It was astounding."[1]

By February 12th, the First and Third Battalions had boarded trains for Genoa. While enduring the familiar discomfort of another boxcar journey, the soldiers found the same physical hardships, but the morale was quite different. Rather than traveling to an uncertain destiny and location, the knowledge that each mile brought them closer to a return to loved ones diminished their misery. Genoa was the first leg of their passage home.

Story described their arrival in Genoa, "the regiment was again reunited [First and Third] and billeted in the beautiful hotel Miramare and for the first time since coming overseas the men enjoyed the luxury of sheets. The Miramare was a new hotel, built just before the war started and had never been occupied until our regiment took over"[2]

As a result of disturbing reports being published in a newspaper back home, an investigation was held in Genoa. The complaints were attributed to soldiers in the Second Battalion. A letter in The Canton Repository written by Corporal J. Homer Ebner described his condition of being in rags with inadequate food while in Cattaro. This was followed by letters from other soldiers who offered no complaints about their time there.[3]

The Company K Log, dated February 20th, detailed the visit of the investigators. "Both of these men were told things which concerned the lives of men that were lost, and things which were certainly not good for the Service, and which could have been avoided. The real decision of the investigators was never made public, but afterward they told us some things which only caused the men to believe that the investigation could have had a more accurate name if some other word had been used to describe it."[4] In the end, the investigation never really amounted to anything.

Corporal Leslie Bender understood the result. He tersely noted in his journal, "The Lt.Col. Gave us a little talk about the investigation of the 332nd In. asked us to say nothing to hurt the organization but forgot to advise us to tell the truth."[5]

Days after the lead elements arrived, the grateful people of the city honored the 332nd. "On February 28th the regiment was presented with a beautiful large flag of St. George, by the Genoese. The Colonel received a gold medal, several officers received silver ones and about a hundred men received bronze ones."[6]

On March 9th, the Second Battalion sailed into Genoa aboard the "Leopolia" an old Austrian boat. Although the mode of transportation and billeting locations differed from those of the First and Third Battalions, all of the men of the 332nd were overjoyed to be reunited with their entire regiment in the same city.

Lieutenant Rendigs recalled the voyage and arrival in Italy:

> Then began one of the most wonderful of sea voyages. The weather was warm, sunshiny, and ideal, while the waves were as calm as the water of an artificial lake. Only once did we have a rainstorm while en route to Genoa, and then only for an hour. From the Bay of Cattaro we crossed the Adriatic Sea, turned down the eastern coast of Italy, round the heel of the "great boot", through the Ionian Sea, and then northwards through the Straits of Messina.

From the deck of our good ship we could see the city of Messina on the Sicilian coast, while opposite it the Italian coast loomed into view. Continuing northwards along the Italian peninsula we passed the Isle of Stromboli, famous for its volcano, and could plainly see a huge, flat surface running from the top of the volcano into the sea, which had evidently been the lava slide. A little later, Elba, famous because of Napoleon's exile, came into view, and after that darkness fell as we prepared to spend our last night on the "Leopilus" (sic). Next morning, Sunday, we came in sight of Genoa about eight o'clock, and as we entered the bay and came up the great harbor, we would see American figures in Khaki, lining the balcony of the Hotel Miramare, overlooking the bay. They were the men of the first and third battalions of our regiment, who had been in Genoa for several weeks awaiting us. We docked at nine o'clock, and were greeted from the pier by the Colonel and a number of officers and men, while the Regimental Band played martial and popular airs."[7]

George Roberts wrote of the Second Battalion "We were greeted by the sound of music; at 12:30 we unloaded and marched through the city among throngs of people to a fine, large school building … this was formerly used as an English hospital and is positively the finest quarters we have had since arriving in Europe … we have no beds but very good mattresses to sleep on … the next day we were busy cleaning up and delousing"[8]

Captain Story noted: "Life was worth living in Genoa. Good food, good quarters, fine weather, a big city and plenty of money formed a combination hard to beat but strange to say everyone wanted to leave. The delay in starting home was most irksome to all. To keep up morale we had drill each morning and afternoons organized sports of various kinds-contests between companies etc."[9]

During the following weeks of March, the soldiers enjoyed a more relaxed schedule. They settled into their new role as stewards of diplomacy in a country that had been so recently disrupted by warring factions. Several men noted in journals that the days in Genoa were pleasant and relaxed. A great number of them took advantage of sightseeing opportunities. Some even traveling to Rome. Roberts described several excursions: "Visited Genoa, saw the Christopher Columbus and Garrabaldi (sic) monuments, as well as many others, the old home of Columbus, and many other places of interest, including churches and the Verdi and Olimpic (sic) wine rooms"[10]

"On March 1st, a few of the much looked for insignias of shoulder patches arrived. Since the regiment was on detached service in Italy, we were permitted to select our own insignia and the Lion of St. Mark was chosen because our time had been spent chiefly in the old Venetian territory."[11]

The 332nd shoulder sleeve insignia quickly became the envy of the A.E.F and is considered to this day as the most aesthetically beautiful of the American military regalia of World War I. The Company Log related the meaning of the regiment's new emblem:

"The regimental insignia made at Milan were now furnished the regiment. We here record a short legendary account of the history of this attractive design, "The Lion of St. Mark."

St. Mark, who is known as "The Historian of the Resurrection," is the patron saint of Venice, and the "The Lion of St. Mark" is his symbol. It is an appropriate symbol, since people in the Middle Ages believed the cub of a lioness was always born dead and after three days the lioness infused breath into the cub. The awakening typified the Resurrection. Since the angels, who are messengers of heaven, are represented as having wings, the lion is winged and represents one who bears good tidings. St. Mark's body was brought from Alexandra, Egypt, about 828 A.D."[12]

Other Americans serving in Italy rushed to get their own version of "The Lion of St. Mark." Many of the elements of Brigadier General Charles Treat's Base Section #8 wanted to make the Lion their own and the enterprising Milan manufacturers were only happy to oblige them. As such, "The Lion of St. Mark" insignia is extant in museum collections with a number of "332" replacement monograms on the bible. These variations include, "A.A.S" for American Ambulance Service, worn by the ambulance drivers immortalized in Hemingway's "A Farewell to Arms;" "M.R.C." for Motor Repair Company; used by the motor repair shop personnel at Mantua and Vicenza; "M.T.C." for Motor Transport Corps personnel, attributed to the supply depot personnel at Alessandria; "A.R.C." for the American Red Cross personnel at Padua, and "Y.M.C.A" for the Young Men's Christian Association who were in support of the troops in theater. Finally, the crafty Italians finally manufactured a version featuring a blank bible for anybody who felt left out. Not to be outdone, some members of the regiment took to wearing their regimental insignia with the 83rd "Ohio" Division insignia sewn on the sleeve directly below and still others wore the regimental, division and Army of Occupation insignia one below the other on the same sleeve. No other unit of the A.E.F wore three shoulder sleeve insignia on one arm!

From that time forward, "The Lion of St. Mark" would be linked with American Forces serving in Italy and specifically the 332nd Infantry Regiment. To this day, the U.S. Army retains the "Lion of St. Mark" as an element of insignia for units assigned in Italy.

Sergeant Major Lettau wrote that while many were experiencing the pleasures of a slower pace in a sizeable city, the atmosphere in the offices was frenetic. "In the offices, especially the Personnel, the work was very heavy as everyone was anxious to be ready when the word came to board the ship."[13]

The day every soldier had longed for finally arrived -and many could not believe what they were told: tomorrow, the regiment would board ships for home! Because the regiment size exceeded the capacity of any one of the available ships, the boys were to sail on three different vessels. "The Second Battalion, "K" and "M" companies and detachments of the Medical, Supply and Machine Gun companies and Base Hospital 102 were to leave first on the "Canopic." Regimental Headquarters, the First

Battalion, "I" Company, Field Hospital 331 and detachments of the Medical, Machine Gun and Supply Companies were to go on the "Duca D'Aosta," March 29th. "L" Company, with detachments, was to remain a few days to conclude all business and to pick up any men returning from leaves."[14] Company L and the stragglers were to sail on the "Dante Alighieri."

Not expecting the regiment to sail from Italy at this early date, Colonel Wallace had released men, some of whom were recent immigrants from Italy and Greece, to visit their families before returning to the states. Sergeant Major Lettau remembered that, "At this time we had men scattered all over Europe and telegrams were dispatched(sic) to them. All except those who went to Greece succeeded in returning in time to go on one of the three ships."[15]

Lieutenant Rendigs was among the men suddenly recalled from their leave of absence:

> "At this time, it being apparent that we were doomed to spend some time in Italy, we decided to request leaves for the purpose of visiting the principal Italian cities. Capt. Craig and I, of our Company, and a dozen officers from other companies of the battalion, put in requests, which were promptly granted, and we were given leave for fourteen days to visit the cities of Naples, Rome, Florence, Bologna, and Milan. Our party left Genoa on the night of the 25th of March, and on the following day, about noon, arrived in Rome. There were two officers from Company E and the Captain and I in our immediate party, and we decided to journey on to Naples at once, and then, starting with that city, which was the one farthest south, gradually work our way northward, taking in the others as we progressed. We reached Naples on the evening of the 26th, and established ourselves in the best hotel we could find – the DeLondres. The other officers of the party remained in Rome, and this later proved to be the wiser move of the two, but of this we were in ignorance at that time. The following morning we procured a guide, and started out bright and early to "do the town".
>
> We visited the three largest cathedrals in the forenoon and the National Art Museum, with its priceless statuary and relics of Pompeii, and in fact from all over Italy. After lunch we visited the King's palace with its extravagantly gorgeous furnishings, and a most remarkable aquarium out on the bay, where we saw an unusually complete variety of undersea life. In the evening we visited a music hall, which is so popular with the average Italian, and witnessed a mediocre performance and ballet. The next morning we had intended to journey to Pompeii and Vesuvius, and return to Naples in the evening, but on arising we found ft raining steadily, so decided to postpone our excursion until the following day. We strolled up town about ten o'clock, intent upon doing a little shopping, but we suddenly received some unexpected and startling news, which promptly changed all of our plans.
>
> We met an "M.P.", which, to the American soldier means "Military Police", who calmly informed us that a telegram had arrived at their office the preceding morning, ordering all officers and men of the 332nd to return to Genoa at once, as the regiment was sailing. We were very much disgruntled to received (sic) this information because we had so carefully planned our trip, and were expecting and hoping to get so much out of it. We were not at all concerned with the news of the regiment sailing inasmuch as our previous experience had convinced us that there was bound to be delay in carrying out orders for embarkation, even if such orders had actually arrived. We all felt that it would be ten days or two weeks before the regiment would really sail, and were greatly tempted to remain at least one day longer in order to visit Pompeii and Vesuvius, but we decided finally to obey our orders and return at once.
>
> We left Naples at noon on the 28th, just an hour and a half after receiving the order, and arrived in Rome that evening at 7 P.M. We learned there that the other officers had received the word a full day sooner than we had, and accordingly had departed the night previously. We remained in Rome two hours, and then boarded a train for Genoa, where we arrived the following morning shortly after ten o'clock. We immediately journeyed out to our billets in the Scuole Mazzini, and upon arriving there learned to our great surprise and chagrin, that our Company, F, along with Companies E, G, M and K, had sailed for America on the liner Canopic, the previous evening at six o'clock.
>
> We could scarcely believe this news, and visited our former quarters only to find them abandoned, which convinced us of the truth of it. We were sorely disappointed, and it would have been difficult to have found more dejected officers in a regiment when, after cutting short our leaves, we had arrived in Genoa only to be denied the pleasure and satisfaction of journeying home with the men of our commands. We learned that a second transport was to sail that evening at six, so we hastened to Regimental Headquarters, hoping that possibly we could get passage on it and rejoin our own troops at Gibraltar where both boats were scheduled to stop over for coaling. However, again we were doomed to disappointment, the Embarkation Officer informing us that every available inch of space on the boat was taken up and that we should be obliged to wait until the third boat sailed with the last quota of the regiment. This was scheduled to leave on the 3rd of April. The prospect of loafing around Genoa for five days did not at all appeal to us and we were also fearful lest we should not rejoin our companies before demobilization, but there was nothing to do but wait, so we settled down at the Hotel Mirramare (sic) with the other troops.
>
> That afternoon the second transport, the "Duc d'Aosta" sailed at six with the first battalion, Regimental Headquarters, and the Supply and I Companies on board, and the Italians gave them a great send-off. We watched the huge liner slowly steam out to sea from the window of our hotel, and it was a sight that none of us would ever care to witness again. However, we were somewhat consoled upon being informed by the Embarkation Officer that the first two transports to sail were slow boats and that the one that

we were to go on, the "Dante Alighieri" was the pride of the Trans-Atlantic Line and should reach New York only three days after the other two had arrived. This news gave us a new hope that after all it would be possible to rejoin our commands in time to say goodbye to the boys with whom we had been so closely associated for so long a time and undergone together so many hardships. We spent the next few days in shopping, going to the Opera, and seeing a little of the town of Genoa, that hitherto we had not had the time to visit. On Wednesday, the 2nd day of April, we were informed that our baggage would be loaded on the "Dante" the following morning, and that we should embark in the afternoon. On Wednesday night we held a big "Party" at one of the downtown cafes, with practically all of the officers still in the city. Next day was a beautifully warm day, with plenty of sunshine, and the sea appeared to be absolutely calm, auguring well for a pleasant homeward voyage."[16]

The ship *Canopic*, which Lieutenant Rendigs missed, left Genoa on March 28th amid torrents of cheers and tears. She sailed for Gibraltar where she would pick up coal fuel for the Atlantic crossing, Duca D'Aosta would follow her, sailing the next day. George Roberts recalled that splendid day:

> "First call at 5 A.M. and at 7 A.M. we were all ready to move out; had dinner at 10:30 and at 12, noon, we had a formation at which seven of our men were decorated, including Sergt. Pahlan of my platoon who was wounded in the battle of Viorio (Sic) Veneto which was fought at the Tagliamento River … at 1:30 P.M. we moved out, proceeding thru the city to the docks in a cold drizzling rain and hail. Large crowds were gathered along the line of march bidding us farewell, and at 2:30 P.M. we arrived at the docks and immediately boarded the British White Star Liner "Canopic," and at 6 P.M. we cut loose from the docks and started on that long desired trip back to the dear old U.S.A. leaving behind the land of macaroni, the battle fields of devastated Belgium, beautiful France, and sunny Italy, where we all experienced hardships galore and pleasures undesirable. We sailed out of the harbor amid throngs of cheering people who had assembled there to bid farewell to the young and daring 332nd as we are now known. We were out only ten minutes when we were hitting waves about as large as houses and many of us got busy feeding the fish."[17]

The next day, the *Canopic* stopped at Marseilles, France to pick up passengers; these new additions created friction on the vessel. Roberts describes the order of protocol that generated resentment among the enlisted soldiers:

"March 29 At 10:30 A.M. we arrived at Marseilles, France, picked up a few casuals, Red Cross nurses and officers, and at 6 P.M. we sailed out of that harbor amid cheers and wishes from the French for a safe and pleasant trip. There is some difference between the nurses of the 332nd and those from the western front. Of course we understand that nurses are not permitted to associate with privates. Our nurses stood for this order but the western front girls do not. For instance, the 332nd nurses do not associate with enlisted men while the western front nurses have but dm [damn] little use for officers, and again, there were signs hanging around on the boat which read, "Nurses are not permitted to associate with enlisted men," but these signs did not last long as the western front girls tore them all down and threw them overboard, then they came down on our deck and had a good time with us and refused to associate with the officers except when absolutely necessary. The officers gave dances on their deck but the western front nurses refused to attend because private soldiers were not allowed there."[18]

Elisabeth Lewis, one of the "Western Front" nurses, was apparently unaware of the brouhaha surrounding herself and her sister nurses. In a string of correspondence to her mother and sister penned aboard the *Canopic*, she makes only two passing references to the regiment. First simply stating, "We have 1700 passengers on board and all except 40 civilians have been in foreign service. Some in Italy and some in France …" Then a few days later, she remarked, "I went to church services this morning. The chaplain of the regiment [the 332nd was the only regiment aboard] holds services every Sunday down in the dining room."[19] Given the forthright nature of her other correspondence to them, it seems she would have shared those details with her most intimate correspondents.

Henry Blank settled in for his journey on the Duca D'Aosta. Already apprehensive about the voyage, he remembered the sea sickness he suffered on the trip over. Noting on March 30, "Got up dizzy this A.M. Stayed in bed till noon. Got up for dinner, shaved and went back to bed again. Nothing new."[20]

Lettau recounted that, "The journey from Genoa to Gibraltar consumed about forty hours, since we reached the "Rock" about 10:00 A. M. March 31st. A library aboard ship afforded the means of recreation to many while, to others, it proved interesting to watch the porpoises (sic) race and play at the prow of the ship as we sped through the water. Then, there were others who refused to be amused. The ship's crew, evidently, had been spoiled by carrying American soldiers before, for various bribes were necessary before the proper amount of food could be obtained, in, at least, the second class dining room … Arriving in the spacious harbor of Gibraltar, we did not dock but cast anchor until such time as the ship could be coaled … There were at least a hundred other vessels at anchor in the splendid harbor. One of these was the Canopic which had left Genoa the day before us. She had stopped at Marseilles but had reached Gibraltar before us [either Lettau or Roberts confused their times as according to Roberts, Canopic arrived after Duca D'Aosta] and, the next day, when we moved into the coal dock we found the Canopic alongside us."[21] Traveling aboard *Canopic*, Roberts noted that:

> "At 4 P.M [March 31]. We sighted the rock of Gibralter and at 4:30 we dropped anchor in the bay just outside the harbor to await our turn for coal. While here we saw the old British battle fleet which is said to be about one hundred years old, and is the same fleet with which England conquered Gibralter (sic) when she took control of it. There

are boats of every description and nationality here including American freighters, Destroyers, and Battle Ships, and again we received a very warm welcome. It is said there are 1700 guns on this fortified rock; two small guns are removed and replaced by one large one each year. One side of this rock is covered with shrubbery and a small city and docks, while the other side is a large water shed, for Gibralter (sic) has three months of almost steady rain each year while during the next nine months there is not a drop of rainfall; during the three months of rainfall they must conserve enough water to provide for their needs during the nine dry months.

April 1, I should have stated that the entire regiment did not sail from Genoa at the same time but instead is sailing by battalions, and twenty-four hours apart, our second battalion taking the lead. We remained at anchor all day just outside the harbor awaiting our turn at the coaling docks and about 9 A.M. the first battalion arrived; they also are to take coal here."[22]

While the vessels were being coaled, the men were allowed to visit Gibraltar. Lettau described the area, "On the morning of the 3rd, half of those aboard the two vessels were sent ashore to walk through Gibraltar. We were glad of a chance to get on land and glad of an opportunity to see the city, but we were compelled to remain in ranks every moment we were off the ship. At any rate, we enjoyed the much needed exercise and also obtained a glimpse of the unique, cosmopolitan city of Gibraltar. It seemed, from the slight acquaintance, to be a very up-to-date city. All of the houses are built of stone and one obtains the impression of cleanliness. Our shore leave was limited to a walk through the main street and the return, when the other half of the men made the trip."[23]

George Roberts, who was now fascinated with his female co-passengers, noted that on, "April 3 Orders were given this morning that passes would be issued to go ashore for the day, half the men to go today and the other half to go tomorrow, so we immediately got busy making dates with nurses to meet them over on the rock as we were not allowed to leave the boat with them, and when the officers asked the girls for dates to visit the rock almost every nurse had a date with a private soldier, and the officers soon found they were out of luck, so to get even with us they let us go ashore by telling us we must march over in a formation and would then be given freedom over there, but instead they marched us over thru the town, turned around and marched us back to the boat. It is useless to describe the feelings we had about that time."[24]

Once again Elizabeth Lewis tells a different story; she shared her day in Gibraltar with her sister in a letter dated that same day, "We are at the docks coaling up and we were given shore passes to-day. We were allowed off from 9 a.m. until 5 p.m. When we got ashore we took a team and road (sic) for an hour and a half and went all around the Rock of Gibraltar. It is a wonderful sight. The guide that drove us around pointed out all the places. There are a great many British soldiers on guard around the town and the rock. We had dinner at a restaurant in the village then we took in the shops. Everything is Spanish. I brought a beautiful collar and so did my pal."[25]

Henry Blank's day was far less eventful, "April 3 Started to coal this morning. Was on guard till 2 P.M. We were taken out to the City. We walked thru the town to the edge of the nutrual (sic) line. Saw some of the Spanish women tying bread on their legs to smuggle it in as the rule is that you can bring in anything that is concealed. The zone of 900 yds belongs to no one, so they say. Saw a Spanish Centry (sic) on duty. Saw the Spanish Barracks across the line. Just passed where they have Bull-Fights. Saw German boats in port, also saw some Moors from Africa. We expect to leave tomorrow. The clocks were set back another hour."[26]

Duca D'Aosta finished coaling first and left on April 4th. Sergeant Major Lettau noted:

> "... at 7:30 we moved out of the harbor. On our left we could see the rocky shores of Africa. Nothing could be distinguished except the mountains over which hung a peculiarly dark, purple haze. On our right lay the green hills of Spain and the dark clouds cast a shadow over the hills, but where there was a break between two clouds, the sun shone through and the little white roofs of the stone houses sparkled as if a spotlight played upon them."[27] Blank added, "Saw some whales off the African coast. Went past several towns on both sides, some in Morocco, some in Spain. This makes the third day at Gibralter and six days from Genova."[28]
>
> "We soon passed the last point of land and were again upon the broad Atlantic. The consequent rocking of the ship, which we now saw was a very different boat from the stately Aquitania, disturbed the feelings of many. The weather also was colder than we had been experiencing."[29]

Following some introspection while waiting for his ship to finish coaling, Roberts' dark mood began to improve:

> "April 4 At 8 A.M. the first battalion was loaded with coal and ready to proceed on their journey to the U.S. and we of the second battalion were a sore and disagreeable bunch that day. However, as the Italian boat Duca de Ostia (sic), carrying the first battalion, is a much slower boat than ours, we expect to beat them to the States. The reason we are so mad is, they gave us the big laugh as they pulled away leaving us behind.
>
> Well, they worked day and night loading our boat with coal and at 7:40 the next morning the last basket of coal was aboard; at 8 A.M. we cut loose from the dock, hooked on to two tugs that helped us out of the harbor, and we were on our last lap towards home, leaving behind the battlefields of France and Italy where thousands of American boys have paid the supreme price that the world might be ruled by Democracy instead of Autocracy, and now I am just beginning to realize how lucky I am, for I am on my way home to see those who are waiting for me, and without a scratch of injury on my body, while some of the boys are returning without arms, legs, eyes, or otherwise disfigured for life, while thousands of our boys will never return to those dear ones and friends who have so patiently waited

for them. After leaving Gibralter (sic) we passed thru the Strait of Gibralter (sic); on one side of this strait to the north lies Spain, the land of bull fights, while on the other side is Africa, the land of the wilds. About noon we were heading out to sea, the water was quiet, and it seemed as if we were standing still while the land slowly drifted away from us, but it did not matter to us which might be moving as long as we were going home towards the American shore."[30]

The next day bad weather set in, "About noon we encountered high winds and of course high winds on the ocean always mean rough water. The old boat put up an awful fight to stay on top but at times it seemed to us she would be dashed to pieces, many of the waves being so large as to cause the boat to rise fifty or sixty feet in the air, then the wave just seemed to disappear and the boat would drop down again so fast it would almost take away one's breath."[31]

After soldiering through several days of bad weather and seasickness, Henry Blank was back on his feet; but like his fellow soldier Roberts, became annoyed after seeing nurses fawn over the dashing 332nd officers, "Feeling better, today. Passed the Astoria Island [a steamship] this morning. Saw Red-Cross Nurse manicuring Capt. Jones' fingernails. Some "Democracy."[32]

The bad weather continued, "April 8 About noon today we ran into another wild storm and again the old boat is bobbing up and down like a cork; waves are washing over the deck, the result being that no one is allowed on deck at the front end of the boat for fear of being washed over board; this storm lasted far into the night."[33]:

> The violent Atlantic storm struck the Duca D'Aosta the next day, Sergeant Major Lettau remembered, "On April 9th we encountered what we thought was quite a storm. The waves rushed over the deck rails and those adventurous spirits who loved to stand in the bow of the ship and allow the water to spray upon them, were ordered inside. The vessel rolled and pitched and standing in the bow of the boat and looking back, it was curious to watch the vessel twist about, almost like a stretched letter "S"."[34]

Although the seas remained rough enough to continue to vex Henry Blank's flatlander disposition, once they passed through this storm the voyage was uneventful. Sergeant Major Lattau remarked:

> "On the twelfth, the sea again became very rough and during the night a heavy fog descended upon us making necessary the weird cry of the fog horn. Upon awakening the next morning, we were relieved to see that the fog had lifted.
>
> All this day we watched eagerly for land and, at last, at 4:45 P. M. the shore of Long Island was visible. As we drew nearer our destination we were in time to witness a sunset behind the Jersey hills, more beautiful, to us, than all of Italy's boasted sunsets. Later, as we passed up the lane marked by buoys, the lights of the Statue of Liberty lighted and a mighty cheer rose on the air.
>
> We cast anchor inside the harbor and slept in the shadow of America once again. It was a most happy night."[35]

Members of Company I , also sailing on the Duca D'Aosta described their feelings as they approached land. "… the Statue of Liberty seemed to us the most beautiful thing in the world when we hove in sight of it on Sunday evening, April 13. More than one man felt a big lump rise in his throat when the next morning the 332nd Inf. Argonauts once more set foot on good old United States soil."[36]

The Company D Log recalled their arrival as their ship pulled into New York Harbor:

> "[We were] met by Mayor's Committee of Welcome aboard police boat "Patrol." Whistles on harbor craft almost burst their metal tongues as they shrieked greetings. Passengers waved their welcome from ferry boats. Passed Statue of Liberty. Band aboard Mayor's boat struck up "Home Sweet Home." A hushed silence fell on board Duc d'Acsta (sic).
>
> As the meaningful strains fell on the water, the men's features became almost immobile, their heartstrings stirred, by a million conflicting surges of emotion. With tremendous effort they struggled for self-mastery; eyes filled with tears of irrepressible joy; breasts heaved and fell under the impulse of emotional struggle within; heads turned aside to hide the tears that trickled down their bronze cheeks.
>
> This was their country, their people; here were their friends, their loved ones. This was the hour they had looked forward to for months; this, judging from their impressions of other countries, is best on earth, and this – this is "Home Sweet Home" – at last!"[37]

Company K, arriving on the *Canopic*, added "Oh! but it is a grand and glorious feeling that sort of "oozes" up through the soles of your shoes when you step on that "Land of the Free and Home of the Brave."And here on the pier it was that we had our first taste of real food for some time in the form of sauerkraut, wieners, pie, candy and coffee, which was served by the Red Cross and we thought it was a banquet."[38]

Roberts added:

> "At 9:30 A.M. we raised anchor and proceeded a short distance up the river to the White Star Landing; we are now a mighty happy bunch. It was just about noon when I stepped from that boat and set my feet on solid American ground once more after being on the water seventeen days. We were met by the Red Cross, Salvation Army, Knights of Columbus, and the YMCA, also by the Mayor of New York and his reception committee who served us a nice, hot lunch. We then crossed the river by ferry, boarded trains and proceeded to Camp Merritt, arriving there about 3 P.M., and when we recall that just ten months ago today we arrived in Liverpool, England, on our way to the battlefields, we realize how much pleasanter this landing is than that of ten months ago. Some of the boys still have a few cooties so we all went over to the delouser and did not get thru there until about one o'clock in the morning,

went to bed about 2 A.M., got up at 7 A.M., ate breakfast, and at 9 A.M. we started to move over to another part of the camp thru a hard rain, and by 12:30 we were all set for at least a few days."[39]

Sergeant Major Lettau remarked that, "Passes were given freely and practically everyone in the regiment enjoyed a visit to New York City. On the 21st, the 332nd Infantry formed at Washington Square, New York, and marched up Fifth Avenue passing thousands of cheering friends and admirers. At the head of the regiment, besides its Commanding Officer and his staff rode General Guglielmotti, royal military attaché to the Italian embassy at Washington, and his staff. Included in the parade were old Garibaldi veterans and representatives of New York's Italian societies. Upon arriving at 102nd Street, the parade passed into Central Park where Mayor Hylan welcomed the men to New York and America. Following this the royal consul general of Italy in New York, Signor Tritoni, presented a gold medal to the regiment."[40]:

> The New York Herald quoted Signor Tritoni's words, "On this medal there stand significantly two figures, one representing Italy, and the other the United States – Italy offering America palms of glory, America moving toward Italy with generous and noble love.
>
> We Italians mean this symbolism to be a hope for the future. Yes, more than a hope, it is a living faith. For the people of Italy love the United States and hope and believe that a brotherhood ever closer, will be established between the two nations.
>
> And so with reverence I salute your glorious flag. You, too, Colonel Wallace, and your gallant regiment I salute. And through you I salute the great leaders of the American army. All hail to the United States! All hail to Italy!"[41]

True to Wallace's high expectations, the regiment turned in the "most precise and inspiring parade performance ever seen in the Avenue of the Allies." The regiment's insignia also made a big impression on the crowd, "Each man wore the Italian service stripe of red, green and white, [Italian War Medal] and upon their left shoulder the handsomest insignia yet seen on a returning unit, the winged lion of St. Mark, embroidered in gold on red background." But it was the soldiers themselves who stole the show 'As one of the thousands along the line of march expressed it, it seemed that every man in the regiment was 'six feet tall and the officers eight feet.'"[42]

Following the presentation, "General Guglielmotti then rehearsed the history of the deeds of the regiment in Italy and the regiment's Commanding Officer replied for the regiment. After these ceremonies (sic), the regiment proceeded to the 69th regiment armory where refreshments were served."[43] When the festivities ended, the regiment returned to Camp Merritt to continue the myriad of tasks necessary before they could leave for Camp Sherman.

"A few days later, the news reached us at Camp that the Pennsylvania men in the regiment were to be sent to Camp Dix to receive their discharges there, so that on April 22nd, we bid farewell to approximately one hundred and fifty men from New Castle, Pa., most of whom had been in Headquarters Company. Several officers and the regular army enlisted men parted with us here."[44]

On April 26th, the regiment boarded Pullman cars one last time; they were headed west for Camp Sherman, Ohio, demobilization, and home. The Company D Log continued the story:

> "The order, "Everybody Out," had been, as a rule, a most unwelcome one in the experience of Co. "D." for it had usually been preliminary to the monotony of drill or the rigors of a long march or hike.
>
> But "Everybody Out" in the early morning of Sunday, the 27th of April, had a different significance – the end of a long journey in the army; it meant the company was again at Sherman, the starting point of its adventures and misadventures. And Camp Sherman spelled demobilization – and Home!"[45]

"A wonderful welcome met us in Cleveland, where our families and friends turned out to greet us. We were permitted to spend the night with our relatives and the following morning, April 26th, we paraded for the last time."[46]

The people of Cleveland turned out in droves to greet the returning heroes of the Italian Campaign, Major General Glenn, their former division commander, made the trip from Camp Sherman to welcome and honor them. The Cleveland Leader wrote that, "… following the biggest strictly military parade Cleveland has had since the country's entry into the world war … a silver loving cup was presented by the Sons of Italy to Col Wallace, who expressed the thanks of his men."[47]

Roberts remembered that:

> "Bombs burst in air, bells rang, flags waved, the crowds cheered from the streets and windows, and shouted greetings to relatives and friends as they marched along, and for one whole square we walked on a carpet of flowers which had been thrown by the crowds in the streets and dropped down on us from an airplane driven by Lieut. Charles Miller. No other regiment has done as much parading as the 332nd and of course the parading always caused much cheering, but none of the cheering sounded so good to us than at Cleveland, for it came from our own folks; fathers, mother, brothers, sisters, wives, sweethearts, and believe me it is indeed great to be home again and in God's country. After the parade and reception we returned to our trains where we discarded our sidearms and rifles and were given freedom of the town until 6 P.M. when we were ready to continue our trip to Camp Sherman. We left Cleveland amid the cheering of great crowds of people."[48]

Captain Story summarized the final days of the regiment. "we made our departure for Camp Sherman, our old home…We were held in Camp Sherman only long enough to close up our records and be demobilized, and on Saturday May 3rd the famous 332nd Infantry Regiment became a thing of the past."[49]

George Roberts wrote his last entry in his wartime journal before leaving for home:

> "Received my discharge and immediately started for old Columbus, Ohio, where many friends were waiting for me. No city in Europe or America ever looked so good to me as Columbus when I am once more located there. Good Old Columbus Town for me ever and always. HAPPY DAY HAPPY EVENING HOME AGAIN. Tonight before I close my eyes, I just want to realize, If this is me or someone else, Laying here without my belts. In this peaceful, quiet home, I can sleep and rest, The man who has a happy home, Is wonderfully blessed."[50]

The last line in Henry Blank's ever optimistic journal stated, "This is the Big-Day we have looked for so long. We are discharged and are now free-men and not slaves of the Military System. About a dozen of the men who left home, together are going home after one year of good screwing. It sure is great to be a "Free-Man," once more."[51]

Joseph Lettau ended his memoir:

> "Beginning on May 2nd, the first companies of the regiment received their discharge papers. On the 3rd several more went through this process and by the evening of the 5th the entire regiment had been discharged, and its members had arrived at the enviable rank of "Mister." No time was lost in boarding the special train for Columbus, home, loved ones and civilian life.
>
> Today, a few months later, the old days and adventures seem like dreams and while few would care to go through the same hardships and experiences again, not one of the regiment, I dare say, regrets the days he wore the unconquerable khaki of Uncle Sam and the proud Lion of St. Mark."[52]

The historian of Company "I" stated, "We at last separated, each man left for home, deloused, discharged and delighted."[53]

Years after the 332nd Regiments' return home to families and routines of civilian life, Colonel Wallace reflected on their experience in Italy:

> "To the opened eye and bright minded the campaign was an experience not to be purchased nor duplicated in a lifetime. Hard work! At times – yes – but none were the worse for it. And fun! – let anyone attend an annual Reunion of the Regiment, listen to the tales in the various Company orderly rooms and he will be convinced that no one died of melancholy on that tour of duty. The Italian Government … bestowed upon us an insignia The Lion of St. Marks. If occasionally any member of the 332nd. finds himself growing a little moody in contemplating that "No man is without honor save in his own country" – let him stroke our lion's golden mane and think, – rightfully, truthfully, smilingly – "We were the soul of a phantom army that saw a wonderful Kingdom arise around it and a mighty Empire crumble at its feet." "[54]

This cartoon proudly depicts the "Lion of St. Mark" insignia of the 332nd U.S. Infantry Regiment. Following the award of the insignia in March 1919, the "Lion of St. Mark" would forever be associated with the deeds of the regiment.

The regiment's standard insignia is gold bullion embroidered on red wool felt. The authors have yet to examine an attributed example using other than gold bullion embroidery. This lovely shoulder sleeve insignia became the envy of the entire A.E.F. This example of the insignia depicts a lion with a windswept mane.

After the war, Private Henry Blank donated his tunic to Military History Institute.

This detail of the tunic sleeve illustrates the use of the 332nd Regiment, 83rd Division, and Army of Occupation shoulder sleeve insignia.

A close view of the collar insignia on Blank's tunic. Note the regimental and Company "I" designation along with the stylized National Army collar disc bearing intertwined "USNA."

Another variant of the 332nd insignia.

The attached elements of the 332nd borrowed the design for their own use; this example substitutes the "332" on the bible with "AAS" denoting American Ambulance Service.

This example is one of the more standard 332nd insignia designs, probably received with the first batch of insignia purchased in Milan.

An unusual variant features an expressionless lion.

This variant depicts a smiling lion.

A slight variation of the "AAS" pattern.

Above: Another "AAS" variation.

Top right: This insignia with "ARC" in lieu of "332" was used by the American Red Cross.

Right: This uncut variant has a frowning lion. Note the cutting mark printed on the felt.

Below: Private Norman J. Riegler and some buddies from Company G, pose with local residents in Brindisi, Italy in 1918. Courtesy Military History Institute.

The standard 83rd Division insignia; embroidered on felt.

A chain Stitched on felt 83rd Division insignia.

This example uses bullion soutache to form the Ohio monogram.

Third Army's insignia; given the Armistice and the Armies' principal mission of the occupation, the insignia was formed from a monogram for Army of Occupation. Here is the standard fully embroidered example.

Another example of the Third Army insignia of much higher quality.

This beautiful example uses bullion and fine embroidery.

At Brindsi, Italy. Courtesy Military History Institute.

Major Scanland on the Canopic. Note the 332nd shoulder sleeve insignia. Courtesy Military History Institute.

Officers and nurses on the Canopic. Courtesy Military History Institute.

In sweet repose on the Canopic. Courtesy Military History Institute.

The 332nd Regimental Band playing at Camp Merritt, New Jersey. Courtesy Military History Institute.

KPs having a spud party at Camp Merritt, New Jersey. Courtesy Military History Institute.

A soldier on the Canopic shot this image of the Rock of Gibraltar. Courtesy Military History Institute.

The Duca-de-Costa in Gibraltar Harbor. Courtesy Military History Institute.

The ship that came out to meet the 332nd in New York Harbor. Courtesy Military History Institute.

Coaling the Canopic in Gibraltar Harbor. Courtesy Military History Institute.

Colonel Wallace addresses the 332nd on board the Canopic. Courtesy Military History Institute.

Merritt Hall, Camp Merritt, New Jersey. Courtesy Military History Institute.

YMCA Hostess House, Camp Merritt, New Jersey. Courtesy Military History Institute.

Souvenir hound! Courtesy Military History Institute.

On Palisade Hill, Rome. British and American soldiers visit the city. Courtesy Military History Institute.

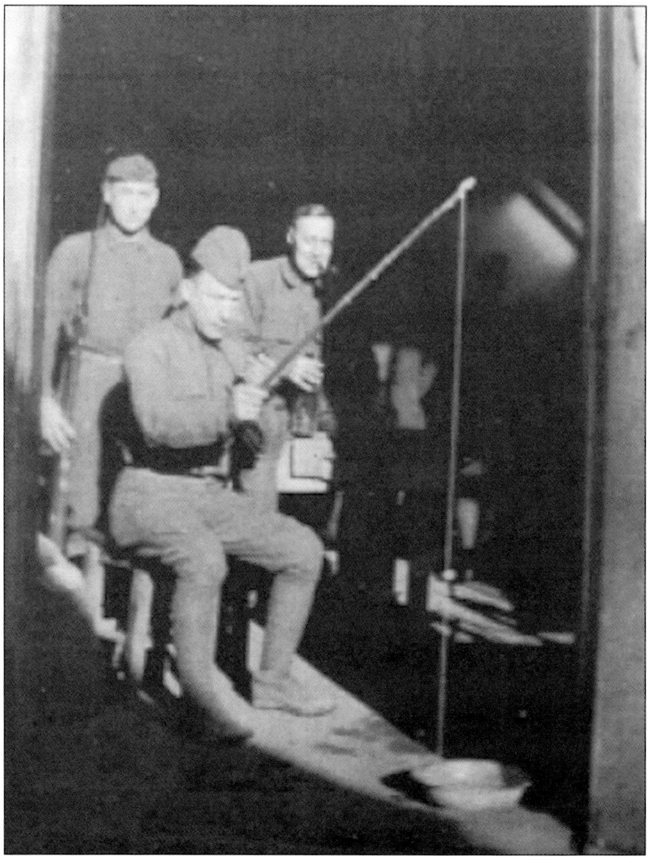

Fishing for a discharge. Courtesy Military History Institute.

Poker hounds of Company G at Camp Merritt, New Jersey. Courtesy Military History Institute.

Men of Company G mustering out. Note that several of the men are wearing all three shoulder sleeve insignia; the 332nd, 83rd Division and the Army of Occupation. Courtesy Military History Institute.

Captain J. P. Dempsey, Commander of Company G, at Camp Merritt, New Jersey. Courtesy Military History Institute.

Lieutenant G.W. Conelly, G Company, at Camp Merritt, New Jersey. Courtesy Military History Institute

Chaplain O'Heeron, Lieutenant Chamberlain and Lieutenant Coffman. Note that both Chamberlain and Coffman are wearing the 332nd Shoulder Sleeve insignia. Courtesy Military History Institute.

Lieutenant M. W. Coffman, G Company, at Camp Merritt, New Jersey. Courtesy Military History Institute.

The S.S. Canopic brought some of the boys home. Courtesy Library of Congress.

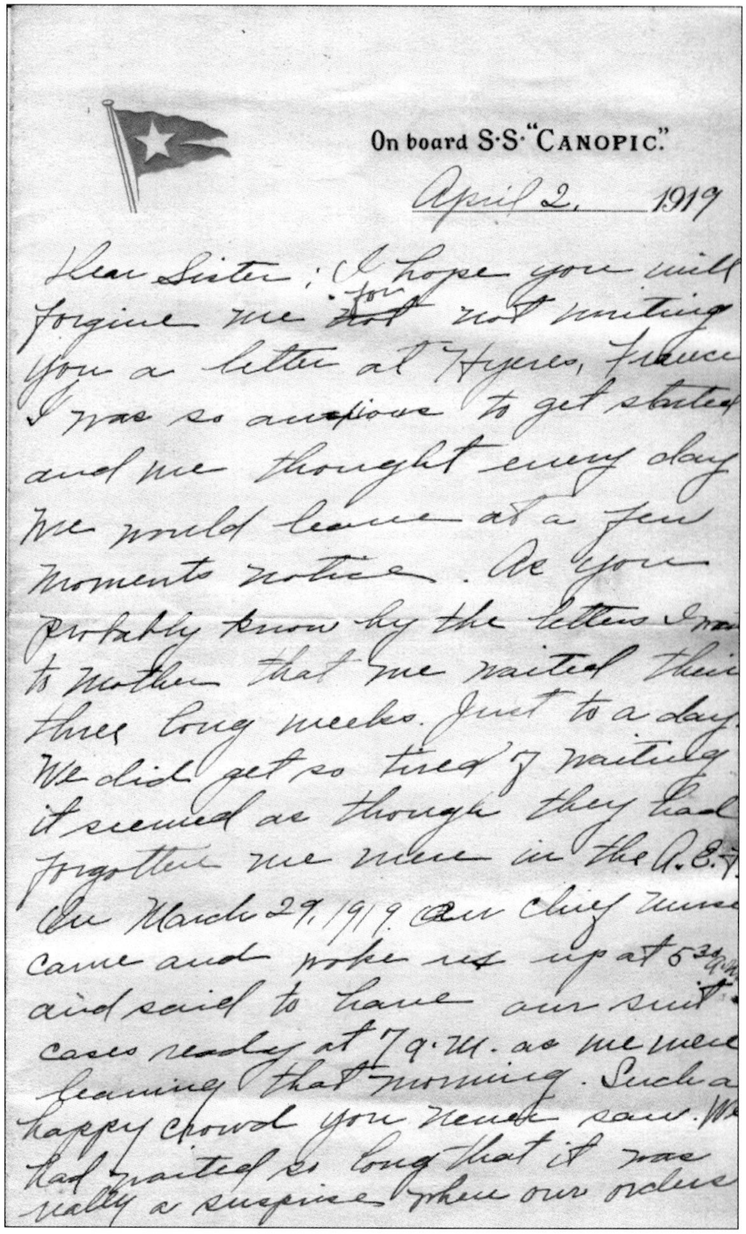

On board S·S·"CANOPIC."

April 2, 1919

Dear Sister: I hope you will forgive me for not writing you a letter at Hyeres, France I was so anxious to get started and we thought every day we would leave at a few moments notice. As you probably know by the letters I wrote to Mother that we waited there three long weeks. Just to a day. We did get so tired of waiting it seemed as though they had forgotten we were in the A.E.F. On March 29, 1919 our chief nurse came and woke us up at 5:30 a.m. and said to have our suit cases ready at 7 a.m. as we were leaving that morning. Such a happy crowd you never saw. We had waited so long that it was really a surprise when our orders

Elisabeth Lewis penned this note on Canopic stationary. Courtesy Military History Institute.

Two 332nd soldiers strike a martial pose while displaying their insignia. Courtesy Private Collection.

First Lieutenant Phillip Edwards wears his 332nd insignia in a studio photograph. Courtesy Private Collection.

Major William G. Everson, the Regimental Executive Officer, sat for this studio portrait in Genoa before returning home. Courtesy Private Collection.

In 1919, before the regiment demobilized, the officers sat for a panoramic photo at Camp Merritt. This extracted section focuses on Colonel Wallace and his field grade commanders. (front row left to right)Major Constant Southworth, Third Battalion Commander, Major Robert B. Burch, First Battalion Commander, Colonel William Wallace, Regimental Commander, Lieutenant Colonel William G. Everson, Regimental Executive Officer, an unidentified major, Major Frank M. Scanland, Second Battalion, Commander, unidentified captain. Courtesy Military History Institute.

This rare studio view shows an unknown soldier proudly displaying his 332nd, 83rd and Army of Occupation insignia upon his return to the United States. Courtesy Private Collection.

PAGE SIX. NEW YORK HERALD, TUESDAY, APRIL 22, 1919.

AMERICANS WHO HELPED TURN WAR TIDE IN ITALY PARADE FIFTH AVENUE TO CHEERS OF VAST THRONG

332ND INFANTRY MARCHING IN FIFTH AVENUE

On April 22, 1919, The New York Herald headlines touted the Regiment's accomplishments in Italy. Courtesy Military History Institute.

MR. ROMOLO TRITONI

MR. ROMOLO TRITONI PRESENTING MEDAL to COL. WILLIAM WALLACE in CENTRAL PARK. GEN. GUGLIELMOTTI on RIGHT.

COL. WILLIAM WALLACE

The Herald article prominently featured pictures of Colonel Wallace and Mr. Tritoni. Courtesy Military History Institute.

The original caption for this photograph reads: "An interesting photograph made in the courtyard of the former home of Christopher Columbus, on the occasion when a group of American doughboys took a trip to this historical spot of interest." The man on the far right and the man fourth from the right are members of the 332nd Infantry with the Lion of St. Mark insignia clearly visible. Courtesy Library of Congress.

Colonel William Wallace poses with General Guglielmotti, Military Attaché of the Italian War Mission, aboard the Duca D'Aosta on the trip back to America. Courtesy Library of Congress.

Colonel William Wallace poses aboard the Duca D'Aosta. Courtesy Library of Congress.

Left: Lieutenant Colonel William Everson aboard the Duca D'Aosta on the trip back to America. Courtesy Library of Congress.

Below: Second Lieutenant John L. Babb of Company K poses wearing his 332nd and Army of Occupation insignia. After the war, Babb lived out his years in Ohio working as an accountant. Courtesy Private Collection.

Opposite
Aboard the Duca D'Aosta, two 332nd boys in full marching order smile knowing they are finally bound for Ohio and home. The soldier on the left is wearing a Mills belt for mounted troops which incorporates the magazine pouch for the M1911 Automatic Pistol. Courtesy Library of Congress.

Opposite, top: Men of the 332nd stand along the decks of the Duca D'Aosta as she pulls into New York harbor. Courtesy Library of Congress. Bottom: Chow time on the Duca D'Aosta; 332nd soldiers eat a hot meal with other returning doughboys. The soldier on the far right wears a Fourth Corps insignia, the second soldier from the left a Sixth Division insignia and the soldier behind him sports a District of Paris shoulder sleeve insignia. Courtesy Library of Congress.

Above: Captain Lemuel N. John, Company A Commander sits with his soldiers in a company photograph. Courtesy Private Collection.

Lieutenant Babb's uniform coat; note Italian ribbon bar awarded to the members of the 332nd. This is the same uniform Lieutenant Babb is wearing in the photograph on page 208. Courtesy Private Collection.

Details of Lieutenant Babb's uniform showing the 332nd Regiment, and Army of Occupation shoulder sleeve insignia along with the red discharge stripe. The discharge stripe was worn to indicate a soldier was no longer in the Army; allowing soldiers free rail transportation and freedom from the ever vigilant Military Police. Courtesy Private Collection.

Second Lieutenant Karns of Company A, second from right, sits for a photo with some friends after his return from the war in Wooster, Ohio. Courtesy Private Collection.

Proud of his regiment, but equally happy that his Army career is at an end, private Fred G. "Harry" Reinert, packs away his 332nd tunic replete with the "Lion of St. Mark" insignia and the coveted discharge stripe; from "With the 332 Reg in Italy". Courtesy Private Collection.

Close-up of Second Lieutenant Karns; he wears the uniform illustrated above. Note the Italian War Service ribbon with black background. Courtesy Private Collection.

The regiment explored Venice prior to their homeward voyage; from "With the 332 Reg in Italy". Courtesy Private Collection.

Genoa proved to be a "real city" to the boys of the regiment; from "With the 332 Reg in Italy". Courtesy Private Collection.

Genoa's social possibilities seem limitless; from "With the 332 Reg in Italy". Courtesy Private Collection.

One of Genoa's most memorable attractions was the Staglieno Cemetery where the many elaborate sculptures awed the boys; from "With the 332 Reg in Italy". Courtesy Private Collection.

An extremely rare, 332nd Infantry Regiment painted helmet displaying the 83rd Division insignia and the "Lion of St. Mark." Courtesy Private Collection.

Below: Company L sits for a panoramic photograph before discharge from the Army at Camp Merritt. Courtesy Private Collection.

The rear of the helmet documents the travels of the regiment. Courtesy Private Collection.

Lieutenant Colonel William G. Everson was the executive officer and second in command of the regiment; in this studio portrait, he wears the 332nd Infantry Regiment and 83rd Division shoulder sleeve insignia. Courtesy Lilly Library, Indiana University, Bloomington, IN.

The uniform of Company A Lieutenant Stanley Karns; Karns wore a sewn on Italian service ribbon along with pin-back Victory and Occupation ribbons. This is the same uniform he is shown wearing on page 214. Courtesy Private Collection.

Detail photograph of Lieutenant Stanley Karns 332nd Regiment and Army of Occupation shoulder sleeve insignia; note the high quality embroidering of the Army of Occupation insignia. Courtesy Private Collection.

Company K Lieutenant John L. Babb fondly remembered the regiment in later years, this was his personalized auto plate. Courtesy Private Collection.

The Brodie helmet that Lieutenant John L. Babb wore in Italy. Courtesy Private Collection.

Company K Lieutenant John L. Babb brought this Austrian helmet back from the war. He most probably picked it up at the depot at Codroipo. Courtesy Private Collection.

Detail of the liner of Babb's Austrian helmet. The helmet shell is a German Model 1916, supplied to the Austrian Army by their allies. Austrian helmets employed a unique liner and chinstrap. This example, a combat veteran, is missing one of the head band pads – the strap is also broken. Courtesy Private Collection.

A.E.F. MAJOR KILLED; NO TRACE OF SLAYER

Frank M. Scanland of Kentucky Found Dead in Lonely Wood at Alexandria, Va.

BODY BRUTALLY BATTERED

Veteran, Gassed and Wounded in Italy, Was in Washington, Seeking Reinstatement.

Special to The New York Times.

WASHINGTON, Oct. 23.—A bruised

Just eighteen months after his return to the states, Major Frank M. Scanland's body was found in Alexandria, Virginia. Although his murder was never solved, some believed there was a direct link to the accidental shooting death of racecar driver John T. Hutchings, for which Scanland was responsible. Courtesy Private Collection

The monumental cemetery at Staglieno in Genoa. This cemetery has many remarkable funerary sculptures and was a popular attraction for the 332nd soldiers billeted in the city. Courtesy Military History Institute.

Below: This rare panoramic photograph of the officers of the 332nd Infantry Regiment was taken at Camp Merritt upon the regiment's return from Europe in 1919. Courtesy Military History Institute

Left: A stunning example of one of the sculptures at the Cimitero di Staglieno in Genoa; the cemetery was a popular attraction for the soldiers of the 332nd. Courtesy Private Collection Above: This example of funerary art from the Cimitero di Staglieno is an allegorical representation of a young maiden staring at the skull and contemplating the future that all mortals face. Courtesy Private Collection

Majors Everson and Scanland, along with several other members of the regiment, were awarded the Italian Croce al Merito di Guerra (War Merit Cross). This award, instituted by King Victor Emanuel III in January 1918, recognized acts of valor equivalent to the American Silver Star. Courtesy Private Collection

Every member of the regiment received the Medaglia Dell Guerra 1915-1918 (War Medal 1915-1918). This medal was awarded to any person serving on the Italian front during the war. The regiment was awarded the medal after it was instituted in July 1920; replacing the "Macaroni Ribbon" that they received while in the Italian theater. Courtesy Private Collection

Corporal, Roy A. Sheil of Company H embossed the cover of his meat can (mess kit) to commemorate his travels and adventures with the regiment. Sheil joined the regiment at Camp Sherman, Ohio in September 1917 and remained with the unit until demobilization. Note the private purchase folding cup and unique homemade fork and spoon combination. Courtesy Private Collection.

The men of Company F held a reunion at Brady Lake in 1925; Lieutenant Rendigs was in attendance. He is seated in the top row, third from the left with the other company officers. Courtesy Rendigs, Fry, Kiely & Dennis, LLP.

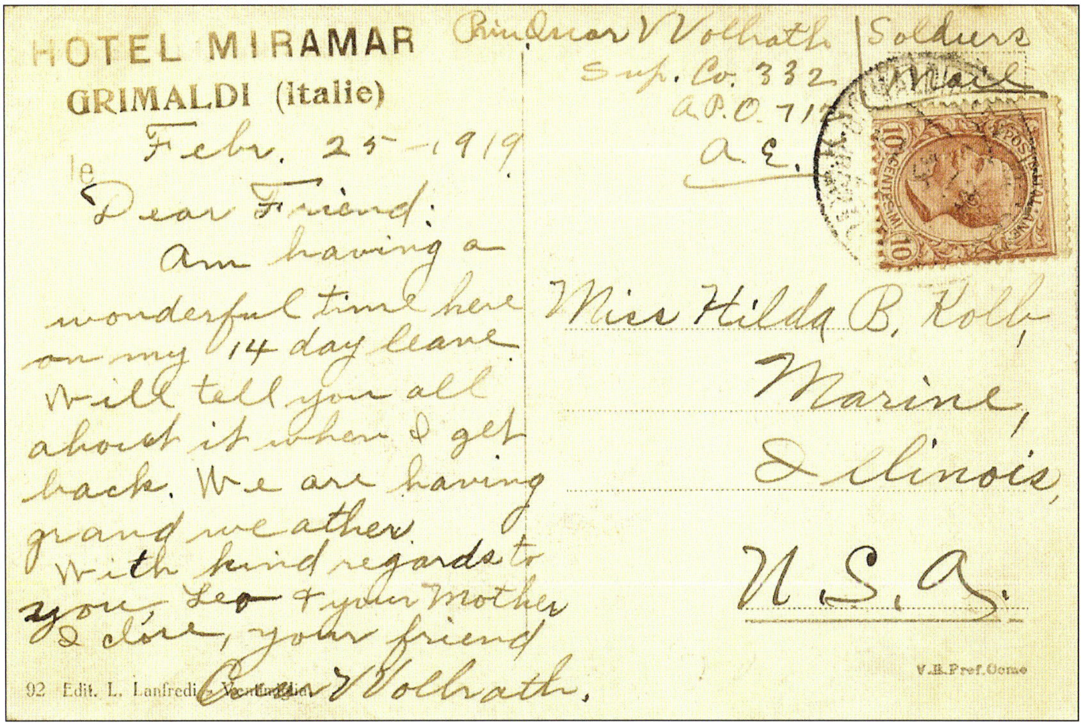

HOTEL MIRAMAR
GRIMALDI (italie)

Feb. 25-1919

Dear Friend:
Am having a wonderful time here on my 14 day leave will tell you all about it when I get back. We are having grand weather.
With kind regards to you, Leo & your Mother I close, your friend
Oscar Vollrath.

Pvt. Oscar V Vollrath
Sup. Co. 332
A.P.O. 71
A.E.

Soldiers Mail

Miss Hilda B. Kolb,
Marine,
Illinois,
U.S.A.

92 Edit. L. Lanfredi

V.E.Pref.Ocme

Private Oscar Vollrath of the Supply Company reported that he was "having a wonderful time" at the Hotel Miramar where the regiment stayed before boarding ships for home. Courtesy Private Collection.

This unidentified medical sergeant displays the regiment's shoulder sleeve insignia. Courtesy Private Collection.

The 332nd was authorized to wear the Victory Medal with two bars: Vittorio-Veneto and Defense Sector. Here is an example belonging to a soldier in the regiment. Courtesy Private Collection.

All other troops assigned to Italy, including those in Base Section 8, wore the Victory Medal with only the Italy bar, 332nd soldiers were not authorized wear this bar. Courtesy Private Collection.

Right: This view of the shoulder sleeve insignia of L Company cook Elmer I. Thompson shows how the 83rd division insignia was trimmed to accommodate the application of the 332nd regiment and Army of Occupation insignia. Courtesy Private Collection.

332nd Reunion medal. The cord colors represent Italian service. Courtesy Private Collection.

Details of 332nd Reunion medal. Courtesy Private Collection.

M Company commander Captain McKinney's presentation watch. Courtesy Jack McKinney.

Appendices

Appendix 1
Roster of the 332nd Regiment from the 1926 Reunion.

REVISED CONSTITUTION
--- of the ---
332nd INFANTRY ASSOCIATION
(Adopted at Columbus, Sept. 5, 1926)

• • •

ARTICLE I

The name of the Association is The 332nd Infantry Association.

ARTICLE II

The purpose of this Associaion shall be to further and encourage loyalty so the Flag of the United States, to promote good fellowship and mutual assistance between former members of the 332nd Infantry, United States Army, and to preserve the records and memories of the service and experience of this Regiment in camp and field during the World War.

ARTICLE III

Any person who has been enrolled as a member of the 332nd Infantry, U. S. A., ar any time during the years 1917-1919 may become a member of this Association on the payment of dues in the sum of $2.00 per annum. The privilege of membership is extended to include anyone who had been enrolled as a member of tbe 331st Field Hospital during its service in Italy.

ARTICLE IV

The Executive Officers of the Association shall be a Chairman, Vice- Chairman, Stcretary, and Recorder, who, except the Recorder, shall be elected at the annual meeting of the Associ~ation. Each Company and the Medical Detachment shall be entitled to appoint one Council Delegate. Such appointments shall be made by each of said units not later than the time of the annnal meeting of the Association, but, if not so made, such delegates may be appointed by the other members of the Council. The Executive Officers and the delegates shall be elected for one year and shall a serve until their successors are elected and qualified.

ARTICLE V

The Executive Officer, and the Delegate, shall constitute the Council. The Council shall be the governing body of this Association, when this Association is not in session, the Executive Officers shall exercise all the powers of the Council between its meetings. The Council may adopt bylaws for its own government and shall appoint a Recorder who shall be custodian of the funds of the Association and of its records, and from whom a bond may be required. He may be paid a reasonable compensation in the discretion of the Council. The Council may also appoint from time to time assistant officers, standing committees, local and ocher repreaenratives as it may judge appropriate.

ARTICLE VI

This Constitution may be amended ar any Annual Meeting of the Association by a two-thirds vote of those present.

• • •

NAMES *and* ADDRESSES *of* OFFICERS *and* MEN WHO SERVED *in the* 332nd INFANTRY REGIMENT

OFFICERS

Alfs, William F. 4217 28th St., Cincinnati, Ohio.
Alston, Harry G., 3401 Shadeland Ave., Pittsburgh, Pa.
Alvord, Claude B., 1980 Ford Drive, Cleveland, Ohio.
Babb, John L., 109 W. Water St., Troy, N. Y.
Bayles, Leo W., 2588 Glenmawr Ave., Columbus, Ohio.
Beery, Harold, 76 Mill River Ave., Rockville Center, L. I., N.Y.
Bentley, Lloyd W., 1823 Roxiord Rd., East Cleveland, Ohio.
Berry, Clarence F., St. Paris, Ohio.
Blair, Guy M., 703 Washington St., Portsmouth, Ohio.
Blumenstiel, Frederic I., 9 B. Liberty St., Springfield, Ohio.
Bourbon, Rolle P., 3811 College Ave., Kansas City, Mo.
Brand, Garnett W., 317 Reynolds St., Urbana, Ohio.
Bratt, Harry C., 4 Mendenhall Ave., Dayton, Ohio.
Brock, Ray M., 209 Central Ave., Dayton, Ohio.
Burch, Robert B., 3135 Menlo Ave., H. P., Cincinnati, Ohio.
Buser, Oliver J., West LaFayette, Ohio.
Caplan, Prank, 208 Vicksburg Ave., Detroit, Mich.
Carroll, Humbert J., 4220 B. 98th St.
Chamberlain, Harold F., 221 N. Professor St., Oberlin, Ohio.
Crouch, Lawrence A., 448 W. Water St., Kalamazoo, Mich.
Childers, Arthur, Jackson, Ky.
Cless, George H., Jr., Worthington, Ohio.
Clinger, Ralph H., Upper Sandusky, Ohio.
Coffin, William M., 1032 Russell Ave., Covington, Ky.
Coffman, William M., 217 B. Northwood Ave., Columbus, Ohio.
Cone, Don H., 578 Scioto St., Urbana, Ohio.
Conelly, George W., 15309 Maculey Ave., Cleveland, Ohio.
Copelan, Robert W., 4314 Langland St., Cincinnati, Ohio.
Craig, Samuel A., Jr.. 800 Wheeling Ave., Cambridge, Ohio.
Crawford, William F., East Ohio Gas Co., Cleveland, Ohio.
Dennison, David S., Sunnyside, Poland, Ohio.
Davidson, Harold M., 11915 Ashbury Ave., Cleveland, Ohio.
Dederich, Robert J., 2619 Scootwood Ave., Toledo, Ohio.
Dempsey, John P., 1618 Hollyroad Rd., Cleveland, Ohio.
DeWerif, Henry A., Farina, Ill.
Donahoe, Joseph 0., 2412 N. Alabama St., Indianapolis, Ind.
Dunbar, Donald 0., 619 Parl Ave., Meadville, Pa.
Edwards, Philip P., 261 W. Lorain St., Oberlin. Ohio.
Ervein, Clarence W., Ogontz, Pa.
Everson, William G., 2448 Mound Ave., Norwood, Ohio.
Flannery, Thomas, 1104 Sexton Ave., Cincinnati, Ohio.
Geowey, Washington I., Jr., 227 Hamilton St., Albany, N. Y.
Gravely, Spottswood F., '794 B. Patton St., Danville, Va.
Grossman, Abraham B., 10519 Pasadena Ave., Cleveland, Ohio.
Hamilton, Herman R., 10326 St. Clair Ave., Cleveland, Ohio.
Havemann, Felix T., 623 Boone St., Piqua, Ohio.
Higgins, Frank J., Jr., 640 Howard Ave., New Haven, Conn.
Higinbotham, Fay, Bridgeport, W. Va.
Hird, James P., 16010 Detroit Ave., Lakewood, Ohio.
Hooper, Arthur L., Dillonvale, Ohio.
Hill, Howard R., 373 Washington Ave., Brooklyn, N. Y.
Huddleson, Harvey W., 3905 Kansas Ave. NW., Washington, D. C.
Irwin, John W., Seaman, Ohio.
John, Lemuel N., Morgantown, W. Va.
Johns, Wallace W., 427 Seventh St., Huntington, W. Va.
Jones, Edward A., Clayville, N. Y.
Karns, Stanley, 902 Mulberry St., Springfield, Ohio.
Keifer, Horace 5., 1230 E. High St., Springfield, Ohio.
Kelley, Frederick 0., Billings, Mont.
Kennedy, Earl B., 9 S. Main St., Findlay, Ohio.
Klingler, Ralph R., Ada, Ohio.
Krum, Charles L., 622 Leader Bldg., Cleveland, Ohio.
Lytle, Lafayette D., 6635 Washington Blvd., St. Louis, Mo.
McConnell, James R., Macksburg, Ohio.
McGowan, Robert R., 1037 LaBelle Ave., Steubenville, Ohio.
McGraw, Andrew J., 57 Broadway Ave., Taunton, Mass.
McKinney, Jasper, 375 Boulevard, Akron, Ohio.
McLain, Chester A., 1572 Massachusetts Ave., Cambridge, Mass.
McMaster, Earl B., 1528 W. Market St., Steubenville, Ohio.
Mackay, Alfred B., 30 F. 58th St., New York, N. Y.
Maurer, Edgar W., 1414 Rockefeller Bldg., Cleveland, Ohio.
Moldrum, Douglas C., 2100 Surrey Road, Cleveland, Ohio.
Menees, Thomas W., 148 Fifth Ave., North Nashville, Tenn.
Miller, Floyd V., 21 W. Euclid Ave., Springfield, Ohio.
Miller, John W., 3435 Cornell P1., Cincinnati, Ohio.
Minkle, Frank, Fairmont, North Dakota.
Mock, John E., Hays, Kansas.
Moldenhauer, Arthur, 1704 W. Marquette Rd., Chicago, Ill.
Moore, John R., 304 W. Washington St., Medina, Ohio.
Munsick, David R., 596 S. Prospect, Maplewood, N. J.
Myers, Elbron H. B., 9814 Marietta Ave., Cleveland, Ohio.
Nearn, Alfred C., Halls, Tenn.
Oberlin, Benjamin C., 1012 Walnut Ave. N.E., Canton, Ohio.
O'Donnell, Charles L., Notre Dame, Ind.
O'Heoron, John K., 8 N. First St., Columbia, Mo.
Quensen, John F., 19 Jeffress St., South Boston, Va.
Ramsey, John R., Huntington, W. Va.
Ranney, Percival K., 12556 Lake Ave., Cleveland, Ohio.
Rendigs, August A., Jr., 6315 Grandvista Ave., Cincinnati, Ohio.
Robbins, William H., 300 E. High St., Springfield, Ohio.
Rubin, David, 2052 F. 82nd St., Cleveland, Ohio.
Sargent, John C., corner Center and Sargent Sts., Marion, Ohio.
Scanland, Frank M., Youngstown, N. Y.
Seymour, Kenneth L., Ramond, Ill.
Smith, Ray F., Burrows, Ind.
Smith, Robert O., 434 Main St., Conneaut, Ohio.
Southworth, Constant, 1st Nat'l Bank Bldg., Cincinnati, Ohio.
Spaulding, Carrie A., 51 5. Main St., Frankfort, Ind.
Speakman, Harold, 43 Washington Square, New York, N. Y.
Stathers, Birk S., Weston, W. Va.
Stathers, William C., Clarksburg, W. Va.
Stern, Louis IL, 3457 Buffalo Ave., Chicago, Ill.
Story, Austin P., 147 Caldwell St., Chillicothe, Ohio.
Strouse, John N., Pine City, New York.
Sullivan, Charles J., 2219 N. 42nd St., Seattle, Wash.
Tippy, Thurman J., Tippecanoe City, Ohio.
Trik, Carl H., 502 Queen Lane, Philadelphia, Pa.
Vail, Herman L., 8406 Euclid Ave., Cleveland, Ohio.
Vorys, Webb I., 441 E. Town St., Columbus, Ohio.
Wallace, William, Fort Leavenworth, Kansas.
Whionery, Karl F., Supt. of Schools, Sandusky, Ohio.
Wigdahl, Almer B., Moorland, Iowa.
White, Wilbur M., 316 5. Plum St., Springfield, Ohio.
Williams, Clarence H., 1322 Sloane Ave., Lakewood, Ohio.
Wilson, Frank B., 726 11th St., Wilmette, Ill.
Yetter, Estel H., 621 Stanley Ave., Middletown, Ohio.

HEADQUARTERS COMPANY

Acker, William, Montgomery, N. Y.
Allum, Robert C., 111 S. Morgan Ave., Waynesburg, Pa.
Ames, Clarence F., 68 N. Summit St., Akron, Ohio.
Angelo, Peter, 1734 F. 19th St., Cleveland, Ohio.
Anderson, Harry K., 4623 Pierce Ave., Cleveland, Ohio.
Art, Jacob, 329 Tuscarawas St. B., Canton, Ohio.
Armacost, Harold, 2360 Eastern Ave., Cincinnati, Ohio.
Allen, Earnest L., 233 Locust St., Marysville, Ohio.
Aigler, Alfred, 215 Kilbourne St., Bellevue, Ohio.
Amann, Joseph, 393 Oakhill Ave., Youngstown, Ohio.
Bailey, Robert, 3129 Warsaw St., Toledo, Ohio.
Ballard, Robert, 210 High Ave. S. W, Canton, Ohio.
Barnthnuse, Herbert, 543 S. Jefferson St., Montpelier, Ind.
Barach, Samuel, 1009 John St., Cincinnati, Ohio.
Bauer, Arnold, Brooklyn Station R. D. No. 1, Cleveland, Ohio.
Bayless, Elmer, Wakeinan, Ohio.
Berger, Charles, 130 5. Beaver St., Wooster, Ohio.
Bing, Ross, 524 N. 3rd St., Barberton, Ohio.
Blackburn, Floyd, 219 F. Portage St., Cuyahoga Falls, Ohio.
Blakey, Harlan P., W. Monroe St., Pawnee, Ill.
Bloom, Thomas, Swanton, Ohio.
Blubaugh, Sylvester R., R. F. D. No. 1, Buckeye City, Ohio.
Booth, Orvill A., R. F. D. No. 2, Black Run, Ohio.
Borman, Earl 0., 3446 Colerain Ave., Cincinnati, Ohio.
Bossong, Walter J., 3383 Detroit Ave., Toledo, Ohio.
Bottlander, Jacob J., Ford City, Pa.
Boughton, Elbert C., Lakemore, Ohio.
Bower, Carl C., Box No. 56, Costar, Ohio.
Bowman, Rollie K., Arlington, Ohio.
Boyle, Hugh, 18 Third St., E. Youngstown, Ohio.
Brindle, John C., Connellsville, Pa.
Brothers, Randall L., E. Market Ext., East Akron, Ohio.
Buck, Edmond, 1375 Myrtle Ave., Cincinnati, Ohio.
Butz, Elmer T., 73 5. 6th St., Kenmore, Ohio.
Bronton, James. Hemlock, Ohio.
Butler, George T., R. F. D. No. 10, Cuyahoga Falls, Ohio.
Cale, Edgil L., Caldwell, Ohio.
Callihan, Harry L., Chicora (Ohio), Pa.
Carl, William C., 126 N. Broadway, Geneva, Ohio.
Carver, Benjamin, R. F. D, No. 1, Marietta, Ohio.
Cattrell, Ephriam S., Toronto, Ohio.
Cheney, Theodore R., 212 Spring St., East Liverpool, Ohio.
Chenoweth, Max, 37 S. Warren Ave., Columbus, Ohio.
Clifford, Earl C., 91 N. 2nd St., Cuyahoga Falls, Ohio.
Cline, Faunt L., R. F. D. No. 3, Sardis, Ohio.
Cocumelli, John, 321 Hill Ave., Steubenville, Ohio.
Colgrove, Floyd R., Mt. Oliver Station, Pemberville, Ohio.
Colton, Leo A., 121 Rosswell St., Akron, Ohio.
Colvin, Earl, 393 5. Arlington St., Akron, Ohio.
Connely, Harold, 961 F. McMillon, Cincinnati, Ohio.
Comer, Elmer N., New Paris, Ohio.
Converse, Samuel R., 1555 State St., Westerville, Ohio.
Coomer, James H., Bernside, Ky.
Corey, Charles F., Winterdale, Pa.
Courtney, James, R. F. D. No. 11, Cuyahoga Falls, Ohio.
Crawford, Forest, R. F. D. No. 3, Woodsfield, Ohio.
Crayne, Leslie J., Waynesburgh, Pa.
Critchfield, Walter R., 50114 Second St., Barberton, Ohio.
Cross, Arthur, R. F. D. No. 5, Memphis, Tenn.
Cruise, Edward M., 137 Carst St., Dayton, Ohio.
Davis, Edward L., 133 Therman St., Zanesville, Ohio.
Davidson, John J., R. F. D. No. 2, Toronto, Ohio.
Deedlow, Henry W., 6718 Bonna Ave. N. B., Cleveland, Ohio.
Dambach, Wilbert, 224 4th St., Ellwood City, Pa.
Dickerhoof, Edward, 21 N. Howard St., Akron, Ohio.
Dickinson, Earl, New Virginia, Iowa.
Diehl, Carl, 405 W. High St., Springfield, Ohio.
Dietrick, Emil, 311 N. Mill St., Massillon, Ohio.
Dillon, Ray, 920 Scovill Ave., Cleveland, Ohio.
Dixon, Henry 825 Kelley Ave., Springfield, Ohio.
Dodt, Eugene, 3132 Hackberry St., Cincinnati, Ohio.
Donaldson, Harry A., 528 Hazel Ave., Ellwood City, Pa.
Dormish, Joseph, 432 Boliver Lake Ave., Barberton, Ohio.
Dotson, Edmond B., Creenwood, W. Va.
Downer, Marshall A., Sawyerwood, East Akron, Ohio.
Dreisbach, Andrew, 183 Frederick St., Barberton, Ohio.
Dresser, Clarence L., 19 N. Balch St., Akron, Ohio.
Duggan, Stanley, 66 Frost Ave., Frostburg, Md.
Dunn, John, 717 Poster St., Youngstown, Ohio.
Dunn, Frederick W., North River Road, Route 6, Warren, Ohio.
DiCrecoq, Francis, 228 5. Main St., Akron, Ohio.
Eastland, Elmer C., Macedonia, Ohio.
Edwards, Wilson, R. P. D. No. 1, Sunbury, Ohio.
Eckroad, Lawrence C., 248 Cuyahoga Palls Ave., Akron, Ohio.
Eghert, John L., R. F. D. No. 16, Everett, Ohio.
Elder, Alexander D., 104 Range St., Barberton, Ohio.
Elliott, Paul, Delroy, Ohio.
Ellis, Charles, Roxbury, Ohio.
Emch, Joseph D., Youngstown, Ohio.
Enfield, William F., R. F. D. No. 24, Delta, Ohio.
Englehardt, August F., care of Police Station, Youngstown, Ohio
Falknor, Walter C., 101 5. High St., Covington, Ohio.
Filter, Raymond 0., 718 Second St., Milwaukee, Wis.
Fitzgerald, Samuel, Old Washington, Ohio.
Fix, William J., 1623 Caroll St., Cincinnati, Ohio.
Fox, Alfred, R. F. D. No. 33, Barberton, Ohio.
Frank, Charles M., 1389 F. Market St., Akron, Ohio.
Frazier, Lon, Leslie, Georgia.
French, Clifton D., Mt. Gilead, Ohio.
Freeman, Abe L., 2260 B. 85th St., Cleveland, Ohio.
Freudmann, Karl F., 1511 B. Market St., Akron, Ohio.
Gensner, Carl F., 800 5. Third St., Columbus, Ohio.
Gascoyne, William M., 320 First St., Barberton. Ohio.
Geduldig, Charles, 9503 Bessemer Ave., Cleveland, Ohio.
Gibbons, Charles C. Rockport, Ind.
Gibbons, Thomas M., 8902 Meridian Ave., Cleveland, Ohio.
Gilmore, Marquis B., Millersburg, Ohio.
Gilson, Karl W., 2024 Glenwood Ave., Toledo, Ohio.
Gloer, Lawrence, R. F. D. No. 3, Fremont, Ohio.
Gibbon, Frank M., 1025 Himrod Ave., Youngstown, Ohio.
Green, Hiram W., New Straitsville, Ohio.
Green, Ray J., Sebring, Ohio.
Gross, Bdward J., Monroeville, Ohio.
Hall, Earl K., 4224 29th St., Oakley, Cincinnati, Ohio.
Hall, Frank, Woodsfield, Ohio.
Harding, Claude W., 2082 W. 81st St., Cleveland, Ohio.
Hanna, Robert, Hillcrest Ave., New Castle, Pa.
Haren, Richard L., 1141 Fulton St., Akron, Ohio.
Hartung, Paul W., 2810 Tuscarawas St., Canton, Ohio.
Harrison, Donald B., 3210 Chestnutdale Ave. S. W., Cleveland, Ohio.
Hays, Francis M., 314 Ave. D, San Antonio, Texas.
Healy, Thomas B., 2983 B. 57th St., Cleveland, Ohio.
Henning, C., 996 Snyder St., Akron, Ohio.
Henrich, Ernest F., Newcomerstown, Ohio.
Herman, Henery L., R. F. D. No. 1, Gibsonburg, Ohio.
Hess, Frank, Jr., 686 Sumner St., Akron, Ohio.
Headrick, Edmond, P. 0. Box 297, East Akron, Ohio.
Hille, Herman J., 208 Washington St., Ironton, Ohio.
Himelright, Ray, R. F. D. No. 11, Akron, Ohio.
Hogsett, Otis C., 968 Fifth Ave., Akron, Ohio.

Homan, Albert F., Tiffin, Ohio.
Hopfe, Roy F., 308 Collins Ave., Columbus, Ohio.
Hudson, Roy F., 35 June Ave., Akron, Ohio.
Hunt, Carl R., R. F. D. No. 10, Cuyahoga Falls, Ohio.
Hunt, Cregory, 927 Court St., Fremont, Ohio.
Hyde, James E., R. F. D. No. 8, Cuyahoga Falls, Ohio.
James, William E., Jr., Brownsville Rd., Mt. Oliver Sta., Pittsburgh, Pa.
Johnson, Charles S., Lakeside, Ohio.
Johnson, mvan C., 249 Berman Ave., East Akron, Ohio.
Jones, Hester C., 308 Calhoon St., Mt. Vernon, Ohio.
Johnson, Chalmers A., 74 Lavelette Ave., Elkins, W. Va.
Julanus, James F., 27 Rockingham St., Cambridge, Mass.
Kammer, Ferdinand L., 334 5. Main St., St. Marys, Ohio.
Kaye, Adam, 416 S. Walnut St., Ravenna, Ohio.
Keeper, William P., Jr., 18406 Melville Rd. N. F., Cleveland, Ohio
Kelleher, Daniel B., R. F. D. No. 31, Copley, Ohio.
Kimble, Ira m., Trinway, Ohio.
Kinch, Paul B., 435 Main St., Hamilton, Ohio.
Knott, William D., 1212 Hickory St., Fremont, Ohio.
Knowlton, Harry D., Mogadore, Ohio.
Koester, Clarence L., 1116 Michigan St., Toledo, Ohio.
Kottka, Leopold F., 724 Allen St., Akron, Ohio.
Krause, Martin M., 3116 W. 17th Place, Cleveland, Ohio.
Keener, Ernest J., 309 Wood St., Paynesville, Ohio.
Lafalce, Joseph, 365 E. Federal St., Youngstown, Ohio.
Leach, Lyell B., 549 Warren Ave., Youngstown, Ohio.
Lee, Frank T., R. F. D. No. 2, Mechanscstown, Ohio.
Lennig, Clarence R., 1619 Hudson Ave., New Castle, Pa.
Leonard, Samuel, R. F. D, No. 4, Canton, Georgia.
Lettau, Joseph L., 461 Edward St., Youngstown, Ohio.
Linder, Henry L., R. P. D. No. 17, Everett, Ohio.
Little, Delbert, Old Fort, Ohio.
Lorman, Edward, Cleveland, Ohio.
Ludwig, John, 746 Sophia St., East Liverpool, Ohio.
Lutz, Jay L., Ira, Ohio.
Lorenz, Alfred C., 1029 Franklin St., Fremont, Ohio.
McAvinew, Charles, 84 22nd St., W. Kenmore, Ohio.
McCleary, Ralph M., 221 Park Way. Akron, Ohio.
McIntyre, Bert, Creston, Ohio.
McIntyre, Lawrence A., 307 Sturges Ave., Mansfield, Ohio.
McKillop, William, 902 5. Main St., Akron, Ohio.
McKitrick, Charles A., R. F. D. No. 1, Amlin, Ohio.
McManus, George, 923 Alger St., Fremont, Ohio.
Marcellus, Elton L., Clayton, New York.
Marschand, Philip A., East Orwell, Ohio.
Mathis, Walter L., 4929 Plainfield Pike, Madisonville, Ohio.
Maute, William A., 1519 Pearl St., Springfield, Ohio.
Meister, Harry C., 7th St., Marietta, Ohio.
Merchant, Monroe F., Sharpsville, Pa.
Miller, John H., 4566 E. 71st 5t., Cleveland, Ohio.
Minchm, Ernest L., Whipple, Ohio.
Monok, John, Marblehead, Ohio.
Morris, Thomas C., Peninsula, Ohio.
Mound, Frank, Gen. Delivery, Youngstown, Ohio.
Osterhoudt, Harry C., 875. Park St., Chicago, Ill.
O'Leary, Joseph F., 402 N. Cedar St., New Castle, Pa.
Ostrom, Archie L., Cardington, Ohio.
Overholt, John, 159 Beck St., Wadsworth, Ohio.
Overly, Frederick J., Grand Rapids, Ohio.
Owens, Thomas B, 625 W. 8th St., Lorain, Ohio.
Painter, Albert D., R. F. D. No. 1, Bluifton, Ohio.
Palazzesse, Cuiseppe, 2151 Murray Hill, Cleveland, Ohio.
Palmer, Carl, Ellett, Ohio.
Parker, Charles J., 423 7th St., Batberton, Ohio.
Payn, George H., 48 Royal Place, Akron, Ohio.
Perenoud, Albert T., 1028 Melchior Place S. W., Canton, Ohio.
Petee, Walter C., 1007 Patton St., Toledo, Ohio.
Pool, Michael, R. P. D. No. 3, Russellville, Ohio.
Peters, Russell E., 94 Oviatt Place, Akron, Ohio.
Post, Arthur R., North Canton, Ohio.
Preston, Roy F., care of H. C. Preston Co., New Castle, Pa.
Pritchard, Edward D., 509 Waldow St., New Castle, Pa.
Purviance, Carroll M., 767 N. 8th St., Steubenville, Ohio.
Paavola, Alex, 949 Trombly Ave., Detroit, Mich.
Peloro, Marco, Glouster, Ohio.
Rake, Raymond, R. F. D. No, 1, Tulsa, Okla.
Rannells, Edward W., 219 Stanton Ave., Springfield, Ohio.
Reid, Arthur R., R. F. D. No. 5, Napoleon, Ohio.
Rhode, Julius C., 235 Glenwood Ave., Akron, Ohio.
Richards, DeForest A., 1761 F. 31st St., Lorain, Ohio.
Richards, Ralph B., care of B. P. 0. E. 982, Barberton, Ohio.
Richards, James A., Box 1030, Glouster, Ohio.
Richert, Russell F., 2724 Faust St., Kenmore, Ohio.
Rossi, Salvatore, 6418 St. Clair Ave., Cleveland, Ohio.
Rittemeyer, Harry M., 4236 Bertus St., North Avondale, Cincinnati, Ohio.
Roesch, Ralph J., 915 A St., Sandusky, Ohio.
Rothgary, Edward, Fremont, Ohio.
Rummell, Dana H., 2234 Hanniford, Norwood, Ohio.
Rummell, John E., 70 Bllenwood, Youngstown, Ohio.
Rupert, John, 314 W. Center St., Barberton, Ohio.
Ryan, Thomas J., 3532 Main Ave., Evanston, Cincinnati, Ohio.
Sabovik, Joseph J., 20004 Elwell Ave., Cleveland, Ohio.
Salewsky, John D., 714 Spring Ave. N. E., Canton, Ohio.
Sayger, Charles S., Hamilton, W. Va.
Sciance, Floyd, R. P. D. No. 1, Fleming, Ohio.
Schell, Benjamin B., West Alexander, Ohio.
Schmidt, John, Marblehead, Ohio.
Scott, Robert I., 518 Ross St., Steubenville, Ohio.
Schrimplin, Fred, 1396 Wooster St., Barberton, Ohio.
Schweitzer, Richard, 12319 Fairport Ave., Cleveland, Ohio.
Shafer, Thomas, 225 Indiana Ave., Sebring, Ohio.
Sheppard, Chester R., Station L, R. R. No, 7, Cincinnati, Ohio.
Sharp, Oliver L., Zaliski, Ohio.
Sheets, Benjamin H., 408 W. State St., Fremont, Ohio.
Sheka, Andrew F., Patton, Pa.
Sherman, Chester C., Lime City, Ohio.
Seiberling, Charles W., Medina Road, Akron, Ohio.
Smale, Alfred R., Rochester, N. Y.
Smith, Edgar A., Helena, Ohio.
Smith, Harold C., 2010 W. Fremont St., Massillon, Ohio.
Smith, William T, 1027 Spring Ave. N. E, Canton, Ohio.
Snyder, David C., Peninsula, Ohio.
Snyder, Ward C., Box 688, Kenmore, Ohio.
Sorrell, Charles, Scranton, Ky.
Sprague, Welland C., 128 N. Church St., Bowling Green, Ohio.
Sprague, George W., R. P. D. No. 3, Willoughby, Ohio.
Stalter, William M., 374 W. Third St., Columbus, Ohio.
Stella, Carlo, 2505 E. 39th St., Cleveland, Ohio.
Stephenson, Carry B., 16 Walker St., Athens, Ohio.
Stine, Claude S., Burgoon, Ohio.
Stoner, Samuel A., R. F. D. No. 1, Jamestown, Ohio.
Stowe, Fred V., 3519 Sheridan Rd., Youngstown, Ohio.
Straka, Thomas W., Toronto, Ohio.
Stuckey, Carl C., 125 Mugs St., Sandusky, Ohio.
Thinnes, George P., 999 Seventh Ave., East Akron, Ohio.
Tomlinson, Otto L., 617 Richmond St., Cincinnati, Ohio.
Tovey, Albert B., North Manchester, Ind.
Trumphour, Walter G., 2628 Kentucky Ave., Kenmore, Ohio.
Tucker, John R., 207 W. Baird St., Barberton, Ohio.
Ulmer, Earl F., Marietta, Ohio.
Walcutt, William, Toboso, Ohio.
Walls, Arthur, 4530 Lafayette Ave., Norwood, Ohio.
Watson, Charles M., R. F. D. No. 1, Kensington, Ohio.
Wendt, Walter C., 522 Reese St., Sandosky, Ohio.
Wight, Archie, Millbury, Ohio.
Wildermuth, Charles D., 739 Creen St., Marietta, Ohio.
Wirsch, Frank J., 3557 W. 88th St., Cleveland, Ohio.
Woolsey, Pierce B., 112 Montrose Ave., Delaware, Ohio.
Wulfekuhi, Francis H., 10058 Flint St., Cincinnati, Ohio.
Wilhelm, Arthur H., 37 5. 22nd St., Kenmore, Ohio.
Wilson, Fred C., 517 W. Madison Ave., New Castle, Pa.
Wolfe, Earl L., 130 W. Martin St., East Palestine, Ohio.
Wheeland, Earl, 727 Adam St., Chillicothe, Ohio.
Whinnery, Herman B., Salem, Ohio.
Wulfekoetter, Werner C., 1317 Myrtle Ave., Cincinnati, Ohio.
Yager, Charles C., 1074 Lane St., Akron, Ohio.
Yackee, Albert A., 125 Range St., Barberton, Ohio.
Yeck, Fred C., 412 Polk St., Sandusky, Ohio.

MEDICAL DETACHMENT

McGraw, Andrew J., 57 Broadway, Taunton, Mass.
Bentley, Lloyd W., 1625 Roxford Rd., Cleveland, Ohio.
Brossman. Abraham B., 10519 Pasadena Ave., Cleveland, Ohio.
Irvin, John W., Sugartreeridge, Ohio.
Stern, Louis N., 8457 Buffalo Ave., Chicago, Ill.
Berry. Clarence P., St. Paris, Ohio.
Bower, John W., R. F. D, No. I, Kilibuck, Ohio.
Boothe, Benjamin 0., 35 E. Evergreen Ave., Youngstown, Ohio.
Cogsil, Alexander F., Kilgore, Ohio.
Coleman, Ralph E., R. F. D. No. 2, Scio, Ohio.
Cresdor, Lawrence D., Winigan, Mo.
Dissinger, Kirby 0., R, F. D. No. 2, Lake, Ohio.
Everett, Wade D., R. F. D. No., 2, Tyrrell, Ohio.
Fuerst, William A., 1927 Hewitt Ave., Cincinnati, Ohio.
Hold, Donald D., 867 W. Market St., Akron, Ohio.
Herring. William 0., Madison Ave. and Joseph St., Mt. Healthy, Ohio.
Hornberger, Jay W., 397 W. Lora Ave., Youngstown, Ohio.
Hunter, Albert M., R. F. D. No. 55, Sharpsville, Pa.
Jenkins, William, 903 Michael P1. S. W., Canton, Ohio.
Johnston, Frank, Carrollton, Ohio.
Johnston, John J., 1019 Orange St., Youngstown, Ohio.
Krebill, Alfred L., R. F. D. No. 4, Louisville, Ohio.
Leigiminger, Loran B., West Lafayette, Ohio.
Levi, Ruby, 2017 Cherry St., Toledo, Ohio.
Linesch, Joseph A., 109 Washington Ave., St. Bernard Station. Cincinnati, Ohio.
Linchester, Warren L., Ganfield, Ohio.
Meyer, J. Wagnew, Bellefontaine, Ohio.
Miller, Joseph L., Woodrow, Pa.
Moore, Glen J, Lola, Ohio.
Myers, Oral H., 885 F. Main St., Columbus, Ohio.
McCrystal, Thomas R., 815 Connecticut Ave. N. W., Washington, D. C.
McMahon, Arthur F., 265 Miles Ave., Akron, Ohio.
Richards, Charles, Malvern, Ohio.
Schram, George L., 2516 Ritchie Ave., Cincinnati, Ohio.
Sieber, Francis J., 769 Wayne St., Walnut Hills, Cincinnati, Ohio.
Smith, John 5., 219 S. Irvine Ave., Sharon, Pa.
Speraw, Walter N., Coalton, Ohio.
Spoon, Byron C., Forrest, Ohio.
Tate, Joseph M., Bowerston, Ohio.
Toddings, Henry C., 251 F. Lorraine St., Oberlin, Ohio.
Wall, Turner W., Hoytville, Ohio.
Warner, Daniel I., R. F. D. No. 1, Delroy, Ohio.
Watkins, Jasper, McGuffey, Ohio.
Wellington, Frank C., 55 W. South St., Warren, Ohio.
Wilson, Wilbur B., Canfield, Ohio.

A COMPANY

John, Lemuel Nimrod, Morgantown, W. Va.
Alvoid, Claude Bradford, 1980 Ford Drive, Cleveland, Ohio.
Karns, Stanley, 1233 W. Pleasant St., Springfield, Ohio.
Moore, John Ray, 304 W. Washington St., Medina, Ohio.
Moore, Roy B., 206 Adams St., Steuhenville, Ohio.
Allen, Arthur, 1118 Dewey Ave., New Castle, Pa.
Anderson, Earl R., Plymouth, Ohio.
Anderton, Arthur M., Moore, Pa.
Ashbridge, Edward L., 1050 Collingswood St., Akron, Ohio.
Aust, George A., 4030 Bank St., Cincinnati, Ohio.
Aust, James M., 620 Belvaire Rd., Cleveland, Ohio.
Baker, Thomas M., Buchtel, Ohio.
Banzhaf, Fred, 3426 Brotherton Rd., Cincinnati, Ohio.
Barlow, Eugene C., 351 W. Ninth St., Elyria, Ohio.
Barthold, George J., 153 McDowell Ave., Steubenville, Ohio.
Bates, Albert, 807 Highland Ave., Steuhenville, Ohio.
Bearmann, Harry, corner Langland and Glen Parker Ave., Cincinnati, Ohio.
Bennett, Ralph, Penn St., Pa.
Benson, Arney A., 385 Alney Ave., Manon, Ohio.
Berk, Svan, 298 Poland Ave., Struthers, Ohio.
Berninger, Herman, 4338 Lexington Ave., St. Louis, Mo.
Berry, Noff C., 401 Coshocton Ave., Mt. Vernon, Ohio.
Bilkey, Maurice L., South Euclid, Ohio.
Bird, Harry L., Hanlin Station, Pa.
Black, Ralph W., 94 Stew St., Cuyahoga Falls, Ohio.
Blanding, Ford, P. 0. Box 237, Phoenix, R. I.
Beckhoefer, William J., 2201 Victor St., Cincinnati, Ohio.
Beedicker, Clayton L., 885 Avon St., Akron, Ohio.
Bowman, Ode, Alliance, Ohio.
Bradley, F., R. F. D. No. 1, Pulaski, Pa.
Brashear, Harry C., 609 Spring St., Steubenville, Ohio.
Brueggman, Walter L., Sebring, Ohio.
Bronie, Fred, R. F. D. No. 2, Alliance, Ohio.
Buck, Ray, 618 Johnson St., Akron, Ohio.
Buck, William B., 4421 N. Artesian Ave., Chicago, Ill.
Buckingham, Clark, Loveland, Ohio.
Buckles, John H., Jefferson, Ohio.
Buehler, Frank H., R. P. D. No. 3, B. Patterson St., Alliance, Ohio.
Buescher, Robert W., 1607 Mansfield St., Cincinnati, Ohio.
Buene, Broni R., 78 Furnace St., Akron, Ohio.
Byars, Claborn lvi., 114 Rush St., Elyria, Ohio.
Cady, Loran C., R. F. D. No. 3, Buffalo Center, Iowa.
Callihan, Howard B., South Portsmouth, Ky.
Cann, Charles B., Box 454, Windber, Pa.
Cataldo, Vincent, 2831 N. 39th St., Cleveland, Ohio.
Chvatal, Charles C., 500 Lamson Ave., Bedford, Ohio.
Clay, Stephen M., 921 Portage St., Gallitria, Pa.
Coghlan, James B., 260 Furnace St., Elyria, Ohio.
Conley, George E., 68 Franklin Ave., Salem, Ohio.
Connor, Daniel F., 176 Lincoln Park Drive, Youngstown, Ohio.
Conroy, David R., 212 S. Sixth St., Steubenville, Ohio.
Coon, George R., P. 0. Box 53, Elyria, Ohio.

Correy, Eugene J., 252 Lake Ave., Conneaut, Ohio.
Costello, James L., 11 York St., Ashtabula, Ohio.
Daltorio, L. Dominick, 139 Hall St., Kent, Ohio.
Dawson, Samuel, 500 Gridley Ave., Akron, Ohio.
Defendifer, Benjamin, Center St., Struthers, Ohio.
Deluse, Harry C., 117 E. McMicken Ave., Cincinnati, Ohio.
Dibble, Frank C., 208 Woodbine Ave., Struthers, Ohio.
Dunlevy, Roscoe A., 730 N. Fourth St., Steubenville, Ohio.
Ernst, John N., Rd. L, Sardinia, Ohio.
Faidley, Pete L., R. F. D. No. 1, Markletown, Pa.
Falce, Vincenzo, 84 Furnace St., Akron, Ohio.
Feldman, Albert P., 1622 Highland Ave., Cincinnati, Ohio.
Ferguson, Clifford, R. F. D. No. 2, Prichard, W. Va.
Finney, John B., 2008 F. Furnace St., New Castle, Ind.
Fithian, Lewis A., Box 21, Poland, Ohio.
Floyd, Roscoe, 50 F. Market St., Akron, Ohio.
Forssell, Herbert G., Box 4, Broadacre, Ohio.
Frazzer, Craig W., 1528 Ridge Ave., Steubenville, Ohio.
Fuque, Oscar, 73 S. Sixth St., Kenmore, Ohio.
Gaffney, Stephen J., 422 McFarland Ct., Akron, Ohio.
Gallabrose, Michael, 146 N. Seventh St., Steubenvilie, Ohio.
Goetz, Joseph P., 1018 B. Kentucky St., Louisville, Ky.
Goodfriend, Nathan H., Mingo Junction, Ohio.
Gordon, Charles, 531 Hilker St., Youngstown, Ohio.
Grant, William M., 109 N. Third St., Cuyahoga Falls, Ohio.
Graul, Harry W., 939 N. Seventh St., Steubenville, Ohio.
Gribble, Booth F., Akron, Ohio.
Hainzel, William J., 106 Columbus St., Massillon, Ohio.
Hannan, James P., Gen. Delivery, Youngstown, Ohio.
Heiner, August, 1029 Casseplia St., Elkhart, Ind.
Herbruck, Earl J., 1311 17th St. N. W., Canton, Ohio.
Hippely, Amos A., R. F. D. No. 6, Salem, Ohio.
Henigsfeld, Leo, 1715 Parkwood Drive, Cleveland, Ohio.
Irvin, Stanley P., Griffith, Ind.
Jackson, Thomas, Neshobe, Miss.
Jenkins, William, 302 B. Liberty St., Gerard, Ohio.
Jewett, Ralph, Furnace Run, Pa.
Johnson, Alva L., Allentown, Mo.
Johnston, Wiofield O., 113 Adolph Ave., Akron, Ohio.
Jones, Alonzo W., Sylacauga, Ala.
Jones, Roy C., R. F. D., Sugar Creek, Ohio.
Juroka, John, 1738 W. Gladstone St., Youngstown, Ohio.
Keeshan, Frank A., 635 W. McMillen St., Cincinnati, Ohio.
Kelly, Ceciel, 31 S. Ninth St., Kenmore, Ohio.
Kennedy, Raymond, Laman, Ind.
Kieffer, Herman R., Georgetown, Ohio.
Kimmel, Clyde A., 42 Lily St., Mansfield, Ohio.
Kinnear, Russell, 2131 F. 83rd St., Cleveland, Ohio.
Kenicek, Yaroslav, 2899 E. 14th St., Cleveland, Ohio.
Leighten, Frank C., P. 0. Box 81, Mansquan, N. J.
Leiberth, George J., 205 Peste St., Cincinnati, Ohio.
Liederbaugh, James J., 11400 Woodland Ave., Cleveland, Ohio.
Linten, Peral E., R. F. D. No. 1, Nelsonville, Ohio.
Lewry, William J., 1844 Huron Ave., Cincinnati, Ohio.
Lyttle, Oscar, 75 Hamilton Ave., Akron, Ohio.
Maag, John, 1349 Emma St., Youngstown, Ohio.
Mall, Frederick, 1632 Vine St., Cincinnati, Ohio.
Mallies, Paotelis, 1571 B. 16th St., Cleveland, Ohio.
Mallos, Nick J., 58 Tod Lane, Youngstown, Ohio.
Mathias, Berman B., Windsor Hotel, Akron, Ohio.
Mauthe, Howard A., 3107 Jefferson Ave., Cincinnati, Ohio.
McDowell, Samuel B., 606 F. Oak St., Massillon, Ohio.
Mcintosh, Sidney W., 420 W. Chase St., Pensacola, Fla.
McNamara, John P., 9814 Heath Ave., Cleveland, Ohio.
Miller, Paul M., 438 N. Eighth St., Barberton, Ohio.
Mills, George P., R. R. No. 3, Forest, Ave., Maysville, Ky.
Moon, Ruffus, 320 N. Eighth St., Barberton, Ohio.
Marrow, Custer A., R. F. D. No, I, Roundbottom, Ohio.
Moser, Francis I., 212 Church St., St. Bernard, Ohio.
Muehlenhad, Herman F., 43 Maple Ave., Mt. Healthy, Ohio.
Neff, Edwin M., 154 Greenfield St., Tiffin, Ohio.
Nere, Thomas, 221 Crescent St., Bellaire, Ohio.
Neioaber, George F., 2022 Western Ave., Cincinnati, Ohio.
O'Here, William P., 1318 Kensington Ave., Youngstown, Ohio.
Orr, Walter C., 814 Leader Bldg., Cleveland, Ohio.
Orth, Otto F., 450 F. Water St., Chillicothe, Ohio.
Otto, Albert A. C., 966 Windsor St., Cincinnati, Ohio.
Page, Harry., 847 Washington Ave., Chillicothe, Ohio.
Pape, Theo. W., 115 Pearl St., Reading, Ohio.
Pappenetti, Angelo C., 260 Race St., Newark, Ohio.
Pawlowski, Frank, 40 Bridge St., Struthers, Ohio.
Perkins, Hugh V., R. F. D. No, I, Prairie Depot, Ohio.
Pealer, Frank M., Galloway, Ohio.
Perren, Albert C., 242 Ford Ave., Barbertoo, Ohio.
Pinnell, Earnest, Flemington, W. Va.
Pittman, Arthur, 316 Julian Ave., Akron, Ohio.
Pontius, George J., 618 Sixth N. W., Canton, Ohio.
Percellio, James, 44 Ferrington St., Ashtabula, Ohio.
Postle, Lawrence F., 712 F. Howard St., Mt. Vernon, Ohio.
Powell, Joseph J., R. F. D. No. 1, Nelsonville, Ohio.
Raff, George H., Rittman, Ohio.
Ray, Clarence F., 613 Hickory St., Roaring Springs, Pa.
Redington, Glen A., Kent, Ohio.
Reis, George S., R. F. D. No. 2, Amherst, Ohio.
Rethmeier, Edgar P., 1630 Sycamore St., Cincinnati, Ohio.
Rhine, Francis W., R. F. D. No. 2, Lake, Ohio.
Robbins, Albert F., 422 Page Ave., Barberton, Ohio.
Robbins, Leslie C., 91 Park St., Ashtabula, Ohio.
Robbinson, Dennis, Piney Creek, Pa.
Rochow, Lawrence, 65 Willis Ave., Youngstown, Ohio.
Rogman, Albert F., Stop 6, Euclid Ave., Euclid, Ohio.
Rohrbaugh, Mervin J., R. F. D. No. 1, Poland, Ohio.
Roll, Harrison M., 441 Kemper Ave., St. Bernard, Ohio.
Roziak, Andro T., 2622 B. 11th St., Cleveland, Ohio.
Roth, Alfred A., 1430 Jefferson Ave., Reading, Ohio.
Rothius, William H., 1010 Chapel St., Cincinnati, Ohio.
Rowan, Fllsworth, 175 E. Main St., Chillicothe, Ohio.
Roy, James C., 443 10th St. N. B., Washington, D. C.
Rudge, James F., 231 Custer Ave., Youngstown, Ohio.
Ruffman, Frank C., 390 Jackson St., Conneaut, Ohio.
Runyan, Stephen G., R. F. D. No. 8, Athens, Ohio.
Ruthenberg, Carl F., 795 Beacon St., Akron, Ohio.
Sanda, Emil, 3351 W. 95th St., Cleveland, Ohio.
Saperiti, Antonio, 18 Cross St., Akron, Ohio.
Sauer, Albert J., 2425 Fairview Ave., Cincinnati, Ohio.
Scearce, Joe L., 9 San Marco St., Cincinnati, Ohio.
Scheumann, Marcus C., 1502 Merrimac St., Cincinnati, Ohio.
Schimweg, Frank, 415 Dorchester Ave., Cincinnati, Ohio.
Schmidt, Francis X., 1741 Erie St., Toledo, Ohio.
Schreiver, Harry, 224 Walnut St., Reading, Ohio.
Schwietering, Joseph F., 1002 Hatch St., Cincinnati, Ohio.
Sebulsky, Abe, 3847 Wood St., Wheeling, W. Va.
Seiter, William Omar, Main Dana Ave., Cincinnati, Ohio.
Sekarak, John, 77 W. Washington St., Struthers, Ohio.
Shaffer, Leslie, 15 Penn Ave., Youngstown, Ohio.
Seibenaller, Harry, 114 Nichols St., Fostoria, Ohio.
Simkins, Charlei, 226 Broad St., Struthers, Ohio.
Sinsebaugh, Karl F., cor. Ridge and Oakwood Ave., Newark, Ohio.
Smisek, Edward, 4418 Bouse Ave., Cleveland, Ohio.
Sellars, Elwood, 1137 Grace St., Akron, Ohio.
Spinney, Leo J., 512 Prospect Place, Avondale, Cincinnati, Ohio.
Stanton, Clarence H., 2500 Melrose Ave., Cincinnati, Ohio.
Stark, Samuel R., 1333 W. Market St., Steubenville, Ohio.
Stedenfeld, Clifford, 2332 Muriel Court, Cincinnati, Ohio.
Steele, Clarence F., 194 Madeiar St., Chillicothe, Ohio.
Stege, Crist P., Buchtel, Ohio.
Stieber, Robert L., 1712 Madison Road, Cincinnati, Ohio.
Stegewald, George R., 3629 Clarion Ave., Cincinnati, Ohio.
Strader, Oran W., 194 Westwood Ave., Akron, Ohio.
Strehmaier, Charles N., 1019 Dayton St., Cincinnati, Ohio.
Schwarti, John F., 1215 North Bend Rd., Cincinnati, Ohio.
Stroup, Frank F., Hawthorn, Pa.
Stroup, John Albert, 1711 Madison Rd., Cincinnati, Ohio.
Sullivan, Harold M., 247 W. Eighth St., Trenton, N. J.
Sullivan, Joseph J., 1056 Symmes, Cincinnati, Ohio.
Sunthimer, William G., R. P. D. No. 8, Cuyahoga Falls, Ohio.
Tate, George H., 556 Lincoln Ave., Cincinnati, Ohio.
Taylor, Jesse, R. F. D. No. 4, Salem, Ohio.
Todarelie, Frank C., R. F. D. No. 17, Box 163, Grove City, Pa.
Towne, Albert, R. F. D. No. 2, Box 270, Amherst, Ohio.
Traber, William, Jr., 500 Milton St., Cincinnati, Ohio.
Turner, Harold R., 219 Euclid Ave., Greenville, Ohio.
Unger, Clarence A., 175 W. Ohio Ave., Sebring, Ohio.
Urban, Daniel F., 1077 Taylor Rd., South Euclid, Ohio.
Wlahos, Harry J., 2200 Prospect Ave., Cleveland, Ohio.
Wade, John B., 3114 Glender Ave., Cincinnati, Ohio.
Wagers, George C., Millersburg, Ohio.
Walton, Charles F., 671 E. River St., Elyria, Ohio.
Warden, James E., Conneaut, Ohio.
Weaver, Charles F., 844 Livingstone Ave., Columbus, Ohio.
Weaver, Wilson J., 111 Norman St., Barberton, Ohio.
Weeks, R., Box 5, 162 Furnace St., Akron, Ohio.
Weisgerherm, Albert J., 594 Rockdale Ave., Cincinnati, Ohio.
Werbrouck, Victor, 692 Winchester St., Monroe, Mich.
Workinger, George F., Route 37, Clinton, Ohio.
Wright, Harley A., Sarcoxil, Mo.
Yeter, Crist R., 348 School St., Cuyahoga Falls, Ohio.
Zadamsky, Joseph, 5010 Guy S. B., Cleveland, Ohio.
Zakoscielny, Walter, 1380 5. Aubin St., Detroit, Mich.
Zeisler, John F., 2836 Highland Ave., Cincinnati, Ohio.
Zelinsky, Dan S., Berea, Ohio.
Zellner, Sam F., R. R. 12, Box 124, Cincinnati, Ohio.
Zimmerman, Eugene, Harrison, Ohio.
Zink, Fred, 3315 Wabash Ave., Cincinnati, Ohio.

B COMPANY

Havemann, Felix T., 514 W. Green St., Sauna, Ohio.
Williams, Clarence H., 1322 Sloane Ave., Lakewood, Ohio.
Tippy, Thurman J., Tippecanoe City, Ohio.
Abrams, Charles W., 148 Park Place, Painesville, Ohio.
Aker, Russell B., New Paris, Ohio.
Altier, Louis, 1340 Madison Ave., Youngstown, Ohio.
Anderson, Heory G., 6 Scoville Ave., Ashtabula, Ohio.
Arthur, Michael J., 1408 Erie St., Toledo, Ohio.
Baldelli, Nello, 123 Oklahoma St., Youngstown, Ohio.
Barker, Robert, 3413 Highview Ave., Cleveland, Ohio.
Benjamine, Doran, 28 Cook St., Akron, Ohio.
Besilius, Edward, 3914 Ontario St., Toledo, Ohio.
Baitian, Ernest O., 3051 W. 15th St., Cleveland, Ohio.
Biehl, Charles W., Youngstown, Ohio.
Birkmeyer, Julius B., Coldwater, Ohio.
Blair, Floyd, Westerville, Ohio.
Blandiinski, Earnest, 418 Russell St., Toledo, Ohio.
Bodrock, John, 4312 Orchard Ave., Cleveland, Ohio.
Boothe, Lee, Uler, W. Va.
Brady, Verna, 448 N. Main St., Marion, Ohio.
Brands, Bernard B., R. F. D. No. 1, Box 8, Tampa, Fla.
Brokamp, Harry A., 1622 Baymiller St., Cincinnati, Ohio.
Brown, Allen H., 518 W. Thornton St., Akron, Ohio.
Brunetti, Antonio, 241 F. Bayeo Ave., Youngstown, Ohio.
Brunswick, Charles, 418 Albert St., Youngstown, Ohio.
Buehler, John, R. F. D. No. 3, Alliance, Ohio.
Burfield, Loy F., R. P. D. No. 1, Cutler, Ohio.
Busche, Ross H., New Matamoras, Ohio.
Campagna, Fresmo, 712 Dewey St., Martins Perry, Ohio.
Cannon, Ralph 0., 49 Oak Park, Youngstown, Ohio.
Clawson, Donald W., 342 Ruchel Road, Akron, Ohio.
Collett, Jerry C., Elkins, W. Va.
Connor, Raymond N., 3880 W. 83rd St., Cleveland, Ohio.
Conrad, Bernard J., Aahville, Pa.
Conroy, John, 30 Cleveland St., Youngstown, Ohio.
Coombs, Harley A., Chagrin Falls, Ohio.
Coombs, Jack, Chagrin Falls, Ohio.
Cooper, James U., 1709 Shorb Ave. N. W., Canton, Ohio.
Cousin, John, Struthers, Ohio.
Cowie, Thomas F., 452 F. York St., Cleveland, Ohio.
Cregon, George W., 41 Colorado St., Ashtabula, Ohio.
Crissinger, Wilbur P., Box 528, Lowellville, Ohio.
Cunningham, William F., 424 Canton St., Youngstown, Ohio.
Dehiof, John, Patton, Pa.
Davis, Lunn J., Washingtonville, Ohio.
Diefenderfer, Ross H., Pine St., Struthers, Ohio.
Detty, Charles H., Box 83, Gillespieville, Ohio.
Donovan, John J., 1915 Sanders St., Helena, Mont.
Dyer, Walter B., 1615 Hollenden Ave., Cleveland, Ohio.
Edwards, George, 3502 Summit Ave., Toledo, Ohio.
Erck, Franklin P., Jr., 921 Fourth St. N. W., Canton, Ohio.
Erhart, John, R. R. No. 6, Brookwell, Ind.
Fabian, Andy, 52 Morelay Ave., Youngstown, Ohio.
Fanto, Harry, 1629 Iron St., Youngstown, Ohio.
Feezel, Riley L., 51 Cotter Ave., Akron, Ohio.
Fisher, Frank T., R. F. D. No. 2, Sylvania, Ohio.
Plorine, Victor, S. Martha Ave., Akron, Ohio.
Ford, Raymond J., 23 W. Frankfort St., Columbus, Ohio.
Fox, Henry L., 8 Lockwood St., Ashtabula, Ohio.
Frazee, Willard C., 27 Todd St., Youngstown, Ohio.
Fry, Monroe A., Benton, Ohio.
Gabriel, Leo B., 861 5. Main St., Cuyahoga Falls, Ohio.
Garwacki, Edward, 342 Moss St., Toledo, Ohio.
Gates, Charles 5., 545 Shepard St., Columbus, Ohio.
Gelhard, Max J., 242 Cypress Ave., Columbus, Ohio.
Gording, Albert J., 3014 Poe Ave., Cleveland, Ohio.
Ging, Charles A., Kelleyburg, Pa.
Grieshaber, James H., 917 W. Park St., Columbus, Ohio.
Grimsley, Roy B., Box 82, Lakemore, Ohio.
Groff, Walter G., 526 Third St., Columbus, Ohio.
Haddox, Harry M., R. F. D. No. 4, Youngstown, Ohio.
Hagert, Edward F., 426 Arbor Rd., Cleveland, Ohio.
Harper, Walter W., 31 W. Prospect St., Akron, Ohio.
Hausman, Morris H., 2339 E. 46th St., Cleveland, Ohio.
Hawley, Andrew, Kittaoning, Pa.
Heath, Harry L., 428 Cleveland St., Toledo, Ohio.
Heck, John E., Gen. Del., Youngstown, Ohio.
Heinze, William J., Jr., 2318 Forestdale Ave., Cleveland, Ohio.
Helmink, Peter J., 3144 W. 58th St., Cleveland, Ohio.

Henley, Huber L., 2601 Chase St., Toledo, Ohio.
Herling, Frank L., 2217 W. 65th St., Cleveland, Ohio.
Hook, Floyd W., Ashville, Ohio.
Horn, Lenville, 2166 Fastern Ave., Cleveland, Ohio.
Howard, Edgar , R. F. D. No. 3, Marietta, Ga.
Hughson, Roswell W., P. 0. No. 7, Akron, Ohio.
Huosicker, Thomas W., 998 LaCroix St., Akron, Ohio.
Jeffries, Frank J., 637 Crouie St., Akron, Ohio.
Jenkies, Jackson S., 1855 F. 167th St., Cleveland, Ohio.
Johnson, Charles F, Patton, Pa.
Johnson, Melvin, 318 Simpson St., Clarksburg, W. Va.
Jones, Clarence E., Crystal Springs, Miss.
Jones, Howard, Mineral Ridge, Ohio.
Jones, Robert W., 107 Cleveland Ave., Columbus, Ohio.
Kauderer, Paul R., 788 5. Third St., Columbus, Ohio.
King, Joseph, 578 City Park Ave., Columbus, Ohio.
Kirkpatrick, Raymond K., Decatur, Ohio.
Knapik, John A., 392 Broad St., Struthers, Ohio.
Kowiiks, Joe, 497 F. 32nd St., Cleveland, Ohio.
Kuhn, Frank, 2394 W. 32nd St., Cleveland, Ohio.
Lambright, Frank, 36 Hart Pl., Akron, Ohio.
Land, Edward J., 1128 Gilbert St., Cincinnati, Ohio.
Lockliter, Edwin P., 38 Jason Ave., Columbus, Ohio.
Lemke, August J., Martin, Ohio.
Lemrich, Edwin H., 594 5. Park St., Columbus, Ohio.
Leone, Joseph, 820 S. Mercer St., New Castle, Pa.
Levandowski, Edward G., 369 W. 31st St., Cleveland, Ohio.
Lewis, Byrd R., Box 44, Shippenville, Pa.
Liogenfolter, Scott, R. F. D. No. 1, Roaring Springs, Pa.
Longe, Waclaw, 3694 B. 87th St., Cleveland, Ohio.
Lynch, Joseph A., 937 McDonald St., F. Liverpool, Ohio.
Maag, George P., 1549 Emma St., Youngstown, Ohio.
Miller, Harry M., R. F. D. 4, Youngstown, Ohio.
Minotti, Giovenni, c/o Peter Julius, Youngstown, Ohio.
Moore, Scott, Xenia, Ohio.
Muench, Stuart L., 897 S. Park St., Columbus, Ohio.
Mulhall, Dennis, R. F. D. No. 2, N. Lima, Ohio.
Myers, Charles S., Dixie, W. Va.
McCall, Harry, Dilliard, Ohio.
McCormick, Albert H., P. 0. Box 207, Youngstown, Ohio.
McCoy, Earl, Murray City, Ohio.
McChee, Harry, Williamsport, Ohio.
McKeeo, Paul B., 393 N. 10th St., Newark, Ohio.
McKee, Alfred L., Conoeaut, Ohio.
McKenzie, John C., Crosstown, Md.
McKinney, Grover C., Grove City, Ohio.
McPheil, William, Florida Ave., Sebring, Ohio.
Nicholoau, Nestor, P. 0. Box 61, Barbertoo, Ohio.
Nobill, Milio, 5678 F. 7lst St., Cleveland, Ohio.
Nyc, Harold R., 1004 Clark St., Akron, Ohio.
Ody, Robert, 208 Kelley Ave., Akron, Ohio.
O'Leery, Daniel, Gen. Del., Akron, Ohio.
Olsewski, Ben, Stewartsville, Ohio.
Oppelt, Oscar J., 1924 Montrose Ave., Cincinnati, Ohio.
Ord, Clyde 0., Henderson, W. Va.
Palmer, Earl, 717 Lawrence Rd., Canton, Ohio.
Patterson, James B., Killbuck, N. Y.
Pesk, William R., 546 Walnut St., W., Canton, Ohio.
Pfeiffer. Albert F., 132 Pearl St., Columbus, Ohio.
Pfaffenberger, John G., 1822 St. Johns Ave., Toledo, Ohio.
Pidick, Mike, 119 Bridge St., Struthers, Ohio.
Platt, Richard, Sheppard, Ohio.
Poole, Edwin J., Grappes Bluff, La.
Pugh, David J., 1474 B. Long St., Columbus, Ohio.
Quails, Charles R., Wheatland, Md.
Rattenberg, Robert, 2669 Bouidnot Ave., Cincinnati, Ohio.
Beardon, Joseph D., 239 W. Rich St., Columbus, Ohio.
Reedy, George C., Box 186, Lowellville, Ohio.
Reedy, John J., Box 186, Lowellville, Ohio.
Reid, Herbert A., Ashville, Ohio.
Reinert, Fred G., 3832 Carlyle Ave., Cleveland, Ohio.
Reiss, Fred A., 1424 Fifth Ave. N., Canton, Ohio.
Rice, Owen, 1346 W. Third St., Dayton, Ohio.
Riedel, Frank R., 2894 York Ave., Cleveland, Ohio.
Rinaz, Rudolph, 3109 Barber Ave., Cleveland, Ohio.
Roach, Lynn R., R. F. D. 9, Box 8, Toledo, Ohio.
Romeo, Sam, 65 E. 11th St., Youngstown, Ohio.
Roner, William, 1001 Albany St., Schenectady, N. Y.
Rorabeck, Orrin A., R. F. D. No. 9, Cuyahoga Falls, Ohio.
Ross, Lester F., Warriors Mark, Pa.
Rossi, John, Jackson St., Lowellville, Ohio.
Ruby, James F., Lowellville, Ohio.
Ruggles, Ivan B., Andrews, Ind.
Russell, Randall A., 1631 Champlain St., Toledo, Ohio.
Russell, Albert, 1226 Quebec Rd., Cincinnati, Ohio.
Rutowski, Stanley, 2642 Chestnut St., Toledo, Ohio.
Samstag, Jacob J., 2142 W. 41st St., Cleveland, Ohio.
Saunders, Curtis L., Adylett, N. C.
Sauvain, Charles F., 556 F. Market St., Akron, Ohio.
Schenk, William, Beloit, Ohio.
Schmitt, John R., 219 B. Beck St., Columbus, Ohio.
Schneider, George J., 4117 Brooklyn Ave., Cleveland, Ohio.
Schwindling, Joseph, 677 Bowery St., Akron, Ohio.
Seidensticker, William L., 629 S. Third St., Columbus, Ohio.
Sevotino, Luino, 1929 W. Market St. Louisville, Ky.
Shaughnessy, Richard P., 1920 W. Market St., Louisville, Ky.
Sheely, Paul, New Springfield, Ohio.
Sheppard, Homer L., R. R. No. 1, Quaker City, Ohio.
Sheff, John E., R. R. 1, Hazelton Br., Youngstown, Ohio.
Shorey, Frank F., 207 Roberts St., Baltimore, Md.
Shrader, Brown D., 127 Pine St., Wadsworth, Ohio.
Skaggs, Leroy, 46 N. Front St., Columbus, Ohio.
Smith, Cecil M., 38 S. Newberry, Cuyahoga Falls, Ohio.
Sopkvich, Mike, R. F. D. No. 1, Lowellville, Ohio.
Smolark, Joseph, 29 McClure St., Struthers, Ohio.
Spealman, Robert R., Holmesville, Ohio.
Spennay, Aaron D., Middlepoint, Ohio.
Spitzer, George W., 71 Jewett St., Akron, Ohio.
Stevens, Ernest R., Senecaville, Ohio.
Spooner, Lucius S., Cumberland, Ohio.
Stiles, Dell S., R. D. No, 2, Pomeroy, Ohio.
Straub, Herman F., 174 Ira Ave., Akron, Ohio.
Strong, Virgil F., 1805 Vassar Ave., Cleveland, Ohio.
Stren, Edward, 30 N. Garfield Ave., Youngstown, Ohio.
Succop, Charles H., 827 St. Clair St., Pittsburgh, Pa.
Sundell, Gustave A., 1495 Hildroth Rd., Columbus, Ohio.
Swain, Francis F., 43 Chicago St., Columbus, Ohio.
Taylor, Harold B., 223 Springfield St., Dayton, Ohio.
Thorne, Allen G., 14th and Virginia Ave., Sebring, Ohio.
Thornton, Charles A., 115 Martin Ave., Columbus, Ohio.
Todsen, Albert W., 3306 Stickhey Ave., Toledo, Ohio.
Tope, Shorley W., 926 High Ave., N. W., Canton, Ohio.
Toper, Frank A., Slanesville, W. Va.
Tustin, William L., Ashville, Ohio.
Utterback, Carl B., 1017 16th St., Canton, Ohio.
Veno, Daniel, 852 Oak St., Youngstown, Ohio.
Wack, Luther 0., Poland, Ohio.
Warkunes, William, 3307 Devoy Rd., Cleveland, Ohio.
Weaver, Harry R., R. F. D. No, 1, Albany, Ind.
Webb, Harry F., 136 Randolph St., Columbus, Ohio.
West, Harrison G., 2840 Julian Ave., Youngstown, Ohio.
White, Chester K., 1493 F. Market St., Akron, Ohio.
Whitman, James M., 412 13th St., Meridian, Miss.
Wiggioa, David L., Indiana, Pa., R. F. D. No. 3.
Wilcox, Bert, 827 Page St., Toledo, Ohio.
Williams, Herbert L., Jamestown, Ohio.
Williams, Walter, 332 S. Truesdale, Youngstown, Ohio.
Winters, Robert F., 152 C Ave., Elm Grove, W. Va.
Wirth, Grover F., 497 W. Walnut, Columbus, Ohio.
Witt, Fred W., 1166 Holmden Ave., Cleveland, Ohio.
Wodsch, Karl B., 498 Victor St., Toledo, Ohio.
Wortman, Eldred G., 733 F, Market St., Akron, Ohio.
Yarmush, Paul J., 898 Star Ave., Cleveland, Ohio.
Yockey, Ernest L., Shreve, Ohio.

C COMPANY

Blumenstiel, Frederick I., Springfield, Ohio.
Brock, Ray M., 209 Central Ave., Dayton, Ohio.
Davidson, Harold M., 11915 Ashbury Ave., Cleveland, Ohio.
Flannery, Thomas, 1104 Setoo Ave., Cincinnati, Ohio.
Allen, Ernest A., R. F. D. No. 2, Mentor, Ohio.
Allegeier, Henry, R. F. D., Sta. "L," Cincinnati, Ohio.
Arance, Milo C., 536 New Court, Youngstown, Ohio.
Arnold, Forrest W., Middlefield, Ohio.
Bain, Albert, Griest Ave., Cincinnati, Ohio.
Barbison, Roger, 1159 (Ashbury A) Federal St., Youngstown, Ohio.
Barnhart, Homer, South Olive, Ohio.
Barrett, Fmmitt, 533 47th St., Bellaire, Ohio.
Barthelmew, Alexander, Sharonville, Ohio.
Baughman, Carl F., 338 Brown St., Akron, Ohio.
Baughman, Warren D., 338 Brown St., Akron, Ohio.
Beaver, James W., 1347 Paine St., Cleveland, Ohio.
Beckman, Herbert, 712 Wyoming Ave., Lockland, Ohio.
Beckaman, 712 Wyoming Ave., Lockland, Ohio.
Beech, George H., Chardon, Ohio.
Beerman, Lawrence C., 431 Louisa St., Akron, Ohio.
Beccoff, Charles E., R. F. D, 1, Waynsboro, Pa.
Benz, Anthony I., 6204 Manuel St., Madisonville, Ohio.
Berger, Harold, 5012 Scoville Ave., Cleveland, Ohio.
Blistain, Clifford A., 1741 Dexter Ave., Cincinnati, Ohio.
Booth, Frederick M., 418 Seventh St., East Liverpool, Ohio.
Bousi, Frank J., 3505 B. 43rd St., Cleveland, Ohio.
Boley, George W., Hallsville, Ohio.
Brehmer, Herbert, 265 Place St., Chillicothe, Ohio.
Brink, Carl J., 393 Columbus St., Ashtabula, Ohio.
Brown, David W., Verona, Ohio.
Buckland, Everett, Box 22, Leipsick, Ohio.
Bukowaki, Vincent, 208 Hassman St., Toledo, Ohio.
Burghy, Ralph R., St. Clairesville, Ohio.
Butler, Carl J., 482 Sherman St., Akron, Ohio.
Butler, Floyd, 2704 Frotida Ave., Keomore, Ohio.
Campfield, Arthur B., 322 Salt Spring Rd., Niles, Ohio.
Carmany, Elvin F., Sta. "A," Barberton, Ohio.
Carpenter, James, Spencer, W. Va.
Car, Stanley W., 1970 Michigan St., Toledo, Ohio.
Chalker, James W., 66 5. Fourth St., Akron, Ohio.
Clark, Harry K., 516 Monroe St., Toledo, Ohio.
Clegg, Charles, 285 F. Ohio Ave., Sebring, Ohio.
Condi, Steve, 206 Lodz St., Akron, Ohio.
Condon, Raymond R., 128 Carroll St., Youngstown, Ohio.
Cook, Lawrence R., Route '1," Argenta, Ill.
Courtney, William G., 723 McClaren Ave., Lockland. Ohio.
Craig, Theodore L., 1424 Cherry St., Toledo, Ohio.
Crooks, David J, Mineral Ridge, Ohio.
Crothers, John A., R. F. D. No, 5, Marysvillle, Ohio.
Culver, Squire, Bloomfield, Ohio.
Curry, Abe, R. F. D. No. 4, Washington, Pa.
Degidio, Nicola, ll 1/2 N. High St., Akron, Ohio.
Delciello, Dominick, 182 Charles St., Akron, Ohio.
Dehurschere, Oscar, 41 Smith St., Mt. Clemens, Mich.
Dickerman, Paul J., Middlefield, Ohio.
Diss, Ralph, 712 Wayne St., Cincinnati, Ohio.
Dodd, Clarence F., Marengo, Ohio.
Dreyer, Frank J., 917 Glenwood Ave., Youngstown, Ohio.
Drury, Francis C., Harrod, Ohio.
Egan, Charles T., 24 Home Ave., Xenia, Ohio.
Elliott, Richard, R. F. D. 11, Lockland, Ohio.
Elmlioger, Sylvester, 30 South St., Reading, Ohio.
Emerich, Emanuel M., 2108 F. 89th St., Cleveland, Ohio.
Evans, Bert W., R. F. D. No. 1, Mineral Ridge, Ohio.
Copelan, R. W., c-o Times-Star, Cincinnati, Ohio.
Fvans, Carl, R. F. D. No. 1, Middleport, Ohio.
Evick, Edward, 1018 Colburn St., Toledo, Ohio.
Favorite, Charles, 2226 Hazeo Ave., Cleveland, Ohio.
Finnigan, Harry W., Mineral Ridge, Ohio.
Fisher, Frank, 6 Dighy St., Toledo, Ohio.
Flagan, Patrick, 1422 W. 23rd St., Cleveland, Ohio.
Flowers, Thomas, Main St., South Zanesville, Ohio.
Fluegeman, Charles, 3920 Lowell St., Cheviot, Ohio.
Foley, Carl T., 998 Paradome St., Cincinnati, Ohio.
Fontanky, George, 38 N. Howard St., Akron, Ohio.
Forbes, Leroy, Addyston, Ohio.
Frankenberg, Albert, Mainville, Ohio.
Franklin, Washington, 94 Syme St., Sharon, Pa.
Franz, Joseph T., 2091 High Ave. SW., Canton, Ohio.
French, Carl, R. F. D., Cileas, Ohio.
Gabriel, Clement A., 412 F. South St., Akron, Ohio.
Gabriel, Ben, 341 S. Main St., Cuyahoga Falls, Ohio.
Geeding Estell A., Addyston, Ohio.
Gemeiner, George F., 300 Vine St., Reading, Ohio.
Getz, Lloyd, 688 Wonderlick Ave., Barberton, Ohio.
Gillespie, Francis A., 37 S. Lake Ave., Youngstown, Ohio.
Gillespie, Joseph, 37 5. Lake Ave., Youngstown, Ohio.
Glaron, George, 1015 Market St., Reading, Ohio.
Gould, John C., East Claridon, Ohio.
Gray, Forrest F., 3 Arch St., Akron, Ohio.
Graney, Cornelius, 341 Scott St., Youngstown, Ohio.
Green, John W., Coal Run, Ohio.
Grubb, Fred, R, F. D. 2, Little Hocking, Ohio.
Gruber, Martin, 20 Calhoun St., Cincinnati, Ohio.
Gulker, John P., R. F. D. No. 6, Ottawa, Ohio.
Haag, Aloysius J., 121 Glenwood Ave., Akron, Ohio.
Haag, Clarence C., R. F. D. No. 1, Big Run, Pa.
Hansen, Carl C., Newell, Iowa.
Hardin, Clarence H., R. F. D. No. 6, Lima, Ohio.
Harmeyer, William, 206 Maple St., Reading, Ohio.
Harmony, George, 560 Cherry St., Marion, Ohio.
Harriogton, Frank G., Columbia Ave., Williamstown, W. Va.
Hauer, Herman, R. F. D. No. 7, Kent, Ohio.
Hayden, Charles, Flgin Ave., Cincinnati, Ohio.
Heeter, Lawrence M., Mineral Ridge, Ohio.
Hendrickson, Roy F., R. F. D. No, 1, Lewisburg, Ohio.
Hendricks, Walter, Woodville, Ohio.
Herrity, Daniel, 124 Liberty St., Allentown, Pa.

Hess, Clyde, 3 Broadway St., Salem, Ohio.
Henry, Byron F., 388 Warren Ave., Youngstown, Ohio.
Halloway, Noble F., 368 Leader St., Marion, Ohio.
Howell, Karl M., 1020 Oakhill Ave., Youngstown, Ohio.
Hughes, Harry M., 424 Fourth St., Niles, Ohio.
Hura, Charles M., 710 Steele Ave., Youngstown, Ohio.
Hura, Joseph P., 710 Steele Ave., Youngstown, Ohio.
James, Ivor B., 75 Willis Ave., Youngstown, Ohio.
Jaster, Otto F., deceased, R. F. D. No. 3, Farmdale, Ohio.
Johnson, Claude W., Interlawn, N. Y.
Johnson, Cyrus L., Box 6, Powell, Ohio.
Johnson, Carl M., 727 Washington St., Akron, Ohio.
Johnson, Hugh F., 1204 W 47th St., Chicago, Ill.
Jones, Thomas, 5134 Broerman Ave., St. Bernard, Ohio.
Kelly, Charles H., 423 Sherman St., Akron, Ohio.
Keegan, Joseph, Sharon Ave., Glendale, Ohio.
Ketcham, Arthur, Toledo, Ohio.
King, Clarence A., 3602 Summit St., Toledo, Ohio.
Kirsdinski, Fred J., Crystal Springs, Ohio.
Klein, Earl F., 1026 Calhoun St., Toledo, Ohio.
Kieling, John P., 38 Graham St., Cincinnati, Ohio.
Kmet, John F., 510 Andres P1., Cleveland, Ohio.
Knepile, Albert C., Harrison, Ohio.
Koehler, Herman, 1024 Hillman St., Youngstown, Ohio.
Koehler, Oscar M., 564 Norton Ave., Barberton, Ohio.
Koehler, William, Hillman St., Youngstown, Ohio.
Kopke, Albert, Jackson St., Amherst, Ohio.
Kot, Walter M., 1510 Michigan St., Toledo, Ohio.
Kull, August C., 216Bain Ave., Marion, Ohio.
Kunkler, Shirley C., R. F. D. No. 1, Cygnet, Ohio.
Lass, Rupert E., 2304 Ashland Ave., Cincinnati, Ohio.
Lauer, Herman, Wipple, Ohio.
Lemker, Joseph M., 624 W. Court St., Cincinnati, Ohio.
Lindstrom, Earnest, 780 Upson St., Akron, Ohio.
Lavelle, James, 3193 W. 46th St., Cleveland, Ohio.
Lewis, Walter, Cleves, Ohio.
Loughead, Edward, 1614 Clayton St., Cincinnati, Ohio.
Lynch, Neal, 4110 Detroit St., Cleveland, Ohio.
McCarthy, Edward, 742 Wayne St., Cincinnati, Ohio.
McClaren, Wade, Wooster, Ohio.
McCubbins, William, 3170 West First St., Cleveland, Ohio.
McGrachan, John I., 1022 Grant Ave., Akron, Ohio.
McGee, Charles W., 639 Johnson St., Akron, Ohao.
McIntire, William M., deceased, 246 Pike St., Cincinnati, Ohio.
Malamphy, Patrick, 288 S. High St., Akron, Ohio.
Malandio, Henry, 311 Salt Springs Rd., Youngstown, Ohio.
Manus, Stanley, 3431 B. 52nd St., Cleveland, Ohio.
Matre, Oscar H., 655 Jefferson Ave., Reading, Ohio.
May, Lewis V., R. F. D. No. 1, Ellsworth, Ohio.
Mayer, Harry L., 195 Central Ave., Delaware, Ohio.
Mazurky, Anthony, 2604 Vega Ave., Cleveland, Ohio.
Meager, James R., 111 "L" St., Wadsworth, Ohio.
Metz, Frank L., 226 Vine St., Reading, Ohio.
Meyer, Jacob, 203 Vine St., Reading, Ohio.
Milanaki, Steve, 545 Beel St., Akron, Ohio.
Mohler, Clinton, 543 Laclede Ave., Youngstown, Ohio.
Moorfield, John W., 517 5. High St., Akron, Ohio.
Morgan, Edgar F., Sawyerwood, Ohio.
Norhaus, Adolph R., Box 41, Gledorf, Ohio.
Oplinger, Thomas, 25 5. 9th St., Kenmore, Ohio.
Papageorge, N., 86 Public Square, Cleveland, Ohio.
Parker, Grant F., 307 Warren Ave., Youngstown, Ohio.
Parker, Thomas, 203 Regent St., Youngstown, Ohio.
Perdue, Ralph H., 1136 Getz St., Akron, Ohio.
Poor, Lorenzo D., Baerdeen, Ohio.
Pope, Tully J., R. F. D. No. 1, South Solon, Ohio.
Powell, Earnest, R. F. D. 11, Cuyahoga Falls, Ohio.
Quinn, Thomas A., 6908 Carnegie Ave., Cleveland, Ohio.
Rankin, Charles D., R. F. D. No. 1, Phildelphia, Ohio.
Reed, Jacob A., 1302 Andres St., Akron, Ohio.
Retner, Philip H., 225½ High St., Barberton, Ohio.
Rhoadea, Paul L., R. F. D. No. 21, Fast Akron, Ohio.
Rinaldo, Raffaella, Sylvania, Ohio.
Robb, Joseph, 1358 Marquette St., Cleveland, Ohio.
Roth, Arthur A., 2286 B. 101st St., Cleveland, Ohio.
Ryan, John, Congress Ave., Glendale, Ohio.
Sager, Phillip, 210 Fagle St., Akron, Ohio.
Saylor, John, Ottawa, Kentucky.
Schep, William, 2824 Astoria Ave., Cincinnati, Ohio.
Schmit, William F., 210 Jackson Ave., St. Bernard, Ohio.
Schola, Louis, deceased, 3921 Columbia Ave., Cincinnati, Ohio.
Schriever, Herman, 224 Walnut St., Reading, Ohio.
Schumaker, Harry C., 126 Carroll St., Akron, Ohio.
Seig, John, Newton, Ohio.
Senger, George A., 103 W. Thornton St., Akron, Ohio.
Shellenhamor, Clifford, 624 N. Fourth St., Cuyahoga Falls, Ohio.
Shiilett, William, 110 5. Broadway, Akron, Ohio.
Shoemaker, Harry R., Bainbridge, Ohio.
Sirabry, A. , Main and Ross Ave., Norwood, Ohio.
Smith, Carlyle A., 177 W. Delason Ave., Youngstown, Ohio.
Snyder, Maurice H., Hoover Ave., Akron, Ohio.
Spangler, Charles R., 1273 F. Market St., Akron, Ohio.
Stecker, Gottleib, 703 Summit St., Akron, Ohio.
Steinman, Oliver, Montgomery, Ohio.
Steward, Lowell, R. F. D. No. 1, Williamsburg, Ohio.
Stover, Frank J., R. F. D. No. 1, Ottawa, Ohio.
Studer, Leslie B., Bethel, Ohio.
Swanson, Alvin L., Costello, Pa.
Torak, Earnest M., Maywood, Ohio.
Trompter, Harry, 5222 Goeman Ave., Cincinnati, Ohio.
Uhlem, John B., R. F. D. No. 33, Barberton, Ohio.
Ventling, Harry C., Danville, Ohio.
Vincke, Ferdinand N., Ottoville, Ohio.
Vonseelao, Frederick, 1111 Fuller St., Cincinnati, Ohio.
Walsh, Leo V., 177 High St., Barberton, Ohio.
Watterson, Daniel, 1396 F. Market St., Akron, Ohio.
Wein, Michael, 315 F. South St., Akron, Ohio.
Welage, Charles, 4340 Main Ave., Norwood, Ohio.
West, Charles L., Reno, Ohio.
Whitelock, Harry H., 1405 F. 12th St., Cleveland, Ohio.
Whitman, Floyd, Star Route, Lodi, Ohio.
Wilikins, Olive A., Toledo State Hospital.
Williams, Robert A., 338 Baum St., Cincinnati, Ohio.
Willis, Herbert L., 339 W. Market St., Akron, Ohio.
Wilson, Oscar J., 460 Allyn St., Akron, Ohio.
Winder, Bryce, 834 Western Ave., Cincinnati, Ohio.
Wojtowicz, Joseph, 346 F. Striecker St., Toledo, Ohio.
Wyatt, Herbert, Wellston, Ohio.
Wymer, Frank, 210 Betz St., Barberton, Ohio.
Wasseer, Clarence V., 443 Falls Ave., Youngstown, Ohio.

D COMPANY

Stathers, Birk S., Weston, W. Va.
Yetter, Fstel H., c/o American Rolling Mills, Middletown, Ohio.
McConnell, James R., Macksburg, Ohio.
Cone, Don H., Urbana, Ohio.
Addison, William F., R. F. D. No. 3, Box 10, Wendall, Ind.
Adler, Louis B. 1712 Highland Ave., Youngstown, Ohio.
Alleman, John F., R. F. D. No. 2, Rome, Ohio.
Angelikeio, Mine, 1917 Woodland Ave., East Cleveland, Ohio.
Armstrong, Harry B., 118 W. Market St., Akron, Ohio.
Anthenreith, Walter R., 512 F. Exchange St., Akron, Ohio.
Baker, Legrand H., 517 Elban Ave., Akron, Ohio.
Baker, Floyd, Harris Sta., Ross County, Ohio.
Barman, Clarence J., 623 E Fourth St., Chillicothe, Ohio.
Barner, George A., R. F. D. 3, Millertown, Pa.
Bauer, Nicolas J., 35 Elm St., Sharon, Pa.
Bechler, William, R. F. D. 2, Lynden, Ohio.
Berger, Herbert S., 221 Albany St., Cincinnati, Ohio.
Berry, Lester P., 308 Garrison St., Fremont, Ohio.
Beyer, Harold G., 2748 Broadway St., Lorain, Ohio.
Beline, Tony, 3618 F. 54th St., Cleveland, Ohio.
Bitting, Harry F., Middleburg, Pa.
Blanchett, Charles, 519 F. Bucyrus St., Crestline, Ohio.
Bobel, Bert J., 1016 5th St., Lorain, Ohio.
Boho, Frank R., Ellerslie, Ind.
Birgu, John, 6124 Glass St., Cleveland, Ohio.
Botchie, John F., Steelton, Pa.
Bottenhorn, Clifford A., 212 Main St., Elmwood Pl., Cincinnati, Ohio.
Brown, Walter, Senecaville, Ohio.
Busky, Frank, 493 14th St., Lorain, Ohio.
Cady, Sherman J., 150 N. Sixth St., Newark, Ohio.
Capece, Fred, 248 Fourth St., Elwood City, Pa.
Capron, Edward T., 237 Ontario St., Toledo, Ohio.
Carris, Guy D., New London, Ohio.
Carnes, William, 146 Mawille Ave., Bowling Green, Ohio.
Chapan, George F., R. F. D. 7, Point Place Rd., Florence Ave., West Toledo, Ohio.
Chiesa, Victor, 812 Wheeling Ave., Cambridge, Ohio.
Chojnowiki, Frank N., 627 Fullerton Ave., Cleveland, Ohio.
Chlopek, John, 1093 E. 69th St., Cleveland, Ohio.
College, Clarence W., Hopewell, Pa.
Covert, Leland P., 2111 F. 22nd St., Cleveland, Ohio.
Corsey, Joseph M., 1247 W. Seventh St., Cincinnati, Ohio.
Crans, John, 248 5. Seffner St., Marion, Ohio.
Curran, Charles H., 619 W. 22nd St., Lorain, Ohio.
Daily, Carl, 104 Arch St., Akron, Ohio.
Danculevich, 1447 F. 51st St., Cleveland, Ohio.
Davies, Paul H., R. F. D. 2, Pleasant Grove, Youngstown, Ohio.
Davis, Jefferson L., R. F. D. 6, Everett, Ohio.
Deichert, William, 337 Sandusky Ave., Fremont, Ohio.
Dewalt, Clark Z., 639 Cherry St., Galion, Ohio.
Donnell, Floyd F., 117 Stone St., Gibonsburg, Ohio.
Dowling, James J., R. F. D. 3, Fldred, Pa.
Dudley, Gordon, R. F. D. 3, Dudlin, Va.
Dunn, William C., Box 464, Kenmore, Ohio.
Eisenbraurn, William, 302 Poland Ave., Struthers, Ohio.
Erb, Lawrence, R. F. D. 1, Clyde, Ohio.
Earnest, John, 2361 F. 76th St., Cleveland, Ohio.
Farnesworth, James C., 663 Baker St., Grafton, Ohio.
Fetterman, Clifford, 615 Madison St., Conneaut, Ohio.
Fisher, Oscar P., R. F. D. 7, Chillicothe, Ohio.
Fleming, Joseph P., 146 W. Chalmers Ave., Youngstown, Ohio.
Frederick, Everett M., R. F. D. No. 1, Vinton, Ohio.
Gallka, John, 2342 Professor St., Cleveland, Ohio.
Gardner, Phillip P., Sta. 'A," Youngstown, Ohio.
Gerald, Close, Millersburg, Ohio.
Getzinger, Wallace A., R. F. D. No. 3, Kenton, Ohio.
Gillespie, Peter, 1370 B. 93rd St., Cleveland, Ohio.
Goldberg, Milton S., 1157 Indiana Ave., Toledo, Ohio.
Golub, David, 3211 F. 117th St., Cleveland, Ohio.
Gottschalk, Fred, 215 Evans St., Gibonsburg, Ohio.
Crienwald, Frank, 1153 Garrison St., Fremont, Ohio.
Haechker, Adolph P., 12015 Locke Ave., Cleveland, Ohio.
Halter, George A., R. F. D. No. 28, Aultman, Ohio.
Hamenon, Frank S., R. F. D. No. 2, Jewell, Ohio.
Hancock, Lester M., Galena, Ohio.
Haney, Mitchell J., 53 F. Evergreen St., Youngstown, Ohio.
Hart, Walter C., Petersburgh, Ohio.
Hastwell, Frank W., Wiltshire Ave., West Park, Ohio.
Hawley, John, 406 5. McKaw St., Kittanning, Pa.
Hayden, William B., Elgin Ave., College Hill, Cincinnati, Ohio.
Hesnebrodt, Clifford, c/o Lorain Dry Cleaning Co., Lorain, Ohio.
Heaton, Earl L., 2144 Beach Ave., Lorain, Ohio.
Hemler, Edward G., 211 Troy St., Dayton, Ohio.
Hendershot, Harry, 66 Bachtel Ave., Akron, Ohio.
Hibner, Oscar A. F., R. F. D. No. 5, Wapokoneta, Ohio.
Hickel, Robert R., 51 S. Fifth St., Kenmore, Ohio.
Hill, Harley C., 1418 Winchester Ave., Lakewood, Ohio.
Hirt, Lee C., 218 W. Lath St., Lorain, Ohio.
Hoertt, Oscar, 909 Valley St., Dayton, Ohio.
Hosack, Laddie A., Bay Village, Ohio.
Houllam, John, 455 F. Prospect Ave., Cirard, Ohio.
Huffer, Edward C., Michigantown, Ind.
Hungerford, Harry, 369 N. Firestone Bldg., Akron, Ohio.
Jacobucci, Frederick, 10660 Arthur Ave., Cleveland, Ohio.
Jackson, George C., 4 Western Ave., Newark, Ohio.
Jamerson, Lancaster, Bell, Florida.
Jones, Joaiah, 1328 Hawo St., Youngstown, Ohio.
Jones, Thomas W., Sylacauga, Ala.
Joy, W., R. F. D. No. 10, Greysville, Ohio.
Karcieaki, Antoni, 6300 Hosemer Ave., Cleveland, Ohio.
Kazimore, Walter, 3318 Trobridge Ave., Cleveland, Ohio.
Keene, Edward, 11827 Midland Ave., West Park, Ohio.
King, Russell B., 4396 Hamilton Ave., Cincinnati, Ohio.
Kline, Jessie C., 663 Yale Ave., Akron, Ohio.
Kohn, Robert B., R. F. D. No. 1, Lawrence, Ohio.
Koatchrys, Charles, 3022 Victor Ave., Cleveland, Ohio.
Kraft, Raym)nd, 918½ Yankee Rd., Middletown, Ohio.
Kramer, Hary, 105 Seventh St., McKeesport, Pa.
Krider, Ward, Adams Mills, Ohio.
Krzic, Antoni, 1560 F. 43rd St., Cleveland, Ohio.
Laird, Charles H., 1822 Fifth Ave., Beaver Falls, Pa.
Langan, Joseph, 612 5. Webster St., Scranton, Pa.
Lautz, Oscar, 1821 Elbon St., Pittsburgh, Pa.
Lewis, Thomas J., 301 F. Liberty St., Girard, Ohio.
Ligon, Robert B., Mayfield, Ky.
Linnert, Edward H., Noble Rd., South Cleveland, Ohio.
Long, Earl J., 549 Mill St., Conneaut, Ohio.
Longnecker, John A., R. F. D. 5, Marysville, Ohio.
Lucrezi, Marco, Sanford St., Painesville, Ohio.
Luzar, Jacob, 716 B. 96th St., Cleveland, Ohio.
Mahafferty, Carl C., 202 Fifth Ave., Tarentum, Pa.
Mallon, William, 2209 Mahoning Rd., Canton, Ohio.
Mann, Denver C., Graysville, Ohio.
Masters, John, R. F. D. No. 4, Marietta, Ohio.
May, James L., Main St., Mineral Ridge, Ohio.
McCarty, James D., 51 N. Willow St., Montclair, N. J.
McIntyre, Owen, 949 Bell St., Akron, Ohio.
Meagle, Harold, 830 Front St., Marietta, Ohio.
Michaliski, Stanley, 1080 Junction Ave., Detroit, Mich.
Mooney, John, 1017 Seventh St., Lorain, Ohio.
Monteclave, Gulssppi, 203 Hall Ave., Warren, Ohio.
Moore, Paul B., R. F. D. 3, Hamlion Station, Pa.

Morris, Lehue, Belmore, Ohio.
Murphy, Cleophus D., Ballington, W. Va.
Murphy, Willian J., 210 Canal Dover Ave., Canal Dover, Ohio.
Murry, Earnest A., R. F. D. 1, Orrville, Ohio.
Muskowita, Stanley, Blain, Ohio.
Noch, John J., 67 Fullerton Ave., Cleveland, Ohio.
Norpell, Max B, 12 Lansing Bldg., Newark, Ohio.
Nowak, Edward J., 2328 Putnam St., Toledo, Ohio.
O'Brien, Eugene R., 222 W. 18th St., Lorain, Ohio.
O'Brien, Michael, 1268 Onieda Ave., Shamokin, Pa.
O'Doherty, James M., No. 7 Fire Station, Lorain, Ohio.
Olson, Gustave, 1037 Payne Ave., St. Paul, Minn.
Parks, Robert C., 547 Youngstown Ave., Warren, Ohio.
Paterson, Alexander, 406 Kansas Ave., Lorain, Ohio.
Pavelchak, Jack, 1176 Dunane St., Akron, Ohio.
Pedrow, Joieph, 11 Holub St., Akron, Ohio.
Palagalli, Dominico, 1065 B. 77th St., Cleveland, Ohio.
Petrick, Benny, 10625 Arthur Ave., Cleveland, Ohio.
Post, Russel F., 21 W, Broad St., Cuyahoga Falls, Ohio.
Powers, Melvin J., Gibsonburg, Ohio.
Preston, Claude, 172 S. Gift St., Columbus, Ohio.
Pugh, Paul L., Arlington, Ohio.
Purlcey, Milton H., Box 251, Redford, Mich.
Rainer, Joe B., R. F. D. 2, Waynesburg, Ind.
Rattifan, Leo, 2811 Monroe St., Cleveland, Ohio.
Reaac, Edward F., 4501 Roseville St., Cleveland, Ohio.
Rizzo, Frank, 414 Butler Ave., Akron, Ohio.
Roache, Layola J., 3151 Cherry St., Toledo, Ohio.
Roomer, Albert, 427 W. 21st St., Lorain, Ohio.
Russell, Harry, R. F. D. 4, Dawson Springs, Ky.
Russell, Roy A., 420 Sherman St., Toledo, Ohio.
Samples, Richard G., Clenendin, W. Va.
Saucer, Abe, 5611 Scoville Ave., Cleveland, Ohio.
Sapsford, Clyde W., R. F. D. 16, Beaverette, Ohio.
Schiiamo, Frank, 3660 B. 144th St., Cleveland, Ohio.
Schneider, Carl J., 4806 Memphis Ave., Cleveland. Ohio.
Schneider, Frank J., 1007 Harriett St., Cincinnati, Ohio.
Schweda, George, R. F. D. 3, Elyria, Ohio.
Schofield, John B., 701 Milwaukee Ave., South Milwaukee, Wis.
Seebach, John H., R. F. D. 5, Stratford, Ontario, Canada.
Shaffer, Clyde H., R. F. D. 5, Wauseon, Ohio.
Shaffer, Clarence, 136 Eastern Hts, Blvd., Elyria, Ohio.
Shannon, Joseph D., R. F. D. 5, Newark, Ohio.
Shapiro, Jacob, 1079 S. Main St., Akron, Ohio.
Shapiro, Sam, 415 Wyona St., Brooklyn, N. Y.
Sikorski, John, 1900 Woodlawn, Cleveland, Ohio.
Sineioso, Peter, Box 575, Dawson Springs, N. Mex.
Sinicrapi, Antonio, 63 Third Ave., New York City, N. Y.
Smith, Julius G., 516 Monroe St., Toledo, Ohio.
Snyder, Harry K., R. F. D, 34, Box 73, Barberton. Ohio.
Snyder. Lester, R. F. D. 4, Beallsville, Ohio.
Snyder, Wilmer C., F. Mable St., Dallastown, Pa.
Stanley, Charles H., c/o Dinkler Hotel, Macon, Ga.
Stein, Carl, 116 Greer St., Defiance, Ohio.
Stewart, Guthrie L., 407 Machen St., Toledo, Ohio.
Stolz, Arthur C., 12 Lucreoe Ave., Dayton, Ohio.
Stone, Charley, Gayesport, Ohio.
Stromski, William, 5444 Lake Ct., Cleveland, Ohio.
Sturn, Gtorge A., 1216 Budd St., Cincinnati, Ohio.
Sullivan, John P., 703 Cherry St., Nilea, Ohio.
Surface, Leo C., R. F. D. 2, Baton, Ohio.
Svastovich, Frank, Clifton Rd., Box 51, Euclid Village, Ohio.
Tait, Glenn F., 361 Seventh St., Barberton, Ohio.
Taylor, Charles D., Philo, Ohio.
Taylor, Frank W., Clarksburg, Ohio.
Taylor, Noel B., 96 W. Miller Ave., Akron, Ohio.
Taylor, Robert L., 207 5. Main St., Kenton, Ohio.
Tickner, Max J., 229 R. R. Exchange Bldg., Chicago, Ill.
Thomas, John L., 126 Perry St., Saodusky, Ohio.
Thomas, Rowland B., % Central Fire Dept., Delaware, Ohio.
Toothmao, Roy C., 112 5. Second St., Newark, Ohio.
Vanauker, David K., Struthers, Ohio.
Van, Frank, % Ohio Fuel & Supply Co., Xenia, Ohio.
Vatilla, Andy, 345 Melvin St., Barbertoo, Ohio.
Vawter, Fred B., 504 F. Maple St., Jeffersonville, Ind.
Veth, Elmer C., 1517 Dudley St., Cincinnati, Ohio.
Villwock, Harold P., 13 Columbia St., Toledo, Ohio.
Wagner, Anthony, 894 Huron St., Akron, Ohio.
Wagner, Walter W., 1916 N. 12th St., Toledo, Ohio.
Warner, Edward, c/o Alliance Brick Co., Alliance, Ohio.
Weaver, James T., 748 Pine St., Williamsport, Pa.
Weaver, Ralph S., 688 Detroit St., Xenia, Ohio.
Weiler, Edward M., 114 F. 20th St., Lorain, Ohio.
Weis, Paul F., 226 S. Wayne St., Kenton, Ohio.
Weoneman, Raymond, 1106 Beldon Ave., West Park, Ohio.
Wharton, Clarence W., R. F. D. 1, Barnesville. Ohio.
Wigley, Joseph L., 241 W. Ray St., New Philadelphia, Ohio.
Wilbur, Robert A., 32 Kingwood St., Morgantown, W. Va.
Williams, Walter F., 429 Brown St., Columbus, Ind.
Wilson, James, Columbiania, Ohio.
Woucek, Mike, 3058 104th St., Cleveland, Ohio.
Wodich, Milly, R. F. D. 8, Cambridge, Ohio.
Wohlheter, Clarence F., R. F. D. No, 1, Adamsville, Ohio.
Wood, Thomas, 524 York St., Newport, Ky.

MACHINE GUN COMPANY

Beery, Harold, 1486 Rockville Center, Long Island, N. Y.
Coffin, William M., 1012 Traction Bldg., Cincinnati, Ohio.
Johnson, Walter 0. R., 11 B. Woodland Ave., Youngstown, Ohio.
Miller, John W., 3534 Cornell P1., Cincinnati, Ohio.
Ranney, Percival K., 12556 Lake Ave., Cleveland, Ohio.
Vorys, Webb I., 441 B. Town St., Columbus, Ohio.
Abair, Fred A., Toledo, Ohio.
Abbott, Byron, 1221 Trant Ave., Middletown, Ohio.
Ammon, Willis C., Salem, Ohio.
Amundson, Edward C., 1319 W. 95th St., Cleveland, Ohio.
Angevino, Anthony M., 347 Division St., Youngstown, Ohio.
Appel, Clarence P., 1006 Orange Ave., Youngstown, Ohio.
Am, Louis B., Mineral Ridge, Ohio.
Barnes, Guy W., 2476 Putnam St., Toledo, Ohio.
Beck, Karl H., 628 F. Sandusky St., Findlay, Ohio.
Bendien, Fred, 1562 Contont St., Lakewood, Ohio.
Bick, Joseph J., 308 N. Front St., Dowagiac, Mich.
Bletao, Merl S., 922 Glenwood Ave., Youngstown, Ohio.
Bochler, Clifford A., 417 LaClede Ave., Youngstown, Ohio.
Borovsky, John J., 421 Steele St., Youngstown, Ohio.
Bradfield, Donald, R. F. D. No, 1, New Waterfield, Ohio.
Brady, Edward J., 1920 Gayle P1. SW., Canton, Ohio.
Bretschneider, Albert, 1143 B. Summit St., Alliance, Ohio.
Bridgman, Chalmers P., 223 W. Church St., Xenia, Ohio.
Brockhoff, Ben J., 153 Elm St., Struthers, Ohio.
Buchstein, William C., Poland, Ohio.
Burkhart, Ralph W., 23 W. Dewey Ave., Youngstown, Ohio.
Butler, William J., 662 Pine St., Youngstown, Ohio.
Buzard, Harry, Poland, Ohio.
Cary, Cecil C., Albany St., Albany, Ala.
Christiansen, Hans, 1201 Hartford Ave., Canton, Ohio.
Connors, William F., 122 Essex St., Youngstown, Ohio.
Costello, John J., 1628 Overland Ave., Youngstown, Ohio.
Crawford, Clarence, Karns City, Pa.
Crawford, Hara, Fair St., Berea, Ohio.
Crown, Frank J., 642 E. Fifth Ave., Columbus, Ohio.
Davis, Frank, 312 Mercer St., Warren, Ohio.
Davis, George W., 42 Syme St., Sharon, Pa.
Dean, Marshall, P. 0. Strasburg, Va.
Dietrich, Philip J., Rosebud, Pa.
Dodds, James A., 244 N. Fourth St., Steubenville, Ohio.
Dolly, Dayton D., Fernstone, Ind.
Dyarman, Odell M., Big Prairie, Ohio.
Eby, Arthur A., Linglestown, Pa.
Bckleberry, W. Lafayette St., Coshocton, Ohio.
Fvans, Perry E., London, Ky.
Everett, Clarence B., West Newton, Pa.
Fero, Clyde B., 628 Alice St., Youngstown, Ohio.
Fishel, Clyde F., 46 Lafayette St., Niles, Ohio.
Fitzpatrick, Edwin R., Washingtonville, Ohio.
Freison, Peter S., 109 W. Marion Ave., Youngstown, Ohio.
Frk, James V., 5102 Guy Ave., Cleveland, Ohio.
Gassan, Frederick C., 628 Harrison St., Sandusky, Ohio.
Geltch, Fmil F., 81 F. Hylda St., Youngstown. Ohio.
Gensner, George, 800 S. Third St., Columbus, Ohio.
Gill, Dallas, 663 S. Washington St., New Castle, Pa.
Gillespie. Joseph F., 215 Custer Ave., Youngstown, Ohio.
Gilpin, Homer B., Beverly, W. Va.
Green, Carl D., 200 W, Myrtle Ave., Youngstown, Ohio.
Green, Frederick D., 50 Murdock St., Youngstown, Ohio.
Hess, Jacob, 656 High St., Youngstown, Ohio.
Hall, Fred G., 1517 Mahoning Ave., Youngstown, Ohio.
Hallbeng, Thomas I., 115 Princeton Ave., Youngstown, Ohio.
Hannington, John C., 416 Broadway Ave., Youngstown. Ohio.
Halstead, Brott C., North Canton, Ohio.
Hawk, Sherman F., 1116 Medill St., Massillon, Ohio.
Haynes, Rule, Knoxville, Tenn.
Helman, Morris M., 315 N. Park Ave., Warren, Ohio.
Hilbig, Charles, 401 Greenwood Ave., Punxsutawney. Pa.
Hill, Floyd T., Box No. 617, Struthers, Ohio.
Hopkins, John 5., 147 S. 15th St., Sebring, Ohio.
Huebner, Fred, 430 Cleveland St., Toledo, Ohio.
Hull, William R., Canfield, Ohio.
Hutchison, Gordon, Sexton St., Struthens, Ohio.
Irvine, Ellis G., 643 High St., Youngstown, Ohio.
Irvine, Roy L., 643 High St., Youngstown, Ohio.
Jackson, John H., 119 S. 10th St., Kennione, Ohio.
Jenkins, John R., 719 Clement St., Cleveland, Ohio.
Kabulish, Thomas, New Salem (Ohio), Pa.
Kaltenbach, Fred H., 384 S. McArthur St., Chillicothe, Ohio.
Karll, Jim, 120 F. North St., Akron, Ohio.
Kay, Ralph D., 639 Parkwood Ave., Youngstown, Ohio.
Kelley, Albert J., 2747 W. Sixth St., Cincinnati, Ohio.
Keentker, Harry C., 823 York St., Cincinnati, Ohio.
Kopp, William F., 25 High St., Salem, Ohio.
Leesslem, George H., 616 Buckeye St., Chillicothe, Ohio.
Lawson, Robert B., 42 College Ave., Buckhamon, W. Va.
Leonard, Norman, 12403 Nibs Ave., Cleveland, Ohio.
Leroy, Elmer C., 73 Falls Ave., Youngstown, Ohio.
Lindstrom, Charles, 522 Sixth St., Braddock, Pa.
Loomis, Frrott, Peal St., Beavendam, Ohio.
Lowe, John A., Fourth St., Youngwood, Pa.
McAllen, Francis P., 1040 High St., Youngstown, Ohio.
McCallin. Cannington A., 172 Buttles Ave., Columbus, Ohio.
McCafferty, Joseph J., 435 Edgewood. Akron, Ohio.
McConnell, Norman S., Berlin Center, Ohio.
McCoy, Oren G., 121 F. Lakeview Ave., Columbus. Ohio.
McGowan, William, 72 F. Eighth St., Columbus, Ohio.
Malone, James F., 5t1 W. Dewey Ave., Youngstown, Ohio.
May, Josiph P., 1306 W. Federal St., Youngstown. Ohio.
Mallory, Chester F., 7209 Heckler Ave., Cleveland, Ohio.
Melfan, William, 186 Dewey Ave., Youngstown, Ohio.
Metcalk, Walter R., Lakeville, Ohio.
Miller, Clyde B., 2427 W. Chestnut St., Altoona, Pa.
Miller, Graoberry, University Club, Cleveland, Ohio.
Millikin, Charles H., R. F. D. No, 4, Brookville, Ohio.
Mitchell, Edmen W., 1552 Eastern Ave., Cincinnati, Ohio.
Meff, Albert C., Canfield, Ohio.
Morgan, Benjamin F., 1112 Hillman St., Youngstown, Ohio.
Morgan, Charles W., Box 134, Mondale, Ohio.
Morgan, Thomas F., 203 W. South St., Jackson, Ohio.
Morlock, Charles, Lowellville, Ohio.
Myers, Park F., R. F. D. No. 20, Akron, Ohio.
Neel, Theodore W., Burnside, Millburn, N. J.
Nester, Elmer A., 207 Annabelle St., Pittsburgh, Pa.
Nixon, Paul F., 132 Willis Ave., Youngstown, Ohio.
Ogden, Robert, 322 N. High St., Chillicothe, Ohio.
Pabst, Ralph F., 48 Cleveland St., Youngstown, Ohio.
Parker, Mark M., R. F. D. 75, Jamestown, N. Y.
Pernill, Russell G., Ashville, Ohio.
Pierce, Lawrence, 625 Morton Ave., Chester, Pa.
Potter, Ralph F., 263 Lake St., Akron, Ohio.
Price, William, 877 Marshall St., Youngstown, Ohio.
Pukelnick, Andrew S., 3440 W. 45th St., Cleveland, Ohio.
Putnam, John F., Grandin, Mo.
Rentz, William F., 992 S. Champion St., Columbus, Ohio.
Rhodes, Clyde, R. F. D. No, 2, Brookville, Pa.
Rixson, Charles F., 60 Pierce Ave., Norwood, R. I.
Rodomaker, Ben H., New Bloomfield, Pa.
Rosenbloom, Dave, 526 S. Alantic Ave., Lima, Ohio.
Rosser, James B., McArthur, Ohio.
Russ, Raymond C., 16125 Clifton Blvd., Cleveland, Ohio.
Russell, Gervase R., Buchtel, Ohio.
Ruthenberg, Herbert C., 298 Berg St., Akron, Ohio.
Ryhal, Charles F., 121 5. Seventh St., Kenmore, Ohio.
Sanford, Frank J., Station A, East Liverpool, Ohio.
Schall, Forrest G., 290 Poland Ave., Stnuthers, Ohio.
Schiller, Herman, 1030 Hoe Ave., New York City, N. Y.
Shea, Howard A., 3911 Whitman Ave., Cleveland, Ohio.
Shehy, George W., 1252 Wilson Ave., Youngstown, Ohio.
Shelton, George W., 1364 Henry Ave. S.S., Canton, Ohio.
Simons, Arthur D., R. F. D, No. 1, Box 249, Youngstown, Ohio.
Schwing, John, 1421 Park Ave. SW., Canton, Ohio.
Seaver, William A., R. R. No, 3, Fargo, N. Dakota.
Smith, Frederick, V., 9608 Parmelee, Cleveland, Ohio.
Smith, Harry H., 255 W. 10th St., Columbus, Ohio.
Spencer, Ralph, 45 B. Duncan, Columbus, Ohio.
Sprinkle, Arthur W., 382 F. Martin St., East Palestine, Ohio.
Stafford, Earl D., 1442 Mahoning Ave., Youngstown, Ohio.
Stagaman, Edwin W., 4004 Floral, Norwood, Ohio.
Stambaugh, Earl, 1206 Glenwood Ave., Youngstown, Ohio.
Strambe, Otto, 30 5. Evanston Ave., Youngstown, Ohio.
Suchan, Joseph C., 3665 E. 50th St., Cleveland, Ohio.
Sullivan, Harry, Buchtel, Ohio.
Sullivan, Roy, R. F. D. No. 4, Circleville, Ohio.
Swanson, Elmer, Grand Valley, Pa.
Tico, Arthur, c/o Alliance Brick Co., Alliance, Ohio.
Tningas, George, 241 F. Boardman St., Youngstown, Ohio.
Turner, Loren O., Byer, Ohio.

Waddington, John W., 1039 Woodland Ave., Youngstown, Ohio.
Webb, William, Canfield, Ohio.
Weed, Asa H., 1514 Foster St., Youngstown, Ohio.
Wehrle, Charles C., 1733 N. Erie St., Toledo, Ohio.
Wilson, Royal J., 328 Riddle Ave., Ravenna, Ohio.
Whittenbargen, George H., Box 229, Youngstown, Ohio.
Wolf, William G., 2353 E 65th St., Cleveland, Ohio.
Wolfe, Chfford J., 2930 Prospect Ave., Cleveland, Ohio.
Yost, Arthur A., Third St. SW., Canton, Ohio.
Zabel, Arthur H. 121 E Chalmers St., Youngstown, Ohio.
Zalesky, John, 708 Second Ave., New Kensington, Pa.

E COMPANY

Deckerson Richard T., 501½ Guyme Bldg., Cincinnati, Ohio.
Hyre, Raymond B., 809 Soc. for Sav. Bldg., Cleveland, Ohio.
Chamberlain, Harold F., 322 Hall St., Ripori, Wis.
Clinger, Ralph H., 2401 Deming Ave., Columbus Ohio.
McMastens, Earl B., 1528 W. Market St., Steubenville Ohio.
Dunbar, Donald G., P. 0. Box 505, San Angelo, Texas.
Moldenhauer, Arthur, 6422 S. Winchester St., Chicago, Ill.
Adkins, Brinton S., 633 Virginia Ave., Midland, Pa.
Anders, Henry, 1106 Washington St., Sandusky, Ohio.
Apkings, Harry, 403 Linden St., Elm Wood Place, Ohio.
Ayers, Kenner C., Marrow, Ohio.
Batticututa Antonio, 501 Bacon Ave., Akron, Ohio.
Baughn, Thomas L., 195 Dayton Ave., Xneia, Ohio.
Baumgartner, Henry J., 1817 Maple Ave., Norwood, Ohio.
Bender Leslie, c/o Bender Sign Co., Akron, Ohio.
Besancon, Francis A., R. F. D. No. 2, Fredericksburg, Ohio.
Biller, Raymond T., 6114 Crobby St., Cincinnati, Ohio.
Bittecuffer Walter M., Route 3, Dover, Ohio.
Black, George R., Minerva, Ohio.
Bloom, Kenneth L., 544 Kilbounoe Ave., Columbus, Ohio.
Brandon, Frank J., Co. F, 7th Infantry, Camp Lewis, Tacoma, Wash.
Breslin, Fred J., 3723 Leuders Ave., Hyde Park, Cincinnati, Ohio.
Bnidgman, Chalmers P., 223 W. Church St., Xeoia, Ohio.
Broadwell, Ralph A., 3635 Morris P1., Cincinnati, Ohio.
Brockman Flmer C., 608 Foulke St., Cincinnati, Ohio.
Bronson, George B., Box 182, Fayette City, Pa.
Brothers, George A., R. F. D. No. 6, Canrollton, Ohio.
Bundy, Harry A., 179 Sales St., Akron, Ohio.
Burkey, John W., R. F. D., Glenmont, Ohio.
Cahill, George, 745 Market St., Akron, Ohio.
Carter, Lewis, Route 1, No. 52, California, Ohio.
Case, Floyd P., 633 Sherman St., Akron, Ohio.
Chapman, Samuel R., Route 1, Selma, Ohio.
Chastie, George F., 28 Ridge Ave., Washington, Pa.
Clark, Farl W., Hatboro, Pa.
Coberly, Ohley F., 120 Grand Ave., Akron.
Conley, Ray V., Blandville, W. Va.
Conloo, Joseph T., 2808 Melrose St., Cincinnati, Ohio.
Courtney, Harry U., 23 Crosby St., Akron, Ohio.
Crawford Evans N.,c/o W. K. Terry Co., Toledo, Ohio.
Critchl, Joseph, 338 Howe St., Akron, Ohio.
Darguzis, William C., 127 Davis Ave., Jolliet, Ill.
Davis, James C., R. F. D. No. 17, Washington, Ohio.
Deisa, Herman, 240 Cuyahoga St., Akron, Ohio.
Derewychuk, Stephen, 84 N. Forge St., Akron, Ohio.
Detmening George A., 2868 May St., Cincinnati, Ohio.
De Ville, Medard, 510 W. 12th St., Meshaweaka, Ind.
Doersarn, Henry F., 549 Fairwood Ave., Columbus, Ohio.
Dokes, Abner, 4553 Erie Ave., Madisonville Ohio.
Dorner, Henry, 2028 Michigan St., Toledo, Ohio.
Drumm, Charles, No. 8 10th St., Wheeling, W. Va.
Duke, Clarence, 120 Noble Ave., Akron, Ohio.
Eickler F. A., 714 Highland Ave., Toledo, Ohio.
Ellis, Isaac B., Route No 5, Springfield, Ohio.
Emerman Max, 2660 F Sist St., Cleveland Ohio.
Everhart Howard M., 45 Stanley Ave., Cincinnati Ohio.
Fay, Edward L., Cole St., Akron Ohio.
Ferris, Bert, 7712 Lockland Ave., Cincinnati Ohio.
Fischesser Anthony, 1700 West St., Norwood, Ohio.
Fisher, Alden C., 118 N. Adams St., Akron, Ohio.
Flack, Arthur K. F. D. No. 1, Volant, Pa.
Franks, Paul S., Millersburg Ohio.
Freeman, Stephen F., Marthon, Ohio.
Fatack, Frank, 1013 Thomas Ave., Corning, Calif.
Futterer, Paul, 861 Oakland Ave., Akron, Ohio.
Gaffin, Hershel C., c/o Firestone Tire & Rubber Co., Akron, Ohio.
Gauger, Wade H., 437 Woolcott Ave., Kent, Ohio.
Germano, Salvatoni, 342 Owens St., Marion, Ohio.
Gentz, Ernst T., 1606 La Grange St., Toledo, Ohio.
Giacomini, Fred, 908 Dayton St., Akron, Ohio.
Golden Arthur, 1154 Pitkins Ave., Akron, Ohio.
Goodwin John D., 3810 Eastern Ave., Cincinnati Ohio.
Groebly, John F., Lindenhurst N. Y.
Grass, George, 801 Prentice St., Madisonville Ohio.
Grunigen Jake V., c/o Akron Sausage Co., Bowery St., Akron, Ohio.
Gronkemeyer Lawrence, 435 Main St., Covingion Ky.
Hale, Clark, 510 Rhoades Ave., Akron, Ohio.
Hancock, Erasmus D., Peninsula, Ohio.
Hardy, Harold J., Sea Breeze, N. Y.
Harlow, Paul J., 617 Creighton Ave., Dayton, Ohio.
Harmon Victor, Route No. 2, Sugar Creek, Ohio.
Hawke, Albert W., R. R. No. 2, Ripley, Ohio.
Heini, Jacob J., 6000 Madison Ave., Cincinnati, Ohio.
Herren, William A., 7456 Bliss St., Columbus, Ohio.
Hess, Arthur J., 1374 East 91st St., Cleveland, Ohio.
Hess, Earl, Bellbrook, Ohio.
Heupel, Raymond C., Taft Apts., 13th and Monroe Sts. Toledo, Ohio
Hodgetts, Richard S., 1311 Wood St., Covington, Ky.
Holmes, Lewis B., Bishop St., Akron, Ohio.
Housel John F., Oneida, Illinois.
Howard Robert N., 113 18th St., Waynewood, W. Va.
Ives, Charles, 318 Summer St., Elyria, Ohio.
Jackson John F., 6319 Desmont St., Cincinnati, Ohio.
Jones, A., Laurel, Ohio.
Jones, Carl L., Orwell, Ohio.
Jordan Goff c/o N. 0. T, & L. Co., Akron, Ohio.
Jordan William , 2254 Beechmont Ave., Mt. Washington, Cincinnati, Ohio.
Kahn, Alexander, 141 F. Elm St., Kent, Ohio.
Kalinowski, Alexander 8320 Pulaski-Aye, Columbus, Ohio.
Kanable Roy F., 200 Weber Rd., Columbus Ohio.
Kastak, Mathew, 13606 Chapelside Ave, Cleveland, Ohio.
Katsa, Apostolos C., c/o Splendid Restaurant, S. Mill St., Akron, Ohio.
Kissance, Hugh H., 926 Eighth St. NW, Canton, Ohio.
Kittelberger Fred W., 675 Crosby St., Akron, Ohio.
Knight, Ray, K, D. No. 2, Farmersville Ohio.
Koenig, Frank, 7716 Sherman Ave., Cleveland, Ohio.
Kraft, Robert J., 1433 East 93rd St., Cleveland, Ohio.
Krey, Frederick, 518 Locust St., Elmwood Place, Ohio.
Kunkel, James A., 1418 Winchester Ave., Lakewood Ohio.
Lamb Herbert A., 486 Lexington Ave., Columbus Ohio.
Lanter, Clinton A., 130 Penn Ave., California, Ohio.
Ledsome Jay, 330 W, South St., Akron, Ohio.
Littlefield, Cyril O., 420 South Ave., Whitman, Mass.
Logan, Charles O., Malvern, Ohio.
Long, Lawson, Carrollton, Ohio.
Lutz, Homer L., Canrollton, Ohio.
McCoy, Clifford G., 2522 Ravine St., Cincinnati, Ohio.
McDaniels, Russel A., 925 South Third St., Middleport, Ohio.
Macdonough, Clayton G., 3563 Vista Ave., Cincinnati, Ohio.
McDaniel, John B., Washington, D. C.
Mandery, Edward, Pierce St., Delphos, Ohio.
Mart, Isaac, 2606 Payne Ave., Cleveland, Ohio.
Martin, Henry, Talimadge, Ohio.
Mayes, Edgar A., Topeka, Kansas.
Messerly, Carl, 497 Edgewood St., Akron, Ohio.
Micknowitch, Adam, Manifold, Pa.
Miller, George, 6414 Rose St., Madisonville, Ohio.
Miller, William H., 6414 Rose St., Madisonville, Ohio.
Minnick, George H., 145 Grand Ave., Akron, Ohio.
Morris, Charles W., 1960 Fairfax Ave., Cincinnati, Ohio.
Moyer, Cleon W., 199 Sackett St., Cuyahnga Falls, Ohio.
Nevins, Charles, 1349 F 84th St., Cleveland. Ohio.
Neisbaum, Phanes, R. F. D. No. 4, Bluffton, Ohio.
O'Brian Charles, 1521 Brooklyn Ave., Detroit, Mich.
Obenhelman, Harry B., 1550 Pullan Ave., Cincinnati. Ohio.
Oser, Charles J., 4526 Canter St., Nonwood, Ohio.
Overberg, Herbert, 1937 Maple Ave., Norwood, Ohio.
Pagett, Orville, 888 New Wheelock Rd., Cleveland, Ohio.
Patterson, Charles A., 116 Harding Way Fast, Galion, Ohio.
Patton, Bernard J., 1600 Cadillac Square Bldg., Detroit, Mich.
Pietkowski, Joseph G., 428 Everett Ave., Toledo, Ohio.
Pohlman, Irvin G., 5912 Bramble Ave., Madisonville, Cincinnati, Ohio.
Poppe, Edwin, 1957 Elm Ave., Norwood, Ohio.
Pugh, Clyde A., Steubenville, Ohio.
Purwin, Kostanty, 6713 Baxter St., Cleveland, Ohio.
Reagon, Lawrence F., 416 Greenside Ave., Canonsburg. Pa.
Reed, Arnold L., 1098 Wooster Ave., Akron, Ohio.
Reichen, Charles L., 2623 Archer Ave., Cincinnati, Ohio.
Richard, Charles A., 263 S. Tenth St., Philadelphia, Pa.
Richard, Harry L., Malvern, Ohio.
Ricks, Lance, 630 Crosby St., Akron, Ohio.
Rischman, Charles M., 2019 Erie St., Toledo, Ohio.
Roberts, Ollie S., 27 E. Fourth St., Dayton, Ohio.
Roberts, Raymond, R. F. D. Box 155, Gloucester. Ohio.
Rooney, Charles L., 105 S. Tonrence St., Dayton, Ohio.
Ross, Joseph L., 419 F. 19th St., Beaver Falls, Pa.
Sanqoist, John R., Dayton, Ohio.
Schadel, Walter H., 3113 B. Minott Ave., Cincinnati, Ohio.
Scherer, Jake, 201 Main St., Toledo, Ohio.
Schuette, Henry J., R. F. D. No. 4, Napoleon, Ohio.
Scheineguss, Robert H., Standard Savings Bank, Akron, Ohio.
Seibold, Max, 409 Cleveland St., Toledo, Ohio.
Senical, Hector, 927 Noble St., Toledo, Ohio.
Sergi, Tony, 315 McKinley St., Donona, Pa.
Shade, Charles I., No. 874, Harbor Springs, Mich.
Sharpe, Theodore W., Route 8, Athens, Ohio.
Shaw, James R., 180 Castle Blvd., Akron, Ohio.
Shea, Joseph B., 472 Beechwood Drive, Akron, Ohio.
Sherman, Harry B., Monclova, Ohio.
Shuman, Frank S., 421 B. Thornton St., Akron, Ohio.
Simon, Harold F., Barbenton, Ohio.
Sneider, Richard C., 7600 Myron Ave., Cleveland, Ohio.
Snyder, Earlis P., 751 Longview Ave., Akron, Ohio.
Somerville, Harold D., 1104 Laurel Ave., Akron, Ohio.
Sorrell, Rodney F., Olouster, Ohio.
Spiker, Harry G., 27 Everett Ave., Cumberland, Md.
Stansbenry, Lyon B., 274 Locust St., Akron, Ohio.
Steinmetz, Arthur N., 96 Dick St., Akron, Ohio.
Stoelzel, Emil F., 637 W. Central St., Toledo, Ohio.
Susi, Antonio P., 448 Curtiss St., Columbus, Ohio.
Sutton, Jesse H., Hibbetts, Ohio.
Swanker, Sherman C., 1536 Rockway Ave., Lakewood, Ohio.
Thomas, Edward C., Maynard, Ohio.
Tankensley, James K., 211 Portage St. N., Canton, Ohio.
Thomasson, Harry C., 265 Madison Ave., Akron, Ohio.
Thompson, Albert, North Baltimore, Ohio.
Thompson, Carl N., Malvern, Ohio.
Turk, John, Niles, Ohio.
Turner, Ferry D., 218 Hazlewood Ave., Barbenton, Ohio.
Turner, Roy, 1113 Oregon Ave., Columbus, Ohio.
Van Fossen, Raymond, Winona Lake, Ind.
Veon, Samuel A., No. 4, Beaver Falls, Pa.
Wagstaff, Thaddeus W., New Hampshire, Ohio.
Wamack, Albert F., 1643 Myrtle Ave., Columbus, Ohio.
Wanner, Glenn D., 201 Green St., Greenville, Ohio.
Warning, William F., Dayton, Ohio.
Warrell, John W., 306 N. Sixth St., Steubenville, Ohio.
Watson, Charles G., 34 W. Woodland Ave., Youngstown, Ohio.
Weaver, Fred, 304 Market St., Marietta, Ohio.
William, Joseph, Pa. Hospital, Philadelphia, Pa.
Willis, Clyde M., 2204 Fourth St. N.E., Canton, Ohio.
Wilson, Winfield, Star Route, Cannollton, Ohio.
Winum, Charles J., 88 N. Valley St., Akron, Ohio.
Van Skoy, K. J., 655 ½ Buckingham St., Columbus, Ohio.
Wilken, Luther, Mallasia Rd., Akron, Ohio.

F COMPANY

Craig, Samuel A., 800 Wheeling Ave., Cambridge, Ohio.
Miller, Floyd V., 21 W. Euclid Ave., Springfield, Ohio.
Oberlin, Benjamin O., 1012 Walnut Ave. N.E., Canton, Ohio.
Rendigs, August A., Jr., 6315 Grandvista Ave., Cincinnati, Ohio.
Auston, David B., 400 F. Wyoming Ave., Lockland, Ohio.
Badaskie, Felix D., 522 King St., Youngstown, Ohio.
Badger, Lewis F., 248 Neilston St., Columbus, Ohio.
Bailey, Jed B., K. F. D, No. 29, Copley, Ohio.
Baker, Charles W., B., F. D. No. 4, Mansfield, Ohio.
Bauensein, George, 61 F McMicken Ave., Cincinnati, Ohio.
Baughman, Arbie B., 416 Lake Ave., Barbenton, Ohio.
Beall, Harry J., 1180 Cook Ave., Lakewood, Ohio.
Beitel, Charles H., 240 High St., Barbenton, Ohio.
Bennioghaus, William H., 2683 Erie Ave., Cincinnati, Ohio.
Berandi, Vito, 3270 W. 34th St., Cleveland. Ohio.
Bercaw, Carl F., Mason, Ohio.
Bittinger, William W., R. K. No. 4, Mansfield, Ohio.
Blom, Clarence A., Reesville, Ohio.
Bogdanski, Frank A., 62 Haskins St., Toledo, Ohio.
Braddock, David, 725 Huron St., Toledo, Ohio.
Bradley, Paul C., K. F. D. No. 7, Hudson, Ohio.
Brasch, Charles F., 521 N. Seventh St., Hamilton, Ohio.
Bruce, Thomas, 455 Church St., Amherst, Ohio.
Bruse, John 0., R. F. D. No. 2, Amherst, Ohio.
Cafforella, Pacetno, 225 Crescent St., Balaire, Ohio.
Campbell, Carl, 116 Cleveland Ave., Columbus, Ohio.
Campbell, John W., 194 Jupiter St., Atlanta, Ga.
Canter, Earl, R. F. D. No. 2, Box 55, Crooksville, Ohio.
Casselbenry, Arthur E., 212½ Park Ave., Banberton, Ohio.

Chandler, Clarence F., 108 Range St., Barberton, Ohio.
Cochran, Melvin W., Spiller, Ohio.
Cohen, Herman, 4980 S. Washington St., Columbus, Ohio.
Collins, Daniel, 520 Ridgon St., Hamilton, Ohio.
Commings, Stratos, 222 E. Third St., Middletown, Ohio.
Conner, George W., 728 Logan Ave., Middletown, Ohio.
Conmany, Roland F., R. F. D. No. 22, East Akron, Ohio.
Cox, Joshua, Zag, Kentucky.
Coy, Chester A., 148 N. Second St., Cuyahoga Falls, Ohio.
Crum, Wilber B., K. F. D. No. 5, Shelby, Ohio.
Culver, Charles R., 2206 Boulevard, Kenmore, Ohio.
Cummings, William, K. F. D. No, 2, Vickery, Ohio.
Dalton, Richard C., 116 W. Main St., Shelby, Ohio.
Davidson, William B., 110 Garfield Ave., Detroit, Mich.
Demoss, Roy B., K. R. F. D. No. 3, Middletown, Ohio.
Donaldson, Glenn S., 995 N. Howard St., Akron, Ohio.
Drake, Homer, R. F. D. No, 2, Williamspont, Ohio.
Drewier, Silas B., 3440 Gladstone Ave., Toledo, Ohio.
Dniesbach, Ulan, K. F. P. No. 25, We1t Akron, Ohio.
Duenki, Karl W., 914 Baker St., Toledo, Ohio.
Duffie, Reedy, 843 12th St., Augusta, Ga.
Edelstein, Harry, 1324 Colwell St., Pittsburgh, Pa.
Egbert, Burl A., 420 Tenth St., Toledo, Ohio.
Eichenberger, Frank, 703 Macon St., Columbus, Ohio.
Emenick, Grover M., 767 Hazel St., Aknon, Ohio.
Estel, John W., Felicity, Ohio.
Eubanks, Edwin A., Route No. 7, Hamilton, Ohio.
Ewalt, Robert R., 602 W. Chestnut St., Mt. Vernon, Ohio.
Ferrell, Arthur 0., 1412 Florida Ave., Kenmore, Ohio.
Ferres, John L., Toledo, Ohio.
Fiber, John C., 52 Manchester Rd., Keomore, Ohio.
Flack, Oscar, New Holland, Ohio.
Flickingen, Fred E., Route No. 32, Barbenton, Ohio.
Fnaney, Clarence B., Route No. 4, Marietta, Ohio.
Foltz, Charles J., 500 Riddle Rd., Cincinnati, Ohio.
Fonste, Frank, Pleasant Ridge, Cincinnati, Ohio.
Franks, John T., R. F. D. No. 35, Barberton, Ohio.
Freeman, Edwin J., 925 St. John Ave., Toledo, Ohio.
Fritz, Louis J., 101 Gradolph Ave., Toledo, Ohio.
Fritz, William F., 101 Randolph Ave., Toledo, Ohio.
Geer, Homer H., Port Clinton, Ohio.
Genmain, George C., P. O. Station No. 7, Akron, Ohio.
Goldy, Harold R., 2384 W. Fourth St., Williamsport, Pa.
Gordon, Leroy, 1256½ Baltimore St., Middletown, Ohio.
Gordon, Robert, 10504 Cedar Ave., Cleveland, Ohio.
Gnamza, Leo J., 628 Haskins St., Toledo, Ohio.
Grant, Roger S., 185 Maplewood Ave., Cuyahoga Falls, Ohio.
Gray, Ed., Withene, Kentucky.
Gnegony, William H., 589 W. Second Ave., Columbus, Ohio.
Grell, Fnank, 308 S. Fourth St., Cuyahoga Falls, Ohio.
Gnisse, Oscar, Toledo Towel Supply Co., Toledo, Ohio.
Grossman, Harry, 1289 B. 17th St., Toledo, Ohio.
Hale, Joseph D., 170 N. Front St., Cuyahoga Falls, Ohio.
Hamalainen, Launi, 3056 W. Maple Ave., Cleveland, Ohio.
Hangaugh, Russell C., 2128 Dayton St., Chicago, Ill.
Hannaman, Otis G., 690 Florence St., Marion, Ohio.
Harris, James F., R. F. D. No. 1, Eastwood, Ohio.
Hennessey, William, 619 Proury Ave., Toledo, Ohio.
Henry, John, Middletown, Ohio.
Heverly, Carl C., 1530 Michigan St., Toledo, Ohio.
Hicks, Earl, 1302 N. 12th St., Toledo, Ohio.
Hilemao, Earl J., R. R. No. 4, Hamilton, Ohio.
Hoagland, Robert H., R. F. D. No. 5, Bedford, Pa.
Hobert, Irving W., 18 Gill St., Columbus, Ohio.
Holmes; Charles A., 121 lonis Ave., Columbus, Ohio.
Houglan, Hilon B., R. F. D. No. 1, Box 31, Copley, Ohio.
Hull, Lee K., Weston, Wood County, -Ohio.
Hullinger, Paul N., 408 F. Stephenson St., Marion, Ind.
Humphreys, Walter T., Sawyerwood, Ohio.
Hurlbut, Homer F., R, F. D. No. 3, Elyria, Ohio.
Inven, Frank D., Fnancisville, Indiana.
Johnson, Gus, 2821 Church Ave., Cleveland, Ohio.
Johnson, Harry, Third and Logan Sts., Dennison, Ohio.
Jones, David E., Granville, Ohio.
Jones, Stanley H., R. R. No. 2, Bethel, Ohio.
Junk, Beacher, West Jefferson, Ohio.
Keezmanek, Joseph H., 334 Mettlen St., Toledo, Ohio.
Kasserman, Roy F., R. F. D. No. 19, Tallmadge, Ohio.
Keller, Adolph A., 267 Southern Ave., Cincinnati, Ohio.
Korn, Ralph O., 1002 St. John St., Toledo, Ohio.
Kinna, James W., 123 Garden St., Lansing, Mich.
Kinney, Leo S., 127 Fond Ave., Barbenton, Ohio.
Kirchner, Rolland B., 1330 Erie St., Toledo, Ohio.
Kianen, Oaklcy A., 1330 Louisiana Ave., Canton, Ohio.
Koeppe, Oscan J., 1429 Michigan St., Toledo, Ohio.
Konoff, Fnank W., 808 Buckeye St., Toledo, Ohio.
Krantz, John H., K. F. D. No. 4, Dover, Ohio.
Krause, Emil B., 523 Walnut St., Toledo, Ohio.
Kuehl, Charles H., 1831 W. Third St., Davenport, Iowa.
Kulp, John J., 1003 Wilson Ave., Columbus, Ohio.
Kyme, Vram, 425 Sumner St., Toledo, Ohio.
Lain, William B., 629 Spring St., Toledo, Ohio.
Lamb, Lunty H., Route No. 1, McGaheysville, Ohio.
Lankauf, Frank, 1612 Chenny St., Toledo, Ohio.
Leeti, John R., 8607 Cedar Ave., Cleveland, Ohio.
Lehman, Harry A., Elmore, Ohio.
Lemnack, Guat, 44 Oliver St., Detroit, Mich.
Lentz, Charles W., 1013 Magnolia St., Toledo, Ohio.
Lewandowski, Frank S. 1253 Noble St., Toledo, Ohio.
Linebaugh, Leo, R. F. D. No, 34, Barbenton, Ohio.
Lisle, Willie, Racine, Ohio.
Litwin, Mike, 91 Chamberlain Ave., Detroit, Mich.
Lok, Walter, 1115 Newbury St., Toledo, Ohio.
Longmore, George, General Delivery, Murray City, Ohio.
McCamic, Edward P., Wellsburg, W, Va.
McCoy, David B., Masonic Club, Banbenton, Ohio.
McClung, Bunen A., Kenmore, Ohio.
McClymonds, Glenn B., Convoy, Ohio.
McConnell, William J., 3141/2 N. Second St., Barbenton, Ohio.
McDonald, Bernard N., Station A, Banberton, Ohio.
Mcllyar, Raymond, 86 Eighth St., Newark, Ohio.
McKenna, James, 178 Walnut St., Revere, Mass.
Magrane, Frank M., 1430 Orange St., Indianapolis, Ind.
Malikowski, Joseph A., 122 B. Park St., Toledo, Ohio.
Malone, Frank, 356 Pinewood Kve, Toledo, Ohio.
Marion, Philip L., 13614 Glenside Rd., Cleveland, Ohio.
Mesckowski, Wladyslas F., 415 Webben St., Toledo, Ohio.
Meyers, Charles C., 113 Locust St., Barbenton, Ohio.
Michelo, Pasqualone, 1034 B. Binmingham Ave., Columbus, Ohio.
Michaels, Harold F., Canbondale, Ohio.
Micly, Omer V., Butler, Indiana.
Moorhead, Robert R., 371 5. Second St., Cuyahoga Falls, Ohio.
Moll, Ira J., 236 N. Bridge St., Chillicothe, Ohio.
Mosier, Denton, 220 Bette St., Barbenton, Ohio.
Mulvaney, Frank, 1968 Champlain St., Toledo, Ohio.
Murphy, Charles B., 123 Geedmore Ave., Barberton, Ohio.
Newlon, Albert L., Circleville, Ohio.
Nowak, John, 3122 Wansaw St., Toledo, Ohio.
Nulton, Frank W., 1018 Shenman St., Toledo, Ohio.
Oberlin, Frank S., R. F. D. No. 35, Barbenton, Ohio.
O'Brien, Mike, 1732 Victoria Rd., Cleveland, Ohio.
O'Creary, John J., 344 B. High St., Lexington, Ky.
Olinger, Cad L., R. F. D. No. 3, Washington C. H., Ohio.
Orihood, Harry N., New Holland, Ohio.
Ostendonif, Joseph, 503 S. Washington St., Delphos, Ohio.
Palhau, August D., 135 Fernwood Ave., Barberton, Ohio.
Palmer, Henry, 9519 Hought Ave., Cleveland, Ohio.
Pavass, Antonio, 2037 Marion Ave., Cleveland, Ohio.
Pettibone, Oscar, 88 Reed Ave., Columbus, Ohio.
Piper, Carl L., 163 Sylvester St., Barbenton, Ohio.
Pitzen, James F., Sardioia, Brown County, Ohio.
Porter, Edward F., 251 5. Garland Ave., Youngstown, Ohio.
Radancy, Paul, 126 S. 18th St., Kenmone, Ohio.
Raffenty, Henry, 585 S. Prospect Ave., Marion, Ohio.
Rathbun, Warren, 212 W. Crosier St., Akron, Ohio.
Reed, Thomas B., Thompson Station, Tenn.
Richards, Lawrence L., Route No. 4, Georgetown, Ohio.
Rieden, Aloys A., 414 Arch St., Chillicothe, Ohio.
Riley, Earl K., Milfond, Ohio.
Roberts, George A., 146 S. Bunges Ave., Columbus, Ohio.
Roecken, William R., R. R. No. 1, Genoa, Ohio.
Rothenbuhlen, Wilbent F., R. K. No. 1, Luckey. Ohio.
Rowan, Fred, Mabie, W. Va.
Howland, William H., R. F. D, No. 4, Marietta, Ohio.
Ruggieni, Frank, 714 Logan Ave., Middletown, Ohio.
Runyon, Roy, N. Maple St., Baton, Ohio.
Rupert, Blwood B., B. Franklin St., Circleville, Ohio.
Ruthenbeng, William J., 495 Beacon St., Akron, Ohio.
Scattone, Rocco, 1308 Webster St., Cleveland, Ohio.
Schneiden, Albert C., 977 B. Livingston Ave., Columbus, Ohio.
Sharp, Lloyd C., R. D. No, 33, Banbentnn, Ohio.
Shaw, Leland D., 988 Jefferson Ave., Akron, Ohio.
Silvers, Roy M., R. F, D. No. 2, Canton, Ohio.
Sippola, John H., Fairport Harbor, Ohio.
Smiley, James F., 1116 W. Bancroft St., Toledo, Ohio.
Smith, Clarence A., 774 Fainview Ave., Hamilton, Ohio.
Smith, Stacey B., P. 0. Box 413, Elynia, Ohio.
Snively, Clarence A., Loudonville, Ohio.
Spencer, George N., Byesville, Ohio.
Stenden, Edwin B., 1627 Pleasant St., Cincinnati, Ohio.
Staub, Frank B., R. F. D. No. 24, Box 147, South Akron, Ohio.
Storm, Fred W., 3908 W. 34th St., Cleveland, Ohio.
Spiffler, Henry F., 232 Third St., Canton, Ohio.
Stump, Sidney P., K. F. D. No. 36, Clinton, Ohio.
Stunnock, Alexis J., Meadville, Pa.
Terwilleger, Byron C., B. Main St., Milfond, Ohio.
Thesing, Joseph H., 319 Seventh St., Barbertoo, Ohio.
Thomas, John, R. F. D. No. 9, Box 109, West Toledo, Ohio.
Thompson, Frank O., R. F. D. No. 3, Summerfield, Ohio.
Trimble, Leroy B., 136 F. Second Ave., Columbus, Ohio.
Tunni, John B., Fairport Harbor, Ohio.
Ulrich, Harry F., 214 W. South St., Akron, Ohio.
Umstead, Herbert B., 465 N. Front St., Cuyahoga Falls, Ohio.
Voie, Frank, St. Clam Ave., Euclid Village, Cleveland, Ohio.
Wallace, Lue, 1618 S. Sixth St., Columbus, Ohio.
Waterfield, Ramie B., R. F. D. No. 1, Georgetown, Ohio.
Watkins, Daniel, Walnut St., Warren, Ohio.
Watkins, Herbert, 730 Current St., Sandusky, Ohio.
Webb, Harrison B., 115 Palmer St., Toledo, Ohio.
Werne, Leo P., Ferdinand, Indiana.
Wettstein, Harold, 60 Lake St., Toledo, Ohio.
Wisoer, Leon H., 23 Wadsworth St., Cuyahoga Falls, Ohio.
Wolfioger, Charles P., 3203 Chase St., Toledo, Ohio.
Wragg, Charley, R. F. D. No, 2, Amherst, Ohio.
Wright, Homer A., 206 Main St., Wadsworth, Ohio.
Wyvill, Roy S., K. F. D. No. 3, Macedonia, Ohio.
Zarske, Edward, 3449 62nd St., Cleveland, Ohio.

G COMPANY

Adams, Edwin, 2212 Quebeck Road, Cincinnati, Ohio.
Adler, Michael B., K. F. D. No. 1, Custer, Ohio.
Ammerman, Walter, N. Baron St., Eaton, Ohio.
Applefellen, Harry, R. F. D. No, 2, Mt. Victory, Ohio.
Barbitta, Coos, 12010 Rexton St. S.E., Cleveland, Ohio.
Bassett, Leonard C., 741 11th Ave., Long Island City, N. Y.
Bedioghaus, Frank, 611 Church St., Cincinnati, Ohio.
Behringer, Edward C., 414 Lincoln Ave. NW., Canton, Ohio.
Benison, Clinton N., 5659 Hamilton Ave., Cincinnati. Ohio.
Bievenour, Lewis J., 1331 Seventh St. NW., Canton, Ohio.
Black, Calvin, 300 F. Elm St., Lima, Ohio.
Beckman, William B., 505 B. 13th St., Cincinnati, Ohio.
Boniphant, Joseph H., Box 63, Old Washington, Ohio.
Borders, Robert H., R. F. D. No. 4, Belle Center, Ohio.
Bongan, Harry A., 53 Lake St., Akron, Ohio.
Bowen, Lawrence, Circleville, Ohio.
Bnesnen, John M., Boston, Ohio.
Brink, Lewis S., 414 High St., Warren, Ohio.
Brothers, William C., 200 Fifth Ave., Chandon, Ohio.
Buehnle, Alfred J., 535 Tiffin St., Sandusky, Ohio.
Bungen, Nevin T., R. F. D. No. 3, Lewisburg, Ohio.
Burton, George F., 1495 Milesia St., Akron, Ohio.
Caffee, Horace O., Benne, Indiana.
Calen, Timothy R., Beach City, Ohio.
Campagoa, Gust, 1229 Orange Ave., Cleveland, Ohio.
Capple, Albert M., 815 State Ave., Cincinnati, Ohio.
Casselman, Roscoe G., 303 N. Hamilton St., Chardon, Ohio.
Calmer, Robert R., Martville, Ohio.
Callagher, Clyde O., 618 Fifth St. N.W., Canton, Ohio.
Chris, Harry M., R. F. D. No. 6, Bethesda, Md.
Cill, Orrin F., North Canton, Ohio.
Cille, Charles H., R. F. 0. No. 6, Coldhill, Ohio.
Cillette, Charles W., 410 5. Eighth St., Cambridge, Ohio.
Clank, William F., 523 Sherman St., Niles, Ohio.
Clear, Charles, 203 5. Beach St., Eaton, Ohio.
Connelly, Charles S., 217 Second St., Fyreville, Ohio.
Conlod, Coetio W., R. F. D. Wickliff, Ohio.
Corbett, Clarence G., 1186 B. 87th St., Cleveland, Ohio.
Cornell, Homer L., North Canton, Ohio.
Crowl, Roy W., 1606 Third St. N.E., Canton, Ohio.
Davis, Charles F., K. R. 8, Dayton, Ohio.
Dawson, Clancy W., R. F. D. No. 3, Kimboltoo, Ohio.
Denie, Frank O., 2136 W. Eighth St., Cincinnati, Ohio.
DeVanney, Lester A., 1516 Second St. N.E., Canton, Ohio.
Devers, John F., 325 Pike St., Youngstown, Ohio.
Dick, Robert B., 935 McKinley Ave. N.W., Canton, Ohio.
Dudley, Ray G., Buffalo, Ohio.
Dunwoody, William J., 129 Belmont St., Warren, Ohio.
Evans, George M., 207 N. Main St., Indianapolis, Ind.
Evans, Thomas P., 1937 Mahoning Rd. N.E., Canton, Ohio.
Fanwick, Arthur F., 915 Ninth St. N.W., Canton, Ohio.
Fatio, Tony, 2654 Glenmore Ave., Pittsburgh, Pa.
Fenwick, James B., Chardon, Ohio.
Ferguson, William, Ramnshoro, Ohio.
Fiedler, Paul O., 59 Arch St., West Mansfield, Ohio.

Fischer, William P., Carntown, Ohio.
Foley, Thomas F., Deerfield, Mich.
Foser, Benedito, 2608 B 31st St., Cleveland, Ohio.
Freehoor, Frank, Miami St., Urbana, Ohio.
Freeload, Charles M., R. F. 0. No. 1, Wore Union, Ohio.
Fry, B. F., R. R. 3, Dayton, Ohio.
Grablo, Aethar A., R. F. D. No. 7, Canton, Ohio.
Green, John F., Cleveland St., Youngstown, Ohio.
Greig, C. H., R. R. No. 1, Synhane, Ohio.
Gribbro, M., Shiloh, Ohio.
Grettle, George F., R. F. 0. No. 1, West Manchester, Ohio.
Gruber, Fool, 420 Fifth St. N.W., Canton, Ohio.
Gnest, Roy A., 1800 12th Ave., Altoona, Pa.
Goldschmidt, Harold J., 900 Woodlawn Ave., Cincinatti, Ohio.
Hamborg, William S., R. F. D. No. 2, Pleasant City, Ohio.
Hanna, Clem, Loans, Ohio.
Harley, Thomas, Jr., 2412 Mahnning Rd. N.E., Canton, Ohio.
Haryer, Cyrno R., 142 Fety St., Farberton, Ohio.
Harmon, Henry H., North Canton, Ohio.
Hasteich, Walter J., it W. 72nd St., Cincinnati, Ohio.
Hoann, Charles R., 2900 Second St. N.W., Canton, Ohio.
Hob, Elmer F., 024 Arlington Ave. N.W., Canton, Ohio.
Hober, Andrew J., Cincinnati, Ohio.
Hoffman, O., R. F. D. No. 2, Black Run, Ohio.
Hoghes, Edward R., 20 W. 78th St., Cincinnati, Ohio.
Hoish, Herbert J., 3037 Neilson Ave, Youngstown, Ohio.
Hone, Jnneyh H., Forest, Ohio.
Jacobs, Jnhn H., Cocoa, Ohio.
Jensen, Oscar F., Chagrin Falls, Ohio.
Jennings, Earl, R. F. D. No. 2, Mansfield, Ohio.
Johnson. A. L., 1664 Foyer St, Philadelphia, Pa.
Jones, Ronni, Phegland, Ohio.
Kotch, J., Cleveland, Ohio.
Konlman, Elmer M., 1319 Third St. N.E., Canton, Ohio.
Kirechorr, Onvid, Sonman, Indiana.
Koneig, Andrew J., Avon, Ohio.
Kromani, William C., 3410 B. 120th So., Cleveland, Ohio.
Kratnan, Avery J., 320 Forest St., Fairmount, Ohio.
Krahy, Joseph M., 1233 11th St. N.W., Canton, Ohio.
Leith, William O, 712 F. 101st St., Cleveland, Ohio.
Lemmon, Harry C., 122 Rose Conet, Barberton, Ohio.
Lemis, Amos J., Lore City, Ohio.
Lemis, James X., Ororgeenmo, Ohm.
Lillie, Angnet 0., 3641 Borden St., Cincinnati, Ohio.
Loog, Fannie A., 21 Oleesner Ave., Mansfield, Ohio.
Lyerin, William A., 1614 Blmnre Ave., Camp Washington, Ohio.
Lyman, Earl W., R. F. D. Fortno, Ohio.
Lynn, Orith, R. F. D. No. 2, Courtland, Ohio.
McCoy, Roy H., 1522 Second St. N.E., Canton, Ohio.
McDonald, F., 107 W. South St., Warren, Ohio.
McFarland, Harvysno S., 1000 F. 77th St., Cleveland Ohio.
McCram, Harry W., 43 Thied St., Shelby, Ohio.
Mackey, Frank C., N. Ninth St., Cambridge, Ohio.
Malden, Edward N., 220 5. Sixth St., Fryesville, Ohio.
Marquette, William A., R. F. D. Hanesburg, Ohio.
Moratno, Edward B., 311 Dryden Coast N.W., Canton, Ohio.
Martin, Jamee F., 60 B. Ninth St., Chillicothe, Ohio.
Mastoron, Entrich, 1326 W. 28th So., Cleveland, Ohio
Mattan, Robert H., R. R. No. 2, Lewistown, Ohio.
Marmell, Charles R., Richmond, Ohio.
Meinken, Frank F., 700 Heave Ave., Cincinnati, Ohio.
Miller, Stanley, Ohio.
Mischler, Earl C., 1310 Stone Ave., Sandusky, Ohio.
Mihler, Lester, North Canton, Ohio.
Monte, Ralph, R. F. D. No. 1, Tiffin, Ohio.
Morrhead, Frank C., Oeaint, Ohio.
Mullen, Hogh A., Oateo Mills, Ohio.
Nickel, Joseph M., Chestnut St., Swanton, Ohio.
Nickernon, Earnest W., 213 W. Madison Ave., Hanovertown, Pa.
Oberle, Oscar, 304 Cerle Ave., Hamilton, Ohio.
O'Cein, John F., 10 S. Elm St., Warren, Ohio.
O'Connell, Daniel F., 38 Braver St., Nors, Ohio.
Osbrorn, Enford F., 024 F. Sixth St., Middletown, Ohio.
Palmer, Albert L., 1210 Tascarawas St. F., Canton, Ohio.
Parke, Clyde, 1072 Taylor Ave., Akron, Ohio.
Prerino, Peter, 2309 Boone St., Cincinnati, Ohio.
Pittinger, C., Decator, Ohio.
Poetman, Urban F., 613 Sandals Place N.E., Canton, Ohio.
Potter, O. F., 32 Ridge Rd., Lomistown, Pa.
Penoarin, Franca, 1900 Orange Ave., Cleveland, Ohio.
Proteman, John H., R. F. 0. Ho. 1, Lemioborg, Ohio.
Panner, Raymond B., Levittsburg, Ohio.
Pogh, B. H., 042 5. Righy St., Youngstown, Ohio.
Quill, A. F., Ohio.
Rabe, Clarence. 100 Lomne St., Oaton, Ohio.
Raflas, F., 633 Delimare Ave., Colombus, Ohio.
Ranch, William, 2206 B. Fifth St., Dayton, Ohio.
Rayborn, Raymond 0., Son 186, Point Pleasant, W. Va.
Real, J. T., 120 Beard St., Nibs, Ohio.
Ramar, Norbert J., 393 Ciecolar St., Tiffin, Ohio.
Raikanski, William F., 421 Franklin Ct., Warren, Ohio.
Reis, P., 24 Fifth St. N.E., Canton, Ohio.
Reck, Ralph L., Onla, Ohio.
Reynolds, Walter N., 9 Cherry St., Warren, Ohio.
Riegler, F. N., 002 Third St. N.F., Canton, Ohio.
Riegler, Lester J., 602 Third St. N.E., Canton, Ohio.
Rocchi, A., 360 Second Ave., Callopolis, Ohio.
Rook, David C., Mattamana, Pa.
Rooske, Albert W., 914 Tenth St. N.E., Canton, Ohio.
Roth, Carl V., 1902 13th Sn. N.W., Canton, Ohio.
Rothe, Charles O., 679 Delhi Ave., Cincinnati, Ohio.
Rosh, Daniel W., Joyce, Ohio.
Roland, Stanley C., 342 W. Locust St., Newark, Ohio.
Salman, Charles, 90 Ring Ave., Columbus, Ohio.
Salman, Michael F., 2906 Yale Ave., Cleveland, Ohio.
Shnampf, Elmer O., R. F. 0. Na. 5, St. Marys, Ohio.
Scharf, Carl, R. F. D. No. 4, Canton, Ohio.
Schieffer, Earl O., R. R. No. 1, Tyrell, Ohio.
Schimt, Frank J., 2149 Stablee St., Cincinnati, Ohio.
Schmittee, Paul, 797 5. Sixth St., Columbus, Ohio.
Schneider, Charles F., 1142 Line St., Cincinnati, Ohio.
Sahorotiher, Charles H., 3862 Vine St., Cincinnati, Ohio.
Sohenibee, Peter F., 1009 Harrison Ave., Cincinnati, Ohio.
Schwab, Cecil, 1320 Shelby Ave., St. Paul, Minn.
Shadley, James B., R. F. D. No. I, McGuffey, Ohio.
Shaffer, Howard D., 909 Eighth St. N.W., Canton, Ohio.
Shattock, Tracy A., 1869 F. Ninth St., Cleveland, Ohio.
Short, William A., Harnod, Ohio.
Smith, John W., 9502 Empire Ave., Cleveland, Ohio.
Sinclair, Carl A., Myers Lake Park, Canton, Ohio.
Smith, Robert B., 372 F. Federal St., Youngstown, Ohio.
Smith, Harry E., 3948 Vinton St., Pittsburgh. Pa.
Snider, E., R. F. D. No. 2, Ada, Ohio.
Snyder, Edward J., R. F. D. No. 2, Warren, Ohio.
Spencer, Roy, R. F. D. No. 1, Roundhead, Ohio.
Spankle, Lloyd, 710 Correll Ave. N.E., Canton, Ohio.
Sprouse, Wayne, J., R.F.D., No. 2, Willoughby, Ohio.
Stain, David, R. F. D. No. 1, Nola, Ohio.
Stillwell, Cannol, Atlanta, Indiana.
Stinemao, Charles B., R. F. D. No. 1, Palmesville, Ohio.
Stover, John R., North Canton, Ohio.
Stoahl, Frank K., R. F. D. No. 2, Malta, Ohio.
Stratton, Frank L., R. F. D. No. 3, Middlefield, Ohio.
Staeb, Irvin D., 617 Ninth St. N.W., Canton, Ohio.
Stroup, Ohmen K., Ingoman, Ohio.
Sullivan, Frank A., 123 Butler St., Niles, Ohio.
Sumi, Samuel, 510 Arlington Ave. N.W., Canton, Ohio.
Swain, Howard D., 1600 Towland Ave. N.E., Canton, Ohio.
Swaney, Lawrence A., R. D. No. 1, Millport, Ohio.
Taylor, Hanlan W., R. D. No. 1, Galion, Ohio.
Tettlebach, J. A., Bay Village, Ohio.
Texten, Arthur L., 3028 W. 25th St., Cleveland, Ohio.
Thoma, 'Webber D., R. F. D. No. 2, Pomeroy, Ohio.
Tift, Walter, 2902 Wade Ave., Cleveland. Ohio.
Tobin, Chester C., 650 B. Fifth Ave., Columbus, Ohio.
Tornans, Charles D., Heaven, Okla.
Toth, John, High St., Fairport, Ohio.
Utt, Henry, 208 Olive St., Warren, Ohio.
Valenio, Giacinto, 907 Blbenon Ave., Cincinnati, Ohio.
Watts, Herbert K., Main St., Utica, Ohio.
Weber, Bryon M., R. F. D. No. 4, Ada, Ohso.
Wednen, John P., 917 Elberon Ave., Cincinnati, Ohio.
Werbeach, John H., 202 Vine St., Fairport, Ohio.
Wessei, Bernard, 1001 State St., Cincinnati, Ohio.
Wilde, Walter J., 720 Rosemont Ave., Cincinnati, Ohio.
Williamson, Alton L., Main St., Mineral Ridge, Ohio.
Wilson, Arthur, Roxhuny, Ohio.
Withenstine, Harry J., Jay St., Newton Falls, Ohio.
Wolf, Lorin J., North Canton, Ohio.
Wood, Clarence P., R. F. D. No. 1, Iola, Ohio.
Young, Robert M., 17th St., Kenmore, Ohio.
Zimmen, Jake, 3305 B. 49th St., Cleveland. Ohio.
Zollen, August L., 2428 Lehman Rd., Cincinnati. Ohio.
Zwick, Leo W., 2518 Gabriel Ave., Cincinnati, Ohio.

H COMPANY

Dempsey, John P., Cleveland, Ohio.
Bayles, Leo W., 2586 Glenmawn Ave., Columbus, Ohio.
Coffman, William M., 217 F. Northwood Ave., Columbus, Ohio.
Higgins, Frank J., Jr., 640 Howard Ave., New Haven, Conn.
Adams, Richard L., 114 Middlebury Ave., Akron, Ohio.
Amos, Loyd 0., 623 Bowman St., Mansfield, Ohio.
Auld, James, 1730 Third St. S.E., Canton, Ohio.
Baker, Leo, 2014 Ninth St. SW., Canton, Ohio.
Barn, Charles P., 24 Cambridge St., Akron, Ohio.
Bashore, John F., R. F. D. No. 1, New Vienna, Ohio.
Betz, Herbert S., General Delivery, Waynesburg, Ohio.
Betzler, Francis A., 1727 Mahoning Rd. N.E., Canton, Ohio.
Boals, Albert L., 215 Grant St., Mansfield, Ohio.
Bochner, Albert W., Butler County, Ohio.
Bonowski, Walter L., 3001 Hantman St., Toledo, Ohio.
Bousson. Cyril, 369 Meldrum St., Detroit, Mich.
Bouklias,William, 1836 Deuber Ave. S.E., Canton, Ohio.
Boyd, Thomas S., 217½ S. Main St., Warren, Ohio.
Boyer, Sylvester P., 804 Seventh St. N.E., Canton, Ohio.
Breiglo, John F., 1026 Prospect Ave. SW., Canton. Ohio.
Brothers, Carl K., R. F. D. No. 1, North Industry, Ohio.
Brown, Hollie M., Pataskala, Ohio.
Brunnen, John, 2013 Navarre Rd. SW., Canton, Ohio.
Burgess, Arthur, Buchtel, Ohio.
Burns, Harry J., 11603 Thornewood Ave. Cleveland, Ohio.
Burton, George W., Millfield, Ohio.
Byers, Steve, 66 Woodbine Ave., Stuthers, Ohio.
Campbell. Victor L., R. F. D. No. 5, Cambridge. Ohio.
Canlin, Joseph L., 1370 E. 49th St., Cleveland, Ohio.
Canrass, George L., 117 B. Third St., Middletown, Ohio.
Ceider, Charles F., 113 Elwood St., Middletown, Ohio.
Chraczonowski, John, 3547 F. 75th St., Cleveland, Ohio.
Cofta, Benjamin, Peninsula, Ohio.
Colle, Joseph K., 1306 High Ave. SW., Canton, Ohio.
Colwell, Clyde J., 1459 Baird Ave., Camden, Ohio.
Connors, William, 661 5. Market St., Galion, Ohio.
Corey, Norton K., Chagrin Falls, Ohio.
Cotton, Hyman J., 5713 Dibble Ave., Cleveland. Ohio.
Coulias, Gus G., 1889 F. 17th St., Cleveland, Ohio.
Culbentson, Roy A., 1113 Thind St. SW., Canton, Ohio.
Cunningham. Clyde D., 1109 Sixth St. SW., Canton, Ohio.
Custis, Earl J., Sebina, Ohio.
Curnota, Kasper, 244 Oakland St., Toledo, Ohio.
Debald, Joseph J., 4411 Bridge Ave., Cleveland, Ohio.
DeVito, Angelo, 1223 Gonden Ave. SE., Canton, Ohio.
Dulaney. Alonzo, Glouster, Ohio.
Dunaitshik, Philip, R. F. D. No. 5, Mansfield, Ohio.
Dunant, Harmon K., R. F. D. No. 5, Pataskala, Ohio.
Dyer, Joseph A., 1137 Dewalt Ave. S. W., Canton, Ohio.
Ebner, John H., 1329 Oxford Ave. N.W., Canton, Ohio.
Eish, Raymond W., 632 Garfield Ave. SW., Canton, Ohio.
Emch, Martin H., W. Liberty St., Ginand, Ohio.
Enmnick, Philip P., R. F. D. 1, Celina, Ohio.
Emo, Leonard T., 2656 F. 128th St., Cleveland, Ohio.
Entle, Herbert L., 1024 Prospect Ave. SW., Canton, Ohio.
Fields, Claude S., 1439 Roland Ave. N.E., Canton, Ohio.
Filigno, Joseph, 56 Broad St., Struthers, Ohio.
Finefrock. Robert T., Waynesburg. Ohio.
Franko, Louis P., R. F. D. 5, Painesville, Ohio.
Franz, Guisceppe, 2418 Metta Ave., Cleveland, Ohio.
Frazer, John H., 213 Columbus St., Wilmington, Ohio.
Friedman, Frank F., R. F. D. 4, Waco, Ohio.
Fromica, Pietro, 918 Cherry Ave. S.E., Canton, Ohio.
Fry, Rollie L., 182 Hanker St., Mansfield, Ohio.
Gable, Floyd B., 1206 Fifth St. SW., Canton, Ohio.
Goltz, Robert D., 1207 Fifth St. N.E., Canton, Ohio.
Giffin, Loman H., 838 Jeanette St., Parkersbung, W. Va.
Gonden, Ray P., 1615 Garfield Ave SW., Canton, Ohio.
Gorsuch, Gnoven G., R. F. D. 5, Johnstown, Ohio.
Gowdy, George W., 609 Third St. S.W., Canton, Ohio.
Grabowiky, August, 3916 Reading Ave., Cleveland, Ohio.
Grogro, George E., 1904 Tuscarawas Ave. W., Canton, Ohio.
Grohol, Joseph W., 133 Daisy St., Mansfield, Ohio.
Guon, Thomas B., 593 E. 136th St., New York City, N. Y.
Haag, William A., 241 Sycamore St., Mansfield, Ohio.
Harris, Oscar, 523 Market St., Warren, Ohio.
Hatfield, Robert, Railroad St., Nelsonville, Ohio.
Hayden, Clay T., 912 Monroe St., Zanesville, Ohio.
Heinz, Carl, 412 Carroll St., Youngstown, Ohio.
Holmes, Charles A., Lovanna, N. Y
Hoover, John C., 510 Fourth St. N.W., Canton, Ohio.
Homer, Alben L., R. F. D. 2, Canton, Ohio.
Hoslen, Charles H., 134 B St., Carlisle, Pa.
Householder, Albert S., Box 39, Canton, Ohio.
Huberty, Arthur K., R. F. D. 1, Canton, Ohio.
Hunter, William A., 1028 Melchoin P1. SW., Canton, Ohio.
Inskeep, Otis D., Lone City, Ohio.
Iucci, Giocondo, Glencoe, Ohio.
Jackson, James F., K. F. D. 4, Chagrin Falls, Ohio.

Jeffers, Albert, R. F. D. 1, Shade, Ohio.
Kaina, John, Butler, Pa.
Kasnen, Perry, 60 Harker St., Mansfield, Ohio.
Ketchak, James, 6904 Lansing Ave., Cleveland, Ohip.
Kieffer, Charles S., 1116 High St. SW., Canton, Ohio.
Kitchen, Dwight V., 236½ Main St., Coshocton, Ohio.
Knell, Russell T., 78 Pioneer St., Dayton, Ohio.
Kuntiosky, John A., 622 High Ave. SW., Canton, Ohio.
Laughny, Earnest K., R. F. D. 8, Newark, Ohio.
Lightfritz, Samuel F., 212 Dryden Ct., Canton, Ohio.
Long, Earnest E., Bellville, Ohio.
Longfellow, Potten, 788 Main St., Akron, Ohio.
Longstreeh, William A., McLuney, Perry County, Ohio.
Lowry, William D., Athens, Ohio.
McBride, Thomas F., 863 Sullivant Ave., Columbus, Ohio.
McElhiney, Benjamin, 9403 Meech Ave., Cleveland, Ohio.
McKean, Chester, 3036 Sixth St. S.W., Canton, Ohio.
Mandello, Baccilio, 113 Furnace St., Akron, Ohio.
Martindale, Daniel, North Industry, Ohio.
Metzger, William Jr., 1397 E. 59th St., Cleveland, Ohio.
Meyer, Fred A., 2971 F. 116th St., Cleveland, Ohio.
Miller, Ivan D., K. F. D. 3, Canton, Ohio.
Mizen, Floyd K., 909 Smith Ave. SW., Canton, Ohio.
Montgomery, George F., Kimbollton, Ohio.
Moore, Robert W., R. F. D. 8, Kent, Ohio:
Morgan, Harry M., R. F. D. 4, Osborn, Ohio.
Mornom, Clyde M., 1656 Tuscarawas Ave., Canton, Ohio.
Mosinski, Leo, S., 5802 Hosmen Ave., Cleveland, Ohio.
Muckley, Paul B., R. F. D. 2, Waynesburg, Ohio.
Myers, Otto F., Newark, Ohio.
Nelson, Harry, 527 Columbus Ave., Canton, Ohio.
Nye, Simon F., 627 Bedford Ave. S.W., Canton, Ohio.
O'Conner, Michel J., 701 N. Main St., Lima, Ohio.
O'Connor, Theodore T., R. F. D. 67, Sharon, Pa.
Orton, Clyde H., 935 Ramsey St., Wilkinsburg, Pa.
Parrot, George C., 404 Melchoin Pt. N.W., Canton, Ohio.
Patton, Edwin H., R. F. D. 3, Canton, Ohio.
Peabody, Irving W., R. F. D. 2, Elyria, Ohio.
Pearson, Albert L., R. F. D. 1, Osnabung, Ohio.
Pennell, Clifford A., Senecaville, Ohio.
Petit, Comilioo W., 1610 Ninth St. SW., Canton, Ohio.
Phillips, Harry K., 397 Grand St., Patterson, N. J.
Phillips, William, 666 Coventry St., Akron, Ohio.
Pickin, Frank T., 48 James St., Gerard, Ohio.
Poe, Chester B., 985 Cleveland St., Chillicothe, Ohio.
Pokoniky, Stanislaw, 719 E. 70th St., Cleveland, Ohio.
Pope, George F., 219 S. Whitman St., Xenia, Ohio.
Pore, Glen D., K. D. 1, Mansfield, Ohio.
Pudlicki, Walter S., 3173 Legrand St., Toledo, Ohio.
Quillan, George W., R. F. D. 2, Kimbellton, Ohio.
Reed, Earl F., Hebron, Ohio.
Reese, Hanny J., 16 N. Michigan St., Toledo, Ohio.
Reinhart, William D., 701 12th St. N.E., Canton, Ohio.
Reitler, Sylvester, K. F. D. 1, Byesville, Ohio.
Richardson, Alben S., 2921 Fourth St. NW., Canton, Ohio.
Robertson, Frank B., 9501 Yale Ave., Cleveland, Ohio.
Romeo, James V., 65 11th St., Youngstown, Ohio.
Rose, John R., 4400 Carnegie Ave., Cleveland, Ohio.
Ruemmele, Arthur, 811 Vine St., Sandusky, Ohio.
Sanne, Guiseppe, 2604 Scoville Ave., Cleveland, Ohio.
Savage, Joseph H., 2344 W. 41st St., Cleveland, Ohio.
Savage, Leo A., 6202 Utica Ave., Cleveland, Ohio.
Schaffner, Paul B., 736 High Ave. SW., Canton, Ohio.
Shauen, Edward A., 230 Smith Ave. SW., Canton, Ohio.
Schmidt, Jonnie M., Fay, Ohio.
Schneider, Goutfried, 411 14th St. S.E., Canton, Ohio.
Schraeder, Harry M., R. F. D. 1, Butler, Ohio.
Schroeder, Roland F., Blue Stone Rd., South Euclid, Ohio.
Schuler, Howard L., R. F. D. 1, Massillon, Ohio.
Schultz, Franklin H., 304 Burr St., Houston, Texas.
Swartz, Harvey 0., R. F. D. 6, Canton, Ohio.
Seachrist, Leo J., 92 W. Third St., Conning, N. Y.
Senpa, Frank, 266 N. Franklin St., Mansfield, Ohio.
Shaw, Joseph H., 807 Second St. N.E., Canton, Ohio.
Sheil, Roy A., 312 High Ave. SW., Canton, Ohio.
Schsler, Earl, Beech City, Ohio.
Shivers, Anchie B., K. F. D. 4, Kimbellton, Ohio.
Shull, Raymond B., 799 Savannah Ave. N.E., Canton, Ohio.
Shunts, Ralph W., 649 Greenfield Ave. SW., Canton, Ohio.
Skoluda, John, 135 Stnicker St., Toledo, Ohio.
Smato, Tony, 323 S. High St., Akron, Ohio.
Smith, Damon F., 46½ N. Gamble St., Shelby, Ohio.
Smith, Robert T., 592 N. Howard St., Akron, Ohio.
Smith, Verne, St. Louisville, Ohio.
Sneddon, Richard Jr., Lore City, Ohio.
Sounwine, Ross K., Plymouth, Ohio.
Speakman, Raymond, 727 B. Fourth St., Chillicothe, Ohio.
Spencer, Alfred J., 1026 Dueber Ave. SW., Canton, Ohio.
Spitens, Pietre, 3254 Guernsay, Bellaine, Ohio.
Scocynski, Mike M., 3361 E. 71st St., Cleveland, Ohio.
Stage, Herchel M., 211 Fifth St., Byesville, Ohio.
Stallard, Wilfred H., K. F. D. 16, Everett, Ohio.
Stanley, Allen H., 258 Highland Ave., Cambridge, Ohio.
Stark, John V., 10710 Grandview Ave., Cleveland, Ohio.
Stewart, Howard H., Westhono, Ohio.
Stockton, Elmer D., 120 Ohio St., Bellevue, Ohio.
Stocker, Roy F., K. F. D. 1, Mansfield, Ohio.
Stone, Dalton E., 632 Grant Ave., Cambridge. Ohio.
Stnoud, Charles, R. F. D. 1, Byesville, Ohio.
Swigert, B. C., 2026 Ninth St. SW., Canton, Ohio.
Tate, Edward C., Yellow Springs, Ohio.
Temple, Arthur, Loudenville, Ohio.
Teubner, Charles, 1428 Willet Ave. S.F., Canton, Ohio.
Thomas, Walter H., K. F. D. 1, Spring Valley, Ohio.
Thompson, George B., R. F. D. 3, New Matamoris, Ohio.
Tindall, Elton W., Clark County, Ohio.
Tomlinson, Floyd F., R, F. D. 4, Shelby, Ohio.
Tooker, Guy F., 404 B. Locust St., Wilmington, Ohio.
Turner, Dudley P., 406 High Ave. S.W., Canton, Ohio.
Troupe, Walter D., Canton, Ohio.
Trout, Loyd, R. F. D. 1, Alexandria, Ohio.
Valurdus, George, 26 F. 10th St., Youngstown, Ohio.
VanHorn, Adam T., 1109 Garfield Ave. S.W., Canton, Ohio.
Vecchio, Angelo, 2551 B. 39th St., Cleveland, Ohio.
Vlotz, Henry C., 932 Dueben Ave. SW., Canton, Ohio.
Vorhies, Charles B., 230 N. Fourth St., Cambridge, Ohio.
Walker, Claude K., 750 Fourth St., Chillicothe, Ohio.
Ward, Clayton, K. F. D. 12, Box 204, Defiance, Ohio.
Weber, Frank J., K. F. D. 9, Defiance, Ohio.
Weisenberger, Clanence, 1114 Second St. N.W., Canton, Ohio.
Weiss, Jonas, 2122 B. 40th St., Cleveland, Ohio.
Welly, Hanman M., 1565 E. 49th St., Cleveland, Ohio.
Whitcomb, Fred, R. F. D. 1, Denver, Ohio.
Wiley, Parley J., Byesville, Ohio.
Wilhelm, Norman F., 1829 Market Ave. S., Canton, Ohio.
Williams, Kay K., Waynesburg, Ohio.
Wiseman, Hanley, Wilkesville, Ohio.
Wongler, William J., R. F. D. 1, Kimball, Ohio.
Yike, Robert, New Salem, Penny County, Ohio.
Young, William S., Rear 400 W. Fourth St., Mansfield, Ohio.

SUPPLY COMPANY

Johns, Wallace W., 427 Seventh St., Huntington, W. Va.
Meldrum, Douglas G., 2100 Surry Rd., Cleveland, Ohio.
Smith, Robert O., 399 Harbor Ave., Conneaut, Ohio.
Carroll, Humbent J.
Babb, John L., 109 W. Water St., Troy, Ohio.
Almasy, Joseph, Box 178, Struthens, Ohio.
Alvers, William, 169 Maple St., Dayton, Ohio.
Arnold, Arthur, 1916 Main St., Kenmone, Ohio.
Aspros, James, Warwick, Ohio.
Bauer, John, 121 Donsey St., Cincinnati, Ohio.
Baum, Elijah, R. F. D. 1, Osnaburg, Ohio.
Bauman, William I., 3109 Emerson Ave., S. Minneapolis, Minn.
Beaty, David L., Oceola Mills Pa.
Beckley, Emanuel, Kilgore, Ohio.
Beckoer, Raymond, Petroleum, W. Va.
Belecak, Ignace, 1156 Manning Ave., Youngstown, Ohio.
Bican, James, Rocky River, Ohio.
Booth, Francis C., 228 Fulton St., Youngstown, Ohio.
Brooks, Francis, 120 E. Fourth St., East Liverpool, Ohio.
Brudenly, Frank, 335 W. Main St., Salem, Ohio.
Buskink, Wayne, 1729 19th St., Parkersburg, W. Va.
Caputo, John, Carrollton, Ohio.
Candaman, Frank, Stop 5, A. B. C. Line, Bedford, Ohio.
Carley, James, 56 W. Main St., Greenville, Pa.
Canman, Chester B., New Athens, Ohio.
Casey, Alfred W., 670 N. Pearl St., Columbus, Ohio.
Chalk, Francis L., 242 Custer Ave., Youngstown, Ohio.
Chapman, Ernie A., Noveltie, Ohio.
Chapman, Frank, 1639 Glenwood Ave. Youngstown, Ohio.
Cleary, Raymond G., 1209 Charlotte Ave., Youngstown, Ohio.
Condo, John, Germano, Ohio.
Conrad, Frank S., 811 Seventh Ave., Three Rivers, Mich.
Cook, Harold B., 101 Groveland St., Oberlin, Ohio.
Coppersmith, William P., 1906 Oakland Ave., Youngstown, Ohio.
Cowan, Loyal H., R. F. D. 2, Saxonbung, Pa.
Cowles, Frederick W., 11 Sumner Rd., Cambridge, Mass.
Croell, Leo, 1012 Harmony St., Youngstown, Ohio.
Cumsuins, John L., Freedom Station, Portage County, Ohio.
Damron, William, 2802 Ohio Ave., Huntington, W. Va.
Danoer, Harrison, Tallmadge, Ohio.
Darst, Howard W., 946 Fifth Ave., Akron, Ohio.
Davis, James, 729 Clarendon Ave., Middletown, Ohio.
Davis, Merle, R. F. D. 2, Huotsburg, Ohio.
Denemen, Marshall H., Everett, Pa.
Disdonato, Pasquale, 10 State St., Peninsula, Ohio.
Diville, Lewis J., 90 Ohio Ave., Salem, Ohio.
Dodway, Arthur J., 222 E. Shaw Ave., Freemont, Ohio.
Dunfee, Ray, 643 Poplar St., Goshocton, Ohio.
Eibeo, John, 4515 Storer Ave., Cleveland, Ohio.
Ferguson, James W., 539 Foster St., Youngstown, Ohio.
Frazier, Walter F., Canfield, Ohio.
Frey, Frank J., 425 Lucas St., Barberton, Ohio.
Friedl, Gabriel R., 1601 Denison Ave., Cleveland, Ohio.
Friedman, Joseph, 2231 Powers Way, Youngstown, Ohio.
Gamble, Franklin, 365 W. Kayen Ave., Youngstown, Ohio.
Gebhandt, Warren A., R. F. D. 1, New Springfield, Ohio.
Glendining, William, 219 Hickory Ave., Moundsville, W. Va.
Goldstein, Alexander, 1425 Cutter St., Cincinnati, Ohio.
Gottiman, Charles, R. R. 1, Magnolia, Ohio.
Greenawalt, Benjamin, Sebriog, Ohio.
Grischow, Henry, 230 Superior St., Youngstown, Ohio.
Gnodotzky, William, North Bend, Ohio.
Hall, John P., 112 New St., Marietta, Ohio.
Harris, William L., R. F. D. 4, Alliance, Ohio.
Hantment, Clarence J., 1660 B. 55th St., Cleveland, Ohio.
Henderson, Arthur, 1919 Clifton St., Youngstown, Ohio.
Henderson, William R., Mifflin, Pa.
Hinkle, Carl P., R. F. D. 34, Barbertoo, Ohio.
Issac, Kelly, 240 Broadway, Toledo, Ohio.
Jackman, Franklin, 319 Harrison Ave., Harrison, Ohio.
Jendski, Joseph, 10 W. Weber St., Toledo, Ohio.
Jester, William G., 3800 Park Ave., Covington, Ky.
Johnson, Harvey, 423 Maryland St., Sebring, Ohio.
Jones, David, 1140 S. Mahooing Ave., Alliance, Ohio.
Jones, James, 1140 S. Mahooing Ave., Alliance, Ohio.
Joyce, Harry, 1128 Emma St., Youngstown, Ohio.
Katienberg, Morris, 232 Spring St., Youngstown, Ohio.
Keowo, William, R. F. D. 1, Lowellville, Ohio.
Kennan, Thomas F., 613 North Ave., Youngstown, Ohio.
Killian, Walter, Terrehill, Pa.
Knobe, Anchie, Carrollton, Ohio.
Kunz, Arthur F., 1102 Yankee Rd., Middleton, Ohio.
Kunfess, Frank, 17 F. Marion St., Youngstown, Ohio.
Lawlon, Leslie, Orchard Ave., Pleasant Gnove, Ohio.
Leopandi, Pasquale, Water St., Lowellville, Ohio.
Leppert, William J., 1116 St. Gregory St., Cincinnati, Ohio.
Levy, Sidney, 7A Barclay Apts., Cincinnati, Ohio.
Lewis, Kobert A., 1402 N. Montford Ave., Baltimore, Md.
Lewis, William.
Martin, Harrison, 825 5. Main St., Middletown, Ohio.
Matchett, William J., Darien Center, New York.
Maven, Dallas, 117 W. Boardman St., Youngstown, Ohio.
McCone, Luke, 264 Custer Ave., Youngstown, Ohio.
McGlaughlin, William, 1896 N. Fourth St., Columbus, Ohio.
Meyer, Carl H., 1116 Michigan St., Toledo, Ohio.
Meyers, John, 305 Mohawk St., Cincinnati, Ohio.
Meyers. William B., 5803 Grand Ave., Cleveland, Ohio.
Miller, August F., 205 W. Boardman St., Youngstown, Ohio.
Miller, Ernest E., 500½ Ohio St., Akron, Ohio.
Miller, John M., 814 Loucks Ave., Scottdale, Pa.
Neville, Arthur, 1815 Mahoning Ave., Youngstown, Ohio.
O'Neill, Edward, 531 Burnett St., Youngstown, Ohio.
Parry, George W., 511 Hillman St., Youngstown, Ohio.
Peebles, Daniel J., 254 Custer Ave., Youngstown, Ohio.
Pennington, Amos B., Mahaffey, Pa.
Pizzoferrato, Samuel, 465 Rice Ave., Youngstown. Ohio.
Pullan, Albert, 16 Hubbard St., Aslitabula, Ohio.
Randa, Matt, New St., Fairport Harbor, Ohio.
Raymond, James, 3213 Monroe St., Toledo, Ohio.
Reckenberger, John, 523 Eddy Rd., Cleveland, Ohio.
Reesh, Clinton B., New Springfield. Ohio.
Renkert, Ralph W., R. P. D. 2, West Liberty, Ohio.
Rhoades, Charles, 683 N. Third St., Barberton, Ohio.
Rock, George, 646 Erie St., Youngstown, Ohio.
Rose, Fred, Cadiz, Ohio.
Rossow, William, 248 Belmont Ave., Youngstown, Ohio.
Schaffer, John C., R. F. D. 1, Fresno, Ohio.
Schaffer, John B., 605 Finley St., Cincinnati, Ohio.
Schreffler, Gilbert, Newport, Pa.
Schroeder, Herman, 307 Jefferson St., Youngstown, Ohio.
Seabrook, Edward, No. 5, Arlington St., Akron, Ohio.
Shenot, Arthur, No. 3, Young St., Pittsburgh, Pa.
Stark, Henry, 513 Hayman St., Youngstown, Ohio.

Strohman, Richard W., 3435 Jay St., Cincinnati, Ohio.
Taylor, Dennis B., 762 S. Main St., Akron, Ohio.
Thomas, Philip, 532 W. Arlington St., Youngstown, Ohio.
Toben, Royce, Parkman, Ohio.
Underwood, William, 45 B. Town St., Columbus, Ohio.
Unger, Robert, R. R. 3, Lewisburg, Ohio.
Valos, Mike, 1525 South Ave., Youngstown, Ohio.
Waddinton, William, 736 W. Madison Ave., Youngstown, Ohio.
Wahoff, Bernard H., 1109 Dayton St., Cincinnati, Ohio.
Ward, William, 2416 Eastern Ave., Cincinnatti, Ohio.
Waring, Harold B., 2099 W. Broad St., Columbus, Ohio.
Welsh, Martin, 41 N. Lane Ave., Youngstown, Ohio.
Whalen, William, 99 N. Truesdale Ave., Youngstown, Ohio.
Williams, Earle, 205 Jefferson St., Youngstown, Ohio.
Willick, John, 810 Stickney St., Toledo, Ohio.
Winings, Jesse O., R. F. D. 1, Means, Ohio.
Wise, James H., Illinois St., Kenmore, Ohio.
Wolf, Sherman, 26 Hanley Ave., Youngstown, Ohio.
Young, John W., 444 Elmira Ave., Youngstown, Ohio.
Zedaker, Charles, Poland, Ohio.
Zimmerman, 134 Jefferson St., Youngstown, Ohio.
Howell, William D., 2334 Prospect Ave., Cleveland, Ohio.
Kling, Philip, 122 W. Front St., Youngstown, Ohio.
Loue, Robert, 936 Yale St., Akron, Ohio.
Magee, Raymond W., Brewster, Ohio.
Miller, Maurice B., R. F. D. 1, Abbottstown, Pa.
Riley, Forest L., Hilton St., Youngstown, Ohio.
Stowe, Russell, 256 W. Oregon Ave., Sebring, Ohio.
Brand, Garnett W., 317 W. Reynolds St., Urbana, Ohio.
Edwards, Philip P., 267 W. Lorraine St., Oberlin, Ohio.
Hird, James P., 16010 Detroit Ave., Lakewood, Ohio.
Blair, Guy M., 703 Washington St., Portsmouth, Ohio.
Smith, R. F., Burrows, Ind.

I COMPANY

Bratt, Harry C., 6 Mondonhall Apts., Dayton, Ohio.
Kennedy, Earl B., Findlay, Ohio.
Mauror, Edgar W., 1414 Rockerfeller Bldg., Cleveland, Ohio.
Story, Austin P., 147 Caldwell St., Chillicothe, Ohio.
Abraham, William A., 707 Second St. N.E., Canton, Ohio.
Allen, Thomas V., 369 Marshall Ave., Columbus, Ohio.
Amrine, Claude L., 60 N. 21st St., Columbus, Ohio.
Anderson, Howard R., 727 Antoinetta St. W., Detroit, Mich.
Orlando, Arthur, Lakeview, Ohio.
Bahnson, James H., Gypsum, Ohio.
Bailey, Edward R., 12320 Gaccola St., Cleveland, Ohio.
Balser, William P., Rt. 1, Massillon, Ohio.
Bauer, Otto, R. D. No. 3, Crestline, Ohio.
Beck, Frank J., Waynesburg, Ohio.
Beckenbach, Harold E., 7319 Lawnview Ave., Cleveland, Ohio.
Benzing, George S., 1613 Fulton Ave., Cincinnati, Ohio.
Bierley, Emery L., Aberdeen, Ohio.
Blank, Henry S., 210 Oxford Ave., Dayton, Ohio.
Bobo, Benjamin O., 58 Noble St., Delaware, Ohio.
Boehm, Joseph P., 786 Park St., Columbus, Ohio.
Boaskon, Albert L., 4269 Williamson Pl., Cincinnati, Ohio.
Bocher, Clarke W., 131 Daller St., Dayton, Ohio.
Bottoms, William B., 537 5. Jefferson St., Dayton, Ohio.
Bowers, Walter F., R. F. D. 2, Troy, Ohio.
Brain, Leo B., 25 N. Columbus St., Massillon, Ohio.
Bretschneider, Herman W., 1143 B. Summit St., Alliance, Ohio.
Brindley, Willis J., Minerva, Ohio.
Britt, William, 2972 B. 75th St., Cleveland, Ohio.
Britton, William S., Wick, W. Va.
Brockmeyer, John C., 163 Guilford Ave., Columbus, Ohio.
Brown, Elmer H., 4324 Riverside Ave., Cleveland. Ohio.
Bruhn, Carl, Elmore, Ohio.
Brush, David D., 64 W. Lane Ave., Columius, Ohio.
Burnett, Ralph A., 1015 Findlay St., Cincinnati, Ohio.
Burns, Ralph B., 379 Lexington Ave., Columbus, Ohio.
Butler, Raymond W., 3618 Walton Ave., Cleveland, Ohio.
Canterbery, Fred, 582 Oak St., Columbus, Ohio.
Carlin, Edward J., 1370 B. 49th St., Cleveland, Ohio.
Carman, Thomas C., R. D. No. 5, Troy, Ohio.
Cassle, Clarence A., 1011 Hamlet St., Columbus, Ohio.
Clabaugh, Arza M., Rushsylvania, Ohio.
Clark, Albert, Alliance, Ohio.
Clay, Willis H., Quincy, Ohio.
Cochran, Floyd H., Alliance, Ohio.
Collins, Stewart, 39 Elwood St., Tiflin, Ohio.
Colvin, Richard B., 7 B. Williams St. Delaware, Ohio.
Cosier, Harold, R. D. 1, Massillon, Ohio.
Crary, George, 1038 Rittenhouse St., Cincinnati, Ohio.
Crawford, Foster, Minerva, Ohio.
Crawford, George L., 12002 Robertson Ave., Cleveland, Ohio.

Damm, Julius, 1509 E. 66th St., Cleveland, Ohio.
Dartt, Roy B., Byesvitle, Ohio.
Davis, John H., 1222 Wesley Ave., Columbus, Ohio.
DeBolt, Lewis B., N. Main St., Richwood, Ohio.
Decker, Fred, 1819 Wooster St., Massillon, Ohio.
Dianni, Emilio, Box 16, Denbo, Pa.
DiSabatino, Albert, 1239 S. Linden Ave., Alliance, Ohio.
Dixon, John S., 503 N. Hennepin Ave., Dixon, Ill.
Dixon, Samuel O., 439 Hanford St., Columbus, Ohio.
Doll, Forrest A., R. D. No. 4, Massillon, Ohio.
Downing, Frank M., Bellecenter, Ohio.
Duffy, Thomas J., 6217 Webster St., Philadelphia, Pa.
Dvorak, Frank P., 3278 Fulton Rd., Cleveland, Ohio.
Ekelberry, George A., Box 26, Galena, Ohio.
Elliott, James V., 2117 E. 55th St., Cleveland, Ohio.
Ellison, James A., 1418 S. Lincoln Ave., Massillon, Ohio.
Feldman, Edward F., 3032 Warsaw St., Toledo, Ohio.
Fisher, William R., 917 Lindsey St., Toledo, Ohio.
Flack, Wilbur, 8115 Wade Park Ave., Cleveland, Ohio.
Flaughter, Adam H., Ripley, Ohio.
Franks, Ben, 1355 Summit St., Columbus, Ohio.
Frehse, Edwin J., 1402 E. 49th St., Cleveland, Ohio.
Frehman, Joseph J., R. F. D. No. I, Massillon, Ohio.
Gale, William A., 1456 Cleveland Ave., Columbus, Ohio.
Gast, Benjamin H., Prospect, Ohio.
George, Lovell G., Forrest, Ohio.
Gerber, Earl W., R. F. D. No. 3, Navarre, Ohio.
Getz, Karl G., 107 5. West St., Massillon, Ohio.
Geyer, Charles 0., 1739 Hanfield St., Cincinnati, Ohio.
Gill, Frederick R., Canal Pulton, Ohio.
Gobeck, Joseph, 415 E. Central Ave., Toledo, Ohio.
Gossett, Loren S., Seventeen, Ohio.
Gregg, Albert B., 3000 Shadeland Ave. N.S., Pittsburgh, Pa.
Grosjean, Louis N., R. F. D. No. 3, Curtice, Ohio.
Hainee, Howard C., 307 19th Ave., Columbus, Ohio.
Hardy, Thomas C., 1410 S. Erie St., Massillon, Ohio.
Han, John A., 666 Meadow Ave., Alliance, Ohio.
Harris, Reese, R. F. D. No. 2, Massillon, Ohio.
Harris, Stanley, 4833 E. 71st St., Cleveland, Ohio.
Hartman, Albert, 236 Stetson St., Cincinnati, Ohio.
Haudenschild, Willard O., 506 E. Ohio St., Kenton, Ohio.
Hawkins, Chester W., 1585 E. 33rd St., Cleveland, Ohio.
Heimann, Alfred R., 1940 W. Tremont St., Massillon, Ohio.
Heminger, Edwin C., Rushylvania, Ohio.
Herrmann, John K., Amsterdam, Ohio.
Hines, Leo M., 281 Shelby St., Alliance, Ohio.
Hoffman, Raymond S., R. F. P. No. 1, Massillon Ohio.
Hopkins, Raymond W., Box 12, Mentor, Ohio.
Howard, Charles N., R. F. D. No. 3, Sunbury, Ohio.
Howells, William L., 941 B. Patterson, St., Alliance, Ohio.
Huff, James A., Richwood, Ohio.
Inskeep, Howard, Middleburg, Ohio.
Ir, Anthony J., 1666 E. 82nd St., Cleveland, Ohio.
Irwin, Raymond H., R. F. P. No. I, East Canton, Ohio.
Jacobs, Jacob, 1624 Madison Ave., New York City, N. Y.
Jacobs, John P., R. F. P. No. 2, North Lawrence, Ohio.
Jeremis, Carman A., 11108 Ingersoll Rd., Cleveland, Ohio.
Jones, Harry C., Route No. 2, North Lawrence, Ohio.
Keister, Lloyd J., Crestline, Ohio.
Keith, Morris P., 2478 Ridgewood Ave., Alliance, Ohio.
Keller, Doweling, Navarre, Ohio.
Kelly, William H., 7725 Superior Ave., Cleveland, Ohio.
Kerges, William J., Navarre, Ohio.
King, Karl G., Bristolville, Ohio.
Koorber, Harry L., 2242 B. 74th St., Cleveland, Ohio.
Kohn, Richard H., 1822 E. 93rd St., Cleveland, Ohio.
Kraft, Sylvester J., R. F. D. No. 1, Massillon, Ohio.
Krieger, Edward J., 944 Pavilion St., Cincinnati, Ohio.
Krites, Virgil T., Rt. No. 6, Wapakoneta, Ohio.
Krupka, William, 3264 W. 52nd St., Cleveland, Ohio.
Kuntz, Elmer J., North Canton, Ohio.
Landgraver, Don S., West Liberty, Ohio.
Lane, Neal R., 311 W. First Ave., Columbus, Ohio.
Lanning, Lowell R., Dunkirk, Ohio.
Larmer, Fred T., Pinery Fork, Ohio.
Laws, Hamilton F., 555 B. Second St., Lima, Ohio.
Lucieris, Lewis, 26 B. Russell St., Columbus, Ohio.
Luckner, Charles B., 1119 Euclid St., Massillon, Ohio.
McAdoo, Ira W., 1408 State St., Massillon, Ohio.
McCampbell, Ivan M., Dolavan, New York.
McCoy, James, Lakeview, Ohio.
McDonald, Carl L., 211 Hester Ave., Alliance, Ohio.
McLaughlin, Elder B., Shelocta, Pa.
McNutt, Clinton A., R. F. D. No. 5, Forest, Ohio.
McQuaide, Thomas R., Salina, Pa.

Mann, James A., 1800 East Ave., Rochester, N. Y.
Market, William C., Put In Bay, Ohio.
Mathias, Frank M., Stark Hotel, Alliance, Ohio.
Meismer, Earl W., R. F. D. No. 2, Massillon, Ohio.
Menke, Edmund, 6016 Fleet Ave., Cleveland, Ohio.
Merritt, John B., 7924 Gory Ave., Cleveland, Ohio.
Miller, Edward, Rt. No. 3, Navarre, Ohio.
Miller, Harry W., Tile Station, Zanesville, Ohio.
Miller, James P., Dunkirk, Ohio.
Miller, Wade, R. F. D. No. 4, Massillon, Ohio.
Moschgat, Carl, 541 Woodvale Ave., Johnstown, Pa.
Moseley, Earl V., 1853 5. Union Ave., Alliance, Ohio.
Moser, Carl W., 368 Cherry St., Kenton, Ohio.
Moses, Carl L., 94 W. Fourth St., Mansfield, Ohio.
Moutes, George W., 257 5. Lyman St., Wadsworth, Ohio.
Mroczkowski, Wincenty, 3845 E. 53rd St., Cleveland, Ohio.
Myers, Willis W., 440 Market St., Kenton, Ohio.
Nardo, Dominick, 856 West Side Rd., Cleveland, Ohio.
Neal, John B., Nashville, Ind.
Nicholson, Alex, 366 Main St., Akron, Ohio.
Null, Albert, Ashley, Ohio.
Oliver, Arthur B., 8210 Korman Ave., Cleveland, Ohio.
Pastor, John F., Maple Heights, Bedford, Ohio.
Paul, Arthur W., R. F. D. No. 2, Navarre, Ohio.
Penrod, William, Beach City, Ohio.
Peters, Henry A., 3236 Superior Ave., Cleveland, Ohio.
Peterson, Otto, 518 E. Third St., Port Clinton, Ohio.
Phillips, Weller C., 398 W. Thornton St., Akron, Ohio.
Pimsner, Andrew C., 3506 56th St., Cleveland, Ohio.
Plumb, Grant M., Galona, Ohio.
Pocock, Hobert W., 711 North Ave., Dayton, Ohio.
Pollock, Howard S., 3458 W. 25th St., Cleveland, Ohio.
Pooley, Harry, 262 Ira Ave., Akron, Ohio.
Pylick, George A., 1766 W. 43rd St., Cleveland, Ohio.
Quaw, Thomas B., 619 S. Chestnut St., Havanna, Ohio.
Quigley, William P., 1269 B. 99th St., Cleveland, Ohio.
Quint, Abraham A., 10626 Greenlawn Ave., Cleveland, Ohio.
Radtka, Carl H., R. F. D. No. 1, Massillon, Ohio.
Rebillot, Urban L., Louisville, Ohio.
Rehm, David, 808 Dayton St., Cincinnati, Ohio.
Reilly, Patrick, 1197 E, 86th St., Cleveland, Ohio.
Rhine, Roy C., 1123 Wellman St., Massillon, Ohio.
Richards, John W., North Lawrence, Ohio.
Rogers, John L., 24 Mary Ave., Dayton, Ohio.
Rose, Bird, R. F. P. No. 2, Gallia, Ohio.
Ross, Fred, 396 Florence St., Newark, Ohio.
Sarli, Tibenio, 3003 Charle Ave., Cleveland, Ohio.
Scheimann, Joseph A., 1012 B. 72nd St., Cleveland, Ohio.
Schouffler, Ernest W., 717 B. Grant St., Dennison, Ohio.
Schlemmer, Fred, General Delivery, Alliance, Ohio.
Schlumpf, Frank B., 701 S. Elm St., Little Rock, Ark.
Schmelzenbach, Eugene B., Bedford, Ohio.
Schmidt, Edward B., 1905 Arch Ave., Alliance, Ohio.
Schmidt, Frank J., 1430 Raspberry St., Massillon, Ohio.
Schultz, Waiter C., 6731 Edna Ave., Cleveland, Ohio.
Schulze, Albert H., 25 Oak St., Danbury, Conn.
Schwall, Elroy M., Woodsfield, Ohio.
Scott, Blann H., 327 N. Webb St., Alliance, Ohio.
Short, Elmer L., W. Baird St., West Liberty, Ohio.
Smith, Earl M., 555 Lane St., Columbus, Ohso.
Smith, Frank F., 130 B. Fourth St., Marysville, Ohio.
Smurthwaite, Robert K., Bellefontaine, Ohio.
Snavely, Orin, Howells Ave., Massillon, Ohio.
Spletzer, Arthur W., Bryan, Ohio.
Stackhouse, Ralph R., Minerva, Ohio.
Stanley, Frank C., 4002 Nevada Ave., West Nashville, Tenn.
Sterzer, Charles A., 55 B. Third St., Dayton, Ohio.
Stone, Archie, 124 Empire St., Toledo, Ohio.
Sullivan, Joseph J., 5036 E. 79th St., Cleveland, Ohio.
Summers, John L., 1716 Logan Ave., Youngstown, Ohio.
Sventeck, John S., 955 E. 67th St., Cleveland, Ohio.
Tabor, Edwin J., 1854 Arch St., Alliance, Ohio.
Tabor, Waslaw, 4011 Warner Ave., Cleveland, Ohio.
Tague, Ferninand L., Crooksville, Ohio.
Tomaszowski, Stanley, Box 38, Dunham, Ind.
Truman, John W., Elmore, Ohio.
Veniman, Harvey, R. F. D. No. 6, Dayton, Ohio.
Varner, Lloyd C., 16 E. Vine St., Alliance, Ohio.
Vetter, Charles C., 41 Marion St., Massillon, Ohio.
Vollmar, Oscar R., 668 Wilson St., Winona, Minn.
Wahl, Andy, 18 Woodland Ave., Massillon, Ohio.
Warmuth, Charles C., Cumberland Valley Pa.
Webb, Joseph O., 20 W. Tremont St., Massillon, Ohio.
Webster, James L., 3649 W. Fine St., St. Louis, Mo.
Welsh, William H., 33 Auburn Pl., Alliance, Ohio.

Welty, Dan, West Mansfield, Ohio.
Wierzbichi, Tony, 3277 B. 65th St., Cleveland, Ohio.
Williams, Earl, 7504 Cedar Ave., Cleveland, Ohio.
Williams, Roy W., 3309 Riverside Ave., Cleveland, Ohio.
Williams, William J., R. F, D. No. 5, Massillon, Ohio.
Williner, Ernest O., Brewster, Ohio.
Winkhart, Harry W., Navarre, Ohio.
Wise, Harold H., 2115 S. Arch Ave., Alliance, Ohio.
Woodworth, Robert W., 1221 Metcalf St., Lima, Ohio.

K COMPANY
White, Wilbur M., 316 5. Plum St., Springfield, Ohio.
Dedenich, Robert J., 2619 Scottwood Ave., Toledo, Ohio.
Sullivan, Charles J., 908 Ritchie Ave., Lima, Ohio.
Hooper, Arthur L., Dillonvale, Ohio.
Dennison, David S., Sunnyside, Poland, Ohio.
Allison, Alex N., 519 Logan St., Steubenville, Ohio.
Amend, Edward, 785 Ebner St., Columbus, Ohio.
Armetrout, Jonah, Rd. No. 1, Fayetteville, Ohio.
Barrow, Harley F., Hillsboro, Ohio.
Baumberger, Alvin P., R. F. D. 1, Rayland, Ohio.
Beckett, Alva B., 510 South St., Steubenville, Ohio.
Bell, Wilbur B., R. D. 2, Box 24, Rayland, Ohio.
Bertram, Edward R., 408 N. Fourth St., Steubenville, Ohio.
Biggio, Andrew A., 124 N. Seventh St., Steubenville, Ohio.
Blake, Robert, East Ave., Washington Court House, Ohio.
Boggs, John N., 904 Lincoln Ave., Steubenville, Ohio.
Brady, Homer L., 301 E. Broadway St., New Baltimore, Ohio.
Bressler, Brsce H., 550 W. Ordway Ave., Bowling Green, Ohio.
Bristown, Charles, Perrysburg, Ohio.
Brown, George M., Lemoyne, Ohio.
Brown, Stanley S., 136 Second St., Girard, Ohio.
Burns, Robert E., 902 Franklin Ave., Steubenville, Ohio.
Byers, Jonas B., Toronto, Ohio.
Cahill, John J., 9 Lake St., Wakefield, Mass.
Carlile, Don, 112 Mill St., Kent, Ohio.
Cassman, Thomas J., 132 W. Eureka St., Lima, Ohio.
Chamberlin, James E., 331 S. Grove St., Bowling Green, Ohio.
Cilenti, Valentino, 1964 E. 120th St., Cleveland, Ohio.
Marino, Colonna, 841 W. Court St., Cincinnati, Ohio.
Compton, Everett I., Kingsport, Tenn.
Conn, Frank A., 504 5. Fourth St., Steubenville, Ohio.
Cornwall, Cohn, 1120 Beatty Ave., Cambridge, Ohio.
Coyle, Cornelius W., 106 Railroad Ave., Wellston, Ohio.
Crawford, Gilbert, R. P. 1, Williamsport, Ohio.
Cress, Thomas W., Zoe, Ky.
Creviston, Arthur R., 497 Wilson Ave., Marion, Ohio.
Czaika, Frank, 4387 Badgley Ave., Cincinnati, Ohio.
Darrah, Gilbert, 592 Spangler Dr., Zanesville, Ohio.
Davis, Delphos L., Maumee, Ohio.
Davis, Lewis, Bergholz, Ohio.
Dean, Clyde M., Box 191, Mingo Junction, Ohio.
Delia, Carmine, 2549 E. 110th St., Cleveland, Ohio.
DiViase, Venturi, 11323 Ingersol Rd., Cleveland, Ohio.
Dickson, Howard F., 323 Hiett Ave., Toledo, Ohio.
Dickson, John A., 225 N. Third St., Steubenville, Ohio.
Domitrovic, Frank C., Box 171, Mingo Junction, Ohio.
Dougherty, Edward P., 607 N. Third St., Steubenville, Ohio.
Dougherty, John J., 607 N. Third St., Steubenville, Ohio.
Eailey, Charles M., Bloomdale, Ohio.
Edwards, Millard, 919 Central Ave., Cincinnati, Ohio.
Etchell, John, 1794 B. 40th St., Cleveland, Ohio.
Ewing, Harry C., 1612 Ridge Ave., Steubenville, Ohio.
Fackler, Jacob R., Richwood, Ohio.
Feeney, Joseph L., 323 Hill Ave., Steubenville, Ohio.
Ferris, Fred E., N. Fourth St., Toronto, Ohio.
Finearty, John A., 414 New York Ave., Wellston, Ohio.
Floto, George W., 224 North St., Steubenville, Ohio.
Fountell, John B., 802 Lilliam St., Pittsburgh, Pa.
Fox, John A., Smithfield, Ohio.
Frantz, Earl H., 2701 Summit St., Toledo, Ohio.
Gallabrese, Thomas B., 146 N. Seventh St., Steubenville, Ohio.
Gardner, Jerome N., Mingo Junction, Ohio.
Gescheider, Otto J., 639 Sixth Ave., Steubenville, Ohio.
Getts, Andrew F., R. D. 4, Continental, Ohio.
Glady, Lewis, 41 Baldwin St., Youngstown, Ohio.
Gorsuch, Thomas E., Mt. Pleasant, Ohio.
Grabill, John S., R. R. 1, Darbyville, Ohio.
Grable, Orion L., R. R. 1, Unionport, Ohio.
Grafton, Aubrey U., R. D. 32, Barberton, Ohio.
Granger, Joseph W., P. 0. Box 108, Tiltonville, Ohio.
Hallett, William O., 106 Lenox Ave., Warren, Ohio.
Halpny, George P., Mingo Junction, Ohio.
Hanna, Floyd, R. D. 1, Rudolph, Ohio.
Heimsch, Arthur W., 237 Sherman St., Dayton, Ohio.
Henry, Elmore I., R. D. 1, Baltimore, Ohio.
Herbst, Howard D., 937 N. Seventh St., Steubenville, Ohio.
Hileman, James, Confluence, Pa.
Hogue, Ralph J., 428 N. Seventh St., Steubenvi1le, Ohio.
Horrigan, James F., Dillonvale, Ohio.
Hudson, Arthur, 241 Wert St., Ashtabula, Ohio.
Izzoni, James, Middletown, Ohio.
Inman, William, 2123 W. Eighth St., Cincinnati, Ohio.
Johns, Lester A., 2548 E. 128th St., Cleveland, Ohio.
Jones, Wilbur C., 127 N. Seventh St., Steubenville, Ohio.
Karns, Jay, Bowling Green, Ohio.
Keliher, John F., Hotel Sterling, Cincinnati, Ohio.
Ralph B. Keller, 194 Central Ave., Newark, Ohio.
Kirk, Delmer E., Luckey, Ohio.
Kirstein, Henry, 3147 W. 112th St., Cleveland, Ohio.
Khimek, Stanislaw, Mulberry St., Toledo, Ohio.
Kline, Clarence H., 1334 Hildreth Ave., Columbus, Ohio.
Klosterman, Frank J., 4147 Spring Grove Ave., Cincinnati, Ohio.
Kodoczkowicc, William, Bairdstown, Ohio.
Kominski, Steve, 3663 B, 61st St., Cleveland, Ohio.
Kopp, Charles, 115 W. Sixth St., Perrysburg, Ohio.
Koron, Felix, 246 E. Weber St., Toledo, Ohio.
Kvasnicka, Joseph J., 10102 Quebec Ave., Cleveland, Ohio.
Lance, Lloyd R., R. D. 1, Custar, Ohio.
Landwehr, J. H., Luckey, Ohio.
Leist, William H., 409 N. Sixth St., Steubenville, Ohio.
Lewis, Raymond, R. D. 3, Box 18, Batavia, Ohio.
Liberatore, Giovanni A., 1007 Swan St., Parkersburg, W. Va.
Limerick, John, 140 5. Fourth St., Steubenville, Ohio.
Logan, Arthur W., Elmore, Ohio.
Loudy, Thomas H., R. R. 3, Benhame, Va.
Love, Raymond, 320 5. Third St., Steubenville. Ohio.
Lowe, Reno B., 632 5. Main St., Akron, Ohio.
McClain, Wilbur N., 421 N. Sixth St., Toronot, Ohio.
McDonald, Ray B., 147 Friesner Ave., Logan, Ohio.
McElroy, Robert B., R. D. 1, Peroria, Ohio.
McGinnis, Isaac M., Danville, Ky.
McGraw, Patrick B., 68 Denver Ave., Cincinnati, Ohio.
McGuinness, Raymond L., 323 S. Seventh St., Steubenville, Ohio.
McMullen, Hugh J., Mingo Junction, Ohio.
McNeil, Albert, Wilson Ave., Steubenville, Ohio.
MacKeever, Robert, 1049 Labelle Ave., Steubenville, Ohio.
Malerli, Arturo, 1405 Belmont St., Belaire, Ohio.
Marcum, Jesse T., 124 Blame Ave., Marion, Ohio.
Mark, Allan J., 316 Dock St., Steubenville, Ohio.
Mark, John G., 8721 Harkness Rd., Cleveland, Ohio.
Marker, Edward B., 244 S. Fifth St., Steubenville, Ohio.
Marshall, James L., Bergholz, Ohio.
Martin, John, 3637 B. 105th St., Cleveland, Ohio.
Mascoline, Joseph, Steubenville, Ohio.
Massarelli, Vincent, 428 Spring Ave., Steubenville, Ohio.
Meyers, William L., 1554 Ontario St., Toledo, Ohio.
Michel, Edward C., Oak Harbor, Ohio.
Miller, Albert H., 2317 Kinkle Ave., Cleveland, Ohio.
Miller, Ernest S., 1532 B. 66th St., Cleveland, Ohio.
Minier, Carl, R. R. 2. Port Clinton, Ohio.
Montgomery, Howard, Steubenville, Ohio.
Moore, Earnest A., R. P. 2, Larue, Ohio.
Mulrooney, John J., 919 N. Seventh St., Steubenville, Ohio.
Myers, Frank O., 307 Virginia Ave., Steubenville, Ohio.
Naylor, Milton, 117 10th St., Sanbury, Pa.
Nicholson, Willard J., 256 N. 5th St., Steubenville, Ohio.
Nicholas, Harry W., Ripley, Ohio.
Nowak, Steve, 9 Bronson Ave., Toledo, Ohio.
Noyes, O. J., Milford Center, Ohio.
Oborn, Maurice G., 255 Olney Ave., Marion, Ohio.
Orians, William O., 372 Haine Ave., Marion, Ohio.
Palandagis, George, 29 Chaplin St., Youngstown, Ohio.
Farmelee, Jason C., 3952 Lockwood Ave., Toledo, Ohio.
Passonesi, Paul, 575 13th St., Lorain, Ohio.
Patton, Stacy B., 260 Lakewood Ave., Ashtabula, Ohio.
Pavlin, Charles T., 3655 B. 50th St., Cleveland, Ohio.
Peterson, John, Unionport, Ohio.
Petrick, John J., Mingo Junction, Ohio.
Phelps, Bacil B., Springfield, Tenn.
Powell, Friend D., 39 S. Maple St., Akron, Ohio.
Prmsa, Joe, 1935 Ninth St., Columbus, Ohio.
Regal, Levi C., Port Clinton, Ohio.
Ringenbach, Armand A., 530 Austin St., Toledo, Ohio.
Roach, Earl P., Yorkville, Ohio.
Rogers, Alvin, Sparkshill, Ill.
Roosa, Charles A., Mantua, Ohio.
Rosiak, Frank, 157 Bronson St., Toledo, Ohio.
Ross, Charles J, 311 Virginia Ave., Steubenville, Ohio.
Ross, Charles W., 1209 Lincoln Ave., Steubenville, Ohio.
Roush, Clifford B., Mineraville, Ohio.
Ryan, John W., 20 Maple St., Willoughby, Ohio.
Sarver, Chester, 1716 Carrollton Ave., Parkside, Toledo, Ohio.
Schaaf, Carl B., 165 5, Scott St., Lima, Ohio.
Schelich, Robert A., 512 B. Fulton St., Celina, Ohio.
Schrickel, Charles, R. D. 3, Rayland, Ohio.
Schroeder, Frank H., R. D. 1, Sunders, Ohio.
Schroeder, Otto, R. R. 9, Defiance, Ohio.
Shanteau, George, Gypsum, Ohio.
Sheehan, William A, 820 Fernwood Ave., Toledo, Ohio.
Shelt, Francis V., 423 W. Clinton St., Napoleon, Ohio.
Shinn, Emmer H., Deerfield, Ohio.
Slafiak, Steve, 451 Phillipa St., South Bend, Ind.
Smith, Clarence P., Ridgeville Corners, Ohio.
Smith, Daniel R., 527 Main St., Hamilton, Ohio.
Smith, John W., Eastwood, Ohio.
Smith, Milton, R. R. 5, Oxford, Ohio.
Smyth, Gay W., Bergholz, Ohio.
Snyder, Mike A., N. Fifth St., Toronto, Ohio.
Sofra, Vincent, 520 W. 13th St., Lorain, Ohio.
Spain, Carl, R. R. 5, Marysville, Ohio.
Spak, Martin, 148 B. Streiker St., Toledo, Ohio.
Speasmaker, Frederick, 1094 Say Ave., Columbus, Ohio.
Spencer, George H., 722 5. Main St., Bowling Green, Ohio.
Stamper, Marvin M., 403 Reynolds St., Middletown, Ohio.
Stempen, John, 434 B. Central Ave., Toledo, Ohio.
Stein, Carl, 414 Curtis Ave., Middletown, Ohio.
Stephens, Clarence S., Somerville, Ohio.
Stephens, Williams J., Seventh St., Glenwood, Wheeling, W. Va.
Stern, Carl F., 807 North St., Middletown, Ohio.
Swallow, Clarence, St. Versailles, Ohio.
Swank, Charles, Weston, Mich.
Swanson, Malcom, 488 Columbus St., Ashtabula, Ohio.
Thompson, Robert B., 854 Rassett Ave., Columbus, Ohio.
Thorn, Floyd L., 253 5. Fifth St., Steubenville, Ohio.
Timotes, Cuilio, 2029 Scoville Ave., Columbus, Ohio.
Trainer, John H., 616 N. Fourth St., Columbus, Ohio.
Trusiewicz, Stanislaw, 316 Streicker St., Toledo, Ohio.
VanVlerah, P., Napoleon, Ohio.
Varano, Michael A., 727 George St., Toledo, Ohio.
Vining, Charles R., Baltimore, Ohio.
Walker, Channing I., Emerson, Ohio.
Wallace, Ernest A., Bergholz, Ohio.
Walton, Harry, 1432 Palmwood Ave., Toledo, Ohio.
Watson, William R., Napoleon, Ohio.
Wawrzyniak, Stanislaw, 1762 Buckingham St., Toledo, Ohio.
Weaver, David J., Box 116, New Bacaria, Ohio.
Welch, Robert L., 1158 Sycamore St., Steubenville, Ohio.
Westlake, Clarence R., 929 N. Fifth St., Steubenville, Ohio.
Whitten, Charles A., Williamsport, Ohio.
Wightman, Edward W., Port Clinton, Ohio.
Wiley, Price, R, F, D. 1, Broadacre, Ohio.
Willeman, Oscar, Ridgeville Corners, Ohio.
Williams, Arthur M., 3103 Ruby Ave. SW., Cleveland, Ohio.
Williams, Richard, 503 Oak St., Old Forge, Pa.
Williamson, Floyd P., R. F. D. 1, Dunbridge, Ohio.
Williamson, Ralph B., R, F. D. 1, Toronto, Ohio.
Wilson, Harry A., 302 Second St., Perrysburg, Ohio.
Wingert, Leon J., 70 W. Ely St., Alliance, Ohio.
Wolverton, Harry R., 104 N. Main St., Middletown, Ohio.
Wood, Harry S., Port Clinton, Ohio.
Woodard, George V., 626 Neil Ave., Columbus, Ohio.
Woodruff, Francis R., 216 N. Poplar St., Oxford, Ohio.
Wright, Charles H., 193 B. York St., Akron, Ohio.
Wright, Harold D., Empire, Ohio.
Wright, Joseph, R. F. D. 1, Kensington, Ohio.
Wyatt, Lester, 1024 Woodstock Ave., Toledo, Ohio.
Yost, Frank A., Boiling Springs, Pa.
Ziemann, Ferdinand J., 945 Belmont Ave., Toledo, Ohio.

L COMPANY
Myers, Elbron B. B., 9814 Marietta Ave., Cleveland, Ohio.
McGowan, Robert R., 1037 LaBelle St., Steubenville, Ohio.
Rubin, David, 2050 B. 82nd St., Cleveland, Ohio.
Crawford, William P., 1119 Third St., Portsmouth, Ohio.
Allen, David K., Cadir, Ohio.
Abruzzese, Joe, 1964 B. 120th St., Cleveland, Ohio.
Arnold, Andrew W., 369 Waddell St., Leetonia, Ohio.
Barcykowski, Frank, 3554 B. 76th St., Cleveland, Ohio.
Barth, Clifford J., 708 Plum St., Toledo, Ohio.
Barlag, Charles, 1013 W. Liberty St., Cincinnati, Ohio.
Battin, Wilfred A., Box 21, Hanoverton, Ohio.
Baumgard, Jacob, Iclondyke, Ohio.
Beck, Edward J., 100 B, Clifton Ave., Cincinnati, Ohio.
Behrens, Fred W., Deshler, Ohio.